The GUINNESS Book of
Air
Facts and Feats

Three engines have long been considered the optimum number for a transport aeroplane. By adding a third 260 hp piston-engine, mounted on the tail-fin, Britten-Norman converted their ten/twelve-seat Islander into the eighteen-seat Trislander

Three Rolls-Royce RB.211 turbofan engines give the Lockheed TriStar a speed of 595 mile/h (958 km/h) and make it far quieter than earlier jet airliners

"No more plain planes" was the slogan adopted by Braniff when they began painting their jets in the kind of over-all colour schemes that had not been seen since the fabric-covered airliners of the 1920s

The GUINNESS Book of
Air
Facts and Feats

edited by

John W R Taylor FRHistS, MRAeS, FSLAET
Michael J H Taylor – David Mondey

artwork by MIKE ROFFE

GUINNESS SUPERLATIVES LIMITED
2 CECIL COURT, LONDON ROAD, ENFIELD, MIDDLESEX

© 1973 Guinness Superlatives Limited
Second Impression 1975

Published in Great Britain by
Guinness Superlatives Limited, 2 Cecil Court,
London Road, Enfield, Middlesex

SBN 900424 10 9

Set in Monophoto Baskerville Series 169,
printed and bound in Great Britain by
Jarrold and Sons Limited, Norwich

Contents

		Page
	Acknowledgements	6
	Introduction	7
Section 1	Pioneers of the Air	9
Section 2	Military Aviation	41
Section 3	Maritime Aviation	129
Section 4	Route-proving and Commercial Aviation	167
Section 5	Lighter-than-Air	196
Section 6	Rotorcraft	213
Section 7	Flying for Sport and Competition	218
Section 8	Rocketry and Spaceflight	233
Section 9	Appendices	252
	1 *Addenda*	252
	2 *Air Speed Records*	257
	3 *Four remarkable aircraft*	261
	4 *Aviation's worst disasters*	264
	Selected Bibliography	267
	Index	270

Acknowledgements

The compilers wish to extend their thanks to the many organisations and individuals who gave generous assistance during the preparation of this book, and particularly to those listed below in alphabetical order:

Aero Spacelines Inc.
Ronald Barker
Beaumont Aviation Literature
The Boeing Company
Chaz Bowyer
British Aircraft Corporation (all Divisions)
J. M. Bruce, M.A., F.R.Hist.S.
Avions Marcel Dassault – Breguet Aviation
N. L. R. Franks
General Dynamics Corporation
Charles H. Gibbs-Smith
Grumman Corporation
Lt.-Col. J. Harsit, Israeli Defence Force/Air Force
Hawker Siddeley Aviation Ltd. (all Divisions)
Imperial War Museum
Italian Air Ministry
Lockheed Aircraft Corporation

Alec Lumsden
Ministry of Defence (R.A.F.)
Ministry of Defence (R.N.)
P. J. R. Moyes
N.A.S.A.
New York Post Corporation
Novosti Press Agency
Flt.-Lt. Alfred Price
Rockwell International
Rolls-Royce Ltd.
The Smithsonian Institution
Society of British Aerospace Companies Ltd.
Tass
Johannes Thinesen
United States Air Force
United States Marine Corps
United States Navy
Gordon S. Williams

Introduction

Ours is the century of flight. It is also the century of the family car, television, antibiotics, nuclear power, two world wars, and a dozen other major developments which affect the lives of everyone to a greater or lesser degree—including pollution.

Like crime, pollution is not new; it is simply becoming so much worse that we are compelled to take notice of it. This brings us straight back to flying, because excessive noise is now recognised as a form of environmental pollution as damaging as smells or dirt; and everyone knows that aeroplanes are noisy, smelly, dirty things.

Air fact number one coming up: the aircraft jet engines in service today, imperfect though they are, produce only about 1 per cent of the world's air pollution. In this respect they are three times less offensive than the piston-engines they replaced. As for noise, the Rolls-Royce-engined Lockheed Tri-Star airbus provides a good example of current trends. It generates sound some 60 to 75 per cent less annoying than that of older four-engined jets, and 30 to 50 per cent less annoying than earlier two- or three-engined airliners.

Already, Rolls-Royce is conducting a two-year research programme aimed at reducing the TriStar's take-off noise annoyance factor by 30 per cent. The long-range objective is even more ambitious, envisaging a reduction of perhaps another 30 per cent. Noting this, airports like Los Angeles International are considering a ban on all but the newest, quietest good-neighbourly aeroplanes from 1980.

How many people will travel by air each year by then? In 1972, nearly 450 million passengers were carried on scheduled services throughout the world, not counting charter flights. Yet the whole history of practical powered flight is still compressed within the traditional "three score years and ten" of a man's life, for it is not yet quite seventy years since the Wright brothers made their first hesitant hops at Kitty Hawk.

Were they first? What about Carl Jatho, the German civil servant who hopped his primitive biplane distances of up to 196 ft at a height of 11 ft over the Vahrenwalder Heide, a heath to the north of Hanover, in the autumn of 1903? The new facts given in this second edition of *Air Facts and Feats* have come to light since the first edition was published, and are of considerable significance to historians. So are the new facts, uncovered by diligent research in Portugal, which reveal Bartolomeu de Gusmão as the true pioneer of ballooning, three-quarters of a century before the Montgolfiers.

Such facts do not lessen the great achievements of the Montgolfiers, or the Wrights, who put man into the air in safety and confidence; but it is important to get the facts right. That is why such an immense effort has gone into this new edition, correcting the original text in the light of more reliable information and adding an enormous volume of new material. Here are the answers to endless questions—not just on big issues, such as who was first to fly over the Poles, or to fly a jet fighter, but who was the world's first air apprentice? It was, after all, the "Dinger" Bells of this world whose skill and persistence transformed the Wright biplane into the Concorde in their lifetime.

In those same few years, men have walked on the Moon and sent the first probe from earth into outer space, a journey that may take two million years and end near the star Aldebaran. Such periods of time, and distances, are beyond our comprehension; but to start Pioneer 10 on its way was a feat to match those which make our book a record of unrivalled adventure and achievement.

M. de Landelle's design for a flying machine

SECTION I
The Pioneers of the Air

Rummaging among boxes of small artefacts in a store-room at Cairo Museum in 1972, Dr. Khalil Messiha came across a strange-looking wooden bird model that had been found originally at Saqqara in 1898. Unlike a real bird, or any of the other models carved in the third or fourth century B.C., this one had a rear body of narrow elliptical shape, like that of a small modern aeroplane, and ended in a deep vertical tail-fin containing a groove for a horizontal tailplane. No bird can contort its body to such a shape.

Did this chance discovery suggest that the ancient Egyptians built model gliders—perhaps even full-scale gliders? Some sceptics prefer to regard the model as no more than a wind direction indicator, pivoted in such a way that the vertical tail would turn it into wind. Why then, queried Dr. Messiha, had the ancient Egyptian craftsman spent so long giving the wing a finely curved aerofoil section?

This is a book of facts and feats, not theories, however attractive. The little model, some 2,300 years old, spanning 7 in, weighing under 1½ oz, and made of sycamore, is certainly fact. We should be on less firm ground if we listed the ancient myths and legends concerning "bird-men" of antiquity, such as the Greek Daedalus and Icarus, and our own Bladud, ninth King of Britain at the time of the Old Testament prophet Elijah.

Birdmen certainly predated modern V.T.O.L. (vertical take-off and landing) aircraft, even if they achieved little but high-speed vertical descent. Elijah himself did rather better, with the aid of a chariot of fire in which a whirlwind whisked him up to heaven.

There is no evidence to suggest that fiery chariots progressed beyond the prototype stage, but birdmen have continued the sport of leaping off high places, wearing wings of feathers, wax and wood, to the present day. Some of the more far-sighted designers of such man-powered wings, notably the great Italian artist-inventor Leonardo da Vinci (1452–1519), tried to supplement ambition with science. One of Leonardo's carefully drawn designs shows the wings mounted on a wooden structure

Wooden model, possibly a glider, carved in Egypt some 2,300 years ago (Boudewijn Weehuizen)

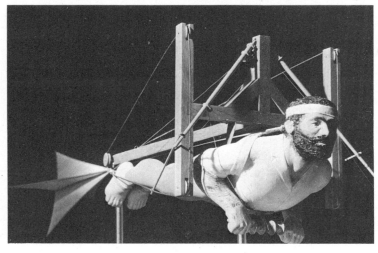

Model of Leonardo da Vinci's man-powered design (Qantas Collection)

fitted with levers and pulleys through which the would-be pilot's muscle-power might be used more effectively. Legs supplemented arms in flapping the wings, and the pilot could even steer up or down by nodding his head.

Leonardo's true cleverness is indicated by the fact that he never tried to fly in such a contraption. Even today, with knowledge, skills and materials beyond the dreams of the sixteenth century, nobody has yet succeeded in building a muscle-powered aeroplane that will fly 1 mile.

By the eighteenth century, as can be seen later in this book, several of the men who longed to fly gave up the search for a human or mechanical power plant. Turning to lighter-than-air balloons, they resigned themselves to mere drifting wherever the wind willed to carry them. Only the more determined, comparing the floating "bubbles" with the crisp, fast wheeling and soaring of the birds, still refused to accept such a pale imitation of real flight.

So, the story of powered flight begins properly in 1799, at the Yorkshire estate of Sir George Cayley, Bart. (1773–1857). This man, who is regarded universally as the "Father of Aerial Navigation", took a small silver disc in that year and engraved it with his first known design for a fixed-wing aeroplane. Still only twenty-six years old, he devised the key to eventual success by suggesting that the lifting system should be left to do its own job efficiently, instead of having also to provide propulsion. If we make allowances for his obsession with paddles rather than a propeller as the medium for producing thrust, his design embodied all the basic features of a modern aeroplane, with a fixed and cambered wing, set at a modest angle of attack, a man-carrying body, and movable cruciform tail surfaces.

These deceptively simple ideas were built into what has always been regarded as the world's first successful model glider in 1804, a successful full-scale glider five years later, and the paddle-equipped glider in which the eighty-year-old Cayley is said to have climaxed his career by flying his aged, and highly reluctant, coachman over a small valley in 1853.

A handful of almost predictable steps led from there to the triumph of Wilbur and Orville Wright, at Kitty Hawk, in December 1903. They spanned half a century mainly because nobody had yet invented a light-weight, powerful engine that would lift into the air a flying-machine based on Cayley's principles.

Most inspired of all the products of the pioneers who followed Cayley was the first of them. We can still see it exactly as its designer, William Samuel Henson (1812–88), conceived it; because his 20 ft span model of the Aerial Steam Carriage is a treasured exhibit in London's Science Museum. It is a monoplane, with enclosed cabin and tricycle undercarriage. Given a power plant more efficient than its steam engine, and perhaps a few degrees of wing dihedral, it looks as if it might have flown, and the course of aviation history would have been changed. Instead, when the model failed to fly, Henson was ridiculed by the sceptics, who poured scorn on drawings of full-scale Steam Carriages in flight over places like the Pyramids and the Taj Mahal.

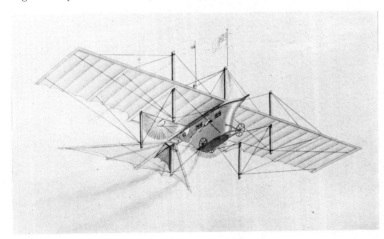

Artist's impression of Henson's Aerial Steam Carriage (Science Museum, London)

Replica of Félix Du Temple's aeroplane, 1874 (Qantas Collection)

It was left to a French naval officer, Félix Du Temple de la Croix, to fly a clockwork model in 1857 and then to scale it up into a sweptforward-wing monoplane which lifted a young sailor into the air at Brest seventeen years later. It was not a proper flight, as the aircraft made only a short hop after gathering speed down a ramp. The huge steam-powered monoplane of Alexander Mozhaisky made a similar ramp-launched leap through the air in Russia in 1884. Ten years later, in Britain, Sir Hiram

*Alexander Mozhaisky
and his aircraft, 1884*

*Sir Hiram Maxim's
biplane, 1894*

Maxim's 3·5 ton biplane lifted itself briefly and unintentionally into the air, from level ground, also under steam-power, but was hardly a practical aeroplane.

Realising that it was now possible to design and build a thoroughly efficient airframe, but that no suitable power plant was available, Otto Lilienthal reverted to powerless gliding flight in Germany. By making more than 2,000 successful glides in 1890–96, he inspired other glider builder/pilots like the American Octave Chanute (1832–1910) and the British Percy S. Pilcher (1866–99). By a tragic coincidence, both Lilienthal and Pilcher died in glider crashes as they were about to fit small, practical engines to their best designs.

So, the race to be first to achieve a powered, sustained, controlled flight was eventually between three Americans, Dr. Samuel Pierpont Langley and the brothers Wilbur and Orville Wright. The odds favoured Langley when he launched his steam-powered pilotless model *Aerodrome No. 5* over the Potomac River on 6th May 1896, for a sustained flight lasting more than 1 min; but two attempts to fly a full-scale piloted version were to prove unsuccessful in the autumn of 1903.

Over in Germany, Carl Jatho (1873–1933) had greater success with a lesser aeroplane. His first machine was a biplane only 11 ft 10 in long, with the elevator mounted triplane-like on top. There were two vertical rudders between the wings, a rubber-tyred undercarriage, and a large propeller driven by a 9·5 hp Buchet engine. Wing area was 581 ft² and the machine weighed 562 lb.

Best flight achieved with this aircraft was 59 ft, at a height of about 2 ft 6 in, on 18th August 1903. Jatho redesigned it as a monoplane, still with a top elevator, to make it easier to control in windy conditions. His second prototype had a reduced wing area of 387·5 ft² and weight of only 408 lb. When tested in the autumn of 1903, it made a number of flights of up to 196 ft, at a height of about 11 ft. It was to be several years before he flew further, in a better design with more power; but it is worth pointing out that his longest hops far exceeded the first of the four flights by the Wright brothers, which they preceded. So Jatho, like the other pioneers who kept enthusiasm alive between the major "milestones" of Cayley and the Wrights, should never be forgotten.

Carl Jatho's second aeroplane, 1903

The first man in the world to identify and correctly record the parameters of heavier-than-air flight was the Englishman, Sir George Cayley, sixth Baronet (born 27th December 1773; died 15th December 1857). Sir George Cayley succeeded to the Baronetcy in a long and distinguished line of Cayleys whose origins are traceable back to Sir Hugo de Cayly, Knight, of Owby, who lived early in the twelfth century. Sir William Cayley was created first Baronet by Charles I on 26th April 1661 for services in the Civil War. The present Baronet, Sir Kenelm Henry Ernest Cayley, tenth Baronet, of Brompton, Yorkshire, was born on 24th September 1896. It was at Brompton Hall, near Scarborough, one hundred years before, that young George Cayley had carried out some of his early experiments with model aeroplanes. The following is a list of notable "firsts" achieved by this remarkable scientist:

(a) He first set down the mathematical principles of heavier-than-air flight (i.e. lift, thrust and drag).

(b) He was the first to make use of models for flying research, among them a simple glider—the first monoplane with fixed wing amidships, and fuselage terminating in vertical and horizontal tail surfaces; this was constructed in 1804.

(c) He was the first to draw attention to the importance of streamlining (in his definition of "drag").

(d) He was the first to suggest the benefits of biplanes and triplanes to provide increased lift with minimum weight.

(e) He was first to construct and fly a man-carrying glider (see page 14).

(f) He was the first to demonstrate the means by which a curved "aerofoil" provided "lift" by creating reduced pressure over the upper surface when moved through the air.

(g) He was the first to suggest the use of an internal-combustion engine for aeroplanes and constructed a model gunpowder engine in the absence of low-flash-point fuel oil.

Reproduction of Cayley's 1804 model glider (Science Museum, London)

The first person to be carried aloft in a heavier-than-air craft in sustained (gliding) flight was a ten-year-old boy who became airborne in a glider constructed by Sir George Cayley at Brompton Hall, near Scarborough, Yorkshire, in 1849. The glider became airborne after being towed by manpower down a hill against a light breeze.

The first man to be carried aloft in a heavier-than-air craft, but not in control of its flight, was Sir George Cayley's coachman at Brompton Hall, reputedly in 1853. A witness of the event stated that after he had landed the coachman struggled clear and shouted "Please, Sir George, I wish to give notice. I was hired to drive, not to fly." No record has ever been traced giving the name of either the ten-year-old or of the coachman. The decennial census of 1851, however, records the name of John Appleby as being the most probable member of Sir George's staff. With regard to the young boy, Sir George had no son or grandson of this age at the time of his experiments, so it may be conjectured that the first "pilot" may have been a servant's son.

Model of Cayley's triplane glider of 1849 (Quantas Collection)

The first model aeroplane powered by a steam engine was that designed and made by W. S. Henson (1812–1888) and John Stringfellow (1799–1883) at Chard, Somerset, England, in 1847. This 20 ft (6·5 m) span monoplane, powered by a steam engine driving twin pusher propellers, was launched from an inclined ramp, but sustained flight was not achieved. Henson subsequently emigrated to America, but both he and Stringfellow remained interested in aeronautics and pursued experiments with powered models. Contrary to former opinion, none of Stringfellow's powered models ever achieved sustained flight.

The first powered model aeroplane to make a successful sustained flight was built and tested in France by Félix Du Temple (1823–1890) in 1857–58. It was powered successively by clockwork and steam.

The first scientist correctly to deduce the main properties (i.e. lift distribution) of a cambered aerofoil was F. H. Wenham (1824–1908) who built various gliders during the mid nineteenth century to test his theories. In collaboration with John Browning, Wenham built **the world's first wind tunnel** in 1871 for the Aeronautical Society of Great Britain.

The first aeronautical exhibition in Great Britain was staged at the Crystal Palace in 1868 by the Aeronautical Society of Great Britain. The exhibits included model engines driven by steam, oil gas and guncotton.

The first powered man-carrying aeroplane to achieve a brief "hop", after gaining speed down a ramp, was a monoplane with sweptforward wings built by Félix Du Temple and piloted by an unidentified young sailor, at Brest in about 1874. The power plant was a hot-air or steam engine, driving a tractor propeller.

The first man-carrying aeroplane to achieve a powered "hop" after rising from supposedly level ground was the bat-winged *Éole* monoplane built and flown by Clément Ader (1841–1925), at Armainvilliers, France, on 9th October 1890. Powered by an 18–20 hp steam engine, the *Éole* covered about 165 ft (50 m), but never achieved sustained or controlled flight. Ader's second aeroplane, the *Avion III*, was tested twice in 1897 but did not fly.

The three most outstanding pioneers of gliding flight prior to successful powered flight were undoubtedly the German Otto Lilienthal (1848–1896), the American Dr. Octave Chanute (1832–1910), and the Englishman Percy S. Pilcher (1866–1899). Their achievements may be summarised as follows:

Otto Lilienthal, German civil engineer, published a classic aeronautical textbook *Der Vogelflug als Grundlage der Fliegekunst* (The Flight of Birds as the Basis of Aviation) in 1889. Although he remained convinced that powered flight would ultimately be achieved by wing-flapping (i.e. in the ornithopter), Lilienthal constructed five fixed-wing monoplane gliders and two biplane gliders between 1891 and 1896. Tested near Berlin and at the Rhinower Hills near Stöllen, these gliders achieved sustained gliding flight; the pilot, usually Lilienthal himself, supported himself by his arms, holding the centre section of the glider. Thus, he could run forward and launch himself off the hills to achieve flight. During this period he achieved gliding distances ranging from 300 ft (100 m) to more than 750 ft (250 m). Although he had been experimenting with a small carbonic acid gas engine he was killed when one of his gliders crashed on the Rhinower Hills on 9th August 1896 before he could progress further with powered flight.

Lilienthal glider

Chanute hang-glider

Octave Chanute, American railroad engineer, was born in Paris, France, on 18th February 1832. His book *Progress in Flying Machines*, published in 1894, was the first comprehensive history of heavier-than-air flight and is still regarded as a classic of aviation literature. As well as providing a valuable information service for pioneers on both sides of the Atlantic, he began designing and building improved Lilienthal-type hang-gliders in 1896. After experimenting with multiplanes fitted with up to eight pairs of pivoting wings and a top fixed surface, he evolved the classic and successful biplane configuration. Flight-testing of his gliders was performed mainly by Augustus M. Herring (1867–1926), as Chanute was too old to fly himself. The Wright brothers gained early inspiration from *Progress in Flying Machines*, became close friends of Chanute, and learned from him the advantages offered by a Pratt-trussed biplane structure and, later, a catapult launching system for their wheel-less aircraft.

Percy S. Pilcher, English marine engineer, built his first glider, the *Bat*, in 1895 and flew that year on the banks of the River Clyde. Following advice by Lilienthal, as well as early practical experiments, Pilcher added a tailplane to the *Bat* and achieved numerous successful flights. This aircraft was followed by others (christened the *Beetle, Gull* and *Hawk*), the last of which was constructed in 1896 and included a fixed fin, a tailplane and a wheel undercarriage. It had a cambered wing with a span of 23 ft 4 in and an area of 180 ft² (7 m and 16·72 m² respectively). Pilcher had always set his sights upon powered flight and was engaged in developing a light 4 hp oil engine (probably for installation in his *Hawk*) when, having been towed off the ground by a team of horses, he crashed in the *Hawk* at Stanford Park, Market Harborough on 30th September 1899, and died two days later.

The box-kite structure was invented in 1893 by an Australian, Lawrence Hargrave (1850–1915). This simple structure provided good lift and stability and formed the basis of aeroplanes such as the Voisin.

The largest aeroplane to lift itself off the ground briefly in the nineteenth century was designed and built by Sir Hiram Maxim (1840–1916). Basically a biplane with 4,000 ft² (372 m²) of lifting area, it was powered by two 180 hp steam engines and ran along a railway track 1,800 ft (550 m) long which was fitted with wooden restraining guard-rails to prevent the machine from rising too high.

On 31st July 1894 during a test run the machine lifted about 2 ft before fouling the guard-rails and coming to rest.

The first man to achieve sustained powered flight with an unmanned heavier-than-air craft was the American Samuel Pierpont Langley (born 22nd August 1834 at Roxbury, Massachusetts; died 27th February 1906, at Aiken, South Carolina). Mathematician and solar radiation physicist, Langley commenced building powered model aeroplanes during the 1890s, launching them from the top of a houseboat on the Potomac River near Quantico. His 14 ft span models (*Aerodrome* Nos. 5 and 6) achieved sustained flights of up to 4,200 ft (1,400 m) during 1896 and incorporated a single steam engine mounted amidships, driving a pair of airscrews. Langley's use of the name *Aerodrome* was derived incorrectly from the Greek αερο-δρόμος (*aerodromos*) supposedly meaning "air runner"; the word, however, is correctly defined as the location of a running event and cannot be held to mean the participant in a running event. Thus in the context of an *airfield* the word "aerodrome", as originally applied to Hendon in Middlesex, England, is correct. In 1898 Langley was requested to continue his experiments with a $50,000 State subsidy and set about the design and construction of a full-scale version. As an intermediate step he built a quarter-scale model which became the world's first aeroplane powered by a petrol engine to achieve sustained flight in August 1903. His full-size *Aerodrome*, with a span of 48 ft (16 m) and powered by a 52 hp Manly-Balzer five-cylinder radial petrol engine, was completed in 1903, and attempts to fly this over the Potomac River with Charles M. Manly at the controls were made on 7th October and 8th December 1903. On both occasions the aeroplane fouled the launcher and dropped into the river. In view of the success achieved by the Wright brothers immediately thereafter, the American Government withdrew its support from Langley and his project was abandoned.

Langley's Aerodrome *on its houseboat launcher, 7th October 1903 (U.S. Army)*

Second unsuccessful launch
of Langley's Aerodrome,
8th December 1903
(Smithsonian
Institution)

The first aeroplane to achieve man-carrying, powered, sustained flight in the world was the
Flyer, designed and constructed by the brothers Wilbur and Orville Wright,
which first achieved such flight at 10.35 h on Thursday, 17th December
1903, at Kill Devil Hills, Kitty Hawk, North Carolina, with an undulating
flight of 120 ft (40 m) in about 12 s. Three further flights were made on the
same day, the longest of which covered a ground distance of 852 ft (230 m)
and lasted 59 s. It should be emphasised that these flights were the natural

The first Wright Flyer *rests on the starting track at Kill Devil Hills prior to the trial of 14th December 1903.*
The four men from the Kill Devil Hills Life Saving Station helped move the machine from the campsite to the hill.
The two boys ran home on hearing the engine start (Library of Congress Collections)

Still flying is this example of
the Curtiss JN-4 "Jenny"
trainer which equipped U.S.
military flying schools
during the First World War

Treasured exhibit in
London's Science Museum is
the little triplane flown by
Britain's greatest pioneer,
A. V. Roe, in 1909
(Air BP)

Another aircraft of 1914–18
that flies regularly at
modern air shows is this
Bristol Fighter

culmination of some four years' experimenting by the Wrights with a number of gliders, during 1899–1903. Details of the powered *Flyer* were as follows:

Wright Flyer No. 1 (1903)
Wing span: 40 ft 4 in (12·3 m).
Over-all length: 21 ft 1 in (6·43 m).
Wing chord: 6 ft 6 in (1·97 m).
Wing area: 510 ft² (47·38 m²).
Empty weight: 605 lb (274 kg).
Loaded weight: Approximately 750 lb (340 kg).
Wing loading: 1·47 lb/ft² (7·2 kg/m²).
Power plant: 12 bhp four-cylinder water-cooled engine lying on its side and driving two 8 ft 6 in (2·59 m) diameter propellers by chains, one of which was crossed to achieve counter-rotation. Engine weight with fuel (0·33 imp. gal), approximately 200 lb (90 kg).
Speed: 30 mile/h (approximately 45 km/h).
Launching: The *Flyer* took off under its own power from a dolly which ran on two bicycle hubs along a 60 ft (20 m) wooden rail.

Rare photograph, taken during the third flight of the Wright Flyer *on 17th December 1903, with Orville at the controls (Library of Congress Collections)*

The first accredited sustained flight (i.e. other than a "hop") achieved by a manned, powered aeroplane in Europe was made on 12th November 1906 by the Brazilian constructor-pilot Alberto Santos-Dumont (1873–1932), a resident of Paris, France, who flew his "*14-bis*" 722 ft (220 m) in 21·2 s; his aeroplane was in effect a tail-first box-kite powered by a 50 hp Antoinette engine, and this flight won for him the Aéro-Club de France's prize of 1,500 francs for the first officially observed flight of more than 100 m. A previous flight, carried out on 23rd October, covered nearly 200 ft (65 m) and had won Santos-Dumont the Archdeacon Prize of 3,000 francs for the first sustained flight of more than 25 m.

The first powered aeroplane flight in Great Britain, though not officially recognised, was almost certainly made by Horatio Phillips (1845–1924) in a 22 hp multiplane in 1907. The aircraft had four of Phillips's unique narrow "Venetian blind" wing-frames in tandem. It covered a distance of about 500 ft (152 m).

The first monoplane with tractor engine, enclosed fuselage, rear-mounted tail-unit and two-wheel main undercarriage with tailwheel was the Blériot VII powered by a 50 hp Antoinette engine. This was Louis Blériot's third full-size monoplane and was built during the autumn of 1907 and first flown by him at Issy-les-Moulineaux, France, on 10th November 1907. Before finally crashing this aeroplane on 18th December that year Blériot had achieved six flights, the longest of which was more than 1,640 ft (500 m). This success confirmed to the designer that his basic configuration was sound—so much so that despite a thirty-year deviation into biplane design, Blériot's basic configuration is still regarded as fundamentally conventional among propeller-driven aeroplanes of today.

The first free flight of a helicopter, with a man on board, was on 13th November 1907 near Lisieux, France. It was built by Paul Cornu and had a 24 hp Antoinette engine driving two rotors. Although this was the first free flight with a man on board, earlier, on 29th September 1907, at Douai, the Breguet-Richet Gyroplane No. 1 had lifted from the ground; but four men were required to steady the machine and so Louis Breguet could not claim a free flight.

The first specification for a military aeroplane ever issued for commercial tender was drawn up by Brigadier-General James Allen, Chief Signal Officer of the

Wright Military Biplane, the world's first military aircraft (Smithsonian Institution)

Horatio Phillips' multiplane, in which he probably made the first brief powered flight in Britain in 1907

U.S. Army, on 23rd December 1907. The specification (main points) was as follows:

● Drawings to scale showing general dimensions, shape, designed speed, total surface area of supporting planes, weight, description of the engine and materials.
● The flying machine should be quick and easy to assemble and should be able to be taken apart and packed for transportation.
● Must be designed to carry two persons having a combined weight of about 350 lb and sufficient fuel for a flight of 125 miles.
● Should be designed to have a speed of at least 40 mile/h in still air.
● The speed accomplished during the trial flight will be determined by taking an average of the time over a measured course of more than 5 miles, against and with the wind.
● Before acceptance a trial endurance flight will be required of at least 1 h.
● Three trials will be allowed for speed. The place for delivery to the Government and trial flights will be Fort Myer, Virginia.
● It should be designed to ascend in any country which may be encountered in field service. The starting device must be simple and transportable. It should also land in a field without requiring a specially prepared spot, and without damaging its structure.
● It should be provided with some device to permit of a safe descent in case of an accident to the propelling machine.
● It should be sufficiently simple in its construction and operation to permit an intelligent man to become proficient in its use within a reasonable length of time.

The first internationally ratified world aeroplane records of performance were those which stood at the end of 1907, both for distance covered over the ground and for flights which followed unassisted take-off from level ground. Thus although the Wright *Flyer* (1905 version) had achieved numerous observed flights across-country, these were not ratified by the F.A.I. for world record purposes as they were, more often than not, commenced by assistance into the air by external means (a falling-weight catapult). The records established up to 31st December 1907 were thus:

12th November 1906	Santos-Dumont ("*14-bis*")	722 ft (220 m)
26th October 1907	Henry Farman (Voisin)	2,530 ft (771 m)

The first circuit flight made in Europe was flown by Henry Farman on 13th January 1908 in his modified Voisin biplane at Issy-les-Moulineaux when he took off, circumnavigated a pylon 500 m away and returned to his point of departure. By so doing Farman won the Grand Prix d'Aviation, a prize of 50,000 francs offered by Henry Deutsch de la Meurthe and Ernest Archdeacon to the first pilot to cover a kilometre. The flight took 1 min 28 s and, owing to the distance taken in turning, probably covered 1,500 m.

The first aeroplane flight in Italy was made by the French sculptor-turned-aviator Léon Delagrange in a Voisin in May 1908. At this time aircraft built by the French brothers Gabriel and Charles Voisin were flown by two pilots, Henry Farman and Léon Delagrange. Henry Farman was born in England in 1874 and retained his English citizenship until 1937 when he became a naturalised Frenchman. Having turned from painting to cycling before the turn of the century, he progressed to racing Panhard motor cars and at one time owned the largest garage in Paris. Gabriel Voisin later remarked that Farman possessed considerable mechanical and manipulative skill, whereas Delagrange "was not the sporting type" and knew nothing about running an engine. Delagrange was killed flying a Blériot monoplane on 4th January 1910. Farman, having abandoned flying to pursue the business of aeroplane manufacture died on 17th July 1958.

Henry Farman on his Voisin biplane, 8th November 1907

Charles and Gabriel Voisin

The first aeroplane flight in Belgium was made by Henry Farman, at Ghent, in May 1908.

The first passenger ever to fly in an aeroplane was Charles W. Furnas who was taken aloft by Wilbur Wright on 14th May 1908 for a flight covering 1,968 ft (650 m) of 28·6 s duration. Later the same morning Orville Wright flew Furnas for a distance of about 2·5 miles (4,000 m) which was covered in 3 min 40 s.

The first passenger to be carried in an aeroplane in Europe was Ernest Archdeacon, the Frenchman whose substantial prizes contributed such stimulus to European aviation, who was flown by Henry Farman on 29th May 1908.

The first American to fly after the Wright brothers was Glenn H. Curtiss, who flew his *June Bug* for the first time on 20th June 1908. During this flight Curtiss covered a distance of 1,266 ft (420 m) and exactly a fortnight later, on 4th July, he

Glenn Curtiss gaining the Scientific American *trophy on the* June Bug

Glenn H. Curtiss

made a flight of 5,090 ft (1,550 m) in 102·2 s to win the *Scientific American* trophy for the first official public flight in the United States of more than 1 kilometre.

The first aeroplane flight in Germany was made by the Dane, J. C. H. Ellehammer, in his triplane at Kiel on 28th June 1908. A development of this triplane was flown by **the first German pilot**, Hans Grade, at Magdeburg in October 1908.

The world's first woman passenger to fly in an aeroplane was Madame Thérèse Peltier who, on 8th July 1908, accompanied Léon Delagrange at Turin, Italy, in his Voisin for a flight of 500 ft (150 m). She soon afterwards became the first woman to fly solo, but never became a qualified pilot.

The first fatality to the occupant of a powered aeroplane occurred on 17th September 1908 at Fort Myer, Virginia, when a Wright biplane flown by Orville Wright crashed killing the passenger, Lieutenant Thomas Etholen Selfridge, U.S. Army Signal Corps. Wright was seriously injured. The accident occurred during U.S. Army acceptance trials of the Wright biplane and was caused by a failure in one of the propeller blades. This imbalanced the good blade, causing it to tear loose one of the wires bracing the rudder-outriggers to the wings, and so sending the aircraft crashing to the ground from about 75 ft (25 m).

The first resident Englishmen to fly in an aeroplane (albeit as passengers) were Griffith Brewer, the Hon. C. S. Rolls, Frank Hedges Butler, and Major B. F. S. Baden-Powell, who were taken aloft in turn by Wilbur Wright in his biplane at Camp d'Auvours on 8th October 1908. Butler had founded the Aero Club of Great Britain in 1901, while Baden-Powell was Secretary of the Aeronautical Society. The "resident" qualification is necessary here as of course the English-born, French-resident Henry Farman had been flying for more than a year by the time the four Englishmen were taken aloft by Wright.

The first officially recognised aeroplane flight in Great Britain was made by the American (later naturalised British citizen) Samuel Franklin Cody (1861–1913) in his *British Army Aeroplane No. 1*, powered by a 50 hp Antoinette engine. The flight of 1,390 ft (424 m) was made at Farnborough, Hants, on 16th October 1908 and ended with a crash-landing, but without physical injury to Cody.

S. F. Cody

Cody's British Army Aeroplane No. 1 (Flight International)

The   longest flight achieved by the end of 1908 was by Wilbur Wright on 31st December 1908, at Camp d'Auvours, where he achieved a stupendous flight of 77 miles (124 km) in 2 hr. 20 min. This won for him the Michelin prize of 20,000 francs—apart from breaking all his own records. A summary of the flights made by Wilbur Wright up to the end of 1908 is as follows:

Wilbur Wright

17th December 1903	Kill Devil Hills	852 ft	260 m	
9th November 1904	Dayton, Ohio	2·75 miles	(4·43 km)	Flew 105 times during 1904
5th October 1905	Dayton, Ohio	24·2 miles	(38·9 km)	Flew 49 times during 1905
14th May 1908	Kill Devil Hills	5 miles	(8 km)	In 7 min 29 s
8th August 1908	Hunaudières, France	—	—	Demonstration flight 1 min 45 s
16th September 1908	Auvours, France	—	—	Flight taking 39 min 18 s
21st September 1908	Auvours, France	41·3 miles	(66·5 km)	First major endurance flight. Flew more than 100 times at this location
3rd October 1908	Auvours, France	34·75 miles	(56 km)	In 55 min 37 s
10th October 1908	Auvours, France	46 miles	(74 km)	In 1 hr 9 min 45 s, with M. Pain-leve as passenger
18th December 1908	Auvours, France	62 miles	(99·8 km)	In 1 hr 54 min 53 s. Climbed to 360 ft (110 m) to establish new altitude record
31st December 1908	Auvours, France	77 miles	(124 km)	In 2 hr 20 min 23 s, to win Michelin prize and set up new world record

As a measure of the Wright biplane's world supremacy at the end of 1908 the following is a list of the more significant flights made by other aviators up to that time:

Alberto Santos-Dumont
12th November 1906
Made the first flight (accredited) in Europe at Bagatelle, covering 722 ft (220 m) in 21·2 s.

Léon Delagrange
5th November 1907 Covered 500 m at Issy-les-Moulineaux.

11th April 1908 Covered 3,925 m (over 2·5 miles) at Issy-les-Moulineaux.

23rd June 1908 Covered 8·75 miles (14·27 km) in 18 min 30 s at Milan, Italy.

6th September 1908 Covered 15·2 miles (24·4 km) in 29 min 53 s at Issy-les-Moulineaux.

17th September 1908 Flight lasting 30 min 27 s at Issy-les-Moulineaux.

Henry Farman
26th October 1907 Covered 2,530 ft (771 m) in 52·6 s.

13th January 1908 Covered a 1 km circuit in 1 min 28 s at Issy-les-Moulineaux.

6th July 1908 Covered 12·4 miles (20 km) in 20 min 20 s.

30th October 1908 Covered 17 miles (27·3 km) in 20 min on cross-country flight from Châlons to Reims.

Glenn H. Curtiss
4th July 1908 Covered 5,090 ft (1,550 m) in 1 min 42 s to win *Scientific American* trophy.

The first aerodrome to be prepared as such in England was the flying-ground between Leysdown and Shellness, Isle of Sheppey (known as "Shellbeach"), where limited established facilities were provided. It was opened in February 1909 by the joint effort of the Aero Club of Great Britain and Short Bros. Ltd.

The first sustained, powered flight by an aeroplane in the British Empire was made on 23rd February 1909 by J. A. D. McCurdy, a Canadian, over Baddeck Bay, Nova Scotia, in his biplane *Silver Dart*, which he had designed. He had made his own first flight at Hammondsport, N.Y., U.S.A., the previous December.

The first aeroplane flight in Austria was made by the Frenchman, G. Legagneux, at Vienna in April 1909 in his Voisin. **The first Austrian** to fly was Igo Etrich, who flew his *Taube* at Wiener-Neustadt in November of that year. His aircraft gave its name to the type of aircraft in fairly widespread use by Germany at the beginning of the First World War.

The first cinematographer to be taken up in an aeroplane was at Centocelle, near Rome, on 24th April 1909, in a Wright biplane flown by Wilbur Wright.

Moore-Brabazon with the "first pig to fly"

The first resident Englishman to make an officially recognised aeroplane flight in England was J. T. C. Moore-Brabazon (later Lord Brabazon of Tara) who made three sustained flights of 450,600 and 1,500 ft (130, 180 and 450 m) between 30th April and 2nd May 1909 at Leysdown, Isle of Sheppey, in his Voisin biplane. He had learned to fly in France during the previous year and on 30th October 1909 won the £1,000 *Daily Mail* prize for the first Briton to cover a mile (closed circuit) in a British aeroplane—a Short-Wright biplane. Shortly afterwards, he carried a pig in a basket on one of his flights, to demonstrate that the sarcastic expression "pigs might fly" was thoroughly outdated. He was awarded the Aero Club of Great Britain's Aviator Certificate No. 1 on 8th March 1910. Lord Brabazon died in 1969.

The first aeroplane flight of over 1 mile flown in Britain was achieved on 14th May 1909 by Samuel Cody who flew the *British Army Aeroplane No. 1* from Laffan's Plain to Danger Hill, Hants—a distance of just over 1 mile—and landed without breaking anything. The Prince of Wales requested a repeat performance during the same afternoon, but Cody, turning to avoid some troops, crashed into an embankment and demolished the tail of his aeroplane.

The Short biplane taking off, 30th October 1909 (Flight International)

The first Briton to fly an all-British aeroplane was Alliott Verdon Roe (1877–1958), in his Roe I triplane on 13th July 1909 at Lea Marshes, Essex. Lack of funds to build the triplane had forced Roe to construct it from wood instead of light-gauge steel tubing, to cover the wings with paper and to use the same 9 hp J.A.P. engine that had powered his unsuccessful biplane. The 100 ft (30 m) flight that was achieved on the 13th was much improved upon on the 23rd, when he flew 900 ft (275 m) at an average height of 10 ft (3 m).

Conquest of the English Channel. In response to an offer by the *Daily Mail* of a prize of £1,000 for the first pilot (of any nationality) to fly an aeroplane across the Channel. **The first attempt** was made by an Englishman, Hubert Latham, flying an Antoinette IV. He took off from Sangatte, near Calais, at 06.42 h on Monday, 19th July 1909, but alighted in the sea after only 6 to 8 miles (10–13 km) following engine failure which could not be rectified in the air. He was picked up by the French naval vessel *Harpon*. The occasion of this attempt was also the **first instance of wireless telegraphy being used to obtain weather reports**, the first report being transmitted

Putting Latham's Antoinette ashore at Calais

from Sangatte, near Calais, to the Lord Warden Hotel, Dover, at 04.30 h on that morning.

Despite working furiously to get a replacement Antoinette, Latham was beaten by Louis Blériot. The Frenchman took off in his Blériot XI monoplane at 04.41 h, from Les Baraques, on Sunday, 25th July 1909, and landed at 5.17·5 h in the Northfall Meadow by Dover Castle to become **the first man to cross the English Channel in an aeroplane.**

Latham did, however, make another attempt to fly the Channel two days later (on 27th July), taking off at 05.50 h from Cap Blanc Nez. When only 1 mile from the Dover cliffs, his engine failed and once again he had to alight in the sea.

Louis Blériot at Dover, 25th July 1909

The first officially recognised aeroplane flight in Russia was made by Van den Schkrouff in a Voisin biplane at Odessa on 25th July 1909.

The first aeroplane flight in Sweden was made by the Frenchman Legagneux at Stockholm in his Voisin biplane on 29th July 1909.

The first woman passenger to fly in an aeroplane in England was Mrs. Cody, wife of Samuel, who was taken up by her husband during the last week of July 1909 over Laffan's Plain, Hants, in the *British Army Aeroplane No. 1*.

The first passenger to be carried by an aeroplane in Canada was F. W. "Casey" Baldwin who was taken aloft on 2nd August 1909 at Petawawa, Ontario, in an aeroplane flown by J. A. D. McCurdy.

Racing at Reims

The first International Aviation Meeting in the world opened on 22nd August 1909 at Reims, and
lasted until 29th August 1909. Thirty-eight aeroplanes were entered to
participate, although only twenty-three managed to leave the ground;
the meeting also attracted aviators and aeroplane-designers from all
over Europe and did much to arouse widespread public interest in flying.
The types and numbers of aeroplanes which flew were: Antoinette (3),
Blériot XI (2), Blériot XII (1), Blériot XIII (1), Breguet (1), Curtiss (1),
Henry Farman (3), REP (1), Voisin (7), Wright (3).

The world's first speed record over 100 km was established by the Englishman, Hubert Latham,
during the Reims International Meeting (see above) between 22nd and
29th August 1909. Flying an Antoinette (powered by a 50 hp 8-cylinder
Antoinette engine) he covered the distance in 1 h 28 min 17 s, at an average
speed of 42 mile/h. In so doing he won the second largest prize of the
meeting amounting to 42,000 francs. First prize went to Henry Farman
who, flying a Gnôme-powered Farman, set up new world records for
duration and distance in a closed circuit, covering 112·5 miles (181·04
km) in 3 h 4 min 56·4 s, winning 63,000 francs.

The first aeroplane flight in the world in which two passengers were carried was made at the
Reims International Meeting (see above) on 27th August 1909 by Henry
Farman who, in his Gnôme-powered Farman biplane, covered a distance
of 6·2 miles (10 km) in 10 min 39 s.

The first pilot to be killed flying a powered aeroplane was Eugène Lefebvre, on 7th September
1909; he crashed while flying a new Wright type A at Port Aviation,
Juvisy. Soon afterwards, on 22nd September, Captain Ferber was killed
when his Voisin hit a ditch while preparing for take-off.

The first aeroplane flight in Denmark was made by Léon Delagrange in September 1909.

The first Aviation Meeting held in Great Britain was that organised by the Doncaster Aviation Committee on the Doncaster Racecourse between 15th and 23rd October 1909. This meeting was not governed by rules laid down by the F.A.I., nor was it officially recognised by the Aero Club of Great Britain. Twelve aeroplanes constituted the field, of which five managed to fly. **The first officially recognised meeting** was held at Squires Gate, Blackpool, between 18th and 23rd October 1909, being organised by the Blackpool Corporation and the Lancashire Aero Club; seven of the dozen participants were coaxed into the air.

The first aeroplane flight in Rumania was made by Louis Blériot in his monoplane at Bucharest on 30th October 1909. It has been said that Blériot's first flights outside France represented the first serious threat to the acknowledged superiority of the Voisin biplane in Europe at that time. However, the Blériot aeroplane was still in effect a prototype, whereas the Voisin had already achieved a degree of series production, about six examples of roughly similar design having been completed.

The first successful still photographs taken from an aeroplane were by M. Meurisse, in December 1909, and showed the flying-fields at Mourmelon and Châlons. The aeroplane was an Antoinette piloted by Latham.

The first aeroplane flight in Ireland is believed to have been carried out by H. G. Ferguson of Belfast during the winter of 1909–10. The aeroplane was of his own design and manufacture; it resembled a Blériot, and was powered by an eight-cylinder 35 hp air-cooled J.A.P. engine.

The first American monoplane to fly was the Walden III, designed by Dr. Henry W. Walden and flown on 9th December 1909 at Mineola, Long Island, N.Y. It was powered by a 22 hp three-cylinder Anzani engine.

The first aeroplane flights in Australia were achieved on 9th December 1909 by Colin Defries, also well known as a motor racing driver. He flew an imported Wright biplane for a mile at a height of 35 ft (11 m) over the Victoria Park Racecourse at Sydney, New South Wales. On the day after his first flight he made a further short flight, this time with a passenger (Mr. C. S. Magennis), **the first to be carried by an aeroplane in Australia.** (It has often been said that Ehrich Weiss, better known as Harry Houdini the escapologist, was the first aeroplane pilot to make a *significant* flight; on 18th March 1910 he flew three times in a Voisin biplane at Digger's Rest, Victoria, achieving a maximum height of over 100 ft (30 m), while his longest flight exceeded 2 miles (3·2 km).

The first aeroplane flight in Egypt was made by Baron de Caters at Cairo on 15th December 1909, flying a Voisin.

The Aero Club of Great Britain had the prefix "Royal" bestowed upon it by H.M. King Edward VII on 15th February 1910. This body had already displayed considerable tact and administrative acumen in the control of flying in Great Britain, and it is quite clear that the King, in bestowing the Royal title upon the club, recognised the position of responsibility it would come to occupy in man's determination to perfect the aeroplane in the coming years.

Mme la Baronne de Laroche

The first certified woman pilot in the world was Mme la Baronne de Laroche, a Frenchwoman, who received her Pilot's Certificate No. 36 on 8th March 1910, having qualified on a Voisin biplane. She was killed in 1919 in an aeroplane accident.

The first night flights were made by Emil Aubrun, a Frenchman, on 10th March 1910 flying a Blériot monoplane. Each of the two flights began and ended at Villalugano, Buenos Aires, Argentina, and was about 12·4 miles (20 km) long.

The first successful seaplane flight was made by Henri Fabre at Martigues, near Marseille, on 28th March 1910. By September 1910 flights of nearly 2 miles were being achieved.

The first aeroplane flight in Switzerland was made by Captain Engelhardt at Saint-Moritz on 13th March 1910.

The first aeroplane flights in Spain were made by Gaudart, Poillot, Le Blond, Mamet and Olieslaegers in March and April 1910.

The first aeroplane flight in Portugal was made by Mamet at Belem on 27th April 1910.

The first recorded night flight in Great Britain was made by Claude Grahame-White during 27th/28th April 1910 in his attempt to overhaul Louis Paulhan in the *Daily Mail* £10,000 London to Manchester air race. During the course of this race Paulhan (who won) thus made the first London to Manchester flight and was **the first to fly an aeroplane over 100 km (62·14 miles) in a straight line in Great Britain.**

The first aeroplane to be "forced down" by the action of another was the Henry Farman biplane of Mr. A. Rawlinson during the Aviation Meeting at Nice, France, in mid April 1910. Mr. Rawlinson was flying his new Farman over the sea when the Russian Effimov passed so close above him (also in a Farman) that his down-draught forced the Englishman into the water. The Russian was severely reprimanded for dangerous flying and fined 100 francs.

The first British woman to fly solo in an aeroplane was almost certainly Miss Edith Maud Cook, who performed various aerial acts under the name of Miss "Spencer Kavanagh". She achieved several solo flights on Blériot monoplanes with the Grahame-White Flying School at Pau in the Pyrenees early in 1910. She was also a professional parachute-jumper, known as "Viola Spencer," and was killed after making a jump from a balloon near Coventry, England, in July 1910.

Charles Rolls preparing to leave Dover for the first double crossing of the English Channel

The first England to France and double crossing of the English Channel was accomplished by the Hon. C. S. Rolls (the "Rolls" of "Rolls-Royce") flying a French-built Wright biplane on 2nd June 1910. He took off from Broadlees, Dover at 18.30·5 h, dropped a letter addressed to the Aero-Club de France near Sangatte at 19.15 h, then flew back to England and made a perfect landing near his starting-rail at 20.06 h. He was thus **first man to fly from England to France in an aeroplane, the first man to make a non-stop double crossing, and the first cross-Channel pilot to land at a pre-arranged spot without damage to his aeroplane.**

The first world record to fall to an Englishman (apart from Henry Farman, and Hubert Latham who established an inaugural record, see above) was the duration record taken by Captain Bertram Dickson who, on 6th June 1910, remained airborne for exactly 2 h with a passenger in his Henry Farman biplane at Anjou, France, thereby establishing a new World Endurance Record with one passenger.

The first British pilot to lose his life while flying an aeroplane was the Hon. Charles Stewart Rolls (born in London, 27th August 1877, the third son of the first Baron Llangattock), who was killed at the Bournemouth Aviation Week on 12th July 1910 when his French-built Wright biplane suffered a structural failure in flight.

The first flight in Australia by an Australian in an indigenous aeroplane was made by John R. Duigan of Mia Mia, Victoria on 16th July 1910 in an aeroplane constructed from photographs of the Wright *Flyer*. On that day Duigan flew only 28 ft (8·5 m), but on 7th October he covered 196 yd (179 m) at a height of about 12 ft (3·65 m).

The first Swedish pilot was Baron Carl Cederström who was granted a Pilot's Certificate at the Blériot Flying School at Pau, France, in 1910. On returning to Sweden he was awarded Certificate No. 1 by the Aero Club of Sweden (Svenska Aeronautiska Sallskapet). He was lost, presumed drowned, while flying as a passenger between Stockholm and Finland in July 1918.

Thulin monoplane in Finnish service

The most famous name in early Swedish aviation was probably that of Dr. Enoch Thulin, D.Phil., who gained his first Pilot's Certificate in France and was subsequently granted Swedish Certificate No. 10. Before the First World War he abandoned full-time flying to concentrate upon aeroplane manufacture, establishing his company at Landskrona in 1915. After the United States entered the war, the Thulin Aircraft Works was probably **the largest aircraft manufacturing concern of any neutral country.** Dr. Thulin was killed in a flying accident on 14th May 1919.

The first aeroplane flights in the Argentine and Brazil were made in 1910 by Voisin and Henry Farman biplanes respectively.

The first mail carried unofficially in an aeroplane in Great Britain was flown by Claude Grahame-White on 10th August 1910 in a Blériot monoplane from Squires Gate, Blackpool; he did not reach his destination at Southport, having been forced to land by bad weather.

The first Channel crossing with a passenger was by J. B. Moisant and his mechanic in a Blériot two-seater aeroplane, from Calais to Dover, on 17th August 1910.

The first use of radio between an aeroplane and the ground was on 27th August 1910 when James McCurdy, flying a Curtiss, sent and received messages via an H. M. Horton wireless set at Sheepshead Bay, N.Y. State.

Claude Grahame-White and passenger

The first crossing of the Irish Sea was made by Robert Loraine who, flying a Farman biplane on 11th September 1910, set off from Holyhead, Anglesey. Although engine failure forced him down in the sea 60 yd offshore from the Irish coast near Baily Lighthouse, Howth, he was generally considered to have been the first to accomplish the crossing.

The first flight over the Alps was made by the Peruvian Georges Chavez in a Blériot on 23rd September 1910. His flight from Brig to Domodossola, via the Simplon Pass, ended in disaster when he crashed on landing and was killed.

The first air collision in the world occurred on 8th September 1910 between two aeroplanes piloted by brothers named Warchalovski at Wiener-Neustadt, Austria. One of the pilots suffered a broken leg. A passenger on one of the aircraft was the Archduke Léopold Salvator of Austria.

Former American President Theodore Roosevelt flew three laps of the aerodrome at St. Louis in a Wright biplane piloted by A. Hoxie in mid October 1910.

Perhaps the greatest feats by a novice pilot were achieved by T. O. M. (later Sir Thomas) Sopwith in 1910. Having purchased a Howard Wright monoplane, he attempted to perform the first test flight on 22nd October, never before having flown as a pilot. It crashed but Sopwith was unhurt. The monoplane was repaired, and he flew it with increasing skill before changing to a Howard Wright biplane. On 21st November, less than a month after his first attempt to fly, he carried out his first-ever taxiing in a biplane before lunch, took off and completed some circuits in the afternoon and qualified for his Pilot's Certificate (No. 31) about tea-time. He carried his first passenger the same evening. Five days later he set up new British Distance and Duration Records, which put him in the lead in the competition for the 1910 British Empire Michelin Cup, offered for the longest distance flown in a closed circuit by a British pilot in a British aeroplane. On 18th December 1910 he won the £4,000 Baron de Forest prize for the longest distance flown in a straight line into Europe by a British pilot in a British machine during that year. His flight covered 177 miles (285 km) from Eastchurch to Beaumont, Belgium. On the last day of the year he regained his lost lead in the Michelin Cup competition by flying 150 miles, only to be beaten at the very last moment by Cody.

T. O. M. Sopwith on his Howard Wright biplane

The largest single crowd to watch a display of flying before the First World War was almost certainly the concourse of nearly 750,000 Indians who turned out to watch M. Henri Jullerot of the Bristol Company in his Military Biplane at Calcutta on 6th January 1911.

The first flight in New Zealand by an aeroplane was made by a Howard Wright type biplane piloted by Vivian C. Walsh at Auckland on 5th February 1911. With his brother Leo, Vivian Walsh imported materials from England with which to build the aircraft and installed a 60 hp E.N.V. engine. Vivian Walsh also made **the first seaplane flight in New Zealand** on 1st January 1914.

The first Government (official) air-mail flight in the world was undertaken on 18th February 1911 when the French pilot Henri Pequet flew a Humber biplane from Allahabad to Naini Junction, a distance of about 5 miles (8 km) across the Jumna River, with about 6,500 letters. The regular service was established four days later as part of the Universal Postal Exhibition, Allahabad, India, the flights being shared by Captain W. G. Windham and Pequet. The envelopes of this first air-mail service were franked "First Aerial Post, U.P. Exhibition, Allahabad, 1911" and are highly prized among collectors.

Eleven passengers were first carried in an aeroplane on 23rd March 1911 by Louis Breguet over a distance of 5 km (3·1 miles) at Douai, France, in a Breguet biplane. **Twelve passengers were first carried in an aeroplane** on 24th March 1911 by Roger Sommer over a distance of 800 m (875 yd) in a Sommer biplane powered by a 70 hp engine.

The first non-stop flight from London to Paris was made on 12th April 1911 by Pierre Prier in 3 h 56 min, flying a Blériot monoplane powered by a 50 hp Gnôme engine. Prier, who was Chief Flying Instructor at the Blériot Flying School, Hendon, took off from Hendon and landed at Issy-les-Moulineaux.

The first air cargo to be carried by an aeroplane was a large case of Osram electric lamps which were delivered by air from Shoreham to Hove, for the General Electric Company, by Horatio Barber in his Valkyrie monoplane on 4th July 1911.

The first Swedish pilot to be awarded a Pilot's Certificate by the Royal Aero Club of Great Britain was Lieutenant C. O. Dahlbeck who qualified at Hendon with the Grahame-White Flying School on a Henry Farman biplane, being awarded Certificate No. 120 on 29th August 1911. Lieutenant Dahlbeck was holder of Swedish Certificate No. 3.

The first British woman to be granted a Pilot's Certificate was Mrs. Hilda B. Hewlett who qualified on a Henry Farman biplane at Brooklands for Certificate No. 122 on 29th August 1911. Her son, Sub-Lieutenant F. E. T. Hewlett, R.N., was taught to fly by her, and was thus **the first and possibly the only naval airman in the world ever to receive his flying tuition from his mother.** His Certificate, No. 156, was gained on 14th November 1911. Young Hewlett was one of the first five officers of the Naval Wing, R.F.C.

The first official mail to be carried by air in Great Britain was entrusted to the staff pilots of the Grahame-White and Blériot flying schools who commenced carrying the mail between Hendon and Windsor on Saturday, 9th September 1911. The first flight was undertaken on that day by Gustav Hamel in a Blériot monoplane, covering the route in 10 min at a ground speed of over 105 mile/h (169 km/h) with a strong tailwind. The service lasted until 26th September, having been instituted to commemorate the Coronation of H.M. King George V. The total weight of mail carried between the Hendon flying-field and Royal Farm, Windsor was 1,015 lb (460·4 kg).

The first Chinese national to receive a Pilot's Certificate was Zee Yee Lee who was awarded Royal Aero Club Certificate No. 148 on 17th October 1911, qualifying on a Bristol Boxkite after receiving his training on Salisbury Plain, England. Lee later became Chief Flying Instructor at the Military Flying School at Nanyuen, Peking. He was followed by Prince Tsai Tao, Wee Gee, Colonel Tsing, Lieutenant Poa and Lieutenant Yoa, at least two of whom gained Certificates in the U.S.A.

The first seaplane competition was held at Monaco in March 1912. Seven pilots attended (Fischer, Renaux, Paulhan, Robinson, Caudron, Benoit, Rugère), the winner being Fischer on a Henry Farman biplane.

The first instance of a Government ordering the grounding of a specific type of aircraft occurred in March 1912 when the French Government ordered all Blériot

monoplanes of the French Army to be prohibited from flying until they had
been rebuilt so that their wings were braced to withstand a degree of
negative-G. Five distinguished French pilots had been killed following the
collapse of the Blériots' wings, but the ban was short-lived and the aircraft
were flying again within a fortnight. The weakness was spotlighted by
Louis Blériot himself who, despite the likely loss of prestige, published a
short report explaining the weakness in his own aeroplanes. There is no
doubt that his frankness increased—rather than detracted from—his very
high standing in aviation circles.

The first American woman to receive her Pilot's Certificate was Harriet Quimby. She was also
the **first woman to pilot an aeroplane across the English Channel**,
in a Blériot monoplane, having taken off from Deal and landed at Cape
Gris-Nez less than an hour later, on 16th April 1912.

The first flight from Paris to Berlin was achieved by Edmond Audemars of Switzerland who flew
a Blériot monoplane from the French capital to the German capital via
Bochum in Westphalia during the spring of 1912.

The first all-metal aeroplane to fly was the Tubavion monoplane built by the Frenchmen Ponche
and Primard in 1912. A fatal accident brought its tests to a halt.

The first flight in Norway by a Norwegian took place on 1st June 1912 when Lieutenant Hans E.
Dons, a submarine officer, flew a German Start across Oslo Fjord from
Horten to Frederikstad, a distance of 37 miles (60 km). As a result of this
achievement the Norwegian Storting (Government) voted the sum of
£900 ($2,160) to send four officers to Paris to learn to fly. Within three
months (in August) one of these officers had established a Scandinavian
distance record.

The first American woman to be killed in an aeroplane accident was Julie Clark of Denver,
Colorado, whose Curtiss biplane struck a tree on 17th June 1912 at Spring-
field, Illinois, and turned turtle. She had qualified for her Pilot's Certificate
on 19th May 1912.

The first crossing of the English Channel by an aeroplane with a pilot and two passengers
was made on 4th August 1912 by W. B. Rhodes Moorhouse (later, as a
Lieutenant in the Royal Flying Corps, the first British airman to be
awarded the Victoria Cross on 26th April 1915) who, accompanied by
his wife and a friend, flew a Breguet tractor biplane from Douai, France,
via Boulogne and Dungeness, to Bethersden, near Ashford, Kent, where
they crashed in bad weather. Nobody was hurt.

The first man to fly underneath all the Thames bridges in London between Tower Bridge and
Westminster was F. K. McClean who, flying a Short pusher biplane from
Harty Ferry, Isle of Sheppey, in mid August 1912, passed between the
upper and lower spans of Tower Bridge, and then underflew all the remaining bridges to Westminster where he landed on the river. No regulations forbade this escapade, but the police instructed McClean to taxi all
the way back to Shadwell Basin before mooring! On the return trip the
aeroplane side-slipped soon after take-off and damaged one of the floats
after hitting a barge. The machine was then towed into Shadwell Dock and
dismantled for the return by road to Eastchurch.

F. K. McClean flying through Tower Bridge

The first officer of the Royal Flying Corps Reserves to be killed while engaged on military flying duties was Second-Lieutenant E. Hotchkiss (the Bristol Company's Chief Flying Instructor at Brooklands) who, with Lieutenant C. A. Bettington, was killed on 10th September 1912 when their Bristol monoplane crashed on a flight from Salisbury Plain. The aircraft suffered a structural failure, after which the wing fabric started to tear away and the aircraft crashed near Oxford. Within three weeks the flying of monoplanes by the Military Wing was banned by Colonel Seely, Secretary of State for War, and although the ban was to last no more than five months it gave rise to an extraordinary prejudice against monoplanes in British military flying circles that was to persist for more than twenty years. (It is usually recorded that Hotchkiss's Bristol crashed on Port Meadow, Oxford, but the memorial tablet confirms that in fact the accident occurred half a mile west of Godstow on the right bank of the River Thames, just north of Port Meadow.)

The number of Pilots' Certificates which had been awarded in the world by the end of 1912 was 2,480, though the number of actual pilots was slightly smaller as some had been awarded certificates in more than one country. One or two others had received certificates in countries which were not members of the

Fédération Aéronautique Internationale. The massive superiority of
France at this time is evident:

1	France	966	10	Holland		26
2	Great Britain	382	11	Argentine Republic		15
3	Germany	335		Spain		15
4	United States of America	193	13	Sweden		10
5	Italy	186	14	Denmark		8
6	Russia	162	15	Hungary		7
7	Austria	84	16	Norway		5
8	Belgium	58	17	Egypt		1
9	Switzerland	27				
					Total	2,480

Two British pilots had been killed during 1910; seven aeroplane occupants were killed in 1911, seventeen in 1912 and fifteen in 1913. By the
outbreak of the First World War seventy-eight British subjects had lost
their lives in aeroplanes at home or abroad.

The first four-engined aeroplane to fly was the Bolshoi (Russian "The Great") biplane designed,
and first flown on 13th May 1913 at St Petersburg, by Igor Sikorsky. It had
a wing span of over 92 ft (28 m) and was powered by four 100 hp Argus
engines.

Strikemaster in action

SECTION II
Military Aviation

The original use of the first military aircraft, nearly two centuries ago, was for battlefield reconnaissance. The aircraft were tethered hydrogen balloons, able to venture no further than the prevailing wind and the length of their cable allowed; but the reports of the observers they carried influenced the course of battles.

When the first practical aeroplanes appeared in the first decade of our present century, it was no coincidence that the first one sold was a Wright biplane delivered to the U.S. Army in 1909. Few people could envisage any real use for the fragile, unreliable early flying-machines. About the only possibility seemed to be as a kind of aerial cavalry, to inform army commanders about enemy movements and dispositions "over the hill" and to give naval commanders long-range eyes to see what was happening over the horizon.

So, when the First World War began, the aeroplanes serving with the armed forces of the belligerents were unarmed and intended primarily for reconnaissance. The reports brought back by their crews proved so valuable that the "other side" quickly appreciated the need to destroy the reconnaissance aircraft or, at least, to prevent them from roaming freely on visual and photographic sorties over the trenches. Fighter aircraft began to enter service to intercept and turn back the reconnaissance aircraft—which themselves acquired protective fighter escorts. This led to fighter-to-fighter combat. Simultaneously, the first bombing raids were directed against the bases from which German Zeppelin airships set out on their reconnaissance missions to find and shadow the Royal Navy at sea.

As the First World War went on, year after year, air fighting and bombing became vital tasks in their own right. By the Second World War, the significance of reconnaissance tended to be overshadowed by the more obvious triumph of R.A.F. fighters in the Battle of Britain and by the immense contributions to final victory made by the bombers of the British, U.S. and Allied forces, including the spectacular actions by carrier-based aircraft in the Pacific.

It was easy to overlook that the Germans might have won the Battle of Britain had their reconnaissance provided a more accurate picture of the effects that successive stages of the Luftwaffe offensive
were, or were not, having. On 12th August 1940, for example, the German Air Force believed it had
destroyed five of the precious radar stations that guided and conserved the strength of R.A.F. fighter
squadrons; in fact, all but one were operational next day. General Stapf reported to his chief that, after
only five days, eight British air bases had been knocked out and the R.A.F. was losing three aircraft
for every German machine lost. It just was not true.

Later, as the great Allied bomber offensive against Europe grew in intensity, so did the need for
sustained, precise reconnaissance. Only the most courageous and skilful sorties by pilots of the camera-
planes could reveal targets like the secret enemy V-weapon centre at Peenemünde. Only hazardous
reconnaissance flights on the day after a heavy raid could show whether a factory, railway yard, rocket
site, airfield, battleship or dam had been destroyed or whether further attacks were necessary.

Nothing has changed in a nuclear age except that, as some of aviation's earliest pioneers predicted,
air-power has made major war virtually inconceivable. Demonstration of the terrifying power of even
small atomic bombs, at Hiroshima and Nagasaki in 1945, provided the basis for a deterrent policy of
"peace through fear". The great power blocs of East and West, accepting that no defence against
nuclear-warhead missiles and bombs is practicable at less than crippling cost, have agreed to a balance
of offensive and defensive nuclear forces.

For the first time in history, it has been admitted that the cost of keeping millions of citizens alive
in war is so high that it cannot be faced, even though the weapons to annihilate those people are poised
permanently, ready for instant launch. The only frail protection is the word of opposing leaders that
they will never be first to launch an attack—backed up by the day-to-day reports of reconnaissance
satellites which, it is believed, would detect any preparations for such attack.

Until the Vietnam War, it appeared that conflict on this kind of more limited, non-nuclear,
scale might be a frequent, unavoidable feature of life in an era deprived of the possibility of a "Third
World War". That long campaign, fought by America on the enemy's terms and with its "nuclear
arm tied behind its back", was ended only by a huge and costly concentrated bombing offensive by
eight-jet B-52s, dropping conventional weapons, in December 1972. The long and weary path to
peace, that nobody really won, should have ensured that no Great Power will ever again allow itself to
become involved in such a confrontation.

This suggests that the only wars that may still be considered worth chancing will be localised
conflicts in or among the newly emergent nations. Hence the current emphasis on tactical non-nuclear
and counter-insurgency combat aircraft, including vertical take-off types able to operate in places
where there are no airfields.

Meanwhile, more than a quarter of a century of relative freedom from major war suggests that the
greatest of all the achievements of the aeroplane, and its offshoot the guided missile, is that they have
made world war seem no longer the mere "continuation of political intercourse by different means"
that seemed so natural to our ancestors a century ago.

"I hope these new mechanic meteors will prove only playthings for the learned and the idle, and not
be converted into new engines of destruction to the human race, as is so often the case of refinements
or discoveries in science."

Horace Walpole (1717–1797) in 1782.

**The first military man to die in an aeroplane crash, and also the first aeroplane casualty in
the world** was Lieutenant Thomas E. Selfridge of the U.S. Signal Corps
on 17th September 1908 at Fort Myer, Virginia; his pilot was Orville
Wright, who was seriously injured in the crash.

The first aeroplane purchased by the American Government was a Wright biplane, *Miss
Columbia*, sold by the Wright brothers on 2nd August 1909. The price was
$25,000, but a bonus of $5,000 was awarded as the specified maximum
speed of 40 mile/h (64 km/h) was exceeded. The aircraft was constructed
at Dayton, Ohio.

The first military pilot to get the Brevet of the Aéro-Club de France was Lieutenant Camerman on 7th March 1910, receiving Brevet No. 33.

The first man to drop missiles from an aeroplane was Glenn Hammond Curtiss on 30th June 1910, when he dropped dummy bombs from a height of 50 ft (15 m) on to the shape of a battleship marked by buoys on Lake Keuka.

The first German active duty officer to receive a Pilot's licence was Leutnant Richard von Tiedemann, a Hussar officer. He first flew solo on 23rd July 1910.

The first serving officer of the British Army to be awarded a Pilot's Certificate in England was Captain George William Patrick Dawes who was awarded Certificate No. 17 for qualification on a Humber monoplane at Wolverhampton on 26th July 1910.

Captain Dawes died on 17th March 1960 aged eighty. He had served in South Africa between 1900 and 1902 when he was awarded the Queen's Medal with three clasps, and the King's Medal with two clasps. He took up flying privately in 1909 and was posted to the R.F.C. on its formation in 1912. He commanded the Corps in the Balkans from 1916 to 1918, during which time he was awarded the D.S.O. and the A.F.C., was mentioned in despatches seven times, and awarded the Croix de Guerre with three palms, the Serbian Order of the White Eagle, the Order of the Redeemer of Greece and created Officer of the Legion d'Honneur. He served with the Royal Air Force in the Second World War as a Wing Commander, retiring in 1946 with the M.B.E. He thus was one of the very few officers who served actively in the Boer War and both world wars.

The first military firearm to be fired from an aeroplane was a rifle fired by Lieutenant Jacob Earl Fickel, U.S. Army, from his single-seater Curtiss biplane at a target at Sheepshead Bay, New York City, on 20th August 1910.

The first explosive bombs dropped by American pilots were those dropped by Lieutenant Myron Sidney Crissy and Philip O. Parmelee, from a Wright biplane, during trials on 7th January 1911 at San Francisco, Calif.

Capitano Piazza with his Blériot (Italian Air Ministry)

The first time an aeroplane was used in war was on 22nd October 1911 when an Italian Blériot, piloted by Capitano Piazza, made a reconnaissance flight from Tripoli to Azizia to view the Turkish positions.

Airship used for reconnaissance by the Italians during the war in North Africa, 1911–12 (Italian Air Ministry)

The first single-seat scout aeroplane was the Farnborough B.S.1 of 1912 which was designed mainly by Geoffrey de Havilland.

Another Farnborough aeroplane, the B.E.1, made **the first successful artillery-spotting flight** over Salisbury Plain in 1912.

FORMATION OF THE FIRST BRITISH MILITARY AEROPLANE SQUADRONS

(The Royal Flying Corps came into being officially on 13th May 1912.)

Squadron	Date	Remarks
No. 1 (Airship and Kite)	13th May 1912	Formed out of No. 1 Airship Company, Air Battalion.
No. 2 (Aeroplane)	13th May 1912	Formed from scratch.
No. 3 (Aeroplane)	13th May 1912	Formed out of No. 2 Aeroplane Company, Air Battalion.
No. 4 (Aeroplane)	16th May 1912	Formed from scratch.
No. 5 (Aeroplane)	26th July 1913	Formed from scratch at Farnborough.
No. 6 (Aeroplane)	31st Jan. 1914	Formed from scratch at Farnborough.
No. 7 (Aeroplane)	May 1914	Formed from scratch.
No. 8 (Aeroplane)	May 1914	Formed out of No. 1 Airship and Kite Squadron, R.F.C.

The first American aeroplane armed with a machine-gun was a Wright biplane flown by Lieutenant Thomas de Witt Milling at College Park, Md., on 2nd June 1912. The gunner, who was armed with a Lewis gun, was Charles de Forest Chandler of the U.S. Army Signal Corps.

The first Swedish military pilot was Captain G. von Porat of the Royal Swedish Engineers who, with two other military pilots, gained his military flying Brevet at the Nieuport School in France in 1912 but did not qualify for a Swedish Certificate. In 1914 he was injured in a flying accident and joined the aeroplane department of Södertalge Verkstäder.

The first Mexican military pilot was Major Alberto Salinas who learned to fly in the U.S.A. and was awarded Pilot's Certificate No. 170 by the Aero Club of America in 1912. He was also founder of Mexican military aviation in that year.

The first military aviation establishment in the Argentine was the Military Flying School at El Palomar, opened on 10th September 1912; the first flying course commenced instruction on Farman biplanes on 4th November that year and was attended by twelve pilots. One of these, Sub-Teniente Manuel Origone, was killed on 19th January 1913 and was thus **the first military air casualty in the Argentine.**

captions for following colour plate

1. B.E.2a *of the Royal Naval Air Service, Eastchurch Squadron, flown by Squadron Commander Charles R. Samson in France and Belgium during the first two years of the First World War. Samson formed an affection for No. 50, and it accompanied him to Tenedos when he was posted to command naval aircraft in the Dardanelles campaign; in the course of the campaign he continued to fly the B.E.2a on reconnaissance, artillery spotting and bombing missions against the Turkish forces. Details of Samson's career may be found in the text.*

2. Nieuport 17 B1566, *flown during the early summer of 1917 by Captain William A. Bishop,* D.S.O., M.C., *of No. 60 Squadron R.F.C. Bishop, whose career is described in fuller detail in the text, is thought to have achieved nearly twenty of his seventy-two confirmed victories while flying B1566.*

3. Sopwith Triplane N5492 Black Maria, *flown during the spring and early summer of 1917 by Flight Sub-Lieutenant Raymond Collishaw as commander of "B" Flight, No. 10 Squadron, R.N.A.S. During twenty-seven days of June 1917 Collishaw flew this aircraft to victory over sixteen enemy machines, including the Albatros D III of Jasta II flown by the ace, Leutnant Karl Allmenröder. N5492 was eventually shot down in July while being flown in combat by another pilot. Details of Collishaw's career may be found in the text.*

4. S.E.5a B4863, *one of the aircraft flown during the summer and autumn of 1917 by Captain James T. B. McCudden,* M.C., M.M., *as commander of "B" Flight, No. 56 Squadron, R.F.C. Details of McCudden's career may be found in the text. During the winter of 1917/18 he is known to have flown S.E.5a B4891, fitted with the red-painted propeller spinner from an LVG C V two-seater which he shot down on 30th November.*

5. Sopwith 7F.1 Snipe E8102, *flown on 27th October 1918 by Major William G. Barker,* D.S.O., M.C., *attached to No. 201 Squadron, R.A.F. Flying alone on the early morning of 27th October, Barker had shot down a German two-seater when he was attacked and wounded in the right thigh by a Fokker D VII. Barker's aircraft lost height in a spin; in the course of the next few minutes he passed through successive layers of a large German formation, being attacked on four separate occasions by groups of at least a dozen Fokker scouts. Before he finally managed to bring his damaged Snipe down for a successful forced landing, Barker had been wounded twice more (in the left thigh and the left elbow); had lost consciousness twice, and twice recovered and regained control of his aircraft; and had shot down three more enemy aircraft. This epic engagement led to the award of the Victoria Cross.*

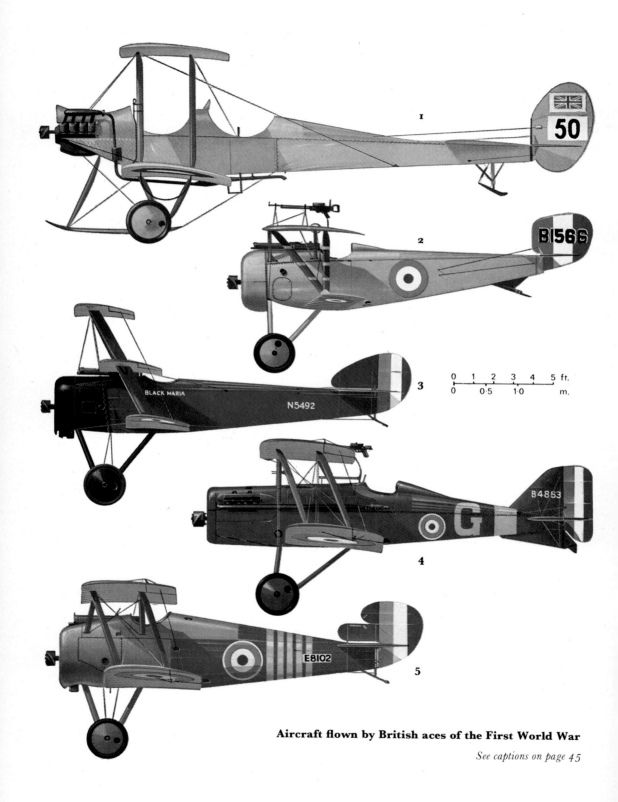

Aircraft flown by British aces of the First World War

See captions on page 45

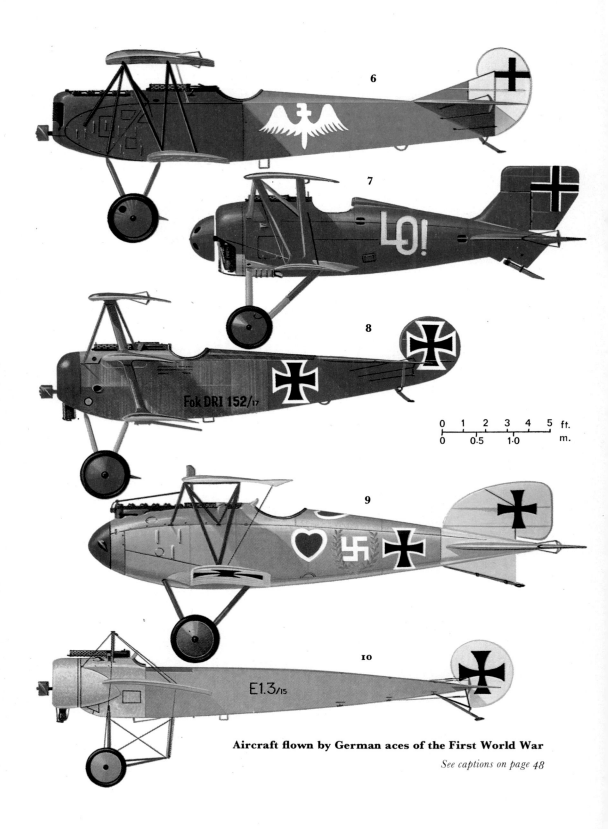

6

7

8

Fok DRI 152/17

9

10

E1.3/15

Aircraft flown by German aces of the First World War

See captions on page 48

6. Fokker D VII *flown during the spring of 1918 by Hauptmann Rudolf Berthold as commanding officer of Jagdgeschwader Nr. 2. Sixth in the roll of German aces, with forty-four confirmed victories, Berthold suffered continual pain from an injury which rendered his right arm useless. He had the controls of his Fokker altered to compensate for his disability and continued to fly, scoring at least sixteen of his victories during a period when his arm refused to heal and was rejecting splinters of suppurating bone almost daily. Active in the Freikorps movement in the immediate post-war period, Berthold led an anti-Communist band known as the "Eiserne Schar Berthold". He was murdered—by strangulation with the ribbon of his Ordre Pour le Mérite—on 15th March 1920, after accepting a safe-conduct offer from a Communist group in Harburg.*

7. Siemens-Schuckert D III *flown late in the summer of 1918 by Oberleutnant Ernst Udet as commanding officer of Jasta 4, based at Metz. This gifted pilot was credited with sixty-two victories, and in this respect was second only to Manfred von Richthofen; his amiable and rather flamboyant disposition made him a popular commander, although an early over-confidence sometimes led him into difficulties. He survived the war, and became well known as a stunt pilot, explorer and international aviation "playboy". His extrovert nature and long friendship with many leading personalities in German aviation led to senior appointments under the Nazi régime; but he eventually found himself playing a role for which he was temperamentally unsuited, and a growing sense of estrangement culminated in his suicide on 17th November 1941. The monogram displayed on his aircraft referred to his fiancée, Fräulein Lola Zink.*

8. Fokker Dr I, *number 152/17, sometimes flown by Rittmeister Manfred, Freiherr von Richthofen as commanding officer of Jagdgeschwader Nr. 1 during the early months of 1918. (Details of Richthofen's career may be found in the body of the text.) Richthofen is known to have been flying this aircraft on 12th March 1918 when he gained the sixty-fourth of his eighty confirmed victories; his victim on that occasion was a Bristol F.2B, number B1251, of No. 62 Squadron, R.F.C. brought down near Nauroy. The crew, Lieutenant L. C. F. Clutterbuck and Second-Lieutenant H. J. Sparks, survived the crash and were made prisoners.*

9. Albatros D III *flown during the spring of 1917 by Leutnant Werner Voss, whose forty-eight confirmed victories place him fourth in the roll of German aces. Voss became a pilot in May 1916 and served his apprenticeship in the famous Jasta Boelcke; he was a born flyer and fighter, but lacked the leadership qualities of Richthofen and Berthold. During the spring of 1917 he is believed to have served briefly with both Jasta 5 and Jasta 14, and it is with the former unit that this Albatros is usually associated. In July 1917, at the request of his friend Richthofen, Voss was posted to command Jasta 10 in Jagdgeschwader Nr. 1. During their lifetimes, Voss was second-ranking ace to Richthofen; he was finally killed on 23rd September 1917 in a prolonged dogfight between himself (flying Fokker Dr I 103/17) and one Albatros scout, against seven S.E.5as, including the whole of "B" Flight, No. 56 Squadron, R.F.C., led by Captain J. T. B. McCudden. Voss was twenty years and five months old when he died.*

10. Fokker E I, *number 3/15, flown by Leutnant Oswald Boelcke of Fliegerabteilung 62, based at Douai in August 1915. (Details of Boelcke's career may be found in the body of the text.) It is believed that this was the machine flown by Leutnant Max Immelmann of the same unit when he gained his first victory on 1st August 1915.*

captions for colour plate on page 47

The first military aircraft acquired by China were six 80 hp and six 50 hp Caudrons ordered from France in March 1913.

The first night flight by a British military aircraft took place either on the night of 15th/16th or 16th/17th April 1913. Lieutenant R. Cholmondeley, of No. 3 Squadron, Military Wing, R.F.C., flew a Maurice Farman biplane from Larkhill to Upavon and back by moonlight.

Sikorsky Ilya Mourometz bomber

The first four-engined bomber to see active service was the Ilya Mourometz biplane, designed by Igor Sikorsky, Head of the Aeronautical Department of the Russian Baltic Railway Car Factory at Petrograd. By the time of the Russian Revolution seventy-three had been delivered to the Military; some 400 bombing sorties were made by the type. It carried up to sixteen crew members and, as with the German R-Type bombers of 1918, routine servicing and minor repairs could be carried out in flight. It is believed that only one was ever shot down by enemy fighters.

The first French airmen to be killed on active service were Capitaine Hervé and his observer, named Roëland. During the colonial campaign in Morocco early in 1914 they made a forced landing in the desert and were killed by local Arabs.

The first military operations involving the use of American aeroplanes were those against Vera Cruz in April 1914 when several Curtiss AB flying-boats were carried to the port aboard the U.S.S. *Mississippi*. The first such military flight was undertaken by Lieutenant (Jg) P. N. L. Bellinger who took off in the Curtiss AB-3 flying-boat on 25th April in order to search for mines in the harbour.

The first Air Service of the U.S. Army was established on 18th July 1914 when an aviation section was formed as part of the Signal Corps with a "paper" strength of 60 officers and 260 men. The entire equipment amounted to six aeroplanes.

Curtiss AB flying-boat (U.S. Navy)

THE FIRST WORLD WAR

The first British airmen to be killed on active service were Second-Lieutenant R. B. Skene and
a mechanic, R. K. Barlow, of No. 3 Squadron, R.F.C., on 12th August
1914. Flying from Netheravon to Dover to form up for the Channel
crossing, their aircraft, a Blériot two-seater of "C" Flight, landed because
of engine trouble. Shortly after taking off again, the aircraft crashed into
trees and both occupants were killed.

The first German Air Service pilot to be killed on active service was Oberleutnant Reinhold
Jahnow. He was fatally injured in a crash at Malmédy, Belgium, on 12th
August 1914. He was holder of German Pilot's Licence No. 80, and a
veteran of several reconnaissance flights for the Turks during the Balkan
campaign of 1912.

B.E.2a No. 347
(Imperial War Museum)

**The first British aeroplane to land on the Continent after the outbreak of the First World
War** was a B.E.2a, No. 347, of No. 2 Squadron, R.F.C., flown by Lieu-
tenant H. D. Harvey-Kelly. He left Dover at 06.25 h and landed near
Amiens at 08.20 h on 13th August 1914.

The first bombs to be dropped upon a capital city from an aircraft fell on Paris, in August 1914. The pilot of the German Taube aeroplane has been variously identified as Leutnant Franz von Hiddeson and Leutnant Ferdinand von Hiddessen. (The confusion between names was caused by the message that was dropped with the bombs reading "The German Army is at your gates—you can do nothing but surrender, Lieut von Heidssen.") The exact date of the attack is believed to have been 30th August, five bombs being dropped, killing one woman and injuring two other persons.

The only British aeroplane fitted with a machine-gun at the outbreak of the First World War was a Henry Farman biplane of No. 5 Squadron, R.F.C., flown by Second-Lieutenant L. A. Strange, which the pilot had fitted with a Lewis gun in the front cockpit. On 22nd August 1914 Strange and his gunner, Lieutenant L. da C. Penn-Gaskell, unsuccessfully pursued an enemy aircraft over Mauberge. Strange was subsequently ordered by his commanding officer to remove both the gun and its mounting, on account of the deterioration in the aircraft's performance caused by their weight.

The first enemy aircraft forced down in combat by British aircraft was a German two-seater forced to land on 25th August 1914 by three aircraft of No. 2 Squadron, R.F.C. The pilot who finally forced it down was Lieutenant H. D. Harvey-Kelly who had been **the first R.F.C. pilot to land in France.**

The first aeroplane to be destroyed by ramming was an Austrian two-seater flown by Leutnant Baron von Rosenthal, rammed over Galicia on 26th August 1914 by Staff Captain Petr Nikolaevich Nesterov of the Imperial Russian XI Corps Air Squadron, who was flying an unarmed Morane Type M. monoplane scout. Both pilots were killed. Nesterov (remembered also as the **first pilot to loop the loop**) was the Imperial Air Service's **first battle casualty.**

The first British air raid on Germany was by four aircraft of the Eastchurch R.N.A.S. Squadron. On 22nd September 1914 two aircraft took off from Antwerp to attack the airship sheds at Düsseldorf, two to attack the airship sheds at Cologne. Only the aircraft flown by Flight-Lieutenant Collet found the target—the sheds at Düsseldorf—and his three 20 lb (9 kg) Hales bombs, while probably on target, failed to explode. All aircraft returned safely.

The first aeroplane in the world to be shot down and destroyed by another was a German two-seater, possibly an Aviatik, shot down at Jonchery, near Reims on 5th October 1914 by Sergent Joseph Frantz and Caporal Quénault in a Voisin pusher of Escadrille V.B. 24. The weapon used is believed to have been a Hotchkiss machine-gun.

The first successful British air raid on Germany took place on 8th October 1914. Squadron Commander D. A. Spenser Grey and Flight-Lieutenant R. L. G. Marix of the Eastchurch R.N.A.S. Squadron flew from Antwerp in Sopwith Tabloids (Nos. 167 and 168) to attack airship sheds at Düsseldorf and Cologne with 20 lb (9 kg) Hales bombs. Grey failed to find the target, bombed Cologne Railway Station and returned to Antwerp. Marix reached his target at Düsseldorf, bombed the shed from 600 ft (200 m) and destroyed it and Zeppelin Z.IX inside. His aircraft was damaged by gun-fire, and he eventually crash-landed 20 miles (30 km) from Antwerp, returning to the city on a bicycle borrowed from a peasant.

The first aeroplane raid on Great Britain, by one aircraft, took place on 21st December 1914. Two bombs fell in the sea near Admiralty Pier at Dover.

The first bomb dropped by an enemy aircraft on British soil, and the second aeroplane raid on Great Britain, again by one aircraft, took place on 24th December 1914. One bomb exploded near Dover Castle.

The first Russian woman to serve as a military pilot (and probably the first in the world) was Princess Eugenie Mikhailovna Shakhovskaya. Gaining her Certificate at Johannisthal, Germany, on 16th August 1911, Princess Shakhovskaya made a personal request to the Tsar on the outbreak of the First World War that she be allowed to serve as a military pilot. In November 1914 she was posted to the 1st Field Air Squadron as a reconnaissance pilot. Princess Shakhovskaya survived both the war and the Revolution; indeed, she subsequently served in the Cheka (Bolshevik secret police) at Kiev, in the post of Chief Executioner—unusual work for a young woman of noble birth.

The first airship raid on Great Britain was carried out on 19th January 1915 by three German Navy Zeppelins, L3, L4 and L6. They took off from Fuhlsbüttel and Nordholz. L6 was forced to return through engine trouble but L3 and L4 arrived over the Norfolk coast at about 20.00 h; nine bombs were dropped in the Great Yarmouth area at 20.25 h by L3, killing two persons and wounding three others. Meanwhile L4 had gone north-west towards Bacton and dropped incendiary bombs on Sheringham, Thornham and Brancaster as well as a high-explosive bomb on Hunstanton wireless-station. Following that, it dropped bombs on Heacham, Snettisham and King's Lynn, where seven high-explosive bombs were dropped and an incendiary, killing two people and injuring thirteen. The two airships were both wrecked on the coast of Jutland on 17th February 1915 after running into a gale on their homeward journey after trying to spot the British Fleet.

The first British bombing raid in direct tactical support of a ground operation occurred on 10th March 1915, comprising attacks on railways bringing up German reinforcements in the Menin and Courtrai areas (Second Wing) and the railway stations at Lille, Douai and Don (bombed by the Third Wing), during the Neuve Chapelle offensive. The Divisional Headquarters at Fournes was also bombed by three aircraft of No. 3 Squadron piloted by Captain E. L. Conran, Lieutenant W. C. Birch and Lieutenant D. R. Hanlon.

Lieutenant W. B. Rhodes Moorhouse, V.C. *(Imperial War Museum)*

The first air Victoria Cross was awarded posthumously to Lieutenant W. B. Rhodes Moorhouse, pilot of a B.E.2 of No. 2 Squadron, R.F.C., for gallantry in a low-level bombing attack on Courtrai Railway Station on 26th April 1915.

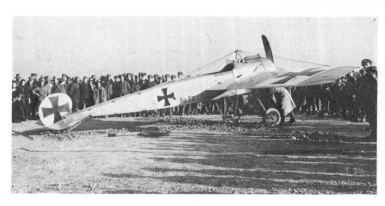

Fokker E III monoplane, the major production version of the first fighter with a synchronised machine-gun

The first air raid on London was by Zeppelin LZ38 on 31st May 1915. The Kaiser had authorised bombing of London, east of the Tower, a few days before and on the night of the 31st 3,000 lb (1,360 kg) of bombs were dropped on north-east London, killing seven people.

The first airship to be shot down was Zeppelin LZ37 on the night of 6th/7th June 1915. In company with LZ38 and LZ39, the airship set out from Bruges to bomb London but adverse weather later forced them to alter course for their secondary targets—railways in the Calais area. LZ37 was located and attacked by Flight Sub-Lieutenant R. A. J. Warneford of No. 1 Squadron, R.N.A.S., flying a Morane-Saulnier Parasol from Dunkirk. Warneford's only means of attack were six 20 lb (9 kg) bombs; he followed the airship from Ostend to Ghent, being forced to keep his distance by fire from the airship's gunners. He made a single pass over the airship dropping all six bombs from about 150 ft (45 m) above it. The sixth exploded, and the airship fell in flames on a suburb of Ghent killing two nuns. Only one member of Oberleutnant Otto van de Haegen's crew survived. Warneford returned safely to base after making a forced landing to repair a broken fuel line. He was informed the following evening that he had been awarded the Victoria Cross; he died twelve days later when the tail of a Henry Farman pusher biplane collapsed in mid-air.

The world's first all-metal cantilever aeroplane was the Junkers J.1 (the "Tin Donkey"), initiated as a private venture by the Forschungsansalt Professor Junkers and flown (on a short "hop") for the first time on 12th December 1915 at Dessau, Germany. Designed by Hugo Junkers, Dr. Mader and Otto Reuter, the J.1 (of which only one was built) had a top speed of 105·5 mile/h (170 km/h).

The first American aeroplanes used in actual military operations were eight Curtiss JNs of the 1st Aero Squadron, U.S. Army, which accompanied the punitive expedition under General John Pershing to Columbus, Mexico on 15th March 1916.

The first U.S. Army pilot to be shot down in the First World War was H. Clyde Balsley who served with the Lafayette Escadrille on the Western Front and who was shot down and wounded near Verdun on 18th June 1916.

The first American pilot to be killed in the First World War was Victor Emmanuel Chapman of the Lafayette Escadrille, who was shot down near Verdun on 23rd June 1916.

The first Peruvian military pilots were Second-Lieutenant Enrique Ruiz and Aspirant Guillermo Protzel who were seconded to El Palomar, Argentina, in 1916 and graduated with the fifth Flying Course. However Argentinian records suggest that Guardia Marina Ismael Montoya and Guardia Marina Roberto Velazco (both Peruvians) also attended this course, and that Ruiz was killed on 13th March 1917 while flying a Blériot monoplane.

The first radio-guided flying-bomb was tested on 12th September 1916. It was called the "Hewitt-Sperry biplane" and was built by Curtiss. Powered by a 40 hp engine, it was capable of covering 50 miles (80 km) carrying a 308 lb (140 kg) bomb-load.

The first British unit to be formed specifically for night bombing operations was No. 100 Squadron, R.F.C., which formed at Hingham, Norfolk, in February 1917, and crossed to France on 21st March. A week later the unit received its first aircraft, twelve F.E.2bs, then being based at Saint-André-aux-Bois. Moving to Le Hameau on 1st April 1917, the squadron received four B.E.2es. The first operations were two raids on the night of 5th/6th April 1917 on Douai Airfield, home base of the "Richthofen Circus". One F.E.2b failed to return; four hangars were badly damaged by bombs.

The first combat aeroplane to enter production in the United States was the British de Havilland D.H.4. The first machine was completed in February 1918, and by 5th November the same year 3,431 had been completed. A total of 4,846 was built before production stopped in 1919. The D.H.4 (or DH-4) was the only American-built aeroplane to fly over enemy territory during the First World War (which excludes of course the operations against Mexico in 1916).

The most successful American pilot to serve exclusively with an American unit in the First World War was Captain Edward Vernon Rickenbacker who was credited with the destruction of twenty-two enemy aeroplanes and four balloons.

Captain Edward V. Rickenbacker, for long Chairman of Eastern Air Lines (Howard Levy)

The first American-trained pilot to shoot down an enemy aircraft was Lieutenant Douglas Campbell, on 14th April 1918. He had received his training at an aviation school in America and was sent to the 94th Aero Squadron on 1st March 1918. In this squadron, with Captain Rickenbacker and Major Lufbery, he participated in the **first patrol over enemy territory by an American unit** on 19th March 1918. He was also **the first American, serving under American colours, to become an ace** by shooting down five enemy aircraft. His fifth German victim was shot down on 31st May 1918.

One of the finest British bombers of the First World War was the Handley Page O/400 which began to arrive for service in numbers in early 1918. The production aircraft were fitted with two engines ranging from 240 hp to 360 hp, giving a maximum speed of about 80–90 mile/h (129–145 km/h). The O/400 could carry a bomb load of 1,800 lb (816 kg) and delivered the "Block-Busters", which were bombs of 1,650 lb (750 kg). The O/400s served with R.A.F. squadrons 58, 100, 115, 207, 214, 215 and 216.

Fokker D VIII

The fastest German aeroplane to reach combat status during the First World War was the Fokker D VIII parasol monoplane single-seater fighting scout, with a top speed of 127·5 mile/h (204 km/h) at sea-level. It was powered by a 110 hp Oberursel U II nine-cylinder rotary engine and was armed with two synchronised Spandau machine-guns. It reached front-line Jastas in August 1918 but was withdrawn shortly afterwards owing to a number of accidents following wing failure. Leutnant Theo Osterkamp of the Marine Jagdgeschwader won his twenty-fifth and twenty-sixth victories while flying a Fokker D VIII.

The largest German aeroplane built during the First World War was the Aviatik R-Type (Riesenflugzeug) giant heavy bomber; basically a Zeppelin Staaken R VI built under licence by Automobil und Aviatik A.G., this colossal aeroplane had a wing span of 180 ft 5·5 in (55·0 m) and a length of 88 ft 7 in (27·0 m). It was powered by four 530 hp Benz Bz VI engines which gave it a maximum speed of 90 mile/h (145 km/h).

The greatest altitude attained by a German aircraft on test during the First World War was
31,160 ft (9,500 m) by the Fokker V 10, which was in effect a Fokker Dr I
triplane powered by a 145 hp Oberursel U III engine. This flight was
probably undertaken early in 1918.

The heaviest German aeroplane built during the First World War is believed to have been the
Siemens-Schuckert R VIII which, with a wing span of 157 ft 6 in (48 m),
weighed 34,980 lb (15,900 kg) fully loaded. It was powered by six 300 hp
Basse und Selve BuS IV engines and had a speed of about 78 mile/h (125
km/h). It was not completed until 1919 and was damaged before flight;
Armistice prohibitions prevented its repair.

The largest aeroplane to be powered by a power plant driving a single propeller was the
Linke-Hofman R II of Germany. This aircraft, of which only one example
ever flew, in January 1919, was designed on the principle of simply scaling
up a conventional single-engine biplane and was due for delivery in July
1918. With a wing span of 138 ft 4 in (42·16 m) and a length of 66 ft 7·875
in (20·32 m), the R II (R55/17) was powered by four 260 hp Mercedes D
IVa engines, arranged in pairs in the nose, driving a single propeller
through a central gearbox. **The propeller was the largest ever used
by an aeroplane** and had a diameter of 22 ft 7·5 in (6·89 m) and was
driven at 545 rev/min. The maximum speed of the aircraft was 81 mile/h
(130 km/h).

THE GREAT AIR FIGHTERS OF THE FIRST WORLD WAR

British and Empire pilots credited with forty or more confirmed victories

Major Edward Mannock, v.c., d.s.o.**, m.c.*	73
Major W. A. Bishop, v.c., d.s.o.*, m.c., d.f.c., l. d'h., c. de g.	72
Major R. Collishaw, d.s.o.*, d.s.c., d.f.c., c. de g.	60
Major J. T. B. McCudden, v.c., d.s.o.*, m.c.*, m.m., c. de g.	57
Captain A. W. Beauchamp-Proctor, v.c., d.s.o., m.c.*, d.f.c.	54
Captain D. R. MacLaren, d.s.o., m.c.*, d.f.c., l. d'h., c. de g.	54
Major W. G. Barker, v.c., d.s.o., m.c.**, c.c., l. d'h., c. de g., v.m.	52
Captain P. F. Fullard, d.s.o., m.c.*, a.f.c.	52
Captain G. E. H. McElroy, m.c.**, d.f.c.*	49
Captain Albert Ball, v.c., d.s.o.**, m.c., c.c., l. d'h., russian order of st george	47
Captain R. A. Little, d.s.o.*, d.s.c.*, c. de g.	47
Major T. F. Hazell, d.s.o., m.c., d.f.c.*	43
Major J. Gilmore, d.s.o., m.c.**	40
Captain J. I. T. Jones, d.s.o., m.c., d.f.c.*, m.m., russian medal of st. george	40

*Bar to award

In addition to the above
    11 pilots gained between 30 and 39 victories
    57 pilots gained between 20 and 29 victories
    226 pilots gained between 10 and 19 victories
    476 pilots gained between 5 and 9 victories

Thus by the "five victory" convention (see page 60), the British and
Empire air forces of the First World War produced 784 aces.

(left) Captain W. G. Barker. An account of the action in which he won the V.C. as a Major appears on page 45 (Imperial War Museum)

(right) Captain G. E. H. McElroy, sometimes called the leading Irish ace

German pilots credited with forty or more confirmed victories

Rittmeister Manfred, Freiherr von Richthofen 80
Oberleutnant Ernst Udet 62
Oberleutnant Erich Loewenhardt 53
Leutnant Werner Voss 48
Leutnant Fritz Rumey 45
Hauptmann Rudolph Berthold 44
Leutnant Paul Bäumer 43
Leutnant Josef Jacobs 41
Hauptmann Bruno Loerzer 41
Hauptmann Oswald Boelcke 40
Leutnant Franz Büchner 40
Oberleutnant Lothar Freiherr von Richthofen 40

All these pilots were decorated with the Ordre Pour le Mérite.

In addition to the above

21 pilots gained between 30 and 39 victories
38 pilots gained between 20 and 29 victories
96 pilots gained between 10 and 19 victories
196 pilots gained between 5 and 9 victories.

Thus by the "five victory" convention, the Imperial German air forces of the First World War produced 363 aces.

(left) Ernst Udet, Germany's second ranking ace

(right) Werner Voss

French pilots credited with forty or more confirmed victories

Capitaine René P. Fonck 75
Capitaine Georges M. L. J. Guynemer 54
Lieutenant Charles E. J. M. Nungesser 45
Capitaine Georges F. Madon 41

In addition to the above
2 pilots gained between 30 and 39 victories
8 pilots gained between 20 and 29 victories
39 pilots gained between 10 and 19 victories
105 pilots gained between 5 and 9 victories.
Thus the French air forces of the First World War produced 158 aces.

The ten most successful American pilots of the First World War

Captain Edward V. Rickenbacker, C.M.H., D.S.C., L. D'H., C. DE G. . 26
Second-Lieutenant Frank Luke Jr., C.M.H., D.S.C., C. DE G. . . 21
Major G. Raoul Lufbery, L. D'H., M.M., C. DE G., M.C. . . . 17
Lieutenant G. A. Vaughn, Jr., D.S.C., D.F.C. 13
Second-Lieutenant F. L. Baylies, L. D'H., M.M., C. DE G. . . 12
Captain F. E. Kindley, D.S.C. 12
Lieutenant D. E. Putnam, D.S.C., L. D'H., M.M., C. DE G. . . 12
Captain E. W. Springs, D.S.C., D.F.C. 12
Major R. G. Landis, D.S.C., D.F.C. 10
Captain J. M. Swaab, D.S.C. 10

In addition to the above 78 pilots gained between 5 and 9 victories; thus America produced during the First World War 88 aces. (It should be noted that the above figures include pilots who served with foreign air forces only, pilots who served with the American forces only, and pilots with mixed service, and all victories gained by these pilots irrespective of service.)

The ten most successful Italian pilots of the First World War

Maggiore Francesco Baracca 34
Tenente Silvio Scaroni 26
Tenente-Colonnello Pier Ruggiero Piccio 24
Tenente Flavio Torello Baracchini 21
Capitano Fulco Ruffo di Calabria 20
Sergente Marziale Cerutti 17
Tenente Ferruccio Ranza 17
Tenente Luigi Olivari 12
Tenente Giovanni Ancillotto 11
Sergente Antonio Reali 11

In addition to the above 33 pilots gained between 5 and 10 victories; thus Italy produced 43 aces during the First World War.

The five most successful Austro-Hungarian pilots of the First World War

Hauptmann Godwin Brumowski 35–40
Offizierstellvertreter Julius Arigi 26–32
Oberleutnant Frank Linke-Crawford 27–30
Oberleutnant Benno Fiala, Ritter von Fernbrugg . . 27–29
Leutnant Josef Kiss 19

(It should be noted that Austrian, Hungarian and Italian sources disagree as to the absolute accuracy of four of these pilot's scores.)

In addition to the above approximately 25 pilots gained between 5 and 18 victories. Thus it can be stated with reasonable certainty that the Austro-Hungarian Imperial air forces produced between 25 and 30 aces during the First World War.

The most successful Imperial Russian pilots of the First World War

Staff Captain A. A. Kazakov, D.S.O., M.C., D.F.C., L. D'H. . . 17
Captain P. V. d'Argueeff 15
Lieutenant Commander A. P. Seversky 13
Lieutenant I. W. Smirnoff 12
Lieutenant M. Safonov 11
Captain B. Sergeivsky 11
Ensign E. M. Tomson 11

In addition to the above either 11 or 12 pilots gained between 5 and 10 victories; thus the Imperial Russian air forces produced either 18 or 19 known aces during the First World War. Other Russian pilots became aces, but the records are incomplete.

The five Belgian aces of the First World War

Second-Lieutenant Willy Coppens, D.S.O. 37
Adjutant André de Meulemeester 11
Second-Lieutenant Edmond Thieffry 10
Captain Fernand Jacquet, D.F.C. 7
Lieutenant Jan Olieslagers 6

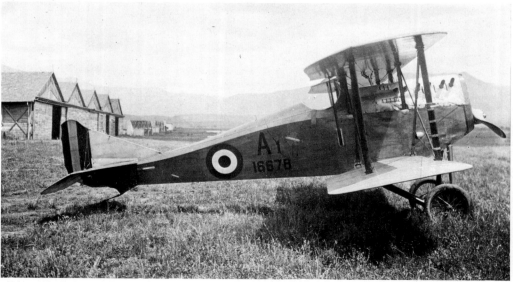

Although Italy produced superb strategic bombers in the First World War, its fighter pilots flew mainly French aircraft. One of the few exceptions was the Ansaldo A-1 Balilla, which could fly at nearly 140 mile/h but had poor manœuvrability (Italian Air Ministry)

Manfred von Richthofen (centre) with pilots of his Jagdstaffel

The confirmation of aerial victories during the First World War was subject to the most stringent regulations, and this has led to confusion over the actual number of victories scored by various pilots. The figures quoted earlier are, with certain exceptions, those officially accepted as accurate in the countries of origin, and refer only to confirmed victories within the letter of the regulations. They are thus more liable to err on the side of under- rather than overstatement. Where certain notable pilots are generally considered to have destroyed significantly more enemy aircraft than are allowed in their official totals, such unconfirmed figures are quoted below in the sections dealing with the pilots by name, or in the captions to the accompanying colour paintings.

The "ace" system, and the policy of public recognition of particularly successful fighter pilots originated in France and was subsequently copied by many nations. Under the French system a pilot who scored five confirmed aerial victories was named in an official communiqué, and thereafter his career was subject to wide publicity. Successful pilots were, as a matter of policy, concentrated in certain units which enjoyed an enormous reputation, for example, the five Escadrilles (3, 26, 73, 103 and briefly 167) which made up the famous "Stork" group, Groupe de Combat No. 12 "Les Cigognes". This latter step might be thought to have had a poor effect on the morale of less prominent units, and was peculiar to the French Air Service. The United States adopted the five-victory rule when their squadrons entered the war, and have applied it ever since. The ace system has never been followed by Great Britain however; while successful pilots naturally tended to become household names through service "grapevines" and normal journalistic activity, it has always been the official view that to single out individuals for massive publicity in this way would be harmful to the morale of the thousands of anonymous service-men whose contribution to the war effort was just as great, if less glamo-rous. In Britain the term "ace" passed into everyday language, but did not and does not depend on any specific number of aerial victories. In Germany the leading fighter pilots were the subject of considerable publicity, and it became normal practice for certain decorations to be awarded to them on the achievement of a certain number of victories, but no rigid mathematical formula was followed. (The German equiva-lent to the term "ace" was *Oberkanone*—loosely "top gun".)

The greatest ace of the First World War, in terms of confirmed aerial victories, was Rittmeister (Cavalry Captain) Manfred, Freiherr von Richthofen—the so-called "Red Baron". The eldest son of an aristocratic Silesian family, he was born on 2nd May 1892 and was killed in action on 21st April 1918, by which time he had been credited with eighty victories, had been awarded his country's highest decoration, commanded the élite unit of the Imperial German Air Service (Luftstreitkräfte), and was the object of universal adulation in his homeland and an ungrudging respect among his enemies. Early in the war Richthofen served on the Eastern Front as an officer in Uhlan Regiment Nr. 1 "Kaiser Alexander III", and transferred to the Air Service in May 1915. His first operational posting was to Feldflie-gerabteilung Nr. 69; with this unit he flew two-seater reconnaissance machines in the East—without apparently any unusual skill—and he continued to serve in general purpose units until September 1916 when he was lucky enough to be selected for Jagdstaffel 2, the single-seater scout squadron trained and led by the brilliant Oswald Boelcke (q.v.). By this time it was probable that Richthofen had already gained two vic-tories, a Maurice Farman S.11 over Champagne in September 1915, and a Nieuport 11 near Douaumont on 25th April 1916—but for lack of ground confirmation these were not included in his official list of victories. His first officially recognised victory was over an F.E.2b, number 7018 of

Von Richthofen, his head bandaged after a recent wound, with Kaiser Wilhelm II

Replica of von Richthofen's Fokker Dr 1 exhibited in Berlin, 1936

No. 11 Squadron, R.F.C.; Richthofen, flying an Albatros D II scout, shot this aircraft down on 17th September 1916, and the crew, Second-Lieutenant L. B. F. Morris and Lieutenant T. Rees, both lost their lives. Richthofen continued to score steadily, and in January 1917 was awarded the coveted "Blue Max", the Ordre pour le Mérite. He was given command of Jagdstaffel 11, and began to enjoy considerable fame. A cold and calculating fighter, he brought to air combat the attitudes of the aristocratic huntsman; he maintained a collection of silver cups, each engraved with the particulars of a victim. His silversmith's most lucrative month was the "Bloody April" of 1917, when he shot down twenty-one aircraft. The most famous pilot to fall to his guns was Major Lanoe G. Hawker, v.c., d.s.o., commanding officer of No. 24 Squadron, R.F.C., who has been called "the English Boelcke" for his skill, vision and organising ability. Major Hawker, flying D.H.2 number 5964, had himself gained several victories when he was shot down after a prolonged and unequal dogfight with Richthofen on 23rd November 1916, to become the "Red Baron's" eleventh victim. Later in June 1917 Richthofen was given command of a new formation, Jagdgeschwader Nr. 1, comprising Jastas 4, 6, 10 and 11; this group of squadrons became known to the Allies as "Richthofen's Flying Circus", partly on account of the bright colours used by various pilots to decorate and identify their aircraft. Contrary to popular legend Richthofen did not invariably fly a personal aircraft painted blood-red over-all; he flew several aircraft, Albatros D IIIs and Fokker Dr Is, and one of each type is thought to have been painted red over-all; but he also used several which were only partially finished in red, an example of one such machine being illustrated in the accompanying colour pages. Richthofen's death on 21st April 1918 has been the subject of controversy ever since. He was flying Fokker Dr I number *425/17* when he became engaged in combat with Sopwith Camels of No. 209 Squadron, R.A.F., over Sailly-le-Sec. At one point, Second-Lieutenant W. R. May was flying at low altitude with Richthofen in pursuit, and the aircraft of Captain A. Roy Brown, d.s.c., diving to attack the German. Brown opened fire in an attempt to save the inexperienced May from the enemy ace, and Richthofen's triplane was then seen to break away and crash-land. The exact relative timing of these events has never been established; but whatever the details, Richthofen was found dead in his cockpit with a bullet wound in the chest. Brown was officially credited with his death, but prolonged research by many amateur and professional historians has failed to settle with any certainty whether the fatal shot was fired by Brown or by a member of an Australian Field Artillery battery which was putting up a considerable volume of small-arms fire at the time. Richthofen's last victim was Second-Lieutenant D. G. Lewis, a Camel pilot of No. 3 Squadron, R.A.F., who was shot down, wounded and taken prisoner near Villers-Bretonneux the day before Richthofen's death.

Captain A. Roy Brown, d.s.c. (Imperial War Museum)

The first true fighter leader of the First World War was Hauptmann Oswald Boelcke, whose name, with those of Richthofen and Immelmann, is still commemorated today in the honour title of a German Air Force combat unit. Boelcke was born on 9th May 1891 and was commissioned in a communications unit in 1912. He became interested in aviation during army manœuvres, and gained his Pilot's Certificate at the Halberstadt Flying School on 15th August 1914. He was posted to La Ferte to join Feldfliegerabteilung No. 13 in September, and, with his brother Wilhelm as observer, soon amassed a considerable number of sorties in Army Co-operation Albatros B II biplanes. By early 1915 he had forty-two missions in his log-book, and

Oswald Boelcke (Imperial War Museum)

had been awarded the Iron Cross, Second Class. The visit of Leutnant Parschau to his unit to demonstrate the Fokker M.8 monoplane scout fired him with enthusiasm; and in April, having received the Iron Cross, First Class, he secured a posting to Hauptmann Kastner's Feldfliegerabteilung No. 62, where he flew an armed machine for the first time–an Albatros C I, number *162/15*. He displayed great spirit, and enabled his observer to shoot down a Morane by his skilful and aggressive flying. His greatest stroke of fortune came when he was selected to fly early examples of Fokker's E-series armed monoplane scouts; few were available, and Boelcke, Kastner and Leutnant Max Immelmann at first took turns to fly them. His success as a combat pilot was matched by his grasp of technical matters and his organising ability. His ideas for the use of squadrons composed entirely of fighting scouts commanded attention in high places; until mid 1916 most units operated mixed equipment, and the concept of an offensive force of single-seater scouts carrying the war directly to the enemy's air forces was entirely new. After a tour of other fronts early in 1916, Boelcke returned to the West and was given command of the new Jagdstaffel Nr. 2 (contracted to Jasta 2). He trained his pilots personally, and revealed a great gift for patient and inspiring instruction, so that his group of highly skilled pilots, flying the sleek new Albatros D I and D II scouts, became the scourge of the Western Front. Many of the greatest aces of the Luftstreitkräfte served their apprenticeship in Jasta 2, and Boelcke commanded great respect and affection among his young subordinates. He was killed on 28th October 1916; in the course of an engagement, during which Boelcke and one of his colleagues, Leutnant Boehme, suddenly had to bank sharply, Boehme's undercarriage struck the wing of his Albatros, and the aircraft spiralled to the ground. He was twenty-five years old, young for his rank, a holder of the Ordre Pour le Mérite and numerous other decorations, the victor of forty aerial combats, and the idol of his country. Since his death he has remained the father-figure of German fighter aviation.

One of Germany's first two great fighter aces was Leutnant Max Immelmann, "The Eagle of Lille". As mentioned above, he was serving with Feldfliegerabteilung No. 62 at Douai when the first Fokker monoplane scouts became available. Hauptmann Kastner instructed Boelcke in the subtleties of the new machine, and Boelcke taught Immelmann. On 1st August 1915 Immelmann scored his first victory while flying an E I (believed to have been one of Boelcke's two machines), when his comrade was forced to drop out of the fight with a defective machine-gun. Thereafter he and Boelcke ranged over their sector of the front, sometimes together, sometimes alone, hunting the enemy from the sky. Even a year later only a comparative handful of German pilots were operating the Fokker scouts; yet so great was the superiority of the agile single-seater, with its synchronised forward-firing machine-gun, that the "Fokker Scourge" became a major disaster for Allied arms. Immelmann and his colleagues were regarded with an almost spectral awe by their enemies (who claimed with straight faces that his aircraft could remain in the air for a week at a time) and were idolised at home. He finally met his death, after shooting down fifteen Allied aircraft, on 18th June 1916; flying near Lens, Immelmann attacked an F.E.2b of No. 25 Squadron, R.F.C. Another F.E., flown by Second-Lieutenant G. R. McCubbin, with Corporal J. H. Waller as gunner, attacked him. The Fokker made an attacking pass, then went into a dive and broke up in mid-air. Some sources claim that his death was caused by technical failure, but the R.F.C. credited Corporal Waller with the victory.

Max Immelmann

As a measure of the recognition accorded to Immelmann by a grateful nation, his full style of address and decorations is quoted:

The Royal Saxon Reserve-Lieutenant Herr Max Immelmann, Commander of the Order of St. Heinrich, Knight of the Ordre Pour le Mérite, Knight of the Iron Cross, First and Second Class, Knight of the Military Order of St. Heinrich, Knight of the Albrecht Order with Swords, Knight of the Hohenzollern House Order with Swords, Knight of the Bavarian Order of Military Merit with Swords, Holder of the Iron Crescent, Holder of the Imbias Medal in Silver, Holder of the Friedrich August Medal in Silver and Holder of the Hamburg Hanseatic Cross.

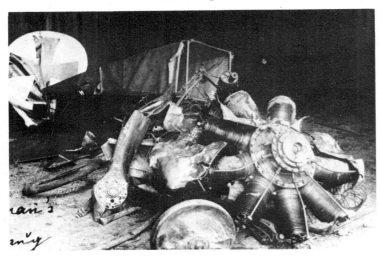

Immelmann's crashed Fokker, 18th June 1916

The first great British ace, Captain Albert Ball occupied a place in the affections of the British public and armed forces analogous to that held by Max Immelmann in Germany. He was the first high-scoring fighter pilot whose exploits became widely known on the home front, and his fighting philosophy— usually involving an unhesitating charge straight at the enemy, whether equally matched or outnumbered six or seven to one—had a unique appeal for his civilian contemporaries whose grasp of the more sophisticated methods adopted by some other pilots was regrettably weak. Born in Nottingham on 21st August 1896, and a good shot while still a boy, Albert Ball joined the Sherwood Foresters on the outbreak of war. During a visit to Hendon he became fired with enthusiasm for flying, and secured a transfer to the R.F.C. He joined No. 13 Squadron in France on 15th February 1916, and flew B.E.2cs on artillery-spotting flights. In May he was posted to No. 11 Squadron, which had in charge a Nieuport scout; he immediately fell in love with the little machine, and was to fly Nieuports by preference throughout his career. His first two successes came on 22nd May; he drove down (but could not get confirmed) an Albatros D I, and forced an L.V.G. two-seater to land. On 1st June he flew over the German airfield at Douai; a Fokker and an Albatros rose to challenge him, and though he did not destroy them he completely outflew them, and returned safely. On 25th June he shot down a balloon, and his M.C. was gazetted two days later. He shot down a Roland C II, later to become his favourite prey, on 2nd July, and while on a brief "rest" with No. 8 Squadron he forced an enemy balloon observer to take to his parachute while on an artillery-spotting flight. Given a new Nieuport on

continued on page 69

captions for p. 66

11. SPAD VII 245 Vieux Charles, *flown by Capitaine Georges Guynemer of Escadrille SPA.3, Groupe de Combat No. 12 "Les Cigognes", Service Aéronautique Française. Guynemer, whose fifty-four confirmed victories place him second on France's roll of aces, flew this aircraft early in 1917; full details of his career may be found in the text. The stork insignia was the badge of SPA.3.*

12. Nieuport 17 1895, *flown by Lieutenant Charles Nungesser of Escadrille N.65 during the summer of 1917. Third among French aces with forty-five confirmed victories, Nungesser was a pilot of enormous determination in the face of constant pain; his career is described in the text. He first used his macabre personal marking in November 1915, and from that time onwards it was painted on all his aircraft. From May 1917 onwards the wings (and later the fuselage top decking) of his aircraft were painted with broad* tricoleur *stripes as an additional identification; as in that month he accidentally shot down a British aircraft which attacked him.*

13. Nieuport 17 *flown during the summer of 1917 by Sergeant Marius Ambrogi of Escadrille N.90. "Marc" Ambrogi was a specialist in shooting down heavily defended observation balloons; these hazardous targets accounted for ten of his fourteen confirmed victories. He survived the war, and later rejoined the colours to fight in the Second World War; in 1940 he was serving as Deputy Commander of Groupe de Chasse I/8 when he shot down a Junkers Ju 52/3m.*

14. Nieuport 28 *flown by Lieutenant Douglas Campbell of the 94th Aero Squadron, American Expeditionary Force, in March 1918. On 19th March he accompanied Major Raoul Lufbery and Lieutenant Edward Rickenbacker on the first patrol over enemy lines by an American unit; and on 14th April he became the first American-trained pilot to score an aerial victory, his victim being an Albatros shot down near the squadron's base at Toul. His fifth victory on 31st May 1918 made him the first ace who had served exclusively with the American forces. He was to score one further victory before a wound put him out of the war on 6th June 1918; he was eventually discharged in 1919 with the rank of Captain.*

15. SPAD XIII 1620, *flown by Lieutenant David E. Putnam of the 139th Aero Squadron, American Expeditionary Force, in the summer of 1918. Putnam was officially credited with twelve victories, but unofficial estimates indicate a considerably higher total. He flew with various French units between December 1917 and July 1918 and gained his first victory on 19th January 1918. On 5th June he fought an epic battle against ten enemy aircraft, sending five down destroyed or damaged. He was transferred in July to the 139th Squadron, in which he served as a Flight Commander until his death in action on 12th September 1918.*

16. SPAD XIII 1719, *flown by Lieutenant Gervais Raoul Lufbery of Escadrille SPA.124—the Escadrille Lafayette—during the winter of 1917–18. With seventeen confirmed victories Lufbery was third in the roll of American aces. Born in France of French parents who later emigrated to America, Lufbery travelled widely as a young man; when war broke out he joined the French Foreign Legion and obtained a quick transfer to the Service Aéronautique. Having successfully applied for pilot training, he received his Brevet on 29th July 1915, and was posted to Escadrille de Bombardement VB.106. In May 1916 he was transferred to the Escadrille Lafayette, and had scored five victories by early October. His subsequent career brought him promotion and many decorations, including the first award of the British Military Cross to an American. With America's entry into the war Lufbery was transferred, with the rank of Major, to the U.S. Air Service, and was subsequently given command of the famous 94th Aero Squadron. He was killed on 19th May 1918; flying a Nieuport 28, he was attacking an Albatros two-seater reconnaissance aircraft over the 94th Squadron's base at Toul when his machine burst into flames. Lufbery fell from the burning aircraft at an altitude of 6,000 ft—whether deliberately or*

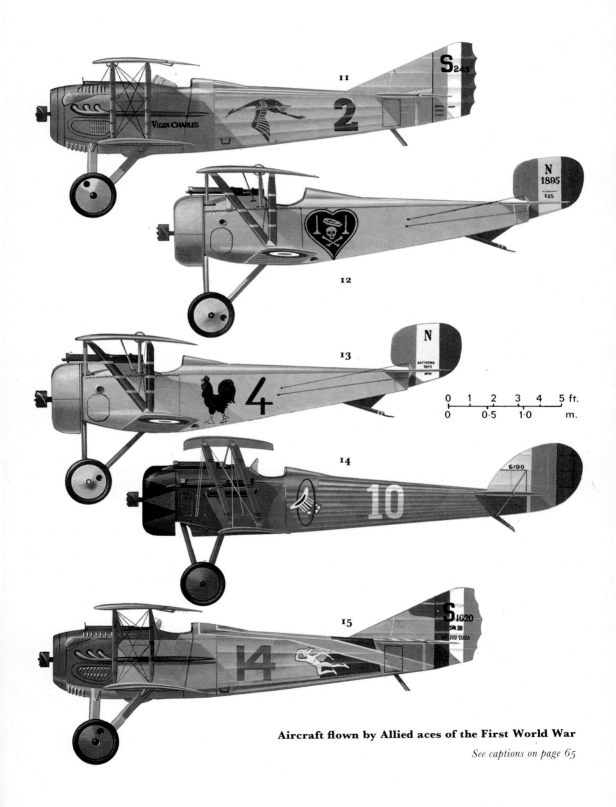

Aircraft flown by Allied aces of the First World War

See captions on page 65

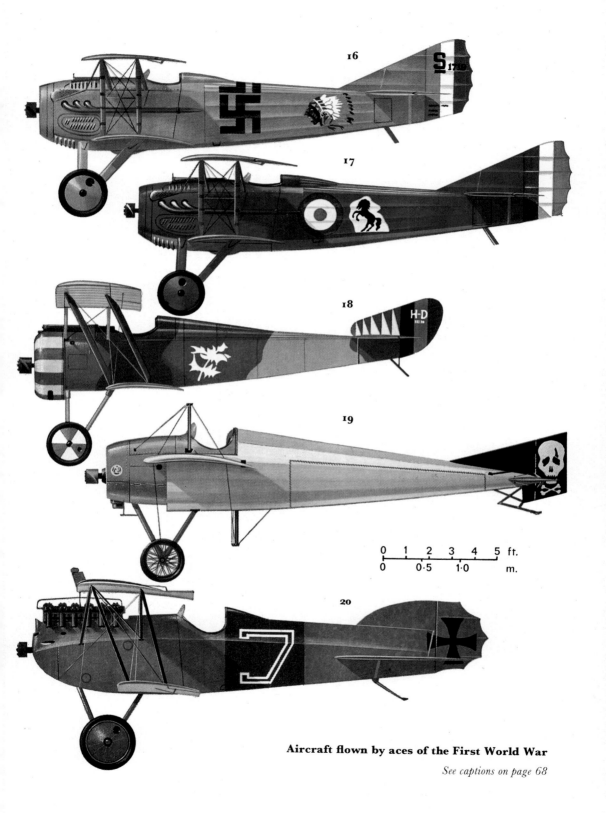

Aircraft flown by aces of the First World War

See captions on page 68

continued from page 65

accidentally will never be known. The Sioux Indian head insignia was the badge of SPA.124; the swastika was Lufbery's personal good luck symbol. At this early date it was naturally innocent of any political significance, and was used widely by pilots on both sides.

17. SPAD XIII *flown by Maggiore Francesco Baracca as commanding officer of the 91a Squadriglia of the Italian Aeronautica del Regio Esercito during the winter of 1917–18. Italy's leading ace with thirty-four confirmed victories, Baracca had qualified as a pilot in 1912, and had flying experience with many types of Italian, French and Belgian aircraft by the time Italy declared war on Austria in May 1915. His first victory was gained on 7th April 1916; leading a dawn patrol of Nieuport 11 scouts from the 70a Squadriglia, he shot down an Aviatik two-seater near Medea. His fifth victory came on 25th November 1916, and from this date onwards he had his famous prancing horse insignia painted on all his aircraft. He continued to score steadily, including two "doubles"—on 21st and 26th October 1917—and was heavily decorated. He failed to return from a ground-strafing mission near Montello on 19th June 1918, and his body and burned-out aircraft were not located until after the Austrian retreat; various theories about his death gained currency, but it seems most probable that, like so many other great air fighters of the First World War, he was killed by ground fire from some nameless infantryman crouching in a trench.*

18. Hanriot HD-1 *flown by Lieutenant Jan Olieslagers of the 1ere Escadrille de Chasse, Aviation Belge Militaire. A pre-war motor-cycle racing star and a pilot since 1909, Olieslagers became one of the great names of Belgian aviation. He served with distinction in Belgium's first all-fighter squadron alongside such aces as Willy Coppens and André de Meulemeester; although his official score was six victories, his contemporaries in the 1ere Escadrille maintained that he scored many more kills behind the German lines, where ground confirmation was seldom possible. Olieslagers died in Antwerp in 1942; the thistle insignia on his aircraft was the badge of the 1ere Escadrille.*

19. Morane-Saulnier MS 5 *scout flown during 1915 by Staff Captain Alexander Alexandrovitch Kazakov as commander of the XIX Corps Air Squadron, Russian Imperial Air Service. Kazakov is acknowledged as Russia's leading First World War ace with seventeen confirmed victories, but unofficial estimates put his true score at thirty-two. He conceived the idea of fixing a steel grapnel on a length of cable to his unarmed Morane scout, and flying low over enemy aircraft to tear away wings, control surfaces or flying wires. He scored his first victory on 18th March 1915, when he brought down an Albatros two-seater near Gusov partly by means of his grapnel, partly by ramming it with his undercarriage. A quiet and deeply religious man, Kazakov went on to command the 1st Fighter Group comprising four squadrons, and to receive sixteen decorations including the British D.S.O., M.C., and D.F.C. During the British intervention in the Russian Civil War he was attached to the R.A.F., flying Sopwith Camels. Shortly after the announcement that British forces were to be withdrawn from the campaign, Kazakov died in a rather ambiguous and inexplicable flying accident on 3rd August 1919.*

20. Phönix D I *flown by Oberleutnant Frank Linke-Crawford as commander of Fliegerkompagnie 60J, Austro-Hungarian Imperial Luftfahrtruppen; this squadron was based at Feltre on the Piave front during the winter of 1917–18. With an official score of twenty-seven to thirty, Linke-Crawford stands third in the roll of Austro-Hungarian aces; little is known of his personal life, beyond the fact that he was a rather earnest and reserved young man who earned promotion at a rate considered phenomenal in the ultra-conservative Imperial forces. He was shot down by Captain J. Cottle of 45 Squadron, R.A.F. on 31st July 1918 near Montello.*

his return to No. 11, on 10th August, Ball resumed his private war against the Rolands. When homogeneous fighting squadrons were formed he took his Nieuport to No. 60 and was given a roving commission, which suited his style admirably. Uncaring of odds, he would charge at enemy formations and deliver a devastating fire at close range, generally from a position immediately below the belly of the enemy machine, with his wing-mounted Lewis gun pulled down and back to fire almost vertically upwards. His D.S.O. and Bar were gazetted simultaneously on 26th September, and a second Bar on 25th November; the record which won him these decorations was impressive enough by any standards. On 15th September he shot down two Rolands; on the 19th he forced down an Albatros; on the 21st, shot down two Rolands and forced a third to land; on the 23rd, destroyed an Albatros; on the 28th, destroyed an Albatros and forced down two more. By the time he left France on 4th October Ball was credited with the destruction of ten enemy aircraft and with forcing down twenty more. On 7th April 1917, after a period spent instructing pupil pilots in England, he returned to the front as a Flight Commander in No. 56 Squadron. This unit flew the new S.E.5 scout, and Ball did not at first view the change of equipment with enthusiasm. He acquired a Nieuport for his personal use, but as he continued to increase his score while using both types of aircraft he became equally attached to the S.E.5. His forty-seventh and last victory, on 6th May 1917, was again achieved by flying close beneath an Albatros scout of Jasta 20 in his Nieuport, sending it crashing to the ground near Sancourt. Later the following evening Ball, flying his S.E.5, dived into dense cloud while chasing a German single-seater near Lens; the enemy later discovered his wrecked aircraft and his body. His death remains a mystery. Lothar von Richthofen was officially credited with the victory, but himself denied it, maintaining that the aircraft he shot down was a triplane—an opinion confirmed by other witnesses. Ball's body bore no wound, and what caused his aircraft to crash has never been established. He was twenty years and nine months old when he died; his Victoria Cross was gazetted on 3rd June 1917.

Captain Albert Ball in the cockpit of an S.E.5. Many of this ace's victories were achieved by firing straight upwards into the belly of an enemy aircraft at short range (Imperial War Museum)

The greatest Allied ace of the First World War was Capitaine René Paul Fonck, who served with Escadrille SPA.103, one of the units of the famous Groupe de Combat No. 12 "Les Cigognes". Officially Fonck is credited with seventy-five victories; his own personal estimate, including aircraft destroyed but not confirmed by Allied ground observers, was 127. Born in the Vosges in

SPAD XIII with the insignia of Les Cigognes *on its fuselage*

1894, Fonck died peacefully in his sleep at his Paris home on 18th June 1953. A keen aviation enthusiast in his boyhood, Fonck was disgusted to find himself posted to the 11th Engineer Regiment on mobilisation in 1914. After unhappy months digging trenches, he finally reported to Saint-Cyr for aviation training in February 1915; and in June, having received his Brevet, he joined Escadrille C.47. He flew Caudron G.IVs on reconnaissance duties and low-level bombing missions, and distinguished himself by his courage. On several occasions he nursed home damaged aircraft, and it is thought that he destroyed a Fokker on 1st March 1916, although this could not be confirmed. In July 1916 he fitted a machine-gun to his aircraft; and on 6th August he forced down a Rumpler, whose crew surrendered. On 14th October 1916 he shot down an Aviatik two-seater, but again failed to secure confirmation. On 17th March 1917 he fought off five Albatroses, destroying one; and this second confirmed victory led to his transfer to the "Cigognes" group a month later. He gained an unconfirmed victory on 3rd May, and a "definite" on 5th May, a Fokker shot down over Laon. His first "double" came on 12th June 1917, when he attacked and destroyed a pair of Albatroses. He repeated this feat on numerous occasions, and on 9th May 1918 he achieved no less than six confirmed "kills"—including three two-seaters destroyed in a total of 45 seconds, the three wrecks being found in a radius of 400 yards. On 26th September he again shot down six aircraft, comprising a two-seater, four Fokker D VIIs, and an Albatros D V. Fonck's last victory was over a leaflet-dropping two-seater on 1st November 1918. He was a thoughtful and analytical pilot, a master of deflection shooting, and his economy of ammunition bordered on the uncanny; he frequently sent an aircraft down for the expenditure of only five or six rounds, placed, in his own words, "comme avec la main"—"as if by hand". His many decorations included the Belgian Croix de Guerre, the French Croix de Guerre with twenty-eight palms, the British Military Cross and Bar, the British Military Medal and the Cross of Karageorge-vitch; his first sextuple victory also brought him the Croix d'Officier de la Légion d'Honneur. There is little doubt that he was in fact **the most successful fighter pilot of any combatant nation in the First World War.**

Britain's most successful fighter pilot in the First World War was Major Edward "Mick" Mannock of Nos. 40, 74, and 85 Squadrons, R.F.C. and R.A.F. His score of combat victories stands at seventy-three, but he is known to have insisted that several additional victories justly attributable to him, should be credited to other pilots in various engagements; his actual total is unknown. Born on 24th May 1887, the son of a soldier, Mannock was working in Constantinople when the war broke out, and was interned by the Turks. He was repatriated in April 1915 on health grounds; rejoined the Territorial Army medical unit to which he had belonged before leaving the country; was commissioned in the Royal Engineers on 1st April 1916; and finally transferred to the Royal Flying Corps in August 1916. His acceptance for flying duties is remarkable; he suffered from astigmatism in the left eye, and must have passed his medical by a ruse. He gained his Pilot's Certificate on 28th November 1916, followed by advanced training and was posted to No. 40 Squadron, France, on 6th April 1917, the unit being equipped at that time with Nieuport scouts. He shot down a balloon on 7th May, and on 7th June scored his first victory over an aeroplane. Returning from leave in July he shot down two-seaters on the 12th and 13th of that month; and his Military Cross was gazetted. He was promoted Captain, and took command of a flight. His score grew rapidly as he was possessed by a bitter and ruthless hatred of the enemy uncommon among his contemporaries, and showed no mercy to any German airman. His care of the pilots under his command, however, was irreproachable, and he has been judged the greatest patrol leader of any combatant air force. He took the greatest pains to plan every sortie in detail, and shepherded less experienced pilots until they gained skill and confidence, often insisting on crediting them with victories to which he was rightfully entitled. His patrols were never on any occasion attacked by surprise. In January 1918 he returned to England to take enforced leave; by that time his score stood at twenty-three. His squadron had recently been equipped with the excellent S.E.5a, an aircraft he later exploited to the full. He returned to France in March as a Flight Commander in the newly formed No. 74—"Tiger"—Squadron, also flying the S.E.5a, and in his three months with the unit added thirty-nine to his score. He was promoted Major in mid June, and was given leave before taking command of No. 85 Squadron. With No. 85 he raised his score to seventy-three by 26th July; on that day his petrol tank was hit by a random shot from the German trenches. His grave has never been found. It was nearly a year later that he was awarded a posthumous Victoria Cross, and his career attracted no great public attention until long after his death.

*"Mick" Mannock
(Imperial War Museum)*

France's second most successful fighter pilot was Capitaine Georges Marie Ludovic Jules Guynemer, who served in the "Cigognes" group with Escadrille N.3/ SPA.3. Although, with a score of fifty-four confirmed victories, he was second to René Fonck in achievement, Guynemer occupied an unrivalled place in the hearts of the French public. He was born on Christmas Eve 1894; a frail and delicate youth, he was twice rejected for military service before finally securing a posting to Pau Airfield as a pupil-mechanic in November 1914. A transfer to flying training followed, and on 8th June 1915 he joined Escadrille MS.3, then flying Morane Bullet monoplanes. (In the French manner, the unit was later designated N.3 and SPA.3 on re-equipment with Nieuport and SPAD scouts respectively.) Guynemer's first victory came on 19th July 1915; by July the following year he had eight victories to his name, and was flying Nieuports. During the latter

Capitaine Georges Guynemer in his Nieuport 23 with "Stork" insignia 1916

half of 1916 his score mounted at ever-increasing speed, bringing decorations and swift promotion; and by the end of January 1917 he was credited with thirty kills. A quadruple victory (two within the space of one minute) on 25th May brought his score to forty-five. His prowess, his pale good looks and dark eyes, his youth and general air of tortured romanticism, all made him a hero the French people could take to their hearts. He continued to fly combat sorties despite attempts to ground him; he was shot down seven times, and his health, never robust, was failing. He finally failed to return from a flight over Poelcapelle (Belgium) on 11th September 1917, and was mourned by his whole nation. No trace of his aircraft or his body has ever been found; no German pilot put in an immediate claim, but a certain Leutnant Wisseman was rather belatedly credited with his death by the German authorities. However the claim is open to question. Wisseman was killed by René Fonck three weeks later.

The third of France's great trio of First World War aces was Lieutenant Charles Eugène Jules Marie Nungesser of Escadrilles VB.106 and N.65. He scored forty-five confirmed victories, and survived the war to die in a record attempt in May 1927. A brilliant athlete and promising scholar, Nungesser left France as a teenage boy and sailed to South America to find an uncle who was reputed to live in Rio de Janeiro. Failing to locate him, the boy found work and stayed in South America for several years, winning a name as a racing motorist and teaching himself to fly. He took part in his first flying display two weeks after climbing into an aeroplane for the first time. He returned to France in 1914, joined the 2nd Hussar regiment, and distinguished himself in a lone battle against a squad of enemy infantry and a car full of German officers during the Battle of the Marne. He transferred to the Service Aéronautique, and reported to the Voisin reconnaissance and bombing unit VB.106 on 8th April 1915. On 26th April he was shot down, and for the next two months devoted himself to vain attempts to lure enemy scouts within range of his lumbering Voisin—usually by imitating a crippled aircraft—in the hope of exacting revenge. He finally scored his first victory late in 1915, on an unauthorised night sortie,

Lieutenant Charles Nungesser (Imperial War Museum)

gaining himself the Croix de Guerre and eight days' detention; and in November he joined Escadrille N.65. His career with N.65 opened with a victory on 28th November, and continued in a series of brilliant successes punctuated by frequent spells in hospital. Nungesser suffered numerous wounds and injuries, and was particularly dogged by the aftermath of a serious crash in January 1916; he sustained multiple fractures which failed to knit satisfactorily, and for the rest of the war was obliged to make periodic trips to hospital to have the bones re-broken and re-set. Despite the appalling pain from which he was seldom free Nungesser continued to fly and to add to his score; many of his total of forty-five kills were gained during a period when he was unable to walk, and had to be carried to and from his aircraft for every flight. After the war he quickly bored of life as an idol of Paris society, and turned first to running a flying school, and later to barnstorming in the United States. Finally he became absorbed in the idea of an East–West Atlantic attempt, and the Levasseur Company prepared a special aircraft designated the "P.L.8." The machine was named *Le Oiseau Blanc*—"The White Bird"—and bore on the fuselage the macabre insignia which Nungesser had made famous in the skies over the Western Front: a black heart charged with a skull and cross-bones, two candles, and a coffin. With Capitaine Coli as navigator, Nungesser flew "The White Bird" out over Le Havre at 06.48 h on 8th May 1927, and was never seen again.

The second most successful British and Empire pilot of the war was the Canadian, William Avery Bishop, born on 8th February 1894 in Ontario. While in England as a cavalry subaltern in the Canadian Mounted Rifles in 1915, Bishop decided he would see more action as a pilot, and transferred to the Royal Flying Corps in July of that year. He flew in France as an observer with No. 21 Squadron for several months, and was hospitalised as the result of a crash-landing and frostbite. He subsequently trained as a pilot and joined No. 60 Squadron in March 1917. The squadron was at that time equipped with Nieuport 17 scouts, an aircraft which Bishop was to handle brilliantly. On 25th March he scored his first victory over an Albatros, and repeated the feat on 31st March. On 7th April destroyed one aircraft and one observation balloon. His M.C. was awarded for this exploit. His score continued to mount at a phenomenal rate; he frequently flew for seven hours a day, and by early May he had claimed twenty enemy machines. His D.S.O. was awarded for his actions on 2nd May, during the course of which day he attacked a total of nineteen enemy aircraft in nine separate engagements, shooting down two. The Nieuport which he usually flew at this time, *B 1566*, is illustrated on an accompanying colour page. On 2nd June he flew alone over an enemy airfield at dawn and shot down three of the aircraft which took off to intercept him, damaged others on the ground, and returned safely to his home base for a late breakfast, thus earning the Victoria Cross. When his score reached forty-five Bishop was promoted Major and awarded a Bar to his D.S.O. Late in 1917 and early in 1918 he carried out a number of non-combat duties, including re-cruiting drives in Canada and instructing at an aerial gunnery school. He was subsequently given command of No. 85 Squadron, flying S.E.5as, and went back to France on 22nd May 1918. Despite orders to avoid risking his life in combat he returned to the fray with characteristic enthusiasm, shooting down twenty-five enemy aircraft in a period of twelve days, twelve of them in the last three days, and all within a total of 36·5 h flying time. He was then recalled to England, and never flew operationally again; his D.F.C. was gazetted on 2nd July. Bishop

William Avery Bishop

remained in the service, rising to the rank of Honorary Air Marshal in the Royal Canadian Air Force. He died in Florida, U.S.A., in September 1956.

The most successful fighter pilot of the Royal Naval Air Service during the First World War, and, with sixty confirmed victories, third in the over-all aces' list, was Raymond Collishaw, born on 22nd November 1893 at Nanaimo, British Columbia. He went to sea at the age of seventeen and served as Second Mate on a merchant ship, and later on fishery protection vessels. He transferred to the R.N.A.S. in January 1916, joining No. 3 Wing in August, and scored his first victory on 12th October. While flying a Sopwith 1½-Strutter with the escort for a Franco-British bombing force, he shot down an enemy scout over Oberndorf. His second and third victories came on 25th October, in the course of a ferry flight; on 27th December he was shot down himself but remained unhurt. In February 1917 he joined a scout unit, No. 3 (Naval) Squadron. He scored one more victory while flying Sopwith Pups with this squadron, and in April was posted to No. 10 (Naval) Squadron as commander of "B" Flight. Equipped with Sopwith Triplanes, the "Black Flight" of "Naval Ten" earned a reputation as one of the most formidable Allied units of the war. The Flight was composed entirely of Canadians; their aircraft were decorated with black paint, and named *Black Maria* (Collishaw), *Black Prince*, *Black Sheep*, *Black Roger*, and *Black Death*. Between May and July 1917 the Flight destroyed eighty-seven enemy aircraft, and during June Collishaw himself shot down sixteen in twenty-seven days. On 6th June he shot down three Albatroses in a single engagement, for which feat he was awarded the D.S.C. On 15th June he scored four victories, and ten days later shot down Leutnant Karl Allmenröder, a thirty-victory ace who flew with von Richthofen in Jasta 11. On 3rd July, his score standing at twenty-eight, Collishaw gained the D.S.O. He shot down ten more victims before the end of the

Raymond Collishaw, brilliant exponent of the Sopwith Triplane and leader of the formidable "Black Flight", who achieved sixty confirmed victories (Imperial War Museum)

Sopwith Triplane painted to represent Raymond Collishaw's Black Maria *(National Aviation Museum, Ottawa)*

month and was shot down himself, for the second time. For the second time, he escaped without significant injury. After home leave Collishaw returned to France on 24th November 1917, taking command of No. 13 (Naval) Squadron, a Sopwith Camel unit. He was posted back to No. 3 (Naval) Squadron as commander in January 1918, by which time his score was forty-one victories. He saw no action until June, but between 11th and 30th added five to his score, and continued to fly and fight brilliantly until reaching his official total of sixty. He was back in England on administrative duties in October, but commanded No. 47 Squadron in the Russian campaign of 1919/20, where he gained two further victories. He remained in the Royal Air Force, serving in the Second World War and reaching the rank of Air Vice-Marshal, C.B., with the D.S.O. and Bar, D.S.C., D.F.C., and Croix de Guerre, as well as both military and civil grades of the O.B.E.

Fourth in the roll of British and Empire aces of the First World War, was Major James Thomas Byford McCudden with fifty-seven confirmed victories although recent research indicates that the actual number may have been higher. He joined the Royal Engineers as a bugler in 1910, transferring to the Royal Flying Corps, Military Wing, in 1913. He arrived in France on 13th August 1914 as a First Class Air Mechanic with No. 3 Squadron. By the summer of 1915 he had reached the rank of Sergeant, had made a few flights as an observer, and was gaining some piloting experience by strictly unofficial flights in a Morane Parasol. McCudden's first combat, as an observer, took place on 19th December 1915, and he was awarded the Croix de Guerre the following month. Late in January 1916 he was promoted Flight Sergeant and posted home for flying training. In July he returned to France and joined No. 20 Squadron, flying reconnaissance and escort missions in F.E.2d aircraft. His first operational mission as a pilot was on 10th July 1916. In August he was posted to a scout squadron, No. 29, equipped with D.H.2s and his first victory, over a two-seater, came on 6th September 1916. He was awarded the M.M. on 1st October, and was commissioned on 1st January 1917. He shot down an Albatros C-type on 6th February, and a Roland C II on the 15th. His M.C. was awarded the following day, and late in the month he was posted home. During the first half of 1917 he served with various training establishments and did a short "refresher course" with No. 66 Squadron, and managed to make a patrol with No. 56 Squadron in July, flying the S.E.5 for the first time. In mid August he joined No. 56 as a Flight Commander, with seven victories to his name. Many of his victims fell after a long "stalk"; he was an instinctive lone hunter, and would wait patiently for the right moment to attack. He was also a sound patrol leader, and his technical background led him to make a thorough study of his engine and guns, and of the potentialities of enemy machines. By 23rd November 1917 he had earned a Bar to his M.C., and his score stood at twenty. Before the end of the year he had destroyed at least a further seventeen aircraft, four of them falling on 23rd December. He repeated this quadruple victory on 16th February 1918, bringing his score to fifty-one. On 25th February 1918 he destroyed his last victim, a Hannover CL III, making a total of fifty-seven kills. He returned to England for an instructional tour, and on 6th April was decorated with the Victoria Cross, the D.S.O. and Bar, and the Bar to his M.C. Five months later, now a Major and commanding officer designate of No. 60 Squadron, he crashed and was killed at Auxi-le-Château shortly after taking off to fly to his new command. His engine failed, and he made the mistake—inexplicable for such a brilliant and experienced pilot—of trying to turn back towards the airfield.

J. T. B. McCudden and "Bruiser" (Air Ministry)

*Still flying in America,
this SPAD XIII is painted
to represent Rickenbacker's
machine (Howard Levy)*

The most successful American pilot of the First World War was Captain Edward Vernon Rickenbacker, whose score totalled twenty-six confirmed aerial victories. Born on 8th October 1890 in Columbus, Ohio, Rickenbacker made a considerable name for himself between 1910 and 1917 as one of America's leading racing motorists. In England to negotiate the establishment of a Sunbeam racing team in 1917, he became interested in flying; and when America's entry into the war sent him back to the United States, he advanced the idea of a squadron composed entirely of racing drivers. The idea did not arouse official interest, but a meeting with General Pershing in Washington led to Rickenbacker's enlistment and sent him to France as the General's chauffeur. In August 1917 he transferred to the Aviation Section, and his mechanical expertise led to a posting to the 3rd Aviation Instruction Center at Issoudun as Chief Engineering Officer—a post he filled with great competence, but much impatience. In his own time he completed advanced flying and gunnery courses, and on 4th March 1918 he finally secured a transfer to the 94th Aero Squadron—the "Hat-in-the-Ring" squadron commanded by Raoul Lufbery, the Escadrille Lafayette ace. With Lufbery and Douglas Campbell (q.v.), Rickenbacker flew the first American patrol over enemy lines on 19th March; and on 29th April he shot down his first victim, an Albatros scout. On 30th May his fifth victory qualified him as an ace, but it was to be his last for four months. An ear infection put him in hospital and convalescence until mid September, when he returned to the squadron as a Captain and Flight Commander. On 14th September he shot down a Fokker, and by the end of the month had sent three more Fokkers, a Halberstadt and a balloon to join it. He took over command of the 94th on 25th September, and continued to score heavily until the Armistice. Captain Rickenbacker was active in the automobile and airline industries between the wars, and was largely responsible for building up Eastern Air Lines, of which corporation he became Chairman in 1953. During the Second World War he toured widely, visiting Air Force units abroad and undertaking various missions for his Government. In the course of a flight over the Pacific his aircraft was forced to ditch, and Rickenbacker and the crew survived twenty-one days on a life-raft before being picked up. He remained active in various public fields until his death in August 1973, at the age of eighty-two. His many American and foreign decorations include his country's highest award for gallantry, the Congressional Medal of Honor.

America's second ranking ace in the First World War was Lieutenant Frank Luke, Jr., who between 16th August and 28th September 1918 scored twenty-one victories and earned immortality as a "balloon-buster". Luke was born in Phoenix, Arizona on 19th May 1897; as a boy he was an excellent athlete, and he is reputed to have been a considerable shot with both rifle and pistol. His early life round the copper-mines of Arizona was not easy, and he acquired a tough reputation. He enlisted in the U.S. Signal Corps (Aviation Section), in September 1917 and was commissioned in January 1918, sailing for France in March. He was then sent to the 3rd Aviation Instruction Center for advanced flying training, and to Cazeau in May for aerial gunnery training. His first duty was ferrying aircraft at Orly, a task which improved his flying skill but frustrated his aggressive spirit. He obtained a posting to the 27th Aero Squadron in late July; and on 16th August broke formation against orders and scored his first victory. This was to be the first of many brushes with authority; Luke was impatient of discipline, and was constantly in trouble with his superiors. He was not a good mixer, and his tough self-confidence did not endear him to his fellow pilots, who considered him a conceited braggart. He was, however, a born combat pilot, whose marksmanship and flying skill were equalled by his aggressive spirit. He became an embittered "loner", and formed a close friendship with only one other pilot, Lieutenant Wehner. Luke shot down his first balloon on 12th September, near Marrieulle, and landed his SPAD so badly damaged that it was written off—the first of five aircraft which he "used up" in his career. On 14th September Luke and Wehner began their short but brilliant partnership; Luke shot down two balloons while Wehner fought off the protective patrol of eight Fokkers. The next day Luke destroyed two more balloons, only to be attacked by seven Fokkers. Wehner, who had shot down a balloon himself, then arrived and shot two of the Fokkers off Luke's tail. The same afternoon Luke accounted for another balloon, and the following evening three more fell to the team-work of Luke and Wehner. On 18th September Luke dived to destroy two balloons near Labeuville while Wehner remained above. On regaining altitude Luke found his comrade engaged with six Fokkers, two of which he promptly shot down. He lost contact with the other pilot, and on his way back to base alone he shot down a Halberstadt two-seater in flames. His elation was short-lived, however; on landing he found that Wehner had been killed. He took a short leave in Paris, but soon returned; and on 26th September he scored again, but again lost his wingman, Lieutenant Roberts. Deeply depressed, Luke went A.W.O.L. for a day. He destroyed another balloon on an unauthorised flight, and then spent the night at a French airfield. His persistent flouting of orders had become a disgrace, and a grounding and arrest order was issued; but it was destined never to be served. Just before sunset, having fuelled his SPAD at a forward airfield, he flew over the American balloon headquarters in Souilly and dropped a note reading "Watch three Hun balloons on the Meuse, Luke." He shot down the first balloon at Dun-sur-Meuse, and a second at Brière Farm; badly wounded in the second action, he nevertheless flew on to Milly and shot the third down in flames. He dived to strafe German troops in the streets of Murvaux, eventually crash-landing on the outskirts of the village. He was surrounded by German troops and called upon to surrender, but preferred to fight it out with his ·45 service pistol. Inevitably he was riddled with rifle bullets and died instantly. It was not until 1919 that his grave was located, and the story of his last fight pieced together from eye-witness accounts. He was awarded a posthumous Congressional Medal of Honor. His habit of making unauthorised sorties has led to some confusion over his actual score, recorded accounts varying between seventeen and twenty-one. The higher score is, however, the more generally accepted, and thus is quoted here.

BETWEEN THE WARS

The first six-engined American aeroplane was the Barling XNBL-1. Powered by six 420 hp Liberty 12A engines, this large experimental "long-range" night bomber triplane had a span of 120 ft (36·5 m) and a maximum loaded weight of 42,569 lb (19,325 kg). First flown on 22nd August 1923, it was found to possess a range of only 170 miles (275 km) with a bomb-load, or 335 miles (540 km) without, and therefore, hardly surprisingly, it was abandoned. The development had cost $350,000.

The Barling XNBL-1
(Howard Levy)

The first fighter to enter service with the Royal Air Force capable of a maximum level speed of more than 200 mile/h (322 km/h) was the Hawker Fury I biplane. Powered by a 525 hp Rolls-Royce Kestrel IIS liquid-cooled engine and armed with two synchronised Vickers machine-guns, the Fury had a top speed of 207 mile/h (333 km/h) at 14,000 ft (4,270 m). Designed by the late Sir Sydney Camm, it first entered service with No. 43 Squadron, at Tangmere, Sussex, in May 1931.

The Hawker Fury I

The first monoplane aircraft with retractable landing gear to enter service with the R.A.F. was the Avro Anson general-reconnaissance aircraft. The prototype of the "Faithful Annie", as the Anson was known in the service, flew for the first time on 24th March 1935. The first production Anson Is were delivered to No. 48 Squadron, at Manston, Kent, on 6th March 1936.

The Polikarpov I-16
(Imperial War Museum)

The first monoplane fighter with a fully enclosed cockpit and a fully retractable undercarriage to enter squadron service anywhere in the world was the Polikarpov I-16 Ishak ("Little Donkey"). The prototype first flew on 31st December 1933, and deliveries of the Type 1 production fighter to Soviet squadrons commenced during the autumn of 1934. The I-16 Type 1 was powered by a 450 hp M22 engine, had a top speed of 224 mile/h (360 km/h) at sea-level, and was armed with two 7·62 mm ShKAS machine-guns.

The first German monoplane fighter with a fully enclosed cockpit and a fully retractable undercarriage to enter squadron service was the Messerschmitt Bf 109B-1. The prototype Bf 109V-1 (D-IABI) first flew in September 1935 powered by a 695 hp British Rolls-Royce Kestrel V engine. The first production Bf 109B-1s were delivered to Jagdgeschwader 2 "Richthofen" in the spring of 1937. The B-1 model was powered by a 635 hp Junkers Jumo 210D engine, had a top speed of 292 mile/h (470 km/h) at 13,100 ft (4,000 m), and was armed with three 7·92 mm MG 17 machine-guns.

The Seversky P-35

The first American monoplane fighter with a fully enclosed cockpit and a retractable, though exposed, undercarriage to enter squadron service was the Seversky P-35, the prototype of which was evaluated at Wright Field in August 1935. The production model, of which deliveries began in July 1937, was powered by a 950 hp Pratt & Whitney R-1830-9 engine. It had a top speed of 281 mile/h (452 km/h) at 10,000 ft (3,050 m), and was armed with one 0·5 in and one 0·3 in machine-gun.

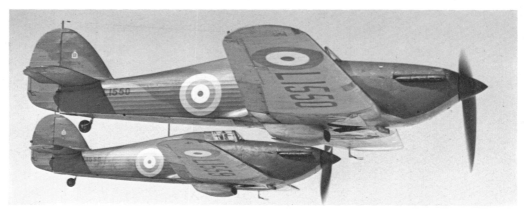

The Hawker Hurricane I (Flight International)

The first British monoplane fighter with a fully enclosed cockpit and a fully retractable undercarriage to enter squadron service was the Hawker Hurricane. It was also
**the R.A.F.'s first fighter able to exceed a speed of 300 mile/h
(483 km/h), and the first of its eight-gun monoplane fighters.** The
prototype made its first flight on 6th November 1935, and initial deliveries
of production aircraft were made to No. 111 Squadron at Northolt,
Middlesex, during December 1937. The Hurricane I was powered by a
1,030 hp Rolls-Royce Merlin II or III engine, had a top speed of 322
mile/h (518 km/h) at 20,000 ft (6,100 m), and was armed with eight
0·303 in Browning machine-guns.

*The Morane-Saulnier
M-S 406*

The first French monoplane fighter with a fully enclosed cockpit and a fully retractable undercarriage to enter squadron service was the Morane-Saulnier M-S 406.
The M-S 405, from which the series was derived, first flew on 8th August
1935, and was the first French fighter aircraft able to exceed a speed of
250 mile/h (402 km/h) in level flight. The first production M-S 406
(N2-66) flew for the first time on 29th January 1939, and by 1st April
1939 a total of twenty-seven had been delivered to the French Air Force.
Powered by an 850 hp Hispano-Suiza HS 12Y-31 engine, the M-S 406
had a maximum level speed of 304 mile/h (490 km/h) at 14,700 ft (4,480 m),
and was armed with one 20 mm HS 59 cannon and two 7·5 mm MAC
machine-guns.

The Macchi C.200

The first Italian monoplane fighter with a fully enclosed cockpit and a fully retractable undercarriage to enter squadron service was the Macchi C.200 Saetta ("Lightning"). First single-seat fighter designed by Dr. Mario Castoldi, the prototype first flew on 24th December 1937. Deliveries of production aircraft began in October 1939, and these were powered by an 870 hp Fiat A.74RC.38 radial engine, giving the C.200 a maximum level speed of 313 mile/h (505 km/h) at 15,750 ft (4,800 m). Armament consisted of two 12·7 mm Breda-SAFAT machine-guns mounted in the upper engine decking.

The first Japanese monoplane fighter with a fully enclosed cockpit and a fully retractable undercarriage to enter squadron service was the Mitsubishi A6M2, popularly known as the "Zero-Sen". The A6M1 prototype first flew on 1st April 1939, and the "12-Shi fighter project", as it had been known, was officially adopted by the Imperial Japanese Navy on 31st July 1940. In commemoration of the anniversary of the 2,600th Japanese Calendar year (A.D. 1940), the new fighter became designated A6M2 Type O Carrier Fighter Model 11. The Zero was first used operationally on 19th August 1940, when a formation of twelve aircraft, led by Lieutenant Tamotsu Yokoyama, escorted a force of bombers attacking Chungking. The A6M2 was powered by a 950 hp Nakajima NK1C Sakae 12 engine, had a top speed of 332 mile/h (534 km/h) at 16,570 ft (5,050 m), and was armed with two 20 mm Type 99 cannon (licence-built Oerlikons) and two 7·7 mm Type 97 machine-guns. Two 30 kg bombs could be carried on an under-fuselage rack.

The Spanish Civil War (1936–39) provided the setting for many significant advances in military aviation. The political background—a rebellion by right-wing elements of the armed forces and population against an extreme left-wing government and popular movement—was such that massive aid was dispatched to the opposing forces by two major international camps. Italy and Germany supported General Francisco Franco y Bahamonde's Nationalists, and the Soviet Union supported the Republican Government, which also drew aid from various other countries and from many volunteer organisations more dedicated in their resistance to Fascism than their outright support of Communism.

German aid, in the form of twenty Junkers Ju 52/3m transport aircraft, six Heinkel He 51b fighter biplanes and eighty-five volunteer air

Heinkel He 51 fighter biplane, one of the first combat types sent by Germany to support General Franco's Nationalist forces in the Spanish Civil War (Hans Obert, via IPMS)

and ground crews, arrived in August 1936, less than a month after the outbreak of war. These aircraft were at once employed in ferrying 10,000 Moorish troops across the Straits of Gibraltar from Tetuan. From this small beginning grew the Legion Cóndor—a balanced force of between forty and fifty fighters, about the same number of multi-engined bombers, and about a hundred miscellaneous ground-attack, reconnaissance, and liaison aircraft, whose first Commander-in-Chief was General-Major Sperrle. Volunteers from the ranks of the Luftwaffe served in rotation, to ensure the maximum dissemination of combat experience. Many of the major combat designs upon which Germany was to rely in the first half of the Second World War were first evaluated under combat conditions in Spain; the Heinkel He 111 bomber, the Dornier Do 17 reconnaissance-bomber, the Messerschmitt Bf 109 fighter, and the Henschel Hs 123 and Junkers Ju 87 ground-attack aircraft were prominent. The contribution of the Legion Cóndor to the eventual Nationalist victory was considerable, but more important still were the inferences drawn by Luftwaffe Staff planners. Valid lessons learned in Spain included the value of the dive-bomber in hampering enemy communications, and the effects of ground-strafing by fighters in the exploitation of a breakthrough by land forces. Less realistic was the impression gained of the relative invulnerability of unescorted bombers and dive-bombers—an impression based on the lack of sophisticated fighter resistance. In the field of fighter tactics, and in terms of combat experience by her fighter pilots, the Spanish Civil War put Germany at least a year ahead of her international rivals.

Italy's intervention in the Spanish Civil War commenced in August 1936, with the arrival by sea at Melilla of twelve Fiat CR. 32 biplane fighters. The eventual strength of the Italian Aviacion del Tercio in Spain was some 730 aircraft (total supplied) including Fiat CR. 32s, SM. 81s, SM. 79s, BR. 20s, Ro. 37s, Ba. 65s, and a squadron of Fiat G. 50s. Of these, 86 aircraft were lost on operations and 100 from other causes, and 175 flying personnel were killed. A total of 903 enemy aircraft were claimed destroyed in aerial combat, and a further 40 on the ground. Total sorties flown were 86,420, and bombing sorties totalled 5,318.

The Spanish Republican Air Force mustered 214 obsolete aircraft at the outbreak of the Civil War. Additionally, the Government had at its disposal 40 civil types of various designs; and between 1937 and 1939, 55 aircraft were built in the Republican zone. Foreign aircraft dispatched to Spain by various friendly nations totalled 1,947, of which 1,409 were sent from Russia. The others included 70 Dewoitine D. 371, D. 500 and D. 510 fighters, 20 Loire-Nieuport 46s and 15 S. 510 fighters from France; 72 aircraft—but no fighters—from the U.S.A.; 72 aircraft from the Netherlands; 57 from Britain; and 47 from Czechoslovakia. Of these some 400 are thought to have been destroyed other than in aerial combat, and 1,520 were claimed shot down by Nationalist, German and Italian pilots.

Polikarpov I-15 in Spanish insignia

The first Russian aircraft to enter combat in Spain were the Polikarpov I-16 Type 6 fighters of General Kamanin's expeditionary command, based at Santander. By September 1936 105 of these aircraft had arrived in Spain—by sea to Cartagena—and had been assembled; some 200 pilots and 2,000 other personnel had also arrived from the Soviet Union. The I-16—known in Spain as the *Rata* ("Rat") and the *Mosca* ("Fly") to Nationalists and Republicans respectively—first entered combat on 5th November 1936. Eventually a total of 475 I-16s were supplied; and from March 1937 they were gathered in one formation designated Fighter Group 31, comprising seven squadrons of fifteen aircraft each. More numerous but inevitably less successful was the I-15 biplane fighter, of which some 550 were supplied. The I-15 was inferior to both the Fiat CR. 32 and the Messerschmitt Bf 109, and no fewer than 415 are believed to have been lost either in combat or on the ground. The most numerous Republican bomber type, the Soviet Tupolev SB-2, also fared badly; of 210 supplied, 178 were lost.

The first maliciously motivated bombs to fall on the U.S.A. were dropped on 12th November 1926 from an aeroplane on a farmhouse in Williamson County, Ill., during a Prohibition gang feud. They were of crude manufacture and failed to explode.

The largest British landplane built prior to the Second World War was the Beardmore Inflexible three-engined monoplane, designed principally by Dr. Adolf Rohrbach at the invitation of the Air Ministry during 1923; built by William Beardmore & Company; and assembled at the R.A.F. Flight Test establishment at Martlesham Heath, Suffolk, during the early months of 1928. It was flown for the first time on 5th March that year by Squadron Leader J. Noakes, M.M. (later Group Captain, A.F.C., M.M.) who reported that the huge monoplane handled extremely well. With a wing span of 157 ft 6 in (48·0 m) and a loaded weight of 37,000 lb (16,780 kg), the Inflexible was somewhat underpowered with three 650 hp Rolls-Royce Condor II engines, which gave it a maximum speed of 109 mile/h (175 km/h).

The Beardmore Inflexible (Ministry of Defence)

The last biplane heavy bomber to serve as such with the Royal Air Force was the Handley Page Heyford which first flew in June 1930 at Radlett, Hertfordshire, entered service with No. 99 (Bomber) Squadron at Upper Heyford, Oxfordshire, on 14th November 1933, and was withdrawn from front-line service in March 1939. The last Heyford was struck off R.A.F. charge in May 1941. Powered by two 575 hp Rolls-Royce Kestrel III engines, the Heyford I had a top speed of 142 mile/h (229 km/h) at 13,000 ft (3,960 m) and could carry a maximum bomb-load of 2,616 lb (1,190 kg).

THE SECOND WORLD WAR

The Polish fighter most widely used at the time of the German invasion in September 1939 was the P.Z.L. P.11, of which 128 were on strength on 1st September 1939. They equipped Nos. 111, 112, 113 and 114 Squadrons of the 1st Air Regiment based on Warsaw, Nos. 121 and 122 Squadrons of the 2nd Air Regiment based at Kraków, Nos. 131 and 132 Squadrons of the 3rd Air Regiment at Poznań, Nos. 141 and 142 Squadrons of the 4th Air Regiment at Torun, No. 152 Squadron of the 5th Air Regiment in the Wilno/Lida area, and No. 161 Squadron of the 6th Air Regiment based at Lwow. The P.11/I prototype was flown for the first time during August 1931, and the first production P.11as entered service in 1934. Definitive version was the P.11c, powered by a P.Z.L.-built Mercury VI S.2 radial engine of 645 hp, giving it a maximum level speed of 242 mile/h (390 km/h) at 18,000 ft (5,485 m). Armament consisted of four 7·7 mm machine-guns, and two 27 lb (12 kg) fragmentation bombs could be carried beneath the wings.

P.Z.L. P.11 (J. B. Cynk)

The greatest losses suffered by the Luftwaffe during the Polish campaign in a single day were those of 3rd September 1939 when twenty-two German aircraft were destroyed (four Dornier Do 17s, three Messerschmitt Bf 110s, two Heinkel He 111s, three Junkers Ju 87s, two Messerschmitt Bf 109s, three Henschel Hs 126s, two Fieseler Fi 156s, one Henschel Hs 123, one Junkers Ju 52 and one Heinkel He 59). One of the Messerschmitt Bf 110s was accidentally shot down by German troops near Ostrolenka. Luftwaffe personnel casualties on this day amounted to thirty-four killed, one wounded and seventeen missing.

The first occasion on which a British aircraft crossed the German frontier during the Second World War was on 3rd September 1939 when Blenheim IV, number N6215, of No. 139 Squadron, flown by Flying Officer A. McPherson, and carrying Commander Thompson, R.N., and Corporal V. Arrowsmith, photographed German naval units leaving Wilhelmshaven.

The first British aircraft to drop bombs on enemy targets during the Second World War was Blenheim IV, number N6204, flown by Flight-Lieutenant K. C. Doran, leading a formation of five aircraft from No. 110 (Hyderabad) Squadron in a raid on the German Fleet in the Schillig Roads, off Wilhelmshaven on 4th September 1939; a formation of five Blenheims from No. 107 Squadron also took part in the attack.

The first British gallantry decorations to be gazetted during the Second World War were two Distinguished Flying Crosses on 10th September 1939 to Flying Officer McPherson and Flight-Lieutenant Doran (see above).

The first German aircraft shot down by British forces during the Second World War was a Dornier Do 18 (Wrk.Nr. 731) of 2 Staffel, Küstenfliegergruppe 506 on 26th September 1939 in German Grid Square 3440 (North Sea). The crew of four was rescued and made prisoner aboard H.M.S. *Somali* (1,870 tons). (H.M.S. *Somali* foundered in tow three days after being torpedoed in a North Russian convoy action, September 1942.)

The first British bombers to fly over Berlin in the Second World War were Armstrong Whitworth Whitleys of No. 10 Squadron, which dropped propaganda leaflets on the night of 1st/2nd October 1939.

The first German aircraft shot down over British soil in the Second World War was a Heinkel
He 111, destroyed by a Spitfire of No. 603 Squadron on 16th October 1939,
over the Firth of Forth.

**The first German aircraft shot down by British forces to land on British soil during the
Second World War** was a Heinkel He 111H-1 (1H+JA) of Stabsstaffel,
Kampfgeschwader 26, shot down by British fighters, which crashed at
Lammermoor Hill, near Dalkeith, 6 miles south of Haddington near the
Firth of Forth on 28th October 1939. This victory was shared by Spitfires
of Nos. 602 and 603 Squadrons. Two of the crew were killed, one wounded
(Leutnant Rolf Niehoff, the commander) and one unwounded.

**The first enemy aircraft shot down by R.A.F. fighters on the Western Front in the Second
World War** was a Dornier Do 17 destroyed over Toul on 30th October
1939. The victorious pilot was Pilot Officer P. W. Mould, flying a Hurricane
of No. 1 Squadron.

*Fokker D. XXI (Finnish
Air Force)*

The first loss suffered by the Finnish Air Force during the "Winter War" with Russia in
1939–40 was Sergeant Kukkonen who, flying a Fokker D.XXI of Fighter
Squadron HLeLv.24 near Viipuri, was shot down by his own anti-
aircraft guns on 1st December 1939.

The first aerial victory claimed during the "Winter War" between Finland and Russia was
claimed by Lieutenant Eino Luukkanen on 1st December 1939; flying a
Fokker D.XXI (*FR-104*) of Fighter Squadron HLeLv.24, he destroyed a
Russian SB-2 bomber.

The first Royal Air Force aircraft to drop bombs deliberately on German soil is believed to
have been an Armstrong Whitworth Whitley, *N1380*, DY-R of No. 102
Squadron, based at Driffield, Yorkshire. No. 102 Squadron, in company
with Whitleys of Nos. 10, 51 and 77 Squadrons, and Handley Page
Hampdens of No. 5 Group, attacked the German mine-laying seaplane
base at Hornum on the night of 19th/20th March 1940.

**The worst losses in aircraft destroyed as the result of air combat and anti-aircraft gunfire
suffered by a single air force on a single day** are believed to have been
those of the Luftwaffe on 10th May 1940. On this day Germany invaded
the Netherlands and Belgium and was opposed simultaneously by the
air forces of Holland, Belgium, France and Great Britain. The Norwegian

campaign, by then nearing its end, also claimed a small number of German victims. On this day the Luftwaffe, according to its own records, lost:

Junkers Ju 52 transports	157 destroyed
Heinkel He 111 bombers	51 destroyed, 21 damaged
Dornier Do 17 bombers	26 destroyed, 7 damaged
Fieseler Fi 156 artillery support aircraft	22 destroyed
Junkers Ju 88 bombers	18 destroyed, 2 damaged
Junkers Ju 87 dive-bombers	9 destroyed
Messerschmitt Bf 109 fighters	6 destroyed, 11 damaged
Dornier Do 215 reconnaissance aircraft	2 destroyed
Henschel Hs 126 reconnaissance aircraft	1 destroyed, 3 damaged
Messerschmitt Bf 110 fighters	1 destroyed, 3 damaged
Dornier Do 18 flying-boat	1 destroyed
Henschel Hs 123 dive-bomber	1 damaged
Other types	10 destroyed, 3 damaged

Total 304 destroyed, 51 damaged

Aircrew casualties amounted to 267 killed, 133 wounded and 340 missing; other Luftwaffe personnel (Flak, engineers, etc.) casualties amounted to 326 killed or missing.

Apart from the purely academic significance of these figures (not previously published), they indicate conclusively that the operations undertaken by the Luftwaffe on this day represented the true commencement of *Blitzkrieg* against substantial opposition. On this day Germany suffered losses in excess of all previous cumulative losses since 1st September 1939, including the Polish campaign. Losses suffered by the Luftwaffe during the invasion of Poland may be summarised as follows:

1st–8th September 1939:
116 aircraft destroyed, 128 aircrew killed, 68 wounded and 137 missing.
9th–13th September 1939:
34 aircraft destroyed, 15 aircrew killed, 15 wounded and 63 missing.
14th–18th September 1939:
23 aircraft destroyed, 24 aircrew killed, 32 wounded and 14 missing.
19th–27th September 1939:
30 aircraft destroyed, 54 aircrew killed, 18 wounded and 4 missing.

The first German aircraft to be destroyed in the air by the Royal Netherlands Air Force during the German invasion of the Low Countries was a Junkers Ju 88A-2 of Kampfgeschwader 30 which was shot down off the Dutch coast by a pilot of 1e Ja.V.A. fighter squadron (the famous "three white mice" unit) on 10th May 1940. On this day Kampfgeschwader 30 was briefed to attack targets at Nijmegen, Rotterdam, Utrecht and Waalhaven.

The greatest single victory achieved by the Royal Netherlands Air Force during the German invasion of the Low Countries was gained at 06.45 h on 10th May 1940 when a force of Fokker D.XXIs intercepted fifty-five Junkers Ju 52/3m transport aircraft of KGzbV 9. The Dutch pilots claimed to have shot down 37 of the formation, but German records indicate a total loss of 39 aircraft, 6 occupants killed, 41 presumed dead, 15 wounded and 79 missing.

The French military aeroplane most widely used at the beginning of the Battle of France on 10th May 1940 belonged to the Potez 630 series, of which a total of 1,250 were built. The main variants were the 630 and 631 fighters and the 63/11 reconnaissance machine. First flown in April 1936, the three-seater Potez 630 fighter, powered by two 640 hp Hispano-Suiza HS 14 Ab 10/11 engines, had a maximum level speed of 280 mile/h (450 km/h) at 13,000 ft (3,960 m). Standard armament comprised two nose-mounted Hispano 9 or 404 cannon, plus one MAC machine-gun for rear defence. Shortage of cannon made it necessary to arm many 630/631s with four machine-guns and when, in February 1940, it was decided to increase the fire-power of these fighters, the cannon were supplemented by six machine-guns mounted beneath the wings.

The first British bombs to fall on the German mainland in the Second World War were dropped by eight or nine Whitleys of 77 and 102 Squadrons, which attacked enemy lines of communication leading to Southern Holland on the night of 10th/11th May 1940.

The first awards of the Victoria Cross to R.A.F. aircrew in the Second World War were to Flying Officer Donald Edward Garland and Sergeant Thomas Gray of No. 12 Squadron, Advanced Air Striking Force. The awards were made posthumously for gallantry when, on 12th May 1940, they dived their Battle aircraft into the bridge at Maastricht, in the Netherlands, in an attempt to delay the German advance.

The first British bombers to attack targets in Italy in the Second World War were Whitleys of Nos. 10, 51, 58, 77 and 102 Squadrons. Crossing the Alps on 11th June 1940, they attacked Genoa and Turin.

The first bombing attack on Berlin was made on the night of 25th/26th August 1940. The attacking force comprised twelve Hampdens of Nos. 61 and 144 Squadrons, seventeen Wellingtons of Nos. 99 and 149 Squadrons, and fourteen Whitleys of Nos. 51 and 78 Squadrons.

THE BATTLE OF BRITAIN

The highest-scoring Allied pilot during the Battle of Britain was Sergeant Josef František, a Czech pilot who served with No. 303 (Polish) Squadron, R.A.F. His confirmed score of seventeen enemy aircraft shot down was achieved entirely during September 1940; he was killed on 9th October 1940. The only British gallantry decoration awarded to František was the Distinguished Flying Medal, but he had previously been awarded the Czech War Cross and the Polish Virtuti Militari.

The Allied pilots who scored ten or more confirmed victories during the Battle of Britain:

†Sgt. J. František, D.F.M.	17	Hurricanes	(303 Sqdn.)	Czech. Top-scoring Czech and Allied pilot
†Plt. Off. E. S. Lock, D.S.O., D.F.C.*	16+1 shared	Spitfires	(41 Sqdn.)	Top-scoring British pilot
Fg. Off. B. J. G. Carbury, D.F.C.*	15+1 shared	Spitfires	(603 Sqdn.)	Top-scoring New Zealand pilot
Sgt. J. H. Lacey, D.F.M.*	15+1 shared	Hurricanes	(501 Sqdn.)	Top-scoring Auxiliary pilot
Plt. Off. R. F. T. Doe, D.S.O., D.F.C.*	15	{ Hurricanes Spitfires	(238 Sqdn.) (234 Sqdn.)	British
†Flt.-Lt. P. C. Hughes, D.F.C.	14+3 shared	Spitfires	(234 Sqdn.)	Top-scoring Australian pilot
Plt. Off. C. F. Gray, D.S.O., D.F.C.**	14+2 shared	Spitfires	(54 Sqdn.)	New Zealander
†Flt.-Lt. A. A. McKellar, D.S.O., D.F.C.*	14+1 shared	Hurricanes	(605 Sqdn.)	British
Fg. Off. W. Urbanowicz, D.F.C.	14	{ Hurricanes Hurricanes	(303 Sqdn.) (601 Sqdn.)	Top-scoring Polish pilot
†Fg. Off. C. R. Davis, D.F.C.	11+1 shared	Hurricanes	(601 Sqdn.)	Top-scoring South African pilot
Flt.-Lt. R. F. Boyd, D.S.O., D.F.C.*	11+1 shared	Hurricanes	(601 Sqdn.)	British
Sgt. A. McDowall, D.S.O., A.F.C., D.F.M.*	11	Spitfires	(602 Sqdn.)	British
Fg. Off. J. W. Villa, D.F.C.*	10+4 shared	{ Spitfires Spitfires	(72 Sqdn.) (92 Sqdn.)	British
Fg. Off. D. A. P. McMullen, D.F.C.**	10+3 shared	{ Spitfires Spitfires	(54 Sqdn.) (222 Sqdn.)	British
Flt.-Lt. R. S. S. Tuck, D.S.O., D.F.C.**	10+1 shared	{ Spitfires Hurricanes	(92 Sqdn.) (257 Sqdn.)	British
Plt. Off. H. C. Upton, D.F.C.	10+1 shared	{ Spitfires Spitfires	(43 Sqdn.) (607 Sqdn.)	Top-scoring Canadian pilot
Flt. Sgt. G. C. Unwin, D.S.O., D.F.M.*	10	Spitfires	(19 Sqdn.)	British

(†=deceased. The ranks shown are those held during the Battle of Britain. The decorations are shown to include *all* gallantry awards won by these pilots before, during and after the Battle.)

The first Victoria Cross to be won during the Battle of Britain was awarded posthumously to

Acting Seaman J. F. (Jack) Mantle, R.N., who was operating an anti-aircraft gun aboard H.M.S. *Foyle Bank* in Portsmouth Harbour on 4th July 1940. The ship, the only one in the port with an anti-aircraft gun, became the focus of an enemy raid and was hit by a bomb which cut the power-supply. Jack Mantle, though severely wounded, continued to fire the gun, operating it manually; despite another direct hit upon the ship, which severed his left leg, he remained at his post until the end of the raid but succumbed to his terrible wounds almost immediately afterwards. His Victoria Cross was only the second to be awarded for an action in or over Great Britain, the first having been awarded to Lieutenant W. Leefe Robinson of No. 39 (Home Defence) Squadron, R.F.C., for his destruction of a Schutte-Lanz airship on the night of 2nd/3rd September 1916 at Cuffley, Hertfordshire.

The first Victoria Cross awarded to a pilot of R.A.F. Bomber Command who survived his act of gallantry was that won by Flight-Lieutenant R. A. B. Learoyd The award was made for gallantry when, on the night of 12th/13th August 1940, Flight-Lieutenant Learoyd was flying Hampden P.4403, one of a force of five from Nos. 49 and 83 Squadrons which dropped delayed action bombs on an aqueduct of the Dortmund-Ems Canal.

The only Victoria Cross ever to be awarded to a member of R.A.F. Fighter Command was that won by Flight-Lieutenant James Brindley Nicolson, R.A.F., on 16th August 1940. A Flight Commander of No. 249 (Hurricane) Squadron, Nicolson was leading a section of three fighters on patrol near Southampton, Hants, when he sighted enemy aircraft ahead. Before he could complete the attack his section was "bounced" from above and behind by German fighters which shot down one Hurricane and set Nicolson's aircraft ablaze. With flames sweeping up through his cockpit, the British pilot remained at his controls long enough to complete an attack on an enemy aircraft which had flown into his sights, and then baled out. Meanwhile on the ground a detachment of soldiers, seeing Nicolson and his wingman descending on parachutes and believing them to be enemy paratroops, opened fire with rifles. Nicolson was hit but survived his wounds and burns, but his colleague was dead when he reached the ground (whether or not he was killed by rifle-fire has never been established).

The first member of the Royal Air Force to be awarded the George Cross (and indeed among the first group of any to be awarded) was Aircraftman Vivian ("Bob") Holloway who, in July 1940, at Cranfield, Bedfordshire, entered a crashed and blazing bomber and extricated the pilot, and in so doing suffered severe burns to his hands. One month later, at the moment of returning from hospital, he again dashed into a blazing aircraft *three times* amidst exploding ammunition, and brought out three crew members. He survived his near-fatal burns despite having been on the danger list for twenty-seven days.

The first regular-serving American pilot to die in action during the Second World War was Pilot Officer William M. L. Fiske, R.A.F., who on 17th August 1940 died of wounds suffered in action at Tangmere, England, during the Battle of Britain against the Luftwaffe on 16th August 1940.

The first air victory scored in the Greek-Italian campaign of 1940–41 was achieved by a Greek pilot of No. 21 Squadron of the Royal Hellenic Air Force, flying a Polish P.Z.L. P.24, when he destroyed an Italian aircraft north of Yannina on 1st November 1940.

The first and only attack in strength by the Italian Air Force on Britain was made on 11th November 1940. Hurricane fighters of Nos. 46, 249 and 257 Squadrons claimed seven Fiat B.R. 20 bombers and four Fiat C.R. 42 fighters destroyed without loss to themselves.

The first 4,000 lb (1,814 kg) "block-buster" bomb to be used on operations was dropped by a Wellington of No. 149 Squadron, during an attack on Emden on 1 April 1941.

The Heinkel He 280 landing after its first test flight, with uncowled engines

The world's first jet fighter, and also the first twin-engined jet aircraft, was the German Heinkel He 280, the first prototype of which, the He 280V-1, first flew on 5th April 1941 powered by two 1,320 lb (600 kg) thrust Heinkel-Hirth HeS 8A turbojets. Maximum speed was estimated to be more than 550 mile/h (885 km/h), though subsequently it has become obvious that the aircraft would have been unable to exceed 400 mile/h (644 km/h). It did not achieve production status.

The largest airborne assault mounted by the Luftwaffe during the Second World War was Operation "Mercury", the landing of 22,750 men on the island of Crete commencing at 07.00 h on 20th May 1941. The Luftwaffe used 493 Junkers Ju 52/3m aircraft and about 80 DFS 230 gliders. The assault was made by 10,000 parachutists, 750 troops landed by glider, 5,000 landed by Ju 52/3ms and 7,000 by sea. The operation, although regarded as a brilliant success, cost Germany about 4,500 men killed and some 150 transport aircraft destroyed or badly damaged, and effectively brought Luftwaffe paratrooping operations to an end.

R.A.F. Fortress I (Boeing B-17C) (Charles E. Brown)

The first combat mission ever flown by the Boeing B-17 Flying Fortress was a raid flown at 30,000 ft (9,150 m) by aircraft of No. 90 (Bomber) Squadron, R.A.F. on Wilhelmshaven on 8th July 1941. Twenty B-17Cs had been supplied to the R.A.F., and were used by this service under the designation "Fortress I".

The first aerial victories claimed during the "Continuation War" between Finland and Russia, which broke out in June 1941, were two Russian DB-3 bombers shot down by six Fokker D.XXIs over the Riihimäki railway junction in the first air battle, which probably took place on 25th June.

The first combat operation carried out by Avro Lancaster heavy bombers was a mine-laying sortie flown by No. 44 (Bomber) Squadron, based at Waddington, Lincolnshire, over the Heligoland Bight on 3rd March 1942. **Their first night-bombing attack** was made on Essen on the night of 10th/11th March 1942.

Commonwealth Boomerang (R.A.A.F.)

The only fighter of Australian design to fire its guns in anger during the Second World War was the Commonwealth CA-12 Boomerang, of which a total of 250 were built between May 1942 and January 1945. The first aircraft *A46-1*, was first flown by Ken Frewin at Fisherman's Bend, Victoria, on 29th May 1942. Powered by an Australian-built 1,200 hp Pratt & Whitney R-1830 engine, which gave it a top speed of 296 mile/h (476 km/h) at 7,600 ft (2,315 m), the Boomerang eventually served with Nos. 4, 5, 83, 84 and 85 Squadrons, Royal Australian Air Force. Although it is true that the Boomerang was used principally as a ground-attack fighter, it is perhaps surprising to record that, frequently in action against Japanese aircraft, it failed to destroy an enemy aeroplane in the air.

The first Boeing B-17E Flying Fortress to arrive in Britain was allocated to the U.S.A.A.F.'s 97th Bombardment Group. This unit made its first operational sortie in Europe on 17th August 1942, when 12 B-17Es attacked Rouen.

The largest-calibre multi-barrelled weapon fired by an aircraft was the six-barrelled 77 mm. Sondergeräte 113A Forstersonde rocket mortar fitted in three Henschel Hs 129 ground-attack aircraft to fire Sabot-type shells vertically downwards. The weapon was triggered by a photo-electric cell actuated by the shadow of a tank beneath the aircraft.

The most successful Russian woman fighter pilot of the Second World War, and thus presumably the most successful woman fighter pilot in the world, served with the mixed-sex 73rd Guards Fighter Air Regiment. She was Junior Lieutenant Lydia Litvak, and she was killed in action on 1st August 1943 at the age of twenty-two with a total of twelve confirmed victories to her name. She flew Yak fighters.

(During the Second World War, most Russian women combat pilots served with the 122nd Air Group of the Soviet Air Force. This all-female unit comprised the 586th Fighter Air Regiment, the 587th Bomber Air Regiment and the 588th Night Bomber Air Regiment. The 586th I.A.P. (Istebitelnyi aviatsionnyi polk=fighter air regiment) was formed at Engels, on the Volga River, in October 1941; it was commanded by Major Tamara Aleksandrovna Kazarinova. The pilots of this unit flew a total of 4,419 operational sorties, took part in 125 air combats, and were credited with 38 confirmed victories. The unit flew Yak-1, -7B and -9 fighters. During the Second World War, thirty Russian airwomen received the gold star of a Hero of the Soviet Union. It is believed that twenty-two of them served with the 588th/46th Guards Night Bomber Air Regiment, which was equipped with PO-2 biplanes.)

The Royal Air Force heavy bomber with the greatest number of operational missions to its credit was the Avro Lancaster B. Mark III, *ED888*, PM-M², of No. 103 (Bomber) Squadron. *Mike Squared*, alternatively known as "The Mother of Them All", made its first operational sortie in a raid on Dortmund on the night of 4th/5th May 1943. By the time the aircraft was retired in December 1944 it had logged 140 missions—the first 66 with No. 103 Squadron, then 65 with No. 576 Squadron, and 9 more with No. 103 Squadron—totalling 974 operational hours. The last two squadrons were based at R.A.F. Elsham Wolds, Lincolnshire.

The only known pilot who has been both gaoled and awarded his country's highest gallantry decoration for the same exploit was Lieutenant Michael Devyatayev, a Soviet fighter pilot shot down by the Luftwaffe over Lvov on 13th July 1944. Taken prisoner by the Germans, Devyatayev escaped and seized a Heinkel He 111 bomber and flew nine other escapees back to Russian-held territory. On regaining his freedom the twenty-three-year-old pilot was gaoled under the U.S.S.R. criminal code which labelled him a traitor for having been taken prisoner. Nine years later, in 1953, he was freed under an amnesty prevailing at the time, and in 1958 was made Hero of the Soviet Union and awarded the Order of Lenin and Gold Star Medal.

Gloster Meteor F Mk I (Ministry of Defence)

The first jet aircraft to enter operational service with any air force was the Gloster Meteor Mark 1, powered by two 1,700 lb (771 kg) thrust Rolls-Royce W.2B/23 Welland I turbojet engines. Twenty Meteor Is were built, one of which was exchanged for an American-built **Bell Airacomet – the first U.S.-designed and built jet fighter.** Three others were used for development purposes and the remainder (*EE213* to *EE222*, and *EE224* to *EE229*) were delivered to No. 616 Squadron. The first two aircraft were

(above) The nuclear deterrent that keeps the peace between East and West is well symbolised by this Boeing B-52 Stratofortress strategic bomber of the U.S.A.F., with Hound Dog missiles under its wings. (below left) Fastest aeroplane ever flown, the air-launched North American X-15 research aircraft reached 4,534 mile/h (7,297 km/h) in 1967. (below right) Sir Barnes Wallis demonstrates a model of his pioneer "swing-wing" aeroplane, the Swallow, which pointed the way to the variable-geometry designs of the present time (Air BP)

delivered on 12th July 1944 to the Squadron, based at Culmhead, Somerset, under the command of Wing Commander A. McDowall, D.S.O., A.F.C., D.F.M.* (see page 89 for top-scoring Battle of Britain pilots). **The first combat sortie** was flown from Manston by the Squadron on 27th July 1944 against V-1 flying-bombs but was unsuccessful owing to gun-firing difficulties. **The first combat success** was scored on 4th August 1944 by Flying Officer Dean who, after his guns had jammed, flew alongside the enemy bomb and, by tipping it with his wing, forced the missile into the ground. The aircraft was *EE216*.

Messerschmitt Me 262A (R. W. Cranham)

The first German jet aircraft to enter operational service was the Messerschmitt Me 262A-1a fighter, powered by two Junkers Jumo 109-004B-1 engines with eight-stage axial-flow compressor, six combustion chambers and single-stage turbine. These engines provided a maximum level speed of 540 mile/h (869 km/h) at 19,685 ft (6,000 m). The swept-wing fighter was armed with four 30 mm MK 108 automatic cannon grouped in the nose; a frequent addition to the armament was a rack of twelve unguided 55 mm R4M rocket projectiles under each wing. These rockets were aimed through the standard gunsight, fired electrically at a range of about 650 yd (595 m) from the target, and proved most effective against bomber formations. The Me 262A-1a entered operational service on 3rd October 1944; a test unit was expanded and renamed Kommando Nowotny—under the command of the Austrian ace, Major Walter Nowotny—and became operational on that date. One of the two Staffeln of the unit was based at Achmer, the other at Hesepe. At approximately the same time the Me 262A-2a Sturmvogel ("Stormbird") fighter-bomber variant

entered operational service with Kommando Schenk, a unit commanded
by Major Wolfgang Schenk and largely drawn from former personnel of
Kampfgeschwader 51 "Edelweiss".

The first jet bomber to enter operational service with any air force—apart from the Me
262A-2a (see above), which was merely a fighter with two bomb pylons
fitted beneath the nose—was the Arado Ar 234B Blitz ("Lightning"),
powered by two Jumo 004B series turbojets. The first prototype Ar
234V1 made its first flight on 15th June 1943, powered by two Jumo
004A turbojets of 1,850 lb (839 kg) thrust. First to enter service were small
numbers of Ar 234B-Os, issued to various Luftwaffe reconnaissance units
during the summer of 1944. The AR 234B entered true bomber squadron
service in October 1944, when deliveries of the type commenced to
Kampfgeschwader 76, then based at Achmer and commanded by Oberstleutnant Robert Kowalewski. A thoroughly practical aircraft with a good
performance, demonstrating a maximum level speed of 461 mile/h (742
km/h) at 19,685 ft (6,000 m), the Blitz entered service too late to prove of
significant value.

The first aerial victory against another piloted aircraft gained by the pilot of a jet aircraft
has never been positively identified, but was certainly achieved in the
first week of October 1944 by a pilot of Kommando Nowotny, the target
being a Boeing B-17 Flying Fortress of the U.S. 8th Air Force.

The first loss of a jet aircraft in aerial combat is thought to have taken place on or about 10th
October 1944, when two Me 262A-1a fighters were shot down by North
American P-51D Mustang escort fighters of the 361st Fighter Group, U.S.
8th Air Force.

The first major operational success by a guided free-falling (i.e. unpowered) bomb was the
sinking of the Italian battleship *Roma* by Dornier Do 217s of 111 Gruppe,
Kampfgeschwader 100, commanded by Major Bernhard Jope, west of
Corsica on 9th September 1943, using Ruhrstahl Fritz-X 3,100 lb (1,406
kg) bombs. The *Roma* was hit by two bombs, the second of which started a
disastrous fire which reached the magazine and caused the battleship to
blow up, break in two and sink with most of her crew. In this Italian fleet,
which was *en route* to surrender to the Allies at Malta, the *Roma*'s sister
ship, the *Italia*, received a direct hit on the bows and took on about
800 tons of water before reaching Malta under her own steam. Fritz-X
bombs later scored hits on the battleship H.M.S. *Warspite*, the British
cruisers H.M.S. *Uganda* and *Spartan* (sunk), and the American cruiser
U.S.S. *Savanna*.

The first jet-fighter ace in the world has not been positively identified, but it is thought that he was
one of the pilots of Kommando Nowotny. The unit was withdrawn from
operations following the death in action of Major Walter Nowotny on
8th November 1944, and later provided the nucleus for the new fighter
wing, Jagdgeschwader 7 "Nowotny"; III Gruppe, JG 7 became operational during December 1944. Hauptmann Franz Schall is known to have
scored three aerial victories on the day of Nowotny's death, and subsequently served with 10 Staffel, JG 7; it is therefore entirely possible that
he was the first pilot in the world to have achieved five confirmed aerial
victories while flying jet aircraft. Other known jet aces of the Second
World War are listed below. The fragmentary records which survived
the final immolation of the Luftwaffe in 1945 prevent the preparation of a

complete list, and the following should therefore be regarded simply as a confirmed framework for future research:

Oberstleutnant Heinz Bär (JV 44)	16
Hauptmann Franz Schall (10./JG 7)	14
Major Erich Rudorffer (II/JG 7)	12
Oberfeldwebel Hermann Buchner (III/JG 7)	12
Leutnant Karl Schnörrer (11./JG 7)	Not less than 8
Leutnant Rudolf Rademacher (II/JG 7)	Not less than 8
Major Theodor Weissenberger (Staff/JG 7)	8
Oberleutnant Walter Schuck (3./JG 7)	8
Oberst Johannes Steinhoff (Staff/JG 7, JV 44)	6
Major Wolfgang Späte (Staff/JG 7)	5
Leutnant Klaus Neumann (JV 44)	5

Messerschmitt Me 163B Komet

The first (and only swept-wing) rocket-engined aeroplane to enter operational squadron service with any air force was the Messerschmitt Me 163B-1 Komet interceptor fighter, powered by a Walter HWK 109-509A-2 bi-fuel liquid rocket motor, giving it a speed of about 600 mile/h (965 km/h). The swept-wing, tailless Me 163B-1 was armed with two 30 mm MK 108 cannon; some machines are known to have carried various experimental armament systems in addition. The Komet equipped only one combat unit, Jagdgeschwader 400; 1 Staffel, JG 400, was established at Wittmundhafen in March 1944, and 2 Staffel at Venlo in May. The whole unit was concentrated on Brandis in July 1944, and operations commenced shortly afterwards; Allied reports mention encounters for the first time on 16th August. The unit's aircraft are thought to have destroyed about a dozen Allied aircraft in all; the only pilot known to have gained two confirmed solo victories was Oberleutnant August Hachtel. The last combat sortie by a Komet was carried out by Oberleutnant Fritz Kelb who took off from Husum on 7th May 1945 and did not return.

The shortest elapsed time for the development of an entirely new jet fighter (which achieved combat status) was sixty-nine days for the Heinkel He 162 Salamander. Conceived in an R.L.M. specification issued to the German aircraft industry on 8th September 1944, the He 162 was the subject of a contract issued on 29th September 1944 for an aircraft capable of being mass-produced by semi-skilled labour using non-strategic materials. Sixty-nine days later, on 6th December 1944, the first prototype He 162V-1 was flown by Heinkel's Chief Test Pilot, Kapitän Peter, at Vienna-Schwechat. On 10th December the prototype broke up in the air and crashed before a large gathering of officials, and Peter was killed. Notwithstanding this set-back, the aircraft entered production and joined I and II Gruppen of Jagdgeschwader I at Leck/Holstein during April 1945. III Gruppe of this Geschwader was under orders to receive the new fighter but was forestalled by the end of the war. Known also as the Volksjäger, or "People's Fighter", it was intended that large numbers would be constructed, but only 116 A-series machines were completed. The Salamander was not a pleasant machine to fly, and as a result few of these aircraft were encountered in combat. Its single BMW 003 turbojet, rated at 1,760 lb (800 kg) thrust, provided a maximum level speed of 522 mile/h (840 km/h) at 19,685 ft (6,000 m).

An Avro Lancaster, Britain's outstanding heavy bomber of the Second World War, warms up for a night take-off (Imperial War Museum)

The first test-drop of the 22,000 lb (9,980 kg) "Grand Slam" bomb was made from an Avro Lancaster on 13th March 1945. **The first operational drop of this bomb** was made by Squadron Leader C. C. Calder of No. 617 (Bomber) Squadron, flying Lancaster B.1 (Special) *PD112*. The bomb was dropped on the Bielefeld Viaduct on 14th March 1945, smashing two of its spans.

The last known enemy piloted aircraft to fall on British soil is believed to have been a Junkers Ju 88G-6 (D5+AX) of 13 Staffel, Nachtjagdgeschwader 3, which had been on intruder operations and crashed at 01.51 h on 4th March 1945 at Elvington, near Pocklington Airfield, Yorkshire. All the crew members perished.

(Left) "Johnnie" Johnson, 38 victories over German fighters and England's leading ace of the Second World War

(right) Wing-Commander B. E. ("Paddy") Finucane

The most successful fighter pilots of the Second World War, by nationality, are listed below: all scores are levelled down to the nearest unit: British gallantry decorations are quoted:

"Screwball" Buerling, the leading Canadian ace

Country of origin		Aircraft destroyed in combat
Australia	Gp. Capt. Clive R. Caldwell, D.S.O., D.F.C.*	28
Austria	Maj. Walter Nowotny.	258
Belgium	Flt.-Lt. Vicki Ortmans, D.F.C.	11
Canada	Sqdn. Ldr. George F. Buerling, D.S.O., D.F.C., D.F.M.*	31
Czechoslovakia	Sgt. Josef František, D.F.M.	28
Denmark	Gp. Capt. Kaj Birksted	either 8 or 10
Finland	F/Mstr. E. I. Juutualainen	94
France	Sqdn. Ldr. Pierre H. Clostermann, D.F.C.*	19
Germany	Maj. Erich Hartmann.	352
Hungary	2nd Lt. Dezjö Szentgyörgyi	43
Ireland	Wg. Cdr. Brendan E. Finucane, D.S.O., D.F.C.**	32
Italy	Maj. Adriano Visconti	26
Japan	Sub-Officer Hiróyoshi Nishizawa	103
Netherlands	Lt.-Col. van Arkel	12 V-1s, and 5
New Zealand	Wg. Cdr. Colin F. Gray, D.S.O., D.F.C.**	27
Norway	Flt.-Lt. Svein Heglund	either 14 or 16
Poland	Jan Poniatowski (rank unknown)	36
Romania	Capt. Prince Constantine Cantacuzino	60
South Africa	Sqdn. Ldr. M. T. St. J. Pattle, D.F.C.*	41
United Kingdom	Gp. Capt. James E. Johnson, D.S.O.**, D.F.C.*	38
United States	Maj. Richard I. Bong	40
U.S.S.R.	Guards Col. Ivan N. Kozhedub	62

The most successful destroyer of flying bombs (V-1s) in flight was Squadron Leader Joseph Berry, D.F.C.**, who shot down sixty during 1944.

Fighter pilots serving with the Royal Air Force during the Second World War who achieved twenty-five or more confirmed aerial victories (countries of origin indicated in parentheses):

Wing Commander R. R. S. Tuck

Sqdn. Ldr. M. T. St. J. Pattle, D.F.C.*	41	(S.A.)
Gp. Capt. J. E. Johnson, D.S.O.**, D.F.C.*	38	(U.K.)
Gp. Capt. A. G. Malan, D.S.O.*, D.F.C.*	35	(S.A.)
Wg. Cdr. B. E. Finucane, D.S.O., D.F.C.**	32	(Ir.)
Sqdn. Ldr. G. F. Buerling, D.S.O., D.F.C., D.F.M.*	31	(Ca.)
Wg. Cdr. J. R. D. Braham, D.S.O.**, D.F.C.**, A.F.C.	29	(U.K.)
Wg. Cdr. R. S. Tuck, D.S.O., D.F.C.**	29	(U.K.)
Sqdn. Ldr. N. F. Duke, D.S.O., D.F.C.**, A.F.C.	28	(U.K.)
Gp. Capt. C. R. Caldwell, D.S.O., D.F.C.*	28	(Au.)
Gp. Capt. F. H. R. Carey, D.F.C.**, A.F.C., D.F.M.	28	(U.K.)
Sqdn. Ldr. J. H. Lacey, D.F.M.*	28	(U.K.)
Wg. Cdr. C. F. Gray, D.S.O., D.F.C.**	27	(N.Z.)
Flt.-Lt. E. S. Lock, D.S.O., D.F.C.*	26	(U.K.)
Wg. Cdr. L. C. Wade, D.S.O., D.F.C.**	25	(U.S.)

(left) "Sailor" Malan

(right) Gregory Boyington of the U.S. Marine Corps in the cockpit of his Corsair fighter

Fighter pilots serving with the United States air forces during the Second World War who achieved twenty-five or more confirmed aerial victories:

U.S.A.A.F.

Major Richard I. Bong (C.M.H.)	40
Major T. B. McGuire (C.M.H.)	38
Colonel F. S. Gabreski	31
Lieutenant-Colonel R. S. Johnson	28
Colonel C. H. MacDonald	27
Major G. E. Preddy	26

U.S.N.

Captain D. McCampbell	34

U.S.M.C.

Major J. J. Foss	26
Lieutenant R. M. Hanson	25
Lieutenant-Colonel G. Boyington	22

(Lieutenant-Colonel Boyington is known to have destroyed an additional six enemy aircraft while serving with the Air Volunteer Group under Chinese command.)

*A Republic P-47
Thunderbolt, the mighty
"Jug", as flown by
Gabreski*

The first operational military use of composite combat aeroplanes was by the German Luftwaffe, during the Allied invasion of France in June–July 1944. Devised originally under a programme designated "Beethoven-Gerät", it was known subsequently as the "Mistel-Programm". Biggest problem was to develop an effective system by which the pilot of the single-seater upper aircraft could control and effect separation of the two components. Initial operational Mistels comprised an upper piloted Bf 109F-4 and a lower Ju 88A-4 which carried 7,700 lb (3,492 kg) of explosives. The weapon was first issued to 2 Staffel of Kampfgeschwader 101, commanded by Hauptmann Horst Rudat, during May–June 1944; and it is thought likely that one or two such weapons struck the old French battleship *Courbet* which was used as a blockship for the British artificial Mulberry Harbour at Courseulles. It is known that about 150 Mistels were built, the majority of the Ju 88G-1 lower components of 125 production versions being captured undamaged when Nordhausen fell to Allied troops.

The most successful fighter pilot in the world, and Germany's leading ace in the Second World War, was Major Erich Hartmann of Jagdgeschwader 52. He was born in Weissach, Württemberg, on 19th April 1922, and was still a seventeen-year-old schoolboy when war broke out. It was 10th October 1942 before he was posted to his first combat unit, 9 Staffel of JG 52, which was operating in the Ukraine. This unit had earned the reputation of being one of the most formidable Staffeln in the Luftwaffe; in the spring of 1942 its pilots, led by the ace Oberleutnant Hermann Graf, had been credited with forty-seven victories in seventeen days. Among the most successful members of the Staffel were Oberfeldwebel Leopold Steinbatz, Graf's wingman, who gained thirty-five victories during the month of May 1942, and was the first N.C.O. to be awarded the Swords and Oak Leaves to the Knight's Cross; Oberfeldwebel Füllgrabe and Süss, both of whom were to score between sixty and seventy victories; and Feldwebel Alfred Grislawski, who was to score 133 kills. In this rarified atmosphere the slim, classically handsome Hartmann, just twenty years old, did not give any immediate signs of future promise. He gained his first victory on 5th November, but by April 1943, when he had amassed a hundred missions in his log-book, his score stood at seven victories only. Like Johnson and many other leading aces, he had a lengthy "running-in" period during which he perfected his technique. His eyesight and co-ordination were excellent, his flying was cool and calculated, and he was economical with his ammunition, usually closing to very short range before opening fire with short bursts. He did not strive for high scores on each sortie, preferring to gain one good, clean textbook kill and then concentrate on his flying and his rear-view mirror. Nevertheless, he was to gain multiple victories on many occasions, his first major success being achieved on 7th July 1943; JG 52 was one of the units involved in covering the great "Zitadelle" tank offensive in the Kursk-Orel-Bielgorod area, and on that day Hartmann

led 7 Staffel's Messerschmitt Bf 109G fighters from their base at Ugrim,
to score seven personal victories in three sorties—three Ilyushin Il-2
ground-attack aircraft, and four Lavochkin LaGG-3 fighters. These were
his twenty-second to twenty-eighth victories; by 20th September his
score had risen to no less than 100; he had been shot down, captured, and
escaped four hours later; and he was clearly emerging as something special,
even among the veterans of JG 52. His Knight's Cross came with his 148th
victory on 29th October 1943, the Oak Leaves on 2nd March 1944 with his
200th, and the Swords on 4th July 1944, with his 239th. The summer of
1944 saw another period of multiple successes; in four weeks he destroyed
seventy-eight enemy aircraft, including eight on 23rd August, and eleven
on the following day, bringing his score to 301—and making him the first
of the only two fighter pilots in the world who ever scored 300 victories.
This feat brought him into the select band of men—numbering twenty-
seven only—who wore the Diamonds to the Knight's Cross, the award
being made on 25th July 1944. In October 1944 he became Staffelkapitän
of 4./JG 52, and took over command of II Gruppe, JG 52 on 1st February
1945. His unit retreated steadily westwards as the Red Army swept across
central Europe in the final great offensive, and Hartmann eventually
surrendered to American forces in Czechoslovakia in May 1945; by this
time he had scored 352 victories, including 260 fighter aircraft, of which
five were American P-51 Mustangs shot down during a brief posting to
Romania. In accordance with a prior political commitment, the American
authorities handed him over to the Russians; he was made to stand trial
as a criminal, and sentenced to ten years' imprisonment. The fact that he
survived this sentence and returned home in 1955 is a considerable
testimony to his character and determination. He rejoined the Luftwaffe,
and rose to high rank during the 1960s; at the time of writing he is still in
uniform.

**The most successful German fighter pilot in combat against the Western Allies during the
Second World War** was Hauptmann Hans-Joachim Marseille, who was
born in Berlin-Charlottenburg in December 1919. As an N.C.O./officer
candidate he saw action on the Channel Coast in 1940, flying with
Lehrgeschwader 2 and 4./JG 52 during the closing stages of the Battle
of Britain. In this campaign he scored his first seven victories, all R.A.F.
fighters, but was himself shot down four times in the process; he was
awarded the Iron Cross First Class in September 1940. In April of 1941
he was posted to I Gruppe Jagdgeschwader 27 in Libya, and it was in
desert warfare that he excelled. He worked with great perseverance to
master his trade, and in the blinding skies of North Africa his superb
depth vision and marksmanship became a legend. He was credited with
many multiple victories, including the astounding total of seventeen
aircraft destroyed on 1st September 1942. He was awarded the Knight's
Cross on 22nd February 1942 for his fiftieth victory; the Oak Leaves on
6th June, for his seventy-fifth; and the Swords only twelve days later, by
which time his score stood at 101. On 8th June he had become Staffelkapitän of 3./JG 27. On 2nd September 1942 he received the Diamonds,
then his country's highest award; he was only the fourth man to receive
the award, the others being Werner Mölders, Adolf Galland, and Gordon
Gollob—the first 150-victory ace. On 30th September the "Star of Africa"
died; returning from an uneventful mission over the Alamein line, he
was forced to bale out when the engine of his Messerschmitt Bf 109G
began to smoke for no apparent reason. He is thought to have been struck
by the tail of his aircraft as he jumped, and his parachute was not seen to

open. He was twenty-two years old, and had been credited with 158 victories, all of them gained in combat against the R.A.F. and Commonwealth air forces.

The most successful English fighter pilot of the Second World War was Group Captain James Edgar "Johnnie" Johnson, credited with thirty-eight confirmed aerial victories over German aircraft. Johnson was born in Loughborough, Leicestershire in 1915; in 1937, a qualified civil engineer, he applied to join the Royal Air Force, but was rejected. In 1939, when the need for aircrew was receiving priority, he was invited to apply once more, and two days later was a Flight Sergeant in the Royal Air Force Volunteer Reserve. He attended flying school at Stapleford Tawney in Essex; with the outbreak of war and the mobilization of the R.A.F.V.R. he was posted to various flying schools, was granted a commission as Pilot Officer, and began training on the Spitfire. Towards the end of August 1940 he was posted to No. 19 Squadron, then based at Duxford, the famous fighter station near Cambridge. He had just twenty-three hours' flying time on Spitfires, and had never fired his guns; and even under the desperate conditions of the Battle of Britain, the squadron was unwilling to send him and the other young replacement pilots into action against the veterans of the Luftwaffe, especially as No. 19 was then experiencing great difficulties with the 20 mm cannon on its aircraft, and losses were high. There was no time to train tyro pilots at Duxford, and Johnson was transferred to No. 616 Squadron, then going through a rest and reorganisation period at Coltishall after being withdrawn from combat. Yet again he was thwarted in his ambition to get into action; an old shoulder fracture began giving trouble, and Johnson was forced to undergo an operation. It was not until January of 1941 that he returned to No. 616 and operational flying. He shared a victory over a Dornier Do 17 with a fellow pilot, and in June 1941 scored his first solo victory—a Messerschmitt Bf 109, shot down over Gravelines. During this period Johnson was flying in the leading section of the three-squadron Tangmere Wing, under the leadership and tutelage of the legless Douglas Bader. His score rose steadily but not spectacularly (six and a half victories by the end of the summer of 1941); he was awarded the D.F.C., and given command of No. 610 Squadron in July 1942. It was while leading this mixed-nationality unit that he began to emerge as one of the brightest stars of Fighter Command. In March 1943 he was given command of the Kenley Wing, flying Spitfires, a formation which included two Canadian squadrons; during the summer of that year the Wing was heavily engaged in daylight operations in support of American bombing raids, and Johnson's personal score between March and September rose by nineteen. An enforced period of non-combat duty followed this successful tour, and it was March 1944 before Johnson returned to operational flying; he was given command of No. 144 Canadian Wing, and in his last air battle—a sortie over Arnhem on 27th September 1944—he scored his thirty-eighth kill. This was, incidentally, the only occasion during his 515 combat missions when his aircraft was hit by enemy fire. All his solo victories had been won in combat with single-engined fighters —Messerschmitt Bf 109s and Focke-Wulf Fw 190s—and the majority of them during a period of Luftwaffe air superiority over the Channel Coast. Johnson remained in the Royal Air Force, finally retiring with the rank of Air Vice-Marshal in 1966; during the Korean War he secured an exchange posting to the U.S.A.A.F. and flew several combat missions. His decorations include the D.S.O. and two Bars, the D.F.C. and Bar, the American D.F.C., Air Medal and Legion of Merit, the C.B. and the

Group Captain Douglas Bader, Britain's famous legless fighter ace, credited with twenty-two victories

C.B.E. From an international point of view, Johnson certainly destroyed the **greatest number of German fighters** of any Allied pilot.

The most successful American fighter pilot of the Second World War was Major Richard Ira Bong, whose forty confirmed aerial victories are unsurpassed by any American military pilot of any war. Born at Superior, Wisconsin, on 24th September 1920, Bong enlisted as a Flying Cadet on 29th May 1941. After flying training at Tulare and Gardner Fields, California, and Luke Field, Arizona, he received his "wings" and a commission (all American military pilots were automatically commissioned) on 9th January 1942. In May he was posted to Hamilton Field, California, for combat training on the Lockheed P-38 Lightning twin-engined fighter, and subsequently joined the 9th Fighter Squadron of the 49th Fighter Group, then based in Australia. In November 1942 Bong transferred to the 39th Fighter Squadron of the 35th Fighter Group; in January 1943 he returned to the 9th, having shot down five Japanese aircraft in the meantime. He remained with the 9th until November 1943, being promoted First-Lieutenant in April and Captain in August. On 11th November he was posted to the Headquarters of V Fighter Command (New Guinea), as Assistant Operations Officer in charge of replacement aircraft; nevertheless, he continued to fly combat missions in P-38s, and by the time he was promoted Major and posted home to instruct in air superiority techniques, in April 1944, his score had risen to twenty-eight confirmed kills. He returned to the Pacific as Gunnery Training Officer of V Fighter Command in September 1944; although not required to continue combat flying, he voluntarily put in thirty further combat missions over Borneo and the Philippines and was credited with a further twelve victories. General George C. Kenney, his commanding officer, ordered him back to the United States in December 1944, with a recommendation for the Congressional Medal of Honor—which award was subsequently granted. Bong became a test pilot for Lockheed at Burbank, California; and on 6th August 1945, the day the world's first atomic bomb was dropped on Hiroshima, he died when the engine of his P-80 jet failed. Apart from his Medal of Honor, Richard Bong was awarded the D.S.C., two Silver Stars, seven D.F.C.s, and fifteen Air Medals. His score of forty kills was achieved during more than 200 combat missions, totalling over 500 flying hours; many of these victories were gained while flying the P-38J *Marge* named after his fiancée, which is illustrated on page 113.

The numbers of aircraft shot down by fighter pilots of the Second World War varied much more widely than was the case in the First World War, due to the enormous differences in conditions and standards of equipment in the various combat areas. Comparison of the list of national top-scoring fighter pilots will immediately reveal the almost incredible superiority of German pilots in terms of confirmed victories—i.e. Major Erich Hartmann, the Luftwaffe's leading ace, is credited with nearly nine times as many victories as the leading British and American pilots, and thirty-five Germans are credited with scores in excess of 150.

Since the end of the war there have been persistent attempts to discredit these scores; but by any reasonable criterion, the figures must now be accepted as accurate. The Luftwaffe's confirmation procedure was just as rigorous as that followed by Allied air forces, and the quoted figures are those prepared at unit level and were not subject to manipulation by the Propaganda Ministry. The phenomenon becomes less astonish-

Left to right: Ernst Udet, Germany's second ranking ace of the First World War, with Adolf Galland and Werner Mölders, first great German ace of the Second World War, who had achieved 115 confirmed victories by the time of his death on 22nd November 1941 (Hanfried Schliephake)

ing if studied in context. The main reasons for the gulf between German and Allied scores were the different conditions of service and the special circumstances which existed on the Russian Front in 1941 and 1942. In Allied air forces an operational tour by a fighter pilot was almost invariably followed by a posting to a second-line establishment for several months. This process of rotating pilots to areas where they could recover from the strain of prolonged combat operations was unknown in the Luftwaffe; apart from very short periods of leave, a German fighter pilot was effectively on combat operations from the day of his first posting until the day his career ended—in death, serious injury, or capture. The Luftwaffe fighter pilot's career was thus, in real terms, about twice as long as his R.A.F. or U.S.A.A.F. counterpart; many of the leading German pilots recorded well over 1,000 combat sorties in their log-books, roughly twice the British average.

When Germany invaded the Soviet Union in June 1941, the Russian Air Forces were equipped with very large numbers of obsolescent aircraft. They had no fighter whose speed and armament approached the performance of the Messerschmitt Bf 109E and Bf 109F, and their bombers in squadron service were markedly inferior to contemporary European designs. The enormous advances achieved by the German Army in the early months of the campaign were accompanied by close air support, and from the first day of the invasion the Luftwaffe enjoyed a measure of air superiority which was quite unprecedented. Operating from forward airfields and keeping up with the advancing tank armies, the German fighters frequently flew five or six sorties every day, and individual scores of four, five or six victories on a single sortie were not uncommon. The Luftwaffe was presented with large numbers of easy targets—the perfect environment for the development of a fighter pilot's skill and confidence. The situation did not become significantly more challenging for many months, by which time many of the Jagdflieger had learned their trade so well that they retained the initiative.

It should be noted, however, that Major Hartmann did not start his combat career until the end of 1942, and that his most consistently successful period of operations fell between August and November 1943, when Russian designs of comparable quality to Western equipment were coming into service in large numbers. It is true that the training of Russian aircrew was still markedly inferior to that of Luftwaffe pilots; but there must come a point at which the search for "special factors" becomes mere rationalisation, and one is left with the inescapable conclusion that Germany simply produced a group of officers who were fighter pilots of exceptional skill and determination.

    This conclusion is borne out by a study of the records of fighter units which were based on the Western Front or in the Mediterranean area throughout the war. While the accompanying table reveals that the vast majority of the most successful pilots saw combat exclusively (or almost exclusively) in Russia, there remain many who spent the whole war in action against the Western Allies, and achieved scores two or three times as great as the leading Allied pilots. After the end of 1942 German and Allied fighter designs were roughly comparable in quality; the explanation must therefore lie in the unbroken combat careers of the Luftwaffe pilots, and in sheer ability. The pilots who scored *100 or more victories against the Western Allies* in northern Europe, southern Europe, the Mediterranean area and North Africa were as follows (Western victories only, in cases of mixed service):

Gerhard Barkhorn, 301 confirmed victories (Imperial War Museum)

Hauptmann Hans-Joachim Marseille	158
Oberstleutnant Heinz Bär	124
Oberstleutnant Kurt Bühligen	112
Generalleutnant Adolf Galland	104
Major Joachim Müncheberg	102
Oberstleutnant Egon Mayer	102
Major Werner Schroer	102
Oberst Josef Priller	101

These figures become even more impressive if one reflects on the fact that Marseille achieved 151 of his victories between April 1941 and September 1942; that Galland did virtually no combat flying between November 1941 and the end of 1944, while he occupied the post of General of Fighters; and that Müncheberg was killed in March 1943.

    Two categories of victories in northern Europe are worthy of special attention; those scored over heavy bombers, and those scored while flying jet aircraft. The achievements of the world's first generation of jet combat pilots are described elsewhere in this chapter. The Luftwaffe placed great value on the destruction of the very heavily armed four-engined Boeing Fortress and Consolidated Liberator bombers which formed the United States 8th Air Force's main equipment in the massive daylight

Yak-9 fighters, standard equipment of Soviet squadrons in the last two years of the war. Unsophisticated by Western standards, the Yak was unbeatable at low altitudes (Imperial War Museum)

bombing offensive of 1943–45. Usually flying in dense formations protected by an enormous combined firepower—and, in the later months, by superb escort fighters—these large aircraft were obviously far more difficult to destroy than smaller aircraft. The leading "heavy bomber specialists" among Germany's daylight home defence pilots included:

Oberleutnant Herbert Rollwage	44
Oberst Walther Dahl	36
Major Werner Schroer	26
Hauptmann Hugo Frey	26
Oberstleutnant Egon Mayer	25
Oberstleutnant Kurt Bühligen	24
Oberstleutnant Heinz Bär	21
Hauptmann Hans-Heinrich König	20
Hauptmann Heinz Knoke	19

The last Victoria Cross won during the Second World War was awarded to Lieutenant Robert Hampton Gray, D.S.C., Royal Canadian Navy Volunteer Reserve (attached to the Fleet Air Arm), and pilot of a Corsair fighter-bomber, who was killed in an attack on a Japanese destroyer in the Bay of Onagawa Wan on 9th August 1945—after both atomic bombs had been dropped upon Japan and only a few days before the Japanese surrender. Gray's V.C. was the only such award to a member of the Royal Canadian Navy during the Second World War.

(It was said, presumably by the then Air Ministry, in 1960 that during the Second World War a total of 19,244 Distinguished Flying Crosses were awarded, as well as 1,576 Bars to the D.F.C. Subsequent research, however, has demonstrated that both these figures are somewhat lower than the actual number of these decorations awarded, as they do not include all those awarded to non-British subjects which were not gazetted in the *London Gazette*.)

Supermarine Spitfire, best-known British fighter of the war and held by many to be the most beautiful aircraft ever built; in all 22,759 Spitfires and Seafires were produced. (Air Portraits)

Two great R.A.F. bomber pilots:
Wing-Commander Guy
Gibson, v.c. (left)
led the famous "Dam-
busting" raid by No. 617
squadron on 17th May 1943

Group Captain Leonard
Cheshire, v.c. (right)
flew more than 100 combat
missions between 1940
and the end of the war;
he was British observer in a
B-29 over Nagasaki when the
second atomic bomb was dropped
(Imperial War Museum)

The Mohne Dam in the
Ruhr on the morning after
the attack by 617
Squadron (Foto-Studio
Euler Werl)

The Second World War
came to a sudden end
following the dropping of
two atomic bombs on
Japanese cities in August
1945. The first bomb was
dropped from the B-29
Enola Gay, commanded by
Colonel Paul Tibbets
(right)

LUFTWAFFE FIGHTER PILOTS WITH 100 OR MORE CONFIRMED VICTORIES DURING THE SECOND WORLD WAR AND THE SPANISH CIVIL WAR

E. = Eastern Front; W = Europe; Afr. = North Africa; Gr. = Greece; * = at least

✠☙⚔◆ = Knight's Cross with Oak Leaves, Swords and Diamonds
✠☙⚔ = Knight's Cross with Oak Leaves and Swords
✠☙ = Knight's Cross with Oak Leaves
✠ = Knight's Cross of the Iron Cross

Name, rank, decorations	Units	Total score	Day/ Night	Fronts	Four-engined	With jet a/c
Major Erich Hartmann✠☙⚔◆	JG 52	**352**	352/0	352 E.	0	0
Major Gerhard Barkhorn✠☙⚔	JG 52, 6, JV 44	**301**	301/1	301 E.	0	?
Major Günther Rall✠☙⚔	JG 52, 11, 300	**275**	275/0	3 W., 272 E.	?	0
Oberleutnant Otto Kittel✠☙⚔	JG 54	***267**	267/0	267 E.	0	0
Major Walter Nowotny✠☙⚔◆	JG 54, Kdo. Nowotny	**258**	258/0	255 E., 3 W.	*1	3
Major Wilhelm Batz✠☙⚔	JG 52	**237**	237/0	232 E., 5 W.	2	0
Major Erich Rudorffer✠☙⚔	JG 2, 54, 7	**222**	222/0	136 E., 60 W., 26 Afr.	10	12
Oberstleutnant Heinz Bär✠☙⚔	JG 51, 77, 1, 3, JV 44	**220**	220/0	96 E., 79 W., 45 Afr.	*21	16
Oberst Hermann Graf✠☙⚔◆	JG 51, 52, 50, 11, 52	**212**	212/0	202 E., 10 W.	10	0
Major Theodor Weissenberger✠☙	JG 77, 5, 7	**208**	208/0	175 E., 33 W.	?	8
Oberstleutnant Hans Philipp✠☙⚔	JG 76, 54, 1	**206**	206/0	177 E., 29 W.	1	0
Oberleutnant Walter Schuck✠☙	JG 5, 7	**206**	206/0	198 E., 8 W.	4	8
Major Heinrich Ehrler✠☙	JG 5, 7	***204**	204/0	204 E.?	?	?
Oberleutnant Anton Hafner✠☙	JG 51	**204**	204/0	184 E., 20 Afr.	5	0
Hauptmann Helmut Lipfert✠☙	JG 52, 53	**203**	203/0	Majority E., *4 W.	2	0
Major Walter Krupinski✠☙	JG 52, 5, 11, 26 JV 44	**197**	197/0	177 E., 20 W.	1	?
Major Anton Hackl✠☙⚔	JG 77, 11, 26, 300, 11	**192**	192/0	105 E., 87 W.	32	0
Hauptmann Joachim Brendel✠☙	JG 51	**189**	189/0	189 E.	0	0
Hauptmann Max Stotz✠☙	JG 54	**189**	189/0	173 E., 16 W.	0	0
Hauptmann Joachim Kirschner✠☙	JG 3, 27	**188**	188/0	167 E., 13 Gr., 6 W., 2 Malta	*2	0
Major Kurt Brändle✠☙	JG 53, 3	**180**	180/0	160 E., 20 W.	0	0
Oberleutnant Günther Josten✠☙	JG 51	**178**	178/0	Majority E.	1	0
Oberst Johannes Steinhoff✠☙⚔	JG 26, 52, 77, 7, JV 44	**176**	176/0	148 E., 28 W. & Afr.	4	6
Oberleutnant Ernst-Wilhelm Reinert✠☙⚔	JG 77, 27	**174**	174/0	103 E., 51 Afr., 20 W.	2	0
Hauptmann Günther Schack✠☙	JG 51, 3	**174**	174/0	174 E.	0	0
Hauptmann Emil Lang✠☙	JG 54, 26	**173**	173/0	148 E., 25 W.	?	0
Hauptmann Heinz Schmidt✠☙	JG 52	**173**	173/0	173 E.	0	0
Major Horst Ademeit✠☙	JG 54	**166**	166/0	165 E., 1 W.	0	0
Oberst Wolf-Dietrich Wilcke✠☙⚔	JG 53, 3	**162**	162/0	137 E., 21 W., 4 Malta	4	0
Hauptmann Hans-Joachim Marseille✠⚔☙◆	JG 52, 27	**158**	158/0	151 Afr., 7 W.	0	0

table continues on page 114

captions for opposite page

1. Gloster Gladiator II *flown late in 1940 by Flight-Lieutenant M. T. St. J. Pattle, D.F.C., as commander of "B" Flight, No. 80 (Fighter) Squadron, R.A.F.; the serial number of this aircraft is believed to have been K7971. Flying from various bases in Greece, Pattle is known to have shot down at least twenty-four enemy aircraft by the end of 1940. Converting on to Hawker Hurricanes early in 1941, he went on to shoot down an estimated total of forty-one enemy machines before his death in action over the Piraeus on 20th April 1941. The South African-born Pattle was thus the most successful fighter pilot to serve with the British air forces during the Second World War.*

2. Supermarine Spitfire IX, *serial EN398, flown by Wing Commander James E. ("Johnnie") Johnson, D.F.C., in April 1943 as Wing Leader of the Kenley Wing —later No. 127 Wing, R.A.F. When Johnson took command of the Wing in March 1943 his score of confirmed victories was six; by the time he relinquished command in September 1943, it stood at twenty-five. Johnson went on to achieve thirty-eight confirmed aerial victories, all single-engined German fighters, and was thus the most successful English fighter pilot of the Second World War, the second most successful R.A.F. fighter pilot, and the most successful Allied fighter pilot in terms of single-engined enemy fighters destroyed in aerial combat.*

3. Lavochkin La 5FN *flown between May and mid July 1944 by Captain Ivan N. Kozhedub, Hero of the Soviet Union; he is believed to have been operating in the Ukraine during this period. By the close of hostilities Kozhedub had attained the rank of Guards Lieutenant-Colonel, and had been awarded the Gold Star of a Hero of the Soviet Union three times. His final score of aerial victories is stated to be sixty-two, which qualifies him as the most successful Allied fighter pilot of the Second World War.*

4. Messerschmitt Bf 109F-4/Trop, 5237, *flown during June 1942 by Oberleutnant Hans-Joachim Marseille, Staffelkapitän of 3 Staffel, Jagdgeschwader 27. Based at Ain-El Gazala in Libya, Marseille scored his 101st confirmed aerial victory on 18th June 1942, and was subsequently awarded the Knight's Cross with Oak Leaves, Swords and Diamonds on 3rd September 1942. His final score of 158 victories qualifies him as the most successful German fighter pilot to see combat exclusively against the British and Commonwealth air forces during the Second World War.*

5. Messerschmitt Bf 109G-14 *flown in February 1945 by Major Erich Hartmann as commanding officer of II Gruppe, Jagdgeschwader 52. During his service on the Russian Front Hartmann achieved a total of 352 confirmed aerial victories, and is thus the most successful fighter pilot the world has ever known. Fuller biographical details may be found in the body of the text.*

6. Junkers Ju 87D-5 *flown during the winter of 1943/44 by Major Hans-Ulrich Rudel as commanding officer of III Gruppe, Schlachtgeschwader 2 "Immelmann" in Russia. The most successful of Germany's Stuka pilots, and probably the greatest ground-attack pilot of that or any other war, Rudel flew a total of 2,530 combat sorties, destroyed 519 Soviet armoured vehicles, and was the only man ever awarded (on 1st January 1945) the Golden Oak Leaves to the Knight's Cross.*

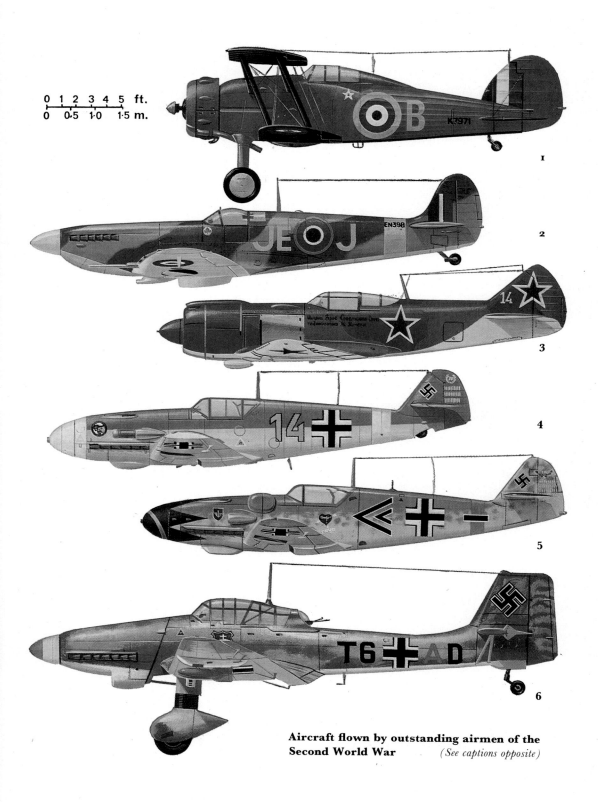

0 1 2 3 4 5 ft.
0 0·5 1·0 1·5 m.

1

2

3

4

5

6

**Aircraft flown by outstanding airmen of the
Second World War** *(See captions opposite)*

captions for opposite page

7. Republic P-47D Thunderbolt, 42-26418, *flown from Boxted, England, during the summer of 1944 by Lieutenant-Colonel Francis S. Gabreski, commanding officer of the 61st Fighter Squadron, 56th Fighter Group, United States 8th Air Force. Gabreski's final score of thirty-one confirmed aerial victories qualifies him as America's leading ace in the European theatre of operations.*

8. Grumman F6F-5 Hellcat "Minsi III", *flown from the carrier U.S.S. Essex during the summer of 1944 by Commander David McCampbell of Fighter Squadron VF-15. McCampbell's final score of thirty-four confirmed aerial victories qualifies him as the U.S. Navy's leading ace of the Second World War.*

9. Lockheed P-38J Lightning, 42-103993 "Marge", *flown between October 1943 and March 1944 by Captain Richard I. Bong, at that time an Assistant Operations Officer at the headquarters of the U.S. 5th Fighter Command in New Guinea. Bong's final score of forty confirmed aerial victories qualifies him as America's leading ace of the Second World War.*

10. Nakajima B5N2 "Kate" *in which Commander Mitsuo Fuchida, General Commander (Air) of the Imperial Japanese Navy 1st Carrier Division, led the first wave of the attack on Pearl Harbor on 7th December 1941, and from the cockpit of which he transmitted the order to attack at 07·49 h that morning.*

11. Mitsubishi A6M2 Reisen (Zero-Sen) *flown in July 1942 from Lae, New Guinea by Petty Officer First Class Saburo Sakai of the Tainan Kokutai, Imperial Japanese Navy Air Force. Sakai, who scored sixty confirmed aerial victories in China and the Pacific before being seriously wounded over Guadalcanal in August 1942, finished the war as Japan's third ranking, and senior surviving, fighter pilot.*

Bomber pilot with the greatest number of sorties over enemy territory in a multi-engined aircraft: Hans-Georg Baetcher, a Major at the end of the Second World War with a total of 658. A Luftwaffe officer, he flew Heinkel 111s during the attacks on Britain in 1940 and 1941 with the pathfinder Kampfgruppe 100, then served in Russia with Kampfgeschwader 100. At the end of the war he commanded III./K.G. 76 equipped with the Arado 234 jet bomber.

Top scoring anti-submarine captain: Squadron-Leader Terrence Bulloch, D.S.O. and Bar, D.F.C. and Bar, who flew Liberators during the Second World War with Nos 120, 224, and 86 Squadrons. Responsible for the destruction of U-597 on 12th October 1942, U-132 on 5th November 1942, and U-514 on 8th July 1943; also caused serious damage to U-89 and U-653

Aircraft flown by outstanding airmen of the Second World War

(See captions opposite)

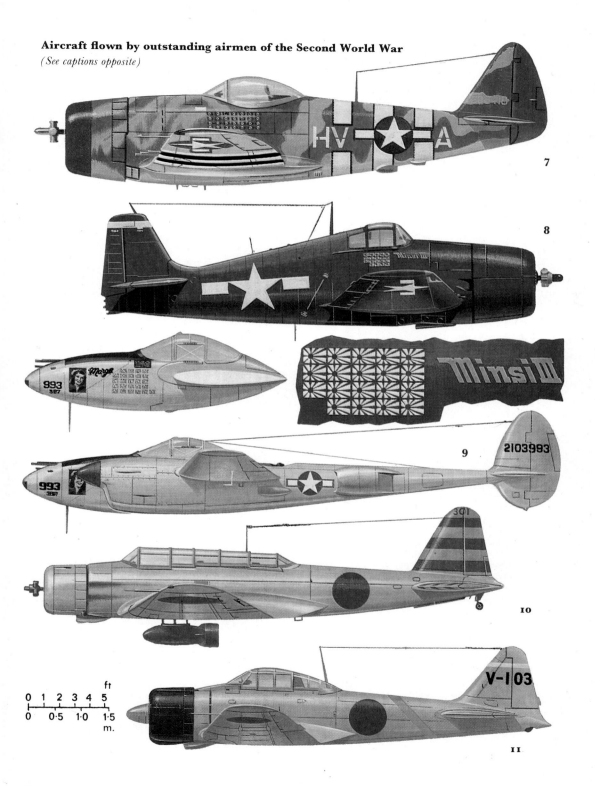

Name, rank, decorations	Units	Total score	Day/ Night	Fronts	Four- engined	With jet a/c
Hauptmann Heinrich Sturm✠	JG 52	**157**	157/0	157 E.	0	0
Oberleutnant Gerhard Thyben✠✎	JG 3, 54	**157**	157/0	152 E., 5 W.	?	0
Oberleutnant Hans Beisswenger✠✎	JG 54	**152**	152/0	152 E.	0	0
Leutnant Peter Düttmann✠	JG 52	**150**	150/0	150 E.	0	0
Oberst Gordon Gollob✠✎✗◆	ZG 76, JG 3, 77	**150**	150/0	144 E., 6 W.	0	0
Leutnant Fritz Tegtmeier✠	JG 54, 7	**146**	146/0	146 E.	0	0
Oberleutnant Albin Wolf✠✎	JG 54	**144**	144/0	144 E.	0	0
Leutnant Kurt Tanzer✠	JG 51	**143**	143/0	126 E., 17 W.	4	0
Oberstleutnant Friedrich-Karl Müller✠✎	JG 53, 3	**140**	140/0	100 E., rest W. and Afr.	*2	0
Leutnant Karl Gratz✠	JG 52, 2	**138**	138/0	121 E., 17 W.	0	0
Major Heinrich Setz✠✎	JG 77, 27	**138**	138/0	132 E., 6 W.	0	0
Hauptmann Rudolf Trenkel✠	JG 77, 52	**138**	138/0	Majority E., *1 W.	1	0
Oberleutnant Walter Wolfrum✠	JG 52	**137**	137/0	137 E.	0	0
Hauptmann Franz Schall✠	JG 52, Kdo. Nowotny, JG 7	**137**	137/0	123 E., 14 W.	?	14
Oberst Adolf Dickfeld✠✎	JG 52, 2, 11	**136**	136/0	115 E., 21 W. and Afr.	11	0
Hauptmann Horst-Günther von Fassong✠	JG 51, 11	**136**	136/0	90 E., 46 W.	4	0
Oberleutnant Otto Fönnekold✠	JG 52	**136**	136/0	Majority E.	0	0
Hauptmann Karl-Heinz Weber✠✎	JG 51, 1	**136**	136/0	136 E.	0	0
Major Joachim Müncheberg✠✎✗	JG 26, 51, 77	**135**	135/0	102 W. and Afr., 33 E.	0	0
Oberleutnant Hans Waldmann✠✎	JG 52, 3, 7	**134**	134/0	121 E., 13 W.	?	2
Major Johannes Wiese✠✎	JG 52, 77	**133**	133/0	133 E.	0	0
Hauptmann Alfred Grislawski✠✎	JG 52, 50, 1, 53	**133**	133/0	109 E., 24 W.	18	0
Major Adolf Borchers✠	JG 51, 52	**132**	132/0	127 E., 5 W.	0	0
Major Erwin Clausen✠✎	JG 77, 11	**132**	132/0	114 E., 18 W.	14	0
Hauptmann Wilhelm Lemke✠	JG 3	**131**	131/0	125 E., 6 W.	0	0
Oberst Herbert Ihlefeld✠✎✗	JG 77, 52, 25, 11, 1	**130**	130/0	67 E., 56 W., 7 Sp.	15	0
Oberleutnant Heinrich Sterr✠	JG 54	**130**	130/0	127 E., 3 W.	?	0
Major Franz Eisenach✠	ZG 76, JG 1, 54	**129**	129/0	129 E.	0	0
Oberst Walther Dahl✠✎	JG 3, 300	**128**	128/0	77 E., 51 W.	36	0
Hauptmann Franz Dörr✠	E. JG 3, JG 5	**128**	128/0	122 E., 6 W.	0	0
Oberleutnant Josef Zwernemann✠✎	JG 52, 77, 11	**126**	126/0	106 E., 20 W.	?	0
Leutnant Rudolf Rademacher✠	JG 54, 7	**126**	126/0	90 E., 36 W.	*10	*8, possibly 25
Leutnant Gerhard Hoffmann✠	JG 52	**125**	125/0	125 E.	0	0
Oberst Dietrich Hrabak✠✎	JG 54, 52, 54	**125**	125/0	109 E., 16 W.	0	0
Oberst Walter Oesau✠✎✗	JG 51, 3, 2, 1	**125**	125/0	73 W., 44 E., 8 Sp.	10	0
Oberleutnant Wolf Ettel✠✎	JG 3, 27	**124**	124/0	Majority E., *4 W.	2	0
Hauptmann Robert Weiss✠✎	JG 26, 54	**121**	121/0	Majority E., 31 W.?	0	0
Major Heinz-Wolfgang Schnaufer✠✎✗◆	NJG 1, 4	**121**	0/121	121 W.	Majority	0

Name, rank, decorations	Units	Total score	Day/Night	Fronts	Four-engined	With jet a/c
Oberfeldwebel Heinz Marquardt✠	JG 51	121	121/0	Majority E.	0	0
Oberleutnant Friedrich Obleser✠	JG 52	120	120/0	111 E., 9 W.	2	0
Oberstleutnant Erich Leie✠	JG 2, 51, 77	118	118/0	75 E., 43 W.	1	0
Leutnant Heinz Wernicke✠	JG 54	117	117/0	117 E.	0	0
Leutnant Jakob Norz✠	JG 5	117?	117/0	117 E.	0	0
Leutnant Hans-Joachim Birkner✠	JG 52, 51	117	117/0	Probably 116 E., 1 W.	0	0
Leutnant Franz-Josef Beerenbrock✠⬥	JG 51	117	117/0	117 E.	0	0
Oberleutnant August Lambert✠	SG 2, 151, 77	116	116/0	116 E.	0	0
Oberst Werner Mölders✠⬥⬥⬥⬥	JG 53, 51	115	115/0	68 W., 33 E., 14 Sp.	0	0
Major Werner Schroer✠⬥⬥	JG 27, 54, 3	114	114/0	102 W., 12 E.	26	0
Leutnant Wilhelm Crinius✠⬥	JG 53	114	114/0	100 E., 14 W.	1	0
Leutnant Hans Dammers✠	JG 52	113	113/0	113 E.	0	0
Leutnant Berthold Korts✠	JG 52	113	113/0	113 E.	0	0
Oberstleutnant Kurt Bühligen✠⬥⬥	JG 2	112	112/0	112 W. and Afr.	24	0
Oberst Helmut Lent✠⬥⬥⬥⬥	ZG 76, NJG 1, 2, 3	110	8/102	110 W.	Majority	0
Major Kurt Ubben✠⬥	JG 77, 2	110	110/0	90 E., 20 W. and Afr.	0	0
Oberleutnant Franz Woidich✠	JG 27, 52, 400	110	110/0	108 E., 2 Afr.	0	0
Major Reinhard Seiler	JG 54	109	93/16	96 E., 4 W., 9 Sp.	1	0
Hauptmann Emil Bitsch✠	JG 3	108	108/0	104 E., 4 W.	0	0
Major Hans "Assi" Hahn✠⬥	JG 2, 54	108	108/0	68 W., 40 E.	4	0
Oberst Günther Lützow✠⬥⬥⬥	JG 3, JV 44	108	108/0	85 E., 18 W., 5 Sp.	0	0
Oberleutnant Bernhard Vechtel✠	JG 51	108	108/0	108 E.	0	0
Hauptmann Werner Lucas✠	JG 3	106	106/0	Probably 100 E., 6 W.	1	0
Oberst Victor Bauer✠⬥	JG 2, 3	106	106/0	102 E., 4 W.	0	0
Generalleutnant Adolf Galland✠⬥⬥⬥⬥	JG 27, 26, JV 44	104	104/0	104 W.	4	?
Leutnant Heinz Sachsenberg✠	JG 52, JV 44	104	104/0	103 E., 1 W.	1?	1?
Major Hartmann Grasser✠⬥	ZG 2, JG 51, 1, 210	103	103/0	86 E., 17 W.	2	0
Major Siegfried Freytag✠	JG 77, 7	102	102/0	Probably 70 E., 32 W. and Afr.	0	0
Hauptmann Friedrich Geisshardt✠⬥	LG 2, JG 77, 26	102	102/0	75 E., 27 W. and Afr.	?	0
Oberstleutnant Egon Mayer✠⬥⬥	JG 2	102	102/0	102 W.	25	0
Oberleutnant Max-Hellmuth Ostermann✠⬥⬥	ZG 1, JG 54	102	102/0	93 E., 9 W.	0	0
Oberleutnant Herbert Rollwage✠⬥	JG 53	102	102/0	91 W. and Afr., 11 E.	44	0
Major Josef Wurmheller✠⬥⬥	JG 53, 2	102	102/0	93 W., 9 E.	*13	0
Oberst Josef Priller✠⬥⬥	JG 26	101	101/0	101 W.	11	0
Hauptmann Rudolf Miethig✠	JG 52	101	101/0	101 E.	0	0
Leutnant Ulrich Wernitz✠	JG 54	101	101/0	101 E.	0	0

AFTER THE SECOND WORLD WAR

The fastest twin piston-engined combat aircraft in the world to reach operational status was the de Havilland Hornet fighter which possessed a maximum speed of 485 mile/h (780 km/h) in "clean" combat configuration. Powered by two 2,070 hp Rolls-Royce Merlin 130 engines, the Hornet was armed with four 20 mm guns, could carry up to 2,000 lb (907 kg) of bombs or rockets on under-wing pylons, and had a maximum range of over 2,500 miles (4,025 km). It was first flown by Geoffrey de Havilland, Jr., on 28th July 1944, but did not reach the first R.A.F. squadron—No. 64 (Fighter) Squadron at Horsham St. Faith, Norfolk—until after the end of hostilities in Europe. The Hornet was also the **last piston-engined fighter to serve with R.A.F. first-line squadrons.**

The de Havilland Hornet (Charles E. Brown)

The first two post-war world absolute air speed records were established by Gloster Meteor F.4 fighters. On 7th November 1945 Group Captain H. J. Wilson established a record speed of 606 mile/h (975 km/h) at Herne Bay, Kent, flying the Meteor EE 454 *Britannia*. On 7th September 1946 Group Captain E. M. Donaldson raised the record to 616 mile/h (991 km/h) near Tangmere, west Sussex in Meteor EE 549. The Meteors featured in the latter speed record had had their wings clipped, reducing wing span from 43 ft 0 in (13.11 m) to 37 ft 2 in (11.33 m). As well as increasing speed, this modification increased the rate of roll, and became standard on all but the earliest F.4s. In 1948 Meteor F.4s superseded F.3s in the R.A.F.'s first-line fighter squadrons until they, in turn, were supplanted by F.8s. In May 1950, the F.4s which equipped No. 222 Squadron at Leuchars became the first jet fighters to be based in Scotland. Meteor F.8s first entered service with No. 245 Squadron at Horsham St. Faith, Norfolk, on 29th June 1950. The Meteor F.4 was powered by two 3,500 lb (1,587 kg) thrust Rolls-Royce Derwent 5 engines, the F.8 by 3,600 lb (1,633 kg) thrust Derwent 8s. Meteor F.8s of the Royal Australian Air Force were the only British jet fighters to see action in the Korean War.

The first Russian jet bomber to achieve production status, but probably on a very limited scale, was the Tupolev Tu-12, little more than a Tu-2 piston-engined bomber re-engined with gas-turbines. The prototype, first flown in 1946, had two RD-10 engines, derived from the Junkers Jumo 004B. Power plant of the production aircraft consisted of RD-500 engines, Russian equivalent of the Rolls-Royce Derwent 5, which each developed 4,400 lb (2,000 kg) thrust.

The Yak-15

The first Russian jet fighter to enter squadron service with the Soviet Air Forces was the Yak-15, designed by Alexander S. Yakovlev. It entered service with the IA-PVO early in 1947, powered by a single RD-10 turbojet (a Russian adaptation of the German Jumo 004B engine) developing 1,980 lb (900 kg) thrust. Armed with two 23 mm Nudelman-Suranov NS-23 guns, the Yak-15 had a top speed of approximately 495 mile/h (800 km/h). Like the first Tupolev jet bombers, the Yak-15 was also the result of adapting a piston-engine airframe for jet propulsion. The prototype retained the wings, cockpit, tailplane and tail wheel landing gear of a Yakovlev Yak-3, the new engine being mounted in the forward fuselage. This meant that the jet efflux was below the pilot's cockpit, and production aircraft had the fuselage under-surface protected by heat-resistant stainless steel and were provided with an all-metal tailwheel. First flight of the Yak-15, with test-pilot M. I. Ivanhov at the controls, was made on 24th April 1946.

The first European swept-wing jet fighter to enter operational service after the Second World War was the Swedish Saab J-29 (first flight, 1st September 1948) which joined the Day Fighter Wing F.13 of the Flygvapnet near Norrkoping in May 1951. Nicknamed *Tunnan* (Barrel) and powered by a British de Havilland Ghost turbojet of 4,400 lb (2,000 kg) thrust, the J-29B possessed a top speed of 658 mile/h at 5,000 ft (1,059 km/h at 1,525 m) or Mach 0·90 at the tropopause.

Saab J-29s, leaving no doubt of why they were nicknamed "Barrels"

First American-built aircraft to enter R.A.F. service after the Second World War were ex-U.S.A.F. B-29 Superfortresses, given the R.A.F. designation "Washington B.Mk 1". No. 149 Squadron at Marham was the first squadron to receive these aircraft, in March 1950.

The first aerial victory to be gained by the pilot of one jet aircraft over another was achieved on 8th November 1950, when Lieutenant Russell J. Brown, Jr., of the 51st Fighter-Interceptor Wing, U.S.A.F., flying a Lockheed F-80C, shot down a MiG-15 jet fighter of the Chinese People's Republic Air Force over Sinuiju on the Yalu River, the border between North Korea and China.

The first jet pilot to achieve five confirmed aerial victories over jet aircraft was Captain James Jabara, an F-86 Sabre pilot of the 4th Fighter-Interceptor Wing, U.S.A.F., who shot down his fifth MiG-15 on 20th May 1951. Captain, later Major Jabara went on to destroy a total of fifteen MiG-15s, thereby becoming the second most successful Allied pilot of the Korean War.

The most successful Allied fighter pilot of the Korean War was Captain Joseph McConnell, Jr., of the 16th Fighter Squadron, 51st Fighter-Interceptor Wing, U.S.A.F.; an F-86 Sabre pilot, McConnell scored his sixteenth and last victory on 18th May 1953, a day on which he destroyed a total of three MiG-15s. He was subsequently killed testing a North American F-86H on 25th August 1954.

*North American F-86
Sabre*

The most successful jet fighter pilot in the world cannot be identified. The record set by Oberstleutnant Bär in 1945 stood, as stated above, until it was equalled by Captain McConnell in 1953. It is thought unlikely that any Communist pilot equalled or surpassed this figure during the Korean War; in general the standard of MiG-15 pilots encountered was not high, though there were some notable exceptions who were assumed to be Russian "advisers". The loss ratio of American jet fighters to MiGs throughout the war was 111 to 807, so it is possible but unlikely that one of the Communist "honchos" surpassed McConnell's achievement. Since the close of hostilities in Korea, encounters between jet combat aircraft have been few and limited in scope. However, although security considerations have prevented the release of details, it is thought likely that at least one jet fighter pilot of the Israeli Defence Force/Air Force has achieved approximately twenty aerial victories over jet aircraft of the Arab Air Forces during and since the Six Day War of June 1967. By November 1972, U.S. aircrews in Vietnam had claimed a total of 174 MiGs shot down since June 1965, of which 63 were destroyed in 1972. Three U.S.A.F. and two U.S. Navy aircrew qualified as aces, with five kills to their credit. Of interest is that two of the U.S.A.F. aces were back-seat weapon systems operators in F-4 fighters, rather than pilots.

The first jet aircraft to fly the Atlantic non-stop and unrefuelled, was an English Electric Canberra B.Mk.2 on 21st February 1951, which was flown from Britain to Baltimore and was later purchased by the U.S.A.F. to become the first Canberra to carry American markings. British Canberras were the first jet bombers produced in Britain and the first to serve with the R.A.F. The type had the unique distinction of being the first aircraft of non-U.S. design to enter operational service with the U.S.A.F. after the end of the Second World War. The first of a pre-production batch of eight B-57As (the original U.S.A.F. designation) made its first flight at Baltimore, Maryland, on 20th July 1953.

The first British transport aircraft specifically designed for air-dropping of heavy loads, and also the R.A.F.'s largest aircraft at the time of its introduction, was the Blackburn Beverley. Powered by four 2,850 hp Bristol Centaurus 173 engines, the prototype (*WZ 889*) flew for the first time on 14th June 1953. Able to carry a payload of almost 22 tons, Beverleys began to equip No. 47 Squadron Transport Command in March 1956.

The first British delta-wing interceptor fighter, and the first twin-jet delta fighter in the world, was the Gloster Javelin. First flown in prototype form (*WD804*) by Squadron Leader W. A. Waterton on 26th November 1951, the Javelin was also **the R.A.F.'s first purpose-built all-weather interceptor fighter**. Flying characteristics of the prototype left much to be desired and when it crashed in July 1952, following the loss of both elevators in flight, Waterton was awarded the George Medal for recovering the auto-observer recordings from the wreck. **The first production Javelin FAW 1** (*XA544*) powered by two 8,150 lb (3,697 kg) thrust Armstrong-Siddeley Sapphire A.S. Sa.6 turbojet engines, made its first flight on 22nd July 1954. First deliveries to No. 46 Squadron at Odiham, Hants, began in February 1956.

The first British V-Bomber (so-called from the wing leading-edge plan-form) was the Vickers Valiant, whose prototype (*WB 210*) first flew on 18th May 1951. Two Mark 1 and one Mark 2 prototypes were built, and were followed by 104 production aircraft, the first of which (*WP 199*) flew on 21st December 1953. They were powered by various versions of the Rolls-Royce Avon axial-flow turbojet, four such engines being located in the wing roots. The Valiant entered R.A.F. service with No. 138 Squadron at Gaydon, Warwickshire, early in 1955 and afterwards equipped Nos. 7, 49, 90, 148, 207, 214 and 543 Squadrons. The production also included versions for photo-reconnaissance (the B. (P.R.) Mark 1) and tankers (B. (P.R.) K. Mark 1 and B.K. Mark 1). Its maximum speed was 567 mile/h (912 km/h) at 36,000 ft (Mach 0·84). Normal loaded weight with a 10,000 lb (4,540 kg) bomb-load was 140,000 lb (63,560 kg). Range without external fuel tanks was 3,450 miles (5,564 km). A Valiant of Bomber Command carried Britain's first operational atomic bomb, which was dropped over Maralinga, Southern Australia, on 11th October 1956.

The world's first large bomber to have a delta-wing plan-form was the Avro Vulcan, the prototype of which (*VX 770*) flew for the first time on 30th August 1952. Production aircraft first entered service with R.A.F. Bomber Command in the Summer of 1956, equipping No. 230 Operational Conversion Unit at Waddington, Lincs.

The world's first high performance variable-geometry military aircraft was the Grumman XF10F-1 Jaguar experimental single-seat carrier-borne fighter which first flew on 19th May 1953. With wings that could be swept back 40° in flight, the Jaguar had a designed top speed of 722 mile/h (1,162 km/h) and was powered by an afterburning Westinghouse J40 turbojet. Although a pre-production batch of thirty aircraft was ordered, the project was abandoned after two prototypes had been completed, owing to the enormous complexity of the problems associated with variable geometry.

The heaviest bomb-load carried by an operational bomber was that of the Boeing B-52 Stratofortress at 75,000 lb (34,019 kg); with this war-load on board, the B-52B possessed a range of approximately 3,000 miles (4,828 km). Dubbed "the big stick", the YB-52 prototype was first flown on 15th April 1952 by A. M. "Tex" Johnson. The first of three production B-52As was delivered to the U.S.A.F.'s Strategic Air Command (S.A.C.) on 27th November 1957. B-52s subsequently became the main flying deterrent of S.A.C. for a dozen years.

The last British heavy bomber powered by piston engines was the Avro Lincoln four-engine aircraft, the Lincoln Mk 1, known originally as the Lancaster Mk IV, being powered by 1,750 hp Rolls-Royce Merlin 85 engines. This version had a maximum level speed of 319 mile/h (513 km/h) at 18,500 ft (5,640

Vickers Valiant

m), could carry 14,000 lb (6,350 kg) of bombs and had defensive armament of six 0·50 in machine-guns in pairs in nose, dorsal and tail turrets. The last Lincoln was retired from Bomber Command in December 1955, when that R.A.F. Command became an all-jet force.

The world's first known air-transportable hydrogen bomb was dropped on 21st May 1956, from a Boeing B-52B flying at 50,000 ft (15,240 m) over Bikini Atoll in the Pacific Ocean.

The first British atomic bomb was dropped by a Vickers Valiant, *WZ366*, of No. 49 (Bomber) Squadron, captained by Squadron Leader E. J. G. Flavell, A.F.C., over Maralinga, Australia, on 11th October 1956.

The first British hydrogen bomb was dropped by a Vickers Valiant of No. 49 (Bomber) Squadron, captained by Wing Commander K. G. Hubbard, O.B.E., D.F.C., A.F.C., on 15th May 1957. The bomb was detonated at medium altitude over the Pacific in the Christmas Island area.

Mirage fighter of the Israeli Air Force, one of the main combat types used in the Six Day War (Stephen P. Peltz)

The greatest measure of superiority in air-to-air combat ever gained by one air force over another, with rough parity of equipment, is undoubtedly attributable to the Israeli Defence Force/Air Force. An official US assessment estimates that Israel destroyed 334 Arab aircraft in air combat during the Yom Kippur War of October 1973, for the loss of only four of its own aircraft. More than half of the Arab aircraft are claimed to have been destroyed by Rafael Shafrir (Dragonfly) infra-red homing missiles, designed and built in Israel. Shafrir resembles the US Sidewinder in appearance, but is specially developed for close-range "dogfighting" at heights up to 60,000 ft (18,000 m).

Total aircraft losses by Egypt and Syria are assessed at 387, plus 41 helicopters. Israeli losses totalled 103 aircraft, made up of 53 Skyhawks, 33 Phantoms, 11 Mirages and 6 Super Mystères. The Israeli DF/AF flew 11,233 sorties during the Yom Kippur War.

ORIGINS OF THE WORLD'S AIR FORCES

Abu Dhabi   The Air Wing of the Abu Dhabi Defence Forces was formed with British help in 1968, following a British decision to withdraw from the Persian Gulf area in 1971. Initial equipment comprised four Agusta-Bell 206A JetRangers, three Britten-Norman Islanders and four DHC Caribou STOL transports. Renamed Abu Dhabi Air Force in 1972, it has since ordered combat types including Mirage fighters.

Afghanistan   The Royal Afghan Air Force was formed in 1924 by King Amanullah with an initial equipment of two Bristol F.2B fighters flown by two German pilots.

Albania   The Albanian Air Force was established in 1947 under Soviet sponsorship with initial equipment of twelve Yak-3 fighters. (An original attempt to form an air force in 1914 had proved abortive.)

Algeria   Force Aérienne Algérienne was formed in 1962, following attainment of Algerian independence from France. Established with Egyptian and Soviet assistance, initial equipment comprised five MiG-15s.

Argentine   The Argentine Air Force was formed on 8th September 1912 with the establishment of the Escuela de Aviacón Militar at El Palomar. The Argentine Naval Aviation Service was formed on 17th October 1919 with the presentation by the Italian Government of facilities established by an Italian mission at San Fernando.

Australia   The origin of Australian military aviation is not well documented. It is known that Senator George Pearce attended the Imperial Conference of 1911, at which political approval was given for the formation of the British Royal Flying Corps. On his return to Australia he sought, and gained, political and financial support for the creation of an Australian Air Force. On 30th December 1911 newspaper advertisements asked for ". . . two competent mechanists and aviators", and Army Order No. 132 of 1912 created a single flight to form a·training school. This flight, comprising four officers, seven warrant officers and sergeants and thirty-two air mechanics, was the first unit of the Aviation Corps. The Australian Flying Corps dates from approximately 27th December 1915, but this was abolished on 31st March 1921 when the Australian Air Force was created. Later in the same year this service gained the prefix Royal, and the Royal Australian Air Force (R.A.A.F.) it has remained to this day.

Austria   Formation of the Deutschösterreichische Fliegertruppe ("Austro-German Flying Troop") took place on 6th December 1918. The current Austrian Air Force (Österreichische Luftstreitkräfte) was founded in 1955 with four Yak-11 and four Yak-18 trainers.

Bangladesh   Bangladesh Defence Force (Air Wing) was established with Indian assistance before the outbreak of hostilities in December 1971. Initial equipment of some half-dozen aircraft included DHC-3 Otters.

Belgium   La Force Aérienne Belge came into effective being on 5th March 1911 with the inauguration of its first airfield at Brasschaet, Antwerp.

Bolivia   The Cuerpo de Aviación was founded in August 1924, although a Flying School had been established at Alto La Paz as early as 1915.

Brazil   The Brazilian Naval Air Force was founded with the establishment of a seaplane school in 1913 at Rio de Janeiro with an Italian Bossi seaplane. The Army Air Service was founded under French training supervision in October 1918 at Rio de Janeiro.

Brunei Sultanate Only former British dependency populated by Malay people that did not join the Federation of Malaysia in 1963, an Air Wing of the Royal Brunei Malay Regiment was formed in 1965. Initial equipment comprised three Westland Whirlwind Mk 10 helicopters.

Bulgaria   A Bulgarian Army Aviation Corps was originally formed in 1912 with Blériot and Bristol monoplanes and fought in the Balkan War of 1912–13. It was resurrected shortly after 12th October 1915 when Bulgaria entered the war as one of the Central Powers.

Burma   Union of Burma Air Force is a small independent air force started with British aid in 1955. Initial equipment 20 Sea Fury FB.11s and some Vampire T.55s.

Cameroun	A small Cameroun Air Force has been established by the Cameroun Republic during the 1960s, but no details of its organisation and equipment are yet known.
Canada	During the first World War, many Canadians served in the British R.N.A.S., R.F.C., and R.A.F. Late in 1918, in Britain, an embryo "Canadian Air Force" was represented by two Canadian squadrons, but the Armistice virtually ended its existence. In 1919 an Air Board was set up to control a "non-permanent militia" basis of part-time flying instruction, and on 19th April 1920 this board began administration of a Canadian Air Force, established with considerable assistance from the Royal Air Force. On 1st April 1924 the Royal Canadian Air Force (R.C.A.F.) came into being.
Central African Republic	As a result of a bilateral defence agreement with France, the Force Aérienne Centrafricaine was established in 1960. Initial equipment comprised a Douglas C-47, three MH Broussards and an Alouette helicopter.
Chile	The Chilean Air Force was formed with the establishment of a flying school at Lo Espejo on 11th February 1913.
China	The Chinese Army Air Arm came into being with the establishment in January 1914 of a flying school at Nan Yuan at which members of the Chinese Army commenced flying instruction under an American, Art Lym.
Colombia	The Fuerza Aérea Colombiana originated in the Escuela de Aviación (flying school) which was founded at Flandes with a Caudron G.IIIA-2 aircraft on 4th April 1922, on the authority of the Colombian Minister of War, Dr. Aristóbulo Archila.
Cuba	Following the Castro revolution in 1958, the Cuban Revolutionary Air Force was modernised and expanded with the assistance of Eastern bloc countries. Initial re-equipment included MiG-17s, MiG-19s, Il-14s and An-2s.
Cyprus	The Air Wing of the Cyprus National Guard was formed after Cyprus became an independent republic on 16th August 1960. Initial equipment included some light aircraft and helicopters.
Czechoslovakia	The Czechoslovak Army Air Force was formed early in 1919 from air components previously serving with the Czech Legions in Russia and France.
Denmark	The Danish Army Air Corps was established on 2nd July 1912 with the formation of a flying school.
Ecuador	The Cuerpo de Aviadores Militares commenced formation in 1920 under the supervision of an Italian Aviation Mission.
Egypt	The Egyptian Army Air Force was originally planned in 1930 under British influence, but its official foundation was not effected until May 1932 with the arrival of its first five aircraft (Gipsy Moths) from Britain.
Ethiopia	The Imperial Ethiopian Air Force commenced formation in 1924 with the procurement of French and German aircraft by Ras Tafari (later Emperor Haile Selassie).
France	The French Army Air Force (originally the Service Aéronautique, and later l'Armée de l'Air) was founded as a separate command in April 1910. By this time several army pilots had learned to fly and the new command had been issued with a Blériot, two Wrights and two Farmans.
Germany	The original German Military Air Force owed its origin to the purchase by the Army of its first Zeppelin dirigible in 1907 and its first eleven aeroplanes in 1910. The Military Aviation Service was formally established on 1st October 1912.
Germany (East)	Organised on tactical lines for army support, under the East German Defence Ministry, the air section of the Nationale Volksarmee, known as the Air Force of the German Democratic Republic, originated in 1950 as a branch of the Volkspolizei.
Ghana	The Ghana Air Force was formed in Accra with the help of instructors from India and Israel, equipped initially with Hindustan HT-2 basic trainers. In late 1960 R.A.F. ground and flying personnel began to provide instruction and the first student pilots were sent to the U.K. for training.
Great Britain	The Royal Air Force owes its origins to the balloon experiments by the Royal Engineers at Woolwich which commenced in 1878. The Air Battalion of the R.E. was established in February 1911, and the Royal Flying Corps in May 1912 with Military and Naval Wings. In November 1913 the Admiralty announced the formation of the Royal Naval

	Air Service. The R.F.C. and R.N.A.S. continued as separate services until amalgamated to form the Royal Air Force on 1st April 1918. The Fleet Air Arm came into being in 1924.
Greece	The Royal Hellenic Army formed its first military squadron of four Farman biplanes in September 1912 at Larissa, its pilots being trained in France. In February 1914 the Naval Air Service was established under the guidance of a British Naval Mission.
Guatemala	Military aeroplanes were first flown by the Guatemalan Army shortly after the First World War, but it was not until 1929 that the Cuerpo de Aeronautica Militar was established as an echelon of the Army.
Republic of Guinea	A small air arm, the Guinea Air Force, is reported to have been formed by the West African Republic of Guinea, with assistance from the Communist bloc, following break-away from French influence in 1958. Equipment includes MiG-15s and MiG-17s and some Ilyushin transport aircraft.
Haiti	The Haitian Corps d'Aviation was formed in 1943 primarily as a national mail-carrying organisation but in the late 1940s air patrols were added to its duties.
Hong Kong Crown Colony	Formed with R.A.F. assistance, the Royal Hong Kong Auxiliary Air Force has been operating since 1st May 1949. Initial equipment comprised some Harvard trainers and Spitfires.
Hungary	Forbidden under the terms of the Treaty of Versailles, Hungary as a separate Republic did not make provision for a small air service until 1936 when it made limited purchases of German and Italian aircraft.
India	Scene of many years of British aviation influence, India established its own air force on 1st April 1933 with one squadron of Westland Wapiti general-purpose aircraft.
Indonesia	After transfer of sovereignty from the Dutch to the United States of Indonesia on 27th December 1949, the Netherlands continued to influence aviation in the area and assisted in the establishment of the Indonesian Republican Air Force (Angkatan Udara Republik Indonesia) which, in the following year, took over from the Netherlands Indies Air Force, which was disbanded.
Iran (Persia)	Aviation in Iran originated in the Air Department of the Army Headquarters established in 1922 by the Prime Minister, Reza Khan. The first military aircraft was a Junkers F-13 transport based at Galeh-Morghi.
Iraq	The Royal Iraqi Air Force was formed in 1931 with five de Havilland D.H.60T Gipsy Moths flown by Cranwell-trained Iraqi pilots.
Ireland	The Irish Army Air Corps was formed in 1922 after the completion of the Anglo-Irish Treaty of December 1921. Its first aeroplane was a Martinsyde Type A Mark II which had been purchased during the truce period to assist General Michael Collins to escape from England had the London talks failed.
Israel	The Israel Defence Force/Air Force owes its origin to the Sherut Avir, a military air service planned in 1947 at the time of Israel's emergence as a Sovereign State. The Sherut Avir gave way to the Israeli Air Force (Chel Ha'avir) in March 1948, and this in turn was integrated with the Army and Navy as the I.D.F./A.F. in 1951.
Italy	Fairly extensive and successful use of aircraft by the Italian Army in the Italo-Turkish War of 1911 led to the formal establishment of the Air Battalion (Battaglione Aviatori) under the Ufficio d'Ispezione Servizi Aeronautici on 27th June 1912. A fully-fledged Military Aviation Service followed on 28th November 1912.
Ivory Coast Republic	Following independence, this former colony received military assistance from France for the establishment of its own armed forces. The Ivory Coast Air Force originated on the receipt of one Douglas C-47 and two Broussard liaison aircraft in 1962.
Jamaica	The Air Wing of the Jamaica Defence Force was established in July 1963, its initial equipment one Cessna 185 Skywagon and one regular pilot. Royal Canadian Air Force personnel trained flying and ground crews needed for subsequent expansion.
Japan	Origins of military aviation in Japan date back to July 1909 with the formation of the Temporary Military Balloon Research Committee. In 1911 the Army and Navy formed separate air services, the Japanese Army Air Force and the Imperial Japanese Naval Air Force. The current Japanese Air Self Defence Force was formed on 1st July 1954.

Jordan	The Royal Jordanian Air Force was formed in 1949 as the Arab Legion Air Force after the Arab-Israeli War of that year. Equipment was initially one de Havilland Rapide.
Kenya	The Kenya Air Force was established following that country's attainment of independence in 1963. Equipped originally with some ex-R.A.F. de Havilland Chipmunks, it was inaugurated officially on 1st June 1964.
Khmer Republic	When Cambodia gained independence from France in 1953, a small air force—Aviation Nationale Khmere—was established with French assistance on 1st April 1954. It has since expanded considerably, equipped with aircraft procured from both East and West.
Korea (North)	Under Russian influence the Korean People's Armed Forces Air Corps (K.P.A.F.A.C.) was formed in October 1948 to absorb the North Korean Army's Aviation Division which, using a small number of ex-Japanese Second World War aircraft had in turn originated in the Soviet-styled North Korean Aviation Society in 1946.
Korea (South)	The Republic of Korea Air Force was established on a limited basis in 1949, the year before North Korean forces crossed the 38th Parallel. The three-year war resulted in rapid expansion by means of massive assistance from the U.S. Air Force.
Kuwait	Originating as an air component formed in the 1950s, the Kuwait Air Force was established in 1960 following assistance given by a British advisory mission.
Laos	Military aviation in Laos originated in 1955 with French aid mainly for training purposes and the provision of some 27 aircraft from America. The Royal Lao Air Force was inaugurated in August 1960, and has since expanded with increasing assistance from the American M.A.P.
Lebanon	The Lebanese Air Force was established in 1949 under R.A.F. influence and supervision, being equipped initially with two Percival Prentice trainers.
Libyan Republic	Military aviation in Libya originated with the receipt of two Gomhuria primary trainers, donated by the United Arab Republic in 1959. The original Royal Libyan Air Force was established in 1963 and was assisted by the U.S. to create a small, but efficient, force. Following overthrow of the Monarchy on 1st September 1969, the Libyan Republican Air Force was created.
Malagasy Republic	Madagascar's armed forces, built up with assistance and equipment from France, established its Malagasy Air Force on 24th April 1961 upon the receipt of seven aircraft, handed over from the French Air Force.
Malaya	Origins of indigenous military aviation in the Federated Malay States date from the Straits Settlements Volunteer Air Force which was born in 1936. Although the R.A.F. assumed the major share of operations against the Communist terrorists, the Malayan Auxiliary Air Force was brought into being in 1950. From this was formed the Royal Malayan Air Force, on 1st June 1958, subsequently renamed the Royal Malaysian Air Force following creation of Malaysia on 16th September 1963.
Mexico	After operations against rebel forces in 1911 by an American mercenary pilot, Hector Worden, the Mexican Government was encouraged to lay the seeds of a small air force which became the Mexican Aviation Corps in 1915, later to be enlarged into the Mexican Air Force (Fuerza Aérea Mexicana).
Morocco	Following the emergence of Morocco as an independent State in 1956, the Royal Moroccan Air Force was established on 19th November that year with a variety of light aircraft and a small number of personnel trained in France and Spain.
Netherlands	Origins of the Royal Netherlands Air Force date back to the last century when, in 1886, the Dutch Army formed a balloon unit for artillery observation duties. Aircraft were first used experimentally during military manœuvres in September 1911, and on 1st July 1913 an Aviation Division of the Royal Netherlands Army was established by Royal Warrant, to be based at Soesterburg. The Naval Aviation Arm (Marine Luchtvaartdienst) was formed on 18th August 1917.
New Zealand	Although originally conceived in 1909, no formal military aviation corps existed in New Zealand during the First World War, pilots serving instead with the R.F.C. and R.N.A.S. Continuing efforts to pursue military aviation during the 1920s led to the formation of the New Zealand Permanent Air Force and Territorial Air Force in June

1923. The Royal New Zealand Air Force was constituted on 1st April 1937.

Nicaragua

In about 1923 the Nicaraguan Army was provided with a small number of Curtiss JN-4s and DH-4s by the U.S.A., but little was done to form a regular air arm until 9th June 1938 when, under American guidance, the Nicaraguan Air Force (Fuerza Aérea de la Guardia Nacional) formally came into being.

Nigeria

Following establishment of the Nigerian Federation in 1960, the Federal Nigerian Air Force was formed in 1964. Initial assistance from an Indian mission was followed by provision of both aircraft and training personnel from West Germany.

Norway

In mid-1912 a German Taube (named *Start*) was purchased by five Norwegian naval officers who presented it to the Royal Norwegian Navy. Almost simultaneously a Maurice Farman (named *Ganger Rolf*) was presented to the Royal Norwegian Army by Norwegians resident in France. Army and Navy flying schools were founded in 1914 and in the following year the Army Air Service (Haerens Flyvåpen) and Naval Air Service (Marinens Flyvevaesen) were formed.

Oman

Following limited support provided by the R.A.F., at the request of the Sultan of Muscat and Oman, to crush the rebellion raised by Imam Ghalib, the Sultan of Oman's Air Force was established in 1958. Initial equipment comprised five Provost trainers and two Pioneer STOL utility aircraft.

Pakistan

The emergence of Pakistan as a dominion in July 1947 was accompanied by the formation of the Royal Pakistan Air Force. Two squadrons were established with former members of the Royal Indian Air Force.

Panama Republic

The Panamanian Air Force was formed in January 1969 with American assistance. Principal tasks are to assist coastguard and police units, and initial equipment comprised Cessna U-17A light planes for liaison duties and two Douglas C-47 transports.

Paraguay

The Paraguayan-Bolivian War of 1932 encouraged the Paraguayan Army to acquire some Potez XXV biplanes and, under the guidance of an Italian Air Mission, these were operated by mercenary pilots; by the end of the war in 1935 a regular Air Force, Fuerzas Aereas Nacionales, had been formed.

Peru

Although financial appropriations were provided for the training of military pilots as early as 1912 it was not until late in 1919 that a military air corps was formed under the aegis of a French Air Mission and with twenty-four British and French aeroplanes. The Peruvian Naval Air Service followed in 1924, but on 20th May 1929 the two were combined to form the Cuerpo de Aeronautica del Perú.

Philippines

The Air Corps of the Philippine Army was formed on 2nd May 1935 as a branch of the Philippine Constabulary. The Philippine Air Force came into being on 3rd July 1947, exactly one year after the inauguration of the Philippine Republic.

Poland

A Polish squadron was incorporated in the Polish Army Corps in 1917, but a fully integrated Air Force was not formed until 29th September 1919 when, under Brigadier-General Macewicz, the new force operated against the U.S.S.R.

Portugal

The Portuguese Air Force (Forca Aérea Portuguesa) owes its origins to funds publicly subscribed in 1912 which were used to purchase a small number of British and French aircraft, and a school was established at Villa Nova da Rainha. In 1917 army and naval air arms (Arma de Aeronáutica and Aviação Maritima) came into being.

Qatar

Following withdrawal of U.K. military forces from the Persian Gulf area at the end of 1971, Qatar elected to build up independent defence forces with British assistance. The inauguration of the Qatar Public Security Forces Air Arm may be dated from the receipt of its first two Westland Whirlwind 3 helicopters in March 1968.

Rhodesia

In 1936 Southern Rhodesia organised the basis of an Air Section of the Permanent Staff Corps at Salisbury. This administered substantial contributions to the R.A.F. during the Second World War. The Southern Rhodesian Air Force changed its title to the Royal Rhodesian Air Force in October 1954. Following dissolution of Federation with Nyasaland in March 1963, the title of this force changed again to the Rhodesian Air Force.

Romania

Romania was one of the first countries in the world to form a regular air force using aeroplanes, its army having established a Flying Corps late in 1910.

Saudi Arabia	The establishment of a small air force was proposed by Ibn Saud in 1923 and this was equipped by Britain with a small number of D.H.9s under an agreement for collaboration which terminated in 1933. The Royal Saudi Air Force in its present form dates from 1950 when a British Mission reorganised the force and supplied light transport and training aircraft.
Senegal	A former French colony, Senegal became independent in November 1958. The Senegal Air Force may be said to date from late 1960 when some C-47s, Broussards and light helicopters were received from France.
Singapore	Following the British Government's decision to withdraw the majority of its armed forces from the Far East before the end of 1971, Singapore began to build up strong military forces. Recruiting for the Singapore Air Defence Command began in April 1968.
South Africa	After six officers of the Union Defence Forces, who had received flying training at a flying school at Kimberley, had been sent to join the R.F.C. on the outbreak of the First World War, the South African Aviation Corps was formed under Major Van der Spuy early in 1915.
South Yemen, Republic of	The Air Force of the Southern Yemen People's Republic dates from the assumption of power by the National Liberation Front in Aden, and British withdrawal on 29th November 1967. Initial equipment consisted of four Douglas C-47s converted from ex-airline DC-3s.
Spain	Spain formed its first military aviation force in 1896 with the establishment of the Servicio Militar de Aerostacion, a captive balloon section. Later, in 1910, plans were laid for the formation of the Aeronáutica Militar Española and in March the following year four French aeroplanes formed the new air force's initial equipment.
Sri Lanka	The original Royal Ceylon Air Force was formed on 10th October 1950 with de Havilland Vampire trainers.
Sudan	After the proclamation confirming Sudan as a Republic on 1st January 1956 steps were taken to form an air force. Four light aircraft were presented by Egypt in the following year with the founding of the Sudanese Air Force.
Sweden	Although the Flygvapnet of today came into being on 1st July 1926, military and naval aviation in Sweden started in 1911 with the presentation of single military and naval aircraft to the nation. Flying schools were formed at Axvall and Oscar Fredriksborg. In 1914 a military flying echelon, the Fälttelegrafkårens Flygkompani ("Field Telegraph Aviation Company") was formed.
Switzerland	The Swiss Fliegertruppe was established on 31st July 1914 at Buedenfeld. Initial equipment comprised one indigenous and three French monoplanes.
Thailand	The Royal Siamese Flying Corps was formed on 23rd March 1914 after three officers of the Royal Siamese Engineers, who had received their flying training in France, returned home. Eight French aircraft provided its initial equipment.
Tunisia	The Tunisian Air Force was established following the attainment of independence in 1956. Fifteen Saab-91D Safir aircraft for *ab initio* training were ordered mid-1960 and the first eight were received on 6th November of that year.
Turkey	Foreign pilots flew the small number of aeroplanes operated during the Balkan Wars of 1912–13. The Turkish Flying Corps came into formal being early in 1915, almost exclusively manned by German crews in German aircraft.
Uganda	Following attainment of independence in 1962, it was decided to form an air force to support the Uganda Rifles. Initial finance was provided in 1964 for formation of the Uganda Army Air Force and for expansion of the Police Air Wing. There is little apparent demarcation between these two forces.
United States of America	Balloons were used by both sides in the American Civil War between 1861 and 1863. An Aeronautical Division of the Signal Corps (with a personnel strength of three) was formed in August 1907, and the first aeroplane, a Wright biplane, was accepted by the Army on 2nd August 1909. A Signal Corps Aviation Section was authorised on 18th July 1914, and following outstanding pioneering maritime flying, a Naval Office of Aeronautics was established on 1st July 1914.

Uruguay	A Department of Military Aviation was created on 20th November 1916 as well as a School of Military Aeronautics at San Fernando.
U.S.S.R.	The Imperial Russian Flying Corps was formed in 1910 together with an Army Central Flying School at Gatchina and a Naval Flying School at Sevastopol. This Flying Corps disintegrated soon after the outbreak of the Revolution in November 1917. In two orders issued on 20th November 1917 and 24th May 1918 the Chief Administration of the Workers' and Peasants' Red Air Fleet (Glavnoe Upravlenie Raboche-Krestyanskogo Krasnogo Vozdushnogo Flota, G.U.R.-K.K.V.F.) was formed.
Venezuela	The Venezuelan Military Air Service was established on 17th April 1920 and a flying school set up at Maracay; the first pilots underwent training in 1921 under French supervision.
Vietnam	The Vietnamese Air Force owes its origins to the setting up under French supervision of flying training facilities at the Armée de l'Air base at Nha Trang in 1951. Observation squadrons were brought into being and these participated with the French against Vietminh forces between 1952 and 1955.
Yugoslavia	Although Yugoslavia as a sovereign State only emerged in 1918, its aviation origins lay in the Serbian Military Air Service formed in 1913 with the return home of six Serbian army officers from France where they had received their flying training.
Zaïre Republic	The Congolese Air Force was formed originally in mid 1961, then equipped with a small number of light aircraft. Has expanded considerably since uniting with the Air Force of the Central Government of Katanga.
Zambia	The Zambian Air Force originates from defence elements allocated to Northern Rhodesia after its secession from the Central African Federation in 1963. Initial equipment comprised four Douglas C-47s and two B.A.C. Pembrokes transferred from the Royal Rhodesian Air Force.

Royal Navy Phantom landing on H.M.S. Ark Royal (Brian M. Service)

SECTION III
Maritime Aviation

The use of aircraft over water stemmed directly from the "purest" application of military aviation—the employment of flying observation platforms. The first generation of shipborne aircraft were intended purely as a means of pushing back the naval commander's horizon, and it was to be many years before the vulnerability of surface vessels to aerial attack—although repeatedly demonstrated by such lonely prophets as "Billy" Mitchell—was recognised by the naval Establishment. It is ironic that America's admirals, the most sceptic of the theory during the inter-war years, should emerge a decade later as commanders of the great carrier task forces which brought Japan to her knees. Imperial Japan's brief but shattering tide of victory swept over the Pacific in the wake of her highly mobile carrier strike aircraft; and it was in the clash of carrier aircraft, whose parent vessels never came within sight or gun-range of one another, that the fate of Japan was sealed. Today the pundits of naval warfare are divided; some say that the future lies with the nuclear-missile-armed submarine, others that nuclear weapons delivered by carrier aircraft offer a greater flexibility of response. Whatever the eventual outcome, those Powers which have the means and the will to support carrier strike forces seem certain to dictate events during the predictable conventional outbreaks of the 1970s.

The world's first aircraft carrier (defined as a waterborne craft used to tether, transport or launch an aircraft) was the *G. W. Parke Custis*, a coal-barge converted during the American Civil War in 1861 under the direction of Thaddeus S. C. Lowe for the transport and towing of observation balloons. The *G. W. Parke Custis* entered service with General McClellan's Army of the Potomac in November 1861, frequently towing balloons on the Potomac River for the observation of the opposing Confederate forces.

The first take-off in the world from water by an aeroplane was made by Henri Fabre, a Frenchman, in his Gnôme-powered monoplane floatplane at Martigues, near Marseille, on 28th March 1910. (See under "Pioneers".)

The first active interest in marine air warfare was displayed by the New York newspaper *World* which established a bombing range on Lake Keuka, near Hammondsport, New York, simulating a battleship target. Glenn Curtiss carried out a demonstration flight, "bombing" this target with lengths of lead pipe on 30th June 1910. (See under "Military Aviation".)

The first naval officer in the world to learn to fly was Lieutenant G. C. Colmore, R.N., who took flying lessons in a Short biplane at Eastchurch, England, at his own expense and was awarded British Pilot's Certificate No. 15 on 21st June 1910.

The first aeroplane to take off from a ship was a Curtiss biplane flown by Eugene B. Ely from an 83 ft (30 m) platform built over the bows of the American light cruiser U.S.S. *Birmingham* (3,750 tons) on 14th November 1910. It has often been averred that the vessel was anchored at the time of take-off; this is not correct as it had been proposed to take off as the ship steamed at 20 knots into the wind. In the event, the *Birmingham* had weighed anchor in Hampton Roads, Virginia, but, impatient to take off, Ely gave the signal to release his aircraft at 15.16 h before the ship was under way. With only 57 ft (17 m) of platform ahead of the Curtiss, the aircraft flew off but touched the water and damaged its propeller; the pilot managed to maintain control and landed at Willoughby Spit, two and a half miles distant. As Ely became airborne from the cruiser, the *Birmingham* sent an historic radio message "Ely's just gone."

Eugene Ely taking off from the U.S.S. Birmingham

captions for
page 132

1. The Wright Flyer of 1903 *is recognised throughout the world as the first aeroplane to have made a powered, controlled and sustained flight. Built by Orville and Wilbur Wright, cycle-making brothers of Dayton, Ohio, USA, it flew for the first time at 10.35 a.m. on 17th December 1903, at Kill Devil Hills, Kitty Hawk, North Carolina. Length of that first flight was 120 ft. (40 m.), which is less than the wing span of most modern airliners. The first* Flyer *logged three further flights on that same day, then was blown over by the wind and damaged, and never flew again. Its total flying lifetime was 98 seconds.*

2. This Blériot XI monoplane *made the first crossing of the English Channel by an aeroplane, by flying from Les Baraques, near Calais, to Northfall Meadow, by Dover Castle, in 36½ minutes on 25th July 1909. More than any previous aviation exploit, this flight made the public aware of the future possibilities of international air travel. Designed and flown by Louis Blériot, the Type XI monoplane had a wing span of 25 ft. 7 in. (7·80 m.), length of 26 ft. 3 in. (8·00 m.), loaded weight of 661 lb. (300 kg.) and speed of 36 m.p.h. (58 km./hr.). It was powered by a 25 h.p. three-cylinder Anzani engine.*

3. Igor Sikorsky's huge biplane, *built in Russia in 1912–13, was officially named* Russian Knight *but is usually remembered as the* Bolshoi *(Grand) because of its great size. First four-engined aeroplane to fly, on 13th May 1913, and the first to have a luxuriously furnished passenger cabin and washroom, it was powered by 100 h.p. Argus engines which gave it a cruising speed of about 55 m.p.h. (88 km./hr.). Wing span was 91 ft. 11 in. (28.00 m.), length 65 ft. 8 in. (20·00 m.) and loaded weight about 9,000 lb. (4,080 kg.). The* Bolshoi *flew 53 times before being damaged by an engine which fell off a crashing aircraft, after which it was dismantled. It could carry eight persons.*

4. The Curtiss flying boat NC-4 *was the first aircraft to cross the Atlantic. It was one of four similar large machines ordered by the US Navy during the First World War, and was launched at Far Rockaway, New York, on 30th April 1919. NC-2 was dismantled to provide spares for NC-1, NC-3 and NC-4, which took off from Trepassy, Newfoundland, on 16th May 1919. NC-1 and NC-3 were both forced down at sea. NC-4, commanded by Lt. Cdr. A. C. Read, reached Horta in the Azores on 17th May, Ponta Delgada on the 20th, Lisbon on the 27th and Plymouth on the 31st. Powered by four 400 h.p. Liberty engines, NC-4 spanned 126 ft. (38·40 m.), had a length of 68 ft. 3½ in. (20·85 m.), loaded weight of 28,500 lb. (12,925 kg.) and maximum speed of 91 m.p.h. (146 km./hr.).*

5. This Vickers Vimy, *still to be seen in the Science Museum, London, made the first-ever non-stop transatlantic flight, flown by Capt. John Alcock and Lt. Arthur Whitten Brown. Both men were knighted for the achievement, which also won a* Daily Mail *prize of £10,000. Powered by two 360 h.p. Rolls-Royce Eagle VIII engines and modified to carry 865 gallons (3,932 litres) of fuel, the Vimy covered the 1,890 miles (3,040 km.) from Newfoundland to Ireland in just under 16 hours on 14–15th June 1919. It had a span of 67 ft. (20·42 m.), length of 42 ft. 8 in. (13·00 m.), weight of 13,300 lb. (6,033 kg.) at take-off in Newfoundland, and normal maximum speed of 100 m.p.h. (161 km./hr.).*

6. Wartime LVG C VI biplanes *were used on the world's first sustained daily passenger services, opened between Berlin and Weimar in Germany, via Leipzig, by Deutsche Luft-Reederei on 5th February 1919. The C VI was normally powered by a 200 h.p. Benz Bz IV engine, had a loaded weight of about 3,086 lb. (1,400 kg.), accommodation for a pilot and two passengers in open cockpits, a speed of just under 100 m.p.h. (161 km./hr.) and span of 42 ft. 7¾ in. (13·00 m.).*

7. Ryan monoplane Spirit of St. Louis *made one of the most celebrated flights of all time when Charles Lindbergh used it for the first solo non-stop transatlantic flight, from New York to Paris, thereby winning a $25,000 prize offered by Raymond*

continued on page 134

See captions on page 131

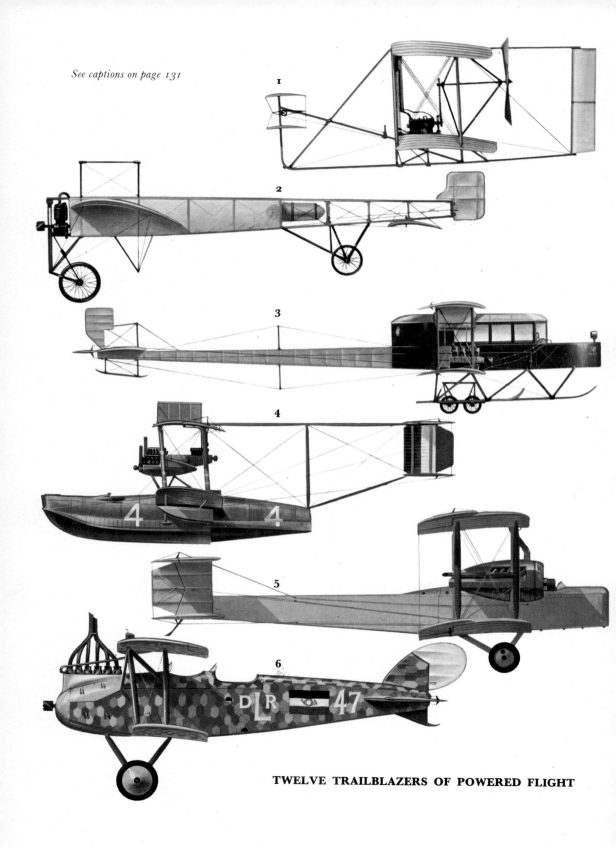

TWELVE TRAILBLAZERS OF POWERED FLIGHT

See captions on page 134

continued from
page 131

Orteig. To make the 3,610 mile (5,810 km.) flight possible, a huge fuel tank was fitted in front of the cabin, making it necessary to use a periscope to see forward, around the tank. Time taken was 33½ hours, on 20th–21st May, 1927. The Spirit of St. Louis *had a 233 h.p. Wright Whirlwind engine, span of 46 ft. (14·02 m.), length of 27 ft. 6 in. (8·38 m.), weight of 5,250 lb. (1,600 kg.) at take-off and average speed of 108 m.p.h. (174 km./hr.).*

8. Eight Handley Page H.P.42s were built *for service with Imperial Airways. First of them was G-AAGX, named* Hannibal, *which flew in November 1930 and became one of the four 18/24-passenger H.P.42Es used on the company's Cairo–Karachi and Cairo–Cape Town routes. G-AAXC* Heracles *(illustrated) was first of the 38-seat H.P.42Ws used on European services from Croydon. Last of the big biplanes, these aircraft remained in use throughout the 'thirties and into the Second World War,* Heracles *alone logging 1¼ million miles and carrying 95,000 passengers in its first seven years. Powered by four 550 h.p. Bristol Jupiter XFBM engines, it spanned 130 ft. (39·62 m.), had a length of 89 ft. 9 in. (27·36 m.), loaded weight of 29,500 lb. (13,380 kg.) and maximum speed of 127 m.p.h. (204 km./hr.).*

9. The Boeing Model 247, *although overshadowed by the later DC-2 and DC-3, was the airliner which set the pattern of "modern" all-metal low-wing monoplane design, with retractable undercarriage, NACA-cowled engines driving controllable-pitch propellers, trim-tabs, a de-icing system and other innovations. Illustrated is NC13347, which survives in the insignia of its original operator, United Air Lines. Seventy-two Boeing 247s were built, of which the first flew on 8th February 1933. Span was 74 ft. (22·55 m.), length 51 ft. 4 in. (15·65 m.), loaded weight 12,650 lb. (5,738 kg.) and maximum speed 182 m.p.h. (293 km./hr.).*

10. The VS-300 helicopter, *first flown on 14th September 1939, was the world's first entirely-practical helicopter and established the now-conventional "single-rotor" (one main rotor and one tail rotor) configuration. Designed and flown by the same Igor Sikorsky who, before he emigrated to America, had built the four-engined Bolshoi in Russia, the VS-300 had up to three tail rotors at one stage. Its fabric covering was not added until quite late in its test flying programme. Powered by a 75 h.p. Lycoming (later 100 h.p. Franklin) engine, the VS-300 was a single-seater with a rotor diameter of 30 ft. (9·14 m.), length of 27 ft. 10 in. (8·48 m.), loaded weight of 1,290 lb. (585 kg.) and speed of 40–50 m.p.h. (64–80 km./hr.).*

11. The Heinkel He 178 *was the first jet-propelled aeroplane to fly, on 27th August 1939, although preceded by the rocket-powered He 176. Because of the imminence of the Second World War, the jet flight was kept secret. Nor did it afford much benefit to the Heinkel company, as Luftwaffe contracts for production jet-fighters went to its competitor, Messerschmitt. Power plant of the He 178 was a Heinkel He S3B turbojet designed by Pabst von Ohain, who ran his first engine only a short time after that of Britain's Frank Whittle. Wing span was 23 ft. 3½ in. (7·20 m.), length 24 ft. 6½ in. (7·48 m.), loaded weight 4,396 lb. (1,998 kg.) and maximum speed about 435 m.p.h. (700 km./hr.).*

12. The Bell X-1 (originally XS-1) research aircraft *is often regarded as second in importance only to the Wright* Flyer *in the history of powered aeroplane flight, as it was the first to exceed the speed of sound (Mach 1) on 14th October 1947. The pilot was Capt. Charles "Chuck" Yeager, USAF, and the X-1 was named* Glamorous Glennis *after his wife. It was air-launched from under the belly of a B-29 bomber "mother-plane", after which the 6,000 lb. (2,722 kg.) thrust rocket-engine consumed the aircraft's 8,177 lb. (3,709 kg.) of fuel in 2½ minutes. Wing span was 28 ft. (8·54 m.), length 31 ft. (9·45 m.) and loaded weight 13,400 lb. (6,078 kg.). The X-1 later attained 967 m.p.h. (1,556 km./hr.).*

The first naval officer sent officially to undergo flying instruction was Lieutenant Theodore G. Ellyson, U.S. Navy, who was ordered to report to Glenn Curtiss in December 1910 at North Island, San Diego, Calif. Ellyson reported to Curtiss on or about 26th January 1911, and was subsequently awarded American Naval Aviator's Certificate No. 1 on 1st July 1911. On 1st March 1911, three officers of the Royal Navy, Lieutenants R. Gregory, C. R. Samson and A. M. Longmore, together with Lieutenant E. L. Gerrard of the Royal Marine Light Infantry, commenced instruction at Eastchurch, England.

Ely's first landing on the U.S.S. Pennsylvania

The first aeroplane to land on a ship was a Curtiss biplane flown by Eugene B. Ely on 18th January 1911 when he landed on a 119 ft 4 in (40 m) long platform constructed over the stern of the American armoured cruiser, U.S.S. *Pennsylvania* (13,680 tons), anchored in San Francisco Bay. It had been intended that the vessel would be under way during the landing, but the Captain considered that there was insufficient sea space to manœuvre and the *Pennsylvania* remained at anchor. Despite landing downwind the Curtiss rolled to a stop at 11.01 h after a run of only 30 ft (10 m). Captain C. F. Pond is reputed to have remarked that "this is the most important landing of a bird since the dove flew back to the Ark". After lunch Ely successfully took off again from the *Pennsylvania* at 11·58 h and returned to his airfield near San Francisco.

The first aeroplane to perform a premeditated landing on water, taxi and then take off was a Curtiss "hydroaeroplane" flown by Glenn Curtiss on 26th January 1911. He took off and then landed in San Diego Harbour, turned round and took off again, flying about 1 mile before coming down near his starting-point.

The U.S. Navy's first aeroplane, a Curtiss A-1 "hydroaeroplane" or seaplane was first flown on 1st July 1911. This of course was not the same aircraft as that flown by Curtiss for his sea landing flight earlier in the year.

The first gallantry decoration to be "earned" by a marine aviator was the Distinguished Flying Cross awarded posthumously to Eugene B. Ely, who was killed while flying on 14th October 1911. The award of the D.F.C. was made twenty-five years later in recognition of his outstanding contributions to marine aviation during 1910 and 1911. His sole reward during his life was an award of $500 made by the U.S. Aeronautical Reserve during 1911.

The first torpedo drop from an aeroplane was achieved in 1911 by the Italian Capitano Guidoni, flying a Farman biplane. The torpedo weighed 352 lb (160 kg).

The first officer of the Royal Navy to negotiate successfully a water take-off in an aeroplane was Commander O. Schwann, R.N., who took off on 18th November 1911, but crashed on landing.

The first officer of the Royal Navy to land successfully on the water in an aeroplane was Lieutenant Arthur Longmore, R.N. (later Air Chief Marshal Sir Arthur Longmore, G.C.B., D.S.O., R.A.F. (Retd.)), who landed a Short S.27 seaplane on the Medway River on 1st December 1911.

The first officer of the Royal Navy to take off from a ship in an aeroplane was Lieutenant Charles Rumney Samson who is said to have made a secret flight in a Short S.27 from a platform on the bows of the British battleship, H.M.S. *Africa* (17,500 tons) moored in Sheerness Harbour during December 1911. His first officially recorded take-off was from H.M.S. *Africa* at 14.20 h on 10th January 1912, flying a modified Short biplane. Commander Samson was appointed Officer Commanding the Naval Wing of the Royal Flying Corps in October 1912.

Samson's Short S.27 taking off from H.M.S. Hibernia

The first pilot in the world to take off in an aeroplane from a ship under way was Commander Samson, who took off in a Short pusher biplane amphibian from the fore-castle of the battleship H.M.S. *Hibernia* while it steamed at 10·5 knots off Portland during the Naval Review of May 1912. At the conclusion of the Review, Commander Samson was one of the officers commanded to dine with H.M. King George V on board the *Victoria and Albert*.

Samson and the S.27 after landing ashore (Flight International)

The first U.S. Marine pilot was Lieutenant Alfred A. Cunningham, U.S. Marine Corps, who qualified for his Pilot's Badge during 1912.

The first Japanese naval pilots began flying instruction during 1912. Three such men were ordered to France and two to America to receive their instruction.

The first naval aeroplanes acquired by the Japanese Navy were two Short-built Maurice Farmans and a Curtiss hydroaeroplane purchased during 1912.

The first naval aeroplane acquired by the French Navy was a Maurice Farman biplane purchased on 12th September 1912, equipped with pontoons. In the same year the French torpedo-boat carrier, *Foudre*, 6,090 tons, was converted to accommodate two seaplanes. Later a platform was added over the ship's bows and from this René Caudron took off on 8th May 1914 while the *Foudre* was anchored in Saint-Raphaël Harbour.

The first naval aviator to gain a Pilot's Certificate in the Argentine was Teniente de Navio Melchor Z. Escola who obtained his Flying Certificate on 23rd October 1912 with the Argentine Aero Club.

The first aeroplane to be successfully catapult-launched from a boat was the Curtiss A-1 floatplane, piloted by Lieutenant T. Ellyson, on 12th November 1912. The operation was performed from an anchored barge, at the Washington Navy Yard, using a compressed-air launcher invented by Captain W. I. Chambers.

The first naval vessel in the world to be commissioned for service as a parent ship for aircraft was H.M.S. *Hermes*, an old light cruiser which was converted to accommodate two seaplanes late in 1912. At the instigation of Winston Churchill, Commander Charles Rumney Samson carried out trials with **the world's first seaplanes with folding wings** for service with the *Hermes*. This ship was followed by the *Empress, Engadine* and *Riviera* which were commandeered ex-cross-Channel steamers adapted to carry seaplanes immediately after the outbreak of the First World War in 1914.

The first Japanese naval vessel converted to support seaplanes was the *Wakamiya Maru* (7,600 tons) converted from a naval transport in 1913. The *Wakamiya Maru* commenced operations against German forces at Kiaochow Bay, China, on 1st September 1914, using Farman seaplanes. Dropping improvised bombs made from naval shells, the pilots of these Farmans succeeded in sinking a German minelayer before the *Wakamiya Maru* struck a mine herself and was damaged.

The first standard naval torpedo dropped by a naval airman in a naval aircraft was a 14 in (35·6 cm) torpedo weighing 810 lb (367 kg), dropped by a Short seaplane flown by Squadron Commander Arthur Longmore, R.N. (Royal Aero Club Pilot's Certificate No. 72), on 28th July 1914.

The first occasion on which naval aeroplanes and aviators participated in combat was the Vera Cruz incident of April 1914 when five Curtiss *AB*s were flown on reconnaissance flights over the Mexican port from the battleship U.S.S. *Mississippi* and cruiser U.S.S. *Birmingham* and came under rifle-fire which caused damage but no loss to aircraft or pilots.

THE FIRST WORLD WAR

The first air operations undertaken by airmen of the Royal Navy during the First World War were reconnaissance flights by Eastchurch Squadron commanded by Wing Commander Charles Samson in support of a Brigade of Royal Marines on the Belgian coast in August 1914.

The first active combat sortie by naval airmen against German territory was a raid undertaken by four aeroplanes of Eastchurch Squadron against German airship sheds at Cologne and Düsseldorf on 22nd September 1914. Only one of the aircraft reached its target at Düsseldorf and its bombs did little damage; all four aircraft returned safely. (See "Military Aviation".)

One of the most distinguished early British airmen (and almost certainly the most distinguished British naval pilot) was Air Commodore Charles Rumney Samson, c.m.g., d.s.o., a.f.c., who was born in Manchester in 1883 and died on 5th February 1931. He entered the Royal Navy in 1898. He served on board H.M.S. *Pomone* (Somaliland, 1903–4, Medal and Clasp), and as First Lieutenant on board H.M.S. *Philomel* (Persian Gulf, 1909–10, Medal and Clasp). He qualified for and was awarded Royal Aero Club Pilot's Certificate No. 71 on a Short biplane at the Naval School, Eastchurch, on 25th April 1911. He was the first British pilot to take off in an aeroplane from a ship (H.M.S. *Africa*, Sheerness, December 1911) and was the first pilot in the world to take off in an aeroplane from a ship under way (H.M.S. *Hibernia*, Royal Naval Review, Portland, May 1912). He commanded the first Naval Wing, R.F.C. in October 1912, and the first

Naval Squadron, R.N.A.S., to be used on operations during the First World War (Belgian coast, August 1914: 1914 Star). He formed and commanded the first Royal Naval Armoured Car Force, September 1914, and commanded the first naval squadron to bomb targets in Germany (see above). He was among the first batch of seven naval officers to be awarded the D.S.O. in the First World War on 23rd October 1914. Served on the Western Front, 1915; Siege of Antwerp; First Battle of Ypres; commanded Brigade of French Territorials at the Battle of Orchies (awarded Chevalier Légion d'Honneur and Croix de Guerre, 14th January 1916); Mentioned in Despatches, October 1914 (Admiralty) and February 1915 (France).

Also during 1915 Samson commanded a squadron of aircraft on the island of Tenedos operating against the Turks early in the Dardanelles campaign and in the same area was later Mentioned in Despatches twice, March 1916 and July 1916 (both Admiralty, Gallipoli). While on a "search-and-bomb" sortie Samson attacked and damaged a staff car carrying Mustafa Kemâl Pasha, the famous Atatürk (1881–1938); he also dropped a 500 lb (227 kg) bomb, the largest bomb hitherto used by an aeroplane. Samson then became the first commander of a "carrier task force" when, as Captain of H.M. Seaplane Carrier *Ben-My-Chree*, he led two other seaplane carriers (*Anne* and *Raven II*) on air operations against Turkish forces in Sinai, Palestine and Arabia. After *Ben-My-Chree* was sunk by Turkish gun-fire off the coast of Turkey, Samson took *Raven* into the Indian Ocean to search for the German raider *Wolf* (awarded a bar to the D.S.O., 23rd January 1917, East Indies). By 1918 Samson was back in home waters and on 1st January that year was promoted to Wing-Captain, R.N.A.S., transferring as Lieutenant-Colonel, temporary Colonel, R.A.F., on 1st April 1918. He proposed a scheme for launching a Sopwith Camel from a towed barge, and attempted the first take-off in July 1918; this failed and the barge rammed the ditched Camel but Samson escaped unhurt. This system was used with success when Lieutenant Stuart Culley took off from the barge on 12th August 1918 and shot down Zeppelin L.53 off the Dutch coast. Promoted Group Captain in 1919, Samson was appointed C.M.G. on 3rd June 1919, and awarded the A.F.C. on 1st January 1919.

The first significant damage inflicted in a raid by naval aircraft was that caused by bombs dropped from a Sopwith Tabloid flown by Flight-Lieutenant R. L. G. Marix on 8th October 1914, in a raid on the airship base at Düsseldorf. His two 20 lb (9 kg) bombs were released from about 600 ft (200 m) and destroyed the Zeppelin Z.IX. (See also "Military Aviation".) *See also page 138 for action by Japanese aircraft.*

Sopwith Tabloid of the kind flown by Flight-Lieutenant R. L. G. Marix

The first operational seaplane unit of the Imperial German Navy was formed on 4th December 1914, moving to its base at Zeebrugge two days later.

The first naval vessel fully converted for aircraft duties, while still under construction was H.M.S. *Ark Royal*, and as such was the first ship in the world to be completed as an aircraft (seaplane) carrier. Launched in 1914 *Ark Royal* became the first aircraft carrier to operate aeroplanes against the enemy in Europe (the *Wakamiya Maru* had launched seaplanes against the Germans in the Far East by this time) when, arriving at the entrance to the Dardanelles on 17th February 1915, one of her seaplanes was sent on reconnaissance against the Turks.

Launching a torpedo from a Short 320 seaplane, which went into service with the R.N.A.S. following the early success of the Short 184

The first air attack using a torpedo dropped by an aeroplane was carried out by Flight Commander C. H. Edmonds flying a Short 184 seaplane from H.M.S. *Ben-My-Chree* on 12th August 1915 against a 5,000 ton Turkish supply ship in the Sea of Marmara. Although the enemy ship was hit and sunk, the captain of a British submarine claimed to have fired a torpedo simultaneously and sunk the ship. It was further stated that the British submarine *E.14* had attacked and immobilised the ship four days earlier. However on 17th August 1915 another Turkish ship was sunk by a torpedo of whose origin there can be no doubt. On this occasion Flight Commander C. H. Edmonds, flying a Short 184, torpedoed a Turkish steamer a few miles north of the Dardanelles. His formation colleague, Flight-Lieutenant G. B. Dacre, was forced to land on the water owing to engine trouble but, seeing an enemy tug close by, taxied up to it and released his torpedo. The tug blew up and sank. Thereafter Dacre was able to take off and return to the *Ben-My-Chree*.

The first launching of an aeroplane by catapult on board ship (excluding anchored barge), took place on 5th November 1915 when an AB2 flying-boat was catapulted from the stern of the American battleship, U.S.S. *North Carolina*, anchored in Pensacola Bay, Florida.

The first major fleet battle in which an aeroplane was used was the Battle of Jutland on 31st May 1916, when Flight-Lieutenant F. J. Rutland (accompanied by his observer, Assistant Paymaster G. S. Trewin) spotted and shadowed a force of German light cruisers and destroyers. Taking off from alongside

H.M. seaplane carrier *Engadine* at about 15.10 h, Rutland sighted the enemy ships and continued to radio position reports to the *Engadine* until a broken fuel pipe forced the seaplane down on to the sea. Having repaired the damage, Rutland took off and returned to his ship. (The following day Rutland performed an act of supreme gallantry, not associated with aviation, which brought him the award of the Albert Medal in Gold, an award so rare that his was one of only three ever made. As the *Engadine* withdrew from the battle she went to the assistance of the crippled armoured cruiser, H.M.S. *Warrior*, and on the next morning went alongside to take off her crew. During this operation a wounded man fell into the sea between the two ships and, despite the great danger of being crushed, Rutland entered the water and rescued the seaman, who was however found to have died from exposure.)

Thereafter Rutland pursued an outstanding, but ultimately tragic career. After the Battle of Jutland, and promoted Flight Commander, Rutland conducted a series of experiments flying Sopwith Pups off short platforms and the decks of H.M. seaplane carriers *Manxman* and *Campania*. These led to the decision to build a platform for the purpose on the light cruiser, H.M.S. *Yarmouth*. However while this construction work was being carried out during the summer and autumn of 1916, Rutland was forced to land near the Danish coast while engaged on an anti-Zeppelin sweep. Having travelled through Denmark, Sweden and Norway, he managed to return to England in 1917 in time to carry out the tests on board the *Yarmouth*. After further wide-ranging trials (which included flying a Pup from a platform on top of the forward 15 in gun turret of the battle-cruiser H.M.S. *Repulse*, on 1st October 1917), Commander Rutland was appointed Senior Flying Officer on board H.M.S. *Furious*, the first aircraft carrier (as distinct from a seaplane or balloon carrier). See below. He was awarded the Distinguished Service Cross and Bar, in addition to the Albert Medal, before the end of the war. Subsequently he went to Japan to advise that nation on naval aviation matters, only to be brought back to the United Kingdom during the Second World War, where he committed suicide shortly after.

The first vessel in the world to be defined as an aircraft carrier (in the modern sense, i.e. equipped with a flying deck for operations of landplanes) was the light battle-cruiser, H.M.S. *Furious*. This ship commenced construction shortly after the outbreak of the First World War, it being intended to arm her with a pair of 18 in guns. In March 1917 authority to alter her design was issued, and at the expense of one of these huge guns she was completed with a hangar and flight deck on her forecastle. With a speed of 31·5 knots, she carried six Sopwith Pups in addition to four seaplanes. Her first Senior Flying Officer was Squadron Commander E. H. Dunning.

H.M.S. Furious, *late 1917*

*Squadron Commander
E. H. Dunning touching
down successfully on
H.M.S. Furious on 2nd
August 1917*

The first landing in the world by an aeroplane upon a ship under-way was carried out by Squadron Commander E. H. Dunning who flew a Sopwith Pup on to the deck of H.M.S. *Furious* on 2nd August 1917. Steaming at 26 knots into a wind of 21 knots, *Furious* thus provided a 47 knot headwind for Dunning who flew his Pup for'ard along the starboard side of the ship before side-slipping towards the deck located on the forecastle. Men then grabbed straps on the aircraft and brought it to a standstill. On 7th August Dunning attempted to repeat the operation in an even greater headwind but stalled as he attempted to overshoot and was killed when his aircraft was blown over the side of the ship.

H.M.S. *Furious* became the **longest-lived active carrier in the world.** Launched in 1916 she featured a flying-deck on her forecastle until mid 1917 when another deck was added aft with interconnecting trackways abaft the superstructure. Between 1921 and 1925 the midships superstructure was eliminated and she emerged as a flush-deck carrier displacing 22,450 tons, with two aircraft lifts and an aircraft capacity of thirty-three. Her over-all length was 786 ft (239 m). After an extraordinarily active and exciting career in the Second World War (and a near head-on collision at night in the Atlantic with a troopship which passed so close as to carry away some of the carrier's radio masts), she was finally scrapped in 1949.

The first enemy airship to be shot down by a landplane launched from a ship was the Zeppelin L.23 which was shot down by Flight Sub-Lieutenant B. A. Smart flying a Sopwith Pup which had taken off from a platform on board the light cruiser H.M.S. *Yarmouth* on 21st August 1917 off the Danish coast.

The first flush-deck aircraft carrier in the world was H.M.S. *Argus* (15,775 tons). Originally laid down in 1914 as the Italian liner *Conte Rosso*, she was purchased by Great Britain and launched in 1917, and completed in 1918. She featured an unrestricted flight deck of 565 ft length (172 m) and could accommodate twenty aircraft. She was ultimately scrapped in 1947. She was **the first carrier in the world to embark a full squadron of torpedo-carrier landplanes,** when in October 1918 a squadron of Sopwith Cuckoos was activated. They did not however see action.

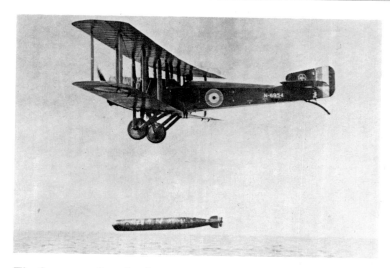

Sopwith Cuckoo (Air Ministry, London)

The first aeroplane in the world designed from the outset as a torpedo-bomber for operation from an aircraft carrier was the Sopwith Cuckoo. First flown in June 1917, the prototype was powered by a 200 hp Hispano-Suiza engine. It could carry an 18 in (45·7 cm) torpedo and entered service when a squadron embarked in H.M.S. *Argus* in October 1918 (see above). Production Cuckoos had a 200 hp Sunbeam Arab or Wolseley Viper engine.

Flight Sub-Lieutenant Culley taking off, 11th August 1918 (Imperial War Museum)

The first pilot to attempt to take off from a towed barge in an aeroplane was Colonel Samson who, as pilot of a Sopwith Camel, attempted in July 1918 to take off from a 40 ft (12 m) barge being towed at 31 knots behind a destroyer. The Camel evidently fouled part of the barge and fell into the water, Samson being fortunate to escape with his life. **The first pilot to perform this feat successfully** was the American-born Flight Sub-Lieutenant Stuart Culley, R.N., who on 1st August 1918 rose from the barge, towed by H.M.S. *Redoubt* at 35 knots. At 08.41 h on 11th August 1918 Culley took off from the barge being towed off the Dutch coast and climbed to 18,000 ft

(6,000 m) to shoot down the German Zeppelin L.53 using incendiary ammunition. He was thus **the first (and probably the only) pilot to shoot down an enemy aircraft having taken off from a towed vessel.** Landing in the sea alongside his towing destroyer, H.M.S. *Redoubt*, he was rescued—and later awarded the D.S.O. for his feat—and his Camel was salvaged by a derrick (invented by Colonel Samson). The only survivor of the Zeppelin baled out from 19,000 ft (6,500 m)—almost certainly a record at that time.

The Porte/Felixstowe Fury

The largest British aircraft constructed and flown during the First World War was the Porte/Felixstowe Fury triplane flying-boat, with a span of 123 ft (37·5 m), a maximum loaded weight of 33,000 lb (15,000 kg) and powered by five 334 hp Rolls-Royce Eagle VII engines. Flown by John Cyril Porte from Harwich harbour in 1918, the Fury never entered service and continued on test until in 1919 it crashed and was almost totally destroyed. On one occasion it was flown with twenty-four passengers, sufficient fuel for 7 h flying and 5,000 lb (2,270 kg) of ballast. (Although the Tarrant Tabor was a larger aircraft and was being constructed during the war, it did not make its first attempt to fly until 26th May 1919 and so cannot be counted.)

The first flight of America's famous Liberty twelve-cylinder engine took place on 21st October 1917, installed in the Curtiss HS-1 flying-boat. The Liberty engine, whose power rose from 375 to 420 hp during development, came to be used by more American aeroplanes than any other prior to 1926, and was one of the world's outstanding aeroplane engines.

The only American naval pilot to shoot down five enemy aircraft during the First World War was Lieutenant David S. Ingalls, U.S. Navy, who, while serving with No. 213 Squadron, R.A.F., in 1918 was credited with the destruction of four enemy aeroplanes and one balloon. He was awarded the British D.F.C. (citation dated 25th October 1918) and the U.S. Distinguished Service Cross (citation dated 11th November 1920). He later served as Assistant Secretary of the Navy for Aeronautics from 1929 until 1932.

BETWEEN THE WORLD WARS

The first American naval pilot to take off from a platform on board an American warship was Lieutenant-Commander Edward O. McDonnell who flew a Sopwith Camel from a turret platform on the U.S. battleship *Texas* on 9th March 1919 anchored in Guantánamo Bay, Cuba. Several American battleships were fitted with aircraft platforms during the 1919–20 period and aeroplanes, including Camels, Nieuport 28s, Hanriot HD-1s and Vought VE-7s, were flown from them.

The first aircraft carrier in the world to introduce the offset "island" superstructure and split-level aircraft hangar was H.M.S. *Eagle*. Originally laid down as the battleship *Almirante Cochrane* (intended for Chile) in 1913, she was purchased and completed as a carrier in 1920, serving with the Royal Navy until in 1942 she was sunk by a German submarine.

The first American aircraft carrier was the U.S.S. *Jupiter*, an ex-collier of 11,050 tons, which was converted to feature a stem-to-stern flight deck of 534 ft length (163 m) in 1920. (Later called *Langley*.)

The first capital warship sunk by bombs dropped by American aeroplanes was the ex-German battleship *Ostfriesland* (22,800 tons) during a demonstration of bombing attacks on a stationary, unmanned target at sea by U.S. Army MB-2 bombers commanded by Brigadier-General William Mitchell on 21st July 1921. During these trials, prior to the sinking of the *Ostfriesland*, U.S. Navy flying-boats had sunk the submarine *U-117*, and U.S. Army bombers had sunk the ex-German destroyer *G-102* and the cruiser *Frankfurt* (5,100 tons). Subsequently Army bombers sank the battleships *Alabama*, *New Jersey* and *Virginia*. The *Washington*, an unfinished battleship of 32,500 tons, was attacked with and hit by all manner of weapons and was finally sunk by naval gunfire.

Brigadier-General William Mitchell

The first American carrier-based fighter to be designed specifically as such was the Naval Aircraft Factory TS-1, the first of which appeared in June 1922, three months after the first U.S. aircraft carrier, the *Langley*, had been commissioned. Designed by the U.S. Bureau of Aeronautics, the TS-1 was built by the Curtiss Aeroplane and Motor Company and first joined the *Langley* in December 1922. It had a top speed of 125 mile/h (200 km/h).

The aircraft carrier limitations imposed by the Washington Treaty (signed on 6th February 1922) permitted the United States and Great Britain to build aircraft carriers up to a total tonnage of 135,000 tons per country; Japan, 81,000 tons, and France and Italy, 60,000 tons each. Aircraft carriers were not permitted to carry guns of greater calibre than 8 in. Moreover, carriers already under construction at the time of the signing of the Treaty were exempt from its provisions. A limit of 27,000 tons was placed on each ship, but each nation might possess up to two vessels each of 33,000 tons. The U.S.S. *Saratoga* and *Lexington* each displaced approximately 33,000 tons, but at full load the figure was nearer 40,000. When no longer considered to be bound by the provisions of the Treaty, Japan rebuilt several of her carriers during the 1930s to displace more than 33,000 tons. Of all the signatory nations (as major Sea Powers) of the Washington Treaty, only Italy chose to ignore the significance of the aircraft carrier, and constructed no such ship between the two world wars.

The first American aircraft carrier to be commissioned for fleet service was the U.S.S. *Langley* (11,050 tons), a converted ex-collier (the *Jupiter*), which was completed in September 1922. **The first pilot to take off from her deck** was Commander Virgil C. Griffin on 17th October that year, and on 26th October Lieutenant-Commander Chevalier carried out **the first landing.**

The first Japanese aircraft carrier to be laid down as such (and second in the world only to H.M.S. *Hermes*) was the *Hosho* (7,470 tons), laid down in December 1919 and completed in December 1922. Her aircraft complement was up to twenty-one and she was not scrapped until 1947.

The first ship in the world to be laid down as an aircraft carrier (but not the first to be completed as such) was H.M.S. *Hermes* (12,900 tons at full load). Laid down in January 1918 and completed in July 1923, she could accommodate twenty-five aircraft and served with the Royal Navy until 1942 when she was sunk by Japanese aircraft off the coast of Ceylon. **She was the first carrier in the world to be sunk by aircraft from another carrier.**

The first squadron of regular U.S. Navy aircraft to embark on an American carrier went on board U.S.S. *Langley* in January 1925.

One of the most remarkable feats of seamanship by the crew of a flying-boat must be that of the crew of the NAF PN-9 flying-boat who, on 1st September 1925, set off from San Francisco Bay to fly to Hawaii, a distance of 2,400 miles (3,860 km) in an attempt to establish a new world seaplane distance record. When 559 miles (964 km) from their destination they were forced to alight on the sea, but completed the voyage by *sailing* the flying-boat after stripping the fabric from the lower wings and making sails. They were sighted by a submarine off Honolulu on 10th September. Nevertheless their flight of 1,841 miles (2,958 km) was recognised as a world seaplane record.

The last occasion on which American pilots flew aircraft designed during the First World War under combat conditions was during the action by the U.S. Marine Corps against the Nicaraguan bandits during 1927. Their aircraft were Naval Aircraft Factory-built de Havilland DH-4Bs and Boeing-rebuilt DH-4Ms.

The first French aircraft carrier was the *Béarn* (25,000 tons), converted from a *Normandie*-class battleship originally laid down in 1914. She was not completed until May 1927 and, although **the longest-lived carrier in the world**, she spent the greater part of the Second World War out of commission and was subsequently converted for use as an aircraft transport. She was ultimately scrapped in 1968.

The first U.S. Marine Corps squadron to serve on board an aircraft carrier was Marine Scouting Squadron VS-14M which embarked in U.S.S. *Saratoga* on 2nd November 1931. Simultaneously VS-15M embarked in U.S.S. *Lexington*.

The Macon *(U.S. Naval Air Station, Moffett Field)*

*A Sparrowhawk 'hooking-on' (U.S.
Naval Air Station, Moffett Field)*

Grumman FF-1

The first and only American operational fighters to serve aboard airships were naval Curtiss F9C Sparrowhawk biplanes which served on board the U.S. airships *Akron* and *Macon* between 1932 and 1935. The prototype Sparrowhawk (*XF9C-1*) achieved the first "hook-on" on the airship *Los Angeles* on 27th October 1931, and the first production aircraft hooked-on to *Akron* on 29th June 1932.

The first aeroplane flown by the U.S. Navy to feature a retractable undercarriage was the Grumman XFF-1 fighter, and as the FF-1 entered service with the Navy in June 1933.

The last operational American biplane to remain in production was the Curtiss SBC Helldiver, whose first flight as the parasol monoplane *XF12C-1* was in 1933 (it was almost immediately redesigned as a biplane), and remained in production in the United States until 1941. At the time of the Japanese attack on Pearl Harbor in December 1941 the U.S. Navy still retained 186 Helldiver biplanes on strength.

PBY Catalina

The flying-boat produced in the greatest numbers anywhere in the world was the Consolidated PBY Catalina. Excluding production in Russia, 1,196 Catalina flying-boats and 944 amphibians were built and these served with the air forces and airlines of more than twenty-five nations. Widely regarded as one of Aviation's classic designs, the PBY in 1973 still continues to give yeoman service in several parts of the world—thirty-five years after the prototype's first flight.

A5M "Claude"

The world's first carrier-based monoplane fighter to achieve operational status was Japan's Mitsubishi A5M *Claude* which entered service with the carrier *Kaga* in 1937 during air operations against the Chinese.

At the outbreak of the Second World War there were twenty aircraft carriers in commission and eleven under construction by the world's major naval powers:

	Under construction	Completed
Great Britain	6	7
Japan	2	6
United States of America	2	6
France	1	1

AIRCRAFT CARRIERS COMPLETED BETWEEN THE WORLD WARS

Name	Displacement at full load tons	Length ft	m	Speed kt	Aircraft accommodation	Completed	Ultimate fate	Remarks
GREAT BRITAIN								
Furious	22,450	786	(239·6)	32·5	33	Recommissioned 1925	Scrapped in 1949	Converted from light battle-cruiser during construction. Originally completed in 1917.
Argus	15,775	565	(172·2)	20·76	20	1918	Scrapped in 1947	Converted from liner *Conte Rosso* during construction.
Eagle	26,400	667	(203·3)	24	21	1920	Sunk by U-Boat, 1942	Converted from battleship *Almirante Cochrane* during construction.
Hermes	12,900	598	(182·3)	25	25	1923	Sunk by Jap. a/c, 1942	World's first carrier designed as such.
Courageous	26,500	786	(239·6)	32	48	1928	Sunk by U-Boat, 1939	Converted from light battle-cruiser.
Glorious	26,500	786	(239·6)	32	48	1930	Sunk by Ger. w/ships, 1940	Converted from light battle-cruiser.
Ark Royal	27,000	800	(243·8)	31·5	60	1938	Sunk by U-Boat, 1941	Max. accommodation 72 aircraft.
UNITED STATES OF AMERICA								
Langley	11,050	542	(165·2)	15	34	1922	Sunk by Jap. a/c, 1942	Converted from collier *Jupiter*, 1920–21.
Lexington	40,000	888	(270·7)	34	80	1927	Sunk by Jap. a/c, 1942	Converted from battle-cruiser during construction. Max. accommodation 120 aircraft.
Saratoga	40,000	888	(270·7)	34	80	1927	Destyd. in A-Bomb test, Bikini 1946	Remarks as for *Lexington*.
Ranger	14,500	769	(234·4)	29·5	80	1934	Scrapped in 1947	
Yorktown	19,900	741	(225·9)	29·5	80	1937	Sunk by Jap. a/c, 1942	
Enterprise	19,900	741	(225·9)	29·5	80	1938	Scrapped in 1958	
JAPAN								
Hosho	7,470	551	(167·9)	25	21	1922	Scrapped in 1947	
Akagi	36,500	855	(260·6)	31·2–32·5	60	1927	Sunk by U.S. a/c, 1942	Converted from battle-cruiser during construction. Accommodation increased to 90 a/c in 1938 on rebuilding.
Kaga	38,200	812	(247·5)	27·5–28·3	60	1930	Sunk by U.S. a/c, 1942	Converted from battleship during construction. Aircraft accommodation increased to 90 in 1936.
Ryujo	10,600	590	(179·8)	29	48	1933	Sunk by U.S. a/c, 1942	
Soryu	15,900	746	(227·4)	34·5	73(max.)	1937	Sunk by U.S. a/c, 1942	
Hiryu	17,300	746	(227·4)	34·3	73(max.)	1939	Sunk by U.S. a/c, 1942	
FRANCE								
Béarn	25,000	599	(182·6)	21·5	40	1927	Scrapped in 1968	Converted from battleship during construction. Not used as aircraft carrier [sic] after Second W.W.

THE SECOND WORLD WAR

The first German aircraft to be shot down by British aircraft during the Second World War was claimed by naval aircraft. Three Dornier Do 18s of *Küstenfliegergruppe 506* were sighted by a patrol of Swordfish aircraft flying from H.M.S. *Ark Royal* over the North Sea on 26th September 1939. Nine Skuas were forthwith launched from the carrier and these succeeded in forcing one of the Dorniers (Werke Nr. 731, of *2 Staffel*, Kü. Fl. Gr. 506) down on to the sea in German Grid Square 3440. The German four-man crew was later rescued and made prisoner on board a British destroyer. The Blackburn Skua was the Fleet Air Arm's first operational monoplane, and the first British aircraft designed specifically as a dive-bomber to enter squadron service.

Blackburn Skua (Charles E. Brown)

The American fighter of the Second World War to remain in production longest was the Vought F4U Corsair which first flew on 29th May 1940, commenced delivery to VF-12 (U.S. Navy Fighter Squadron Twelve) on 3rd October 1942, and remained in production until the last aircraft was completed at Dallas, Texas, in December 1952. It was thus **the last piston-engined American fighter to remain in production.** Fastest of the series was the F4U-5N, powered by a 2,300 hp R-2800-32W two-stage radial engine, which had a maximum level speed of 470 mile/h (756 km/h) at 26,800 ft (8,168 m). Armed with four 20 mm cannon, the F4U-5N could also carry two 1,000 lb bombs on under-wing pylons.

The first American-built fighter aircraft in British service to destroy a German aircraft in the Second World War were two Grumman Martlets (U.S.N. designation F4F-3) of the Royal Navy. Patrolling over Scapa Flow on 25th December 1940, Martlets of No. 804 Squadron, flown by Lieutenant L. V. Carver, R.N., and Sub-Lieutenant Parke, R.N.V.R., intercepted and forced down a Junkers Ju 88.

The first British single-seat monoplane fighter to serve on board aircraft carriers of the Royal Navy was the Hawker Sea Hurricane. The type equipped No. 880 Squadron in January 1941 and was embarked in H.M.S. *Furious* in July of the same year.

The first single-engined American aircraft equipped with a power-operated gun-turret, and also the first to carry a 22 in torpedo, was the Grumman TBF Avenger. First flight of an XTBF-1 prototype was made on 1st August 1941. First operational use of production aircraft was at the Battle of Midway on 4th June 1942.

The first American naval pilot to destroy five enemy aircraft in the Second World War was Lieutenant Edward Henry O'Hare, U.S. Navy, who, on 20th February 1942, attacked single-handed a formation of nine Japanese bombers in the south-west Pacific area and shot down five and damaged a sixth.

The first naval battle in which the issue was decided by aircraft alone was the Battle of the Coral Sea, fought on 7th-9th May 1942, between U.S. Navy Task Force 17 and Vice-Admiral Takeo Takagi's Carrier Striking Force (part of Vice-Admiral Shigeyoshi Inouye's Task Force MO). The battle was fought to prevent Japanese support of an invasion of Port Moresby and disrupt Japanese plans to launch air strikes against the Australian mainland. In this respect the battle must be considered to have been an American victory, although the large American carrier U.S.S. *Lexington* was sunk —**the first American carrier to be lost in the Second World War.** The opposing carrier forces were as follows:

U.S. Navy:

U.S.S. *Lexington*	23 F4F Wildcat fighters, 36 SBD Dauntless dive-bombers and 12 TBD Devastator torpedo-bombers.
U.S.S. *Yorktown*	21 F4F Wildcat fighters, 38 SBD Dauntless dive-bombers and 13 TBD Devastator torpedo-bombers.

Imperial Japanese Navy:

Shoho	12 A6M Zero fighters, 9 B5N Kate torpedo-bombers.
Shokaku	21 A6M Zero fighters, 21 D3A Val dive-bombers and 21 B5N torpedo-bombers.
Zuikaku	21 A6M Zero fighters, 21 D3A Val dive-bombers and 21 B5N torpedo-bombers.

The Japanese carrier *Shoho* was attacked and sunk by Dauntlesses and Devastators from the *Lexington* and *Yorktown* (giving rise to the famous radio call from Lieutenant-Commander Robert Dixon "Scratch one flat-top"). A total of 69 American naval aircraft were lost during the battle while the Japanese losses amounted to about 85 as well as about 400 naval airmen (many of whom went down with the *Shoho*). The Japanese carrier *Shokaku* was also damaged severely, but was able to limp home for repairs. The loss of experienced airmen and the absence of the *Shokaku* critically weakened Japanese naval forces when involved in the vital Battle of Midway, fought between 4th and 7th June 1942.

The first operational American naval aircraft to feature hydraulically-operated folding wings was the Douglas TBD Devastator, which was also the U.S. Navy's first carrier-based monoplane torpedo-bomber to enter production. First flight of the prototype was made on 15th April 1935, but it was not until 5th October 1937 that the first production TBD-1s were delivered to Squadron VT-3. It is perhaps interesting to record that of the total number of seventy-five Devastators on strength with the U.S. Navy on 4th June 1942—the day of the Battle of Midway—thirty-seven were lost during the course of this battle, Squadron VT-8 being destroyed in its entirety and another squadron decimated in combat with Japanese Zero fighters.

Three great U.S. airliners:
This Ford Tri-Motor of late-1920s vintage was
still carrying passengers on scheduled services
forty years after it was built (Harry McDougall)

Best-loved airliner of all time, the Douglas
DC-3 (Dakota) was the workhorse of the
Allied air forces in the Second World War
and the aircraft used to rebuild the airlines
of the world when peace returned in 1945

With the wings, tail-unit, and engines of the
wartime B-29 Superfortress bomber fitted to a
double-deck fuselage, the Boeing Stratocruiser
brought new standards of luxury to the post-
war air routes. Transatlantic passengers
could walk down a spiral stairway to a below-
deck lounge, for a drink and a quiet chat

Grumman F7F Tigercat

The first operational carrier-based fighter in the world with a tricycle undercarriage was the Grumman F7F-1 Tigercat. The first of two XF7F-1 prototypes made its first flight in December 1943, but production aircraft entered squadrons too late to see operational service in the Second World War. Powered by two 2,100 hp Pratt & Whitney R-2800-34W engines, the Tigercat had a top speed of 435 mile/h at 22,200 ft (700 km/h at 6,766 m), and was armed with four 20 mm and four 0·50 in guns. It could carry up to 1,000 lb (454 kg) of bombs under each wing, or a torpedo under the fuselage. A two-seat night-fighter variant (the F7F-2N) was also produced.

The first British twin-engined aircraft to land on the deck of an aircraft carrier, on 25th March 1944, was the pre-prototype of the de Havilland Sea Mosquito (*LR359*). Production Sea Mosquito *TR33s* first entered service with No. 811 Squadron at Ford, Sussex, in August 1946.

The Short Shetland

The largest military flying-boat built by Great Britain was the Short Shetland, of which only two prototypes were built. The first, designated Shetland I (*DX166*), flew for the first time on 14th December 1944, flown by John Parker with Geoffrey Tyson as co-pilot. Designed for long-range maritime reconnaissance, both Shetland prototypes were powered by 2,500 hp Bristol Centaurus engines, and their wing span was 150 ft 4 in (45·82 m). The Shetland I had a maximum take-off weight of 125,000 lb (56,700 kg) and attained a maximum level speed of 263 mile/h (423 km/h). On 28th January 1946 it was destroyed by fire at its moorings. With the end of the war in sight it was decided to complete the second prototype as a civil transport, and this was given the designation Shetland II. It was allocated the last constructor's number issued by Shorts at Rochester, S.1313, and had the civil registration G-AGVD. It flew for the first time on 17th September 1947 and completed its preliminary trials, but lack of interest in flying-boats after the end of the Second World War meant that it was not used in a transport role.

The first aviation unit specifically formed for suicide operations was the *Shimpu* Special Attack Corps, a group of twenty-four volunteer pilots commanded by Lieutenant Yukio Seki, formed within the 201st (Fighter) Air Group, Imperial Japanese Navy, during the third week of October 1944. The unit, equipped with Mitsubishi A6M Zero-Sen single-seat fighters, was formed for the task of diving into the flight decks of American aircraft carriers in the Philippines area, with 550 lb (250 kg) bombs beneath the fuselages of the fighters. (*Shimpu* is an alternative pronunciation of the Japanese ideographs which also represent *kamikaze*, "Divine Wind", the name more generally applied to Japanese suicide operations.) **The first successful suicide attack was carried out** by Lieutenant Seki on 25th October 1944; flying from Mabalacat, he and another pilot crashed into the American escort carrier *St. Lo*, which sank as a result of the damage inflicted.

The first successful use of a purpose-built suicide aircraft is thought to have taken place on 1st April 1945, when three *Ohka* ("Cherry Blossom") piloted rocket-powered bombs of the 721st Air Group, Imperial Japanese Navy, were released over an American naval force near Okinawa (approximate position 26° 15′ N, 127° 43′ E). Damage was inflicted on the battleship U.S.S. *West Virginia*, the attack cargo-ships *Achernar* and *Tyrell*, and the attack transport *Alpine*. **The first ship to be sunk by a purpose-built suicide aircraft** was the destroyer *Mannert L. Abele*, on 12th April 1945, near Okinawa (approximate position 27° 25′ N, 126° 59′ E).

Ohka suicide aircraft, nicknamed Baka *(Fool) by Allies. The first successful use of this weapon was on 1st April 1945 (Imperial War Museum)*

The last sortie by suicide aircraft, according to Japanese accounts, was flown on 15th August 1945 by seven aircraft of the Oita Detachment, 701st Air Group, Imperial Japanese Navy, led in person by Admiral Matome Ugaki, commander of the 5th Air Fleet. United States records fail to confirm any *kamikaze* attacks on this date however.

The total number of suicide aircraft expended, and the results of these attacks, are believed to be as follows:

	Sorties	Aircraft returned	Expended
Philippines area	421	43	378
Formosa area	27	14	13
Okinawa area	1,809	879	930
Total	2,257	936	1,321

It has not proved possible to distinguish between actual suicide aircraft and escort fighters in the Okinawa operations and this must necessarily invalidate the total figures to some extent. A rough estimate would show that the usual ratio of escort fighters to suicide aircraft on most sorties was about three to two, although late in the campaign many sorties were flown entirely without escort.

The total number of American naval vessels sunk by suicide attacks from the air was 34, and 288 damaged. Those which were sunk comprised 3 escort aircraft carriers, 13 destroyers, 1 destroyer escort, 2 high-speed minelayers, 1 submarine chaser, 1 minesweeper, 5 tank-landing ships, 1 ocean tug, 1 auxiliary vessel, 1 patrol craft, 2 motor torpedo-boats and 3 other vessels.

AFTER THE SECOND WORLD WAR

The first twin-engined single-seat fighter to operate from aircraft carriers of the Royal Navy was the de Havilland Sea Hornet F.20, which equipped No. 801 Squadron when it was re-formed at Ford, Sussex, on 1st June 1947. The prototype (*PX212*) made its first flight on 19th April 1945. Production aircraft were powered by two 2,030 hp Rolls-Royce Merlin 133s or 134s, and had a maximum speed of 467 mile/h (742 km/h) at 22,000 ft (6,700 m).

The Ryan Fireball

The first American aeroplane to land under jet power on a ship was a Ryan FR-1 Fireball compound fighter, powered by a conventionally mounted Wright R-1820-72W radial piston-engine, as well as by a General Electric I-16 turbojet installed in the rear fuselage. This combination had resulted from the U.S. Navy's doubts of the suitability of jet-powered aircraft for carrier operations. Flown by Ensign Jake C. West on to the escort carrier U.S.S.

Wake Island on 6th November 1945, it had been intended to fly on using the reciprocating engine, but this failed on the approach and West landed under jet power.

The world's first pure jet aircraft to operate from an aircraft carrier was a de Havilland Vampire I, the third prototype of which (*LZ551*) had been modified for deck-landing trials. It was first flown off H.M.S. *Ocean*, a light fleet carrier of the Colossus Class, by Lieutenant-Commander E. M. Brown, R.N.V.R., on 3rd December 1945. The first deck landing was followed by trials in which fifteen take-offs and landings were made in two days. For the purpose of these trials the aircraft was designated the "Sea Vampire Mk. 10" (not to be confused with the Vampire N.F. Mk. 10 two-seat night fighter).

The first American pure jet aeroplane to operate from a carrier was the McDonnell FH-1 Phantom, the prototype of which (the *XFD-1*) landed for the first time on board the carrier U.S.S. *Franklin D. Roosevelt* on 21st July 1946. The FH-1 Phantom subsequently became the first jet fighter in operation with the U.S. Marine Corps.

The first post-war world long distance record for aeroplanes was set up by a modified Lockheed P2V-1 Neptune maritime reconnaissance aircraft, the *Truculent Turtle*, which flew a distance of 11,236 miles (18,083 km) in September 1946.

The last operational fighter aircraft of the U.S. Navy to use 0·50 in (50 calibre) machine-guns as standard was the North American FJ-1 Fury naval jet fighter which first flew on 27th November 1946. Although only thirty-three of these aircraft were built, the FJ-1 was the progenitor of the F-86 Sabre, one of the world's most successful jet fighters of the 1950s.

The greatest utilitarian range of duties ever applied to a *bona fide* **combat aeroplane** was probably that applied to the Douglas Skyraider. Developed to meet a specification for a carrier-based dive-bomber and torpedo-carrier, it was

The Douglas Skyraider (U.S. Navy)

the first single-seat aircraft in this category. In addition to these basic roles, variants were produced for night attack, airborne early warning, reconnaissance, electronic counter-measures, target-towing, drone control, specialist anti-submarine attack, submarine search, freighter, twelve-seat transport and ambulance. The *XBT2D-1* prototype made its first flight on 18th March 1945, deliveries to the U.S. Navy began in December 1946, and the last was withdrawn in April 1968. Powered by a 2,700 hp Wright R-3350-26W radial engine, the AD-2 Skyraider could carry up to 8,000 lb (3,628 kg) of mixed ordnance on its under-wing or under-fuselage strong points.

The first pure jet fighter to serve with the U.S. Navy and the U.S. Marine Corps was the McDonnell FH-1 Phantom which commenced delivery to VF-17A (U.S. Navy Fighter Squadron Seventeen) in July 1947.

The first British naval aircraft in regular service with power-folding wings, and also the last piston-engined fighter in F.A.A. first-line squadrons, was the Hawker Sea Fury. First flown on 21st February 1945, the type entered service with No. 807 Squadron in August 1947. Operating with distinction throughout the Korean War, the Sea Fury flown by Lieutenant P. Carmichael of No. 802 Squadron destroyed the squadron's first MiG-15 on 9th August 1952.

The largest flying-boat in the world, the largest aeroplane ever flown, and the aircraft with the greatest wing span ever built, was the Hughes H.2 *Hercules.* The 180 ton flying-boat was powered by eight 3,000 hp Pratt & Whitney R-4360 piston-engines, had a wing span of 320 ft (97·54 m), and an overall length of 219 ft (66·75 m). Designed to accommodate up to 700 passengers, it was intended primarily as a freighter and no cabin windows were provided. Piloted by its sponsor, the American millionaire Howard Hughes, it flew on only one occasion, covering a distance of about a mile over Los Angeles Harbor, California, on 2nd November 1947.

Saunders-Roe SR.A/1

The first flying-boat in the world capable of a maximum level speed of over 500 mile/h (805 km/h) was the Saunders-Roe SR.A/1 jet fighter flying-boat of Great Britain which first flew on 16th July 1947. Powered by two Metrovick Beryl axial-flow turbojets, the SR.A/1 had a top speed of 512 mile/h (824 km/h) and an armament of four 20 mm guns. Three prototypes were built, but the project was abandoned when flight tests made it clear that the large flying-boat hull compromised both speed and manoeuvrability.

FJ-1 Fury

The first U.S. Navy jet fighter squadron to go to sea under operational conditions was VF-5A (U.S. Navy Fighter Squadron Five), equipped with North American FJ-1 Fury fighters, on board U.S.S. *Boxer*, on which the aircraft were first landed on 10th March 1948.

The Royal Navy's first all-helicopter squadron was No. 705, formed at Gosport in 1950. Equipped with the Westland Dragonfly, the British-built version of the Sikorsky S-51, it quickly demonstrated its value for "plane-guard" duties and ship-to-shore communications.

The first U.S. Navy jet fighter to take part in air combat was the Grumman F9F-2 Panther, several of which took off from the carrier U.S.S. *Valley Forge* off Korea on 3rd July 1950 and went into action against North Korean forces. A U.S. Navy pilot of a Grumman Panther shot down a MiG-15 on 9th November 1950 and thus became **the first U.S. Navy jet pilot to shoot down another jet aircraft.** The Panther was the first jet fighter designed by the Grumman Corporation, and the first two XF9F-2 prototypes were powered by imported Rolls-Royce Nene turbojets of 5,000 lb (2,268 kg) thrust.

The first standardised jet fighter to serve in F.A.A. first-line squadrons was the Supermarine Attacker, and was also the first aircraft powered by the Rolls-Royce Nene turbojet. The type first entered service with No. 800 Squadron at Ford, Sussex, on 22nd August 1951, and this was the F.A.A.'s first operational jet squadron.

Douglas F3D-2 Skyknight (Gordon S. Williams)

The first jet aircraft in the world to destroy another jet aircraft at night was a U.S. Marine Douglas F3D-2 Skyknight all-weather fighter, which destroyed a night-flying MiG-15 over Korea on 2nd November 1952.

The first American naval pilot to achieve five air victories over Korea was Lieutenant Guy Bordelon who, flying a piston-engined Vought F4U Corsair, shot down his fifth victim on 17th July 1953.

Grumman F11F-1 Tigers

The first supersonic operational carrier-borne naval interceptor in the world was the Grumman F11F-1 Tiger of the U.S. Navy. Designated originally F9F-9, this was changed after the first three production aircraft had been delivered and, in 1962, was finally designated F-11. The prototype, powered by a Wright J65-W-6 turbojet rated at 7,800 lb (3,538 kg) thrust, flew for the first time on 30th July 1954. The F-11A was capable of a speed of 890 mile/h (1,432 km/h) in level flight at 40,000 ft (12,190 m), and was armed with four 20 mm cannon. Two or four Sidewinder missiles could be carried on under-wing pylons. F11F-1s entered service with the U.S. Navy's VA-156 Squadron in March 1957. Two F11F-1Fs were powered by 15,000 lb (6,805 kg) thrust J79-GE-3A engines, and demonstrated Mach 2 performance in level flight.

The first turbojet-powered all-weather fighter to serve with the Royal Navy was the de Havilland Sea Venom, which equipped No. 890 Squadron at Yeovilton, Somerset, in March 1954. At the end of 1958 three Sea Venoms of No. 893 Squadron carried out the first firings of Firestreak missiles by an operational fighter squadron of the Royal Navy.

The first variable-incidence jet fighter in the world was the Chance Vought (LTV, or Ling-Temco-Vought) F-8 Crusader supersonic air-superiority fighter of the U.S. Navy. The object of the variable-incidence wing was to reduce the aircraft's nose-up attitude during landing, while setting the wing in an optimum lift position. The first of two XF8U-1 prototypes, powered by a Pratt & Whitney J57-P-11 turbojet engine, made its first flight on 25th March 1955. Deliveries of the production Crusader, under the designation F-8A, began to VF-32 (U.S. Navy Fighter Squadron Thirty-two) on 25th March 1957. This initial production version was powered by a J57-P-12 or 4A engine, providing a maximum level speed of 1,100 mile/h (1,770 km/h) at 40,000 ft (12,200 m). Armament comprised four 20 mm cannon and, on early models, a fuselage pack of thirty-two air-to-air rockets. Later F-8As carried two fuselage-mounted Sidewinder missiles.

The heaviest aeroplane ever to serve as standardised equipment on board aircraft carriers was the Douglas A3D Skywarrior carrier-based attack-bomber. The first of two XA3D-1 prototypes first flew on 28th October 1952, and initial

production A3D-1s (later A-3A) were first delivered to VAH-1 (U.S.
Navy Heavy Attack Squadron One) on 31st March 1956. The definitive
production version, ultimately designated A-3B, served on board carriers
of the Essex and Midway classes. This latter version had a span of 72 ft
6 in (22·10 m) and a maximum loaded weight of 82,000 lb (37,195 kg).
Powered by two 12,400 lb (5,624 kg) thrust Pratt & Whitney J57-P-10
turbojets, the A-3B Skywarrior had a maximum level speed of 610 mile/h
(982 km/h) at 10,000 ft (3,050 m).

Douglas A3D Skywarrior (Brian M. Service)

The first swept-wing two-seat all-weather fighter to serve with the Royal Navy was the de
Havilland Sea Vixen. The first operational squadron equipped with the
type was No. 892, which commissioned at Yeovilton, Somerset, on 2nd
July 1959. It was also the first British naval aircraft designed as an integrated weapons system, and the first to become fully operational armed
with guided missiles.

The fastest strategic reconnaissance/attack aircraft to serve with the U.S. Navy was the North
American A-5/RA-5C Vigilante. The first flight of the prototype was
made on 31st August 1958. First operational unit to receive production
A-5As, in June 1961, was VAH-7 (U.S. Navy Heavy Attack Squadron
Seven) which took them on board the U.S.S. *Enterprise* in August 1962. The
Vigilante was the first production aircraft to feature variable-geometry air
intakes for its two turbojet engines, and also had a unique linear bomb-bay
located between the tail-pipes of the engines, to allow a free-falling
nuclear weapon to be ejected rearwards. It was intended that a proportion
of the aircraft's fuel-load should be carried in two tanks attached to this
weapon. Consumed before the target was reached, the tanks would then
serve as aerodynamic stabilisers for the weapon. The RA-5C strategic
reconnaissance version had an impressive performance for, powered by
two afterburning General Electric J79-GE-8 turbojets, it had a maximum
speed of Mach 2·1, a range of 3,000 miles (4,820 km) and a service ceiling
of 64,000 ft (19,500 m). It was the second largest aircraft to be accepted for
operational service on board an aircraft carrier, with a gross weight of
61,730 lb (28,000 kg).

The last biplanes in U.S. military or naval service were a small number of NAF N3N-3 primary seaplane trainers of the U.S. Navy, which were retired from service in 1961. The N3N-3 was the last original design of the Naval Aircraft Factory (N.A.F.), the U.S. Navy's first permanent manufacturing and test facility, which was established in 1917 at Philadelphia Navy Yard, Pennsylvania.

The first swept-wing single-seat fighters to be built for the Royal Navy, and the first to be capable of low-level attack at supersonic speed was the Supermarine Scimitar. The first operational squadron, No. 803, was formed at Lossiemouth, Scotland, in June 1958. The Scimitar was also the first British naval aircraft to have a power-operated control system.

The first specially designed anti-submarine helicopter ordered for the Royal Navy was the Westland Wessex, developed from the Sikorsky S-58. Equipped with an automatic pilot, the Wessex could be operated by day or night in all weathers. First first-line squadron to be equipped with the type was No. 815, commissioned at Culdrose on 4th July 1961.

The world's first specially designed low-level strike aircraft was the Blackburn N.A.39, subsequently named Buccaneer. The S.1, powered by de Havilland Gyron Junior turbojets, first entered operational service with the F.A.A.'s No. 801 Squadron at Lossiemouth in July 1962. The developed S.2 version, with more powerful Rolls-Royce Spey turbojets, also entered service with No. 801 Squadron, on 14th October 1965. Prior to that, on 4th October 1965, the first production aircraft (*XN974*) became the first F.A.A. aircraft to make a non-stop crossing of the North Atlantic without flight refuelling. The 1,950 miles (3,138 km) from Goose Bay, Labrador, to R.N.A.S. Lossiemouth were flown in 4 h 16 min.

North American RA-5C Vigilante (Stephen P. Peltz)

FIRST FLIGHT DATES OF THE WORLD'S PRINCIPAL MARITIME AEROPLANES

1918
Supermarine N.1B Baby flying-boat (U.K.)   .   .   February
Navy/Curtiss NC-1 flying-boat (U.S.)   .   .   .   4th October

1926
Blackburn Iris flying-boat (U.K.)   .   .   .   .   June
Short Singapore flying-boat (U.K.)   .   .   .   .   17th August
Boeing Model 69 fighter (U.S.)   .   .   .   .   3rd November

1928
Boeing F4B-1 fighter (U.S.)   .   .   .   .   .   25th June

Short Singapore   *Boeing F4B-1*

1930
Short Rangoon flying-boat (U.K.)   .   .   .   . 24th September

1932
Short Sarafand flying-boat (U.K.)   .   .   .   .   30th June

1933
Grumman XJF-1 Duck (U.S.) .   .   .   .   .   4th May
Grumman XF2F-1 fighter (U.S.)   .   .   .   .   18th October
Supermarine Seagull V/Walrus (U.K.)   .   .   .   21st June

1934
Mitsubishi G3M (*Nell*) bomber (Japan)   .   .   .   April

1935
Mitsubishi A5M (*Claude*) fighter (Japan)   .   .   .   4th February
Consolidated PBY Catalina flying-boat (U.S.)   .   .   28th March
Douglas XTBD-1 Devastator (U.S.) .   .   .   .   15th April
NAF XN3N-3 naval trainer (U.S.)   .   .   .   .   August

1936
Vought XSB2U-1 Vindicator/Chesapeake (U.S.)   .   1st January

1937
Nakajima B5N (*Kate*) bomber (Japan)   .   .   .   January
Grumman XF4F-2 Wildcat fighter (U.S.) .   .   . 2nd September
Short Sunderland flying-boat (U.K.)   .   .   .   16th October
Brewster XF2A-1 Buffalo fighter (U.S.)   .   .   .   December

Grumman XF2F-1

Douglas TBD-1 Devastator

1938

Aichi D3A (*Val*) bomber (Japan)	January
Vought XOS2U-1 Kingfisher (U.S.)	20th July
Supermarine Sea Otter amphibian (U.K.) . . .	August
Fairey Albacore torpedo-bomber (U.K.) . . .	12th December
Blackburn Roc fighter (U.K.)	23rd December

1939

Martin XPBM-1 Mariner flying-boat (U.S.) . .	18th February
Mitsubishi A6M Zero-Sen fighter (Japan) . . .	1st April
Mitsubishi G4M (*Betty*) bomber (Japan) . . .	22nd October

1940

Fairey Fulmar fighter (U.K.)	4th January
Curtiss XSB2C-1 Helldiver (U.S.) . . .	12th December
Yokosuka D4Y dive-bomber (Japan) . . .	December

1941

Brewster XSB2A-1 Buccaneer (U.S.) . . .	17th June
Lockheed PV Ventura bomber (U.S.) . . .	31st July
Grumman Avenger torpedo-bomber (U.S.) . .	1st August
Fairey Firefly fighter (U.K.)	22nd December

1942

Blackburn Firebrand fighter (U.K.) . . .	27th February
Mitsubishi J2M (*Jack*) fighter (Japan) . .	20th March
Grumman XF6F Hellcat fighter (U.S.) . .	26th June
Kawanishi N1K1-J (*George*) seaplane fighter (Japan) .	27th December

Grumman F4F Wildcat

Short Sunderland

Brewster XSB2A-1 Buccaneer

Fairey Firefly prototype

1943
Grumman F7F Tigercat fighter (U.S.) .   .   .   December

1944
Curtiss XSC-1 Seahawk (U.S.)   .   .   .   16th February
Grumman XF8F-1 Bearcat fighter (U.S.) .   .   .   21st August
Martin XBTM-1 Mauler (U.S.)   .   .   .   26th August
Hawker Fury/Sea Fury fighter (U.K.)   .   .   .   1st September
Yokosuka MXY7 Ohka suicide aircraft (Japan) .   .   October
Short Shetland flying-boat (U.K.)   .   .   .   14th December

Hawker Sea Fury

McDonnell XFD-1 Phantom

1945
McDonnell XFD-1 Phantom fighter (U.S.)   .   .   26th January
Douglas XBT2D-1 Skyraider (U.S.) .   .   .   .   18th March
de Havilland Sea Hornet fighter (U.K.)   .   .   .   19th April
Short Seaford flying-boat (U.K.)   .   .   .   .   April
Lockheed Neptune patrol bomber (U.S.) .   .   .   17th May
Grumman XTB3F-1 Guardian (U.S.)   .   .   .   19th December

1946
Supermarine Attacker fighter (U.K.)   .   .   .   27th July
North American FJ-1 Fury fighter (U.S.)   .   .   .   27th December

1947
McDonnell Banshee fighter (U.S.)   .   .   .   .   11th January
Saunders-Roe SR.A/1 flying-boat fighter (U.K.) .   .   16th July
Hawker P.1040 (Sea Hawk) fighter (U.K.)   .   .   2nd September
Grumman Panther fighter (U.S.)   .   .   .   .   24th November
Grumman Albatross amphibian (U.S.)   .   .   .   24th October

1948
Douglas Skyknight fighter (U.S.)   .   .   .   .   23rd March
Martin Marlin flying-boat (U.S.)   .   .   .   .   30th May
Vought Cutlass fighter (U.S.) .   .   .   .   . 29th September

Grumman XTB3F-1 Guardian (Harold G. Martin)

Martin XP5M-1 Marlin

1949
North American T-28 Trojan trainer (U.S.)   .   . 26th September

1951
Douglas Skyray fighter (U.S.) .   .   .   .   . 23rd January
McDonnell Demon fighter (U.S.)   .   .   .   . 7th August
Grumman Cougar fighter (U.S.)   .   .   . 20th September
de Havilland Sea Vixen (D.H.110) fighter (U.K.)   . 26th September
North American FJ-2 fighter (U.S.) .   .   .   . 27th December

1952
Douglas XA3D-1 Skywarrior attack aircraft (U.S.)   . 28th October
Grumman XS2F-1 Tracker anti-submarine
     aircraft (U.S.)   .   .   .   .   .   . 4th December

Douglas XF4D-1 Skyray

Grumman XS2F-1 Tracker (Harold G. Martin)

1954
Douglas A-4 Skyhawk fighter (U.S.) .   .   .   . 22nd June
Grumman Tiger fighter (U.S.) .   .   .   .   . 30th July
North American FJ-4 Fury fighter (U.S.) .   .   . 28th October

1955
Chance Vought (LTV) F8U Crusader fighter (U.S.) .   25th March

1956
Supermarine Scimitar fighter (U.K.)   .   .   . 20th January
Breguet Alizé anti-submarine aircraft (France) .   . 6th October

1957
Canadair Argus maritime patrol aircraft (Canada)   29th March

Douglas A4D-1 (A-4) Skyhawk   *Breguet 1050 Alizé*

1958
North American Buckeye trainer (U.S.)   .   .   7th February
Hawker Siddeley Buccaneer strike aircraft (U.K.)   .   30th April
Dassault Etendard IV-M fighter (France)   .   21st May
McDonnell F4H Phantom II fighter (U.S.)   .   27th May
Lockheed P-3 Orion maritime patrol aircraft (U.S.)   .   19th August
North American A-5 Vigilante bomber (U.S.)   .   31st August

1960
Grumman Intruder attack aircraft (U.S.)   .   .   19th April
Grumman Hawkeye early-warning aircraft (U.S.)   .   21st October

1961
Breguet Atlantic maritime patrol aircraft (France)   .   21st October

1964
Grumman C-2A Greyhound transport (U.S.)   .   . 18th November

1965
LTV A-7A Corsair II attack aircraft (U.S.)   .   . 27th September

1967
Hawker Siddeley Nimrod maritime patrol aircraft (U.K.)   23rd May
Shin Meiwa PS-1 flying-boat (Japan)   .   .   5th October

1969
Sepecat Jaguar M fighter (U.K./France)   .   .   . 14th November

1970
Grumman F-14 Tomcat fighter (U.S.)   .   .   21st December

1972
Lockheed S-3A Viking anti-submarine aircraft (U.S.) .   21st January

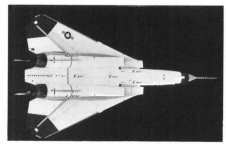

McDonnell F4H-1 Phantom II   *Grumman F-14A Tomcat*

Boeing 747 "Jumbo Jet"

SECTION IV
Route-proving and Commercial Aviation

The first passenger services by air were operated between cities in Germany by five Zeppelin airships in the years 1910–14. More than 35,000 people were carried without injury.

The first recorded carriage of freight by air was a box of Osram lamps carried on 4th July 1911 by a Valkyrie monoplane flown by Horatio Barber from Shoreham to Hove in Sussex, England, on behalf of the General Electric Company who paid £100 ($240) for the flight.

The first official air mail (India, 18th February 1911) and first air mail in Great Britain (9th September 1911): see "Pioneers of the Air"

The first coast-to-coast flight across America was made by Calbraith P. Rodgers between 17th September and 5th November 1911. Rodgers, trying to win a $50,000 prize offered by William Randolph Hearst, flew from New York to Pasadena in a Wright biplane. Making a series of short flights, he arrived at the destination nineteen days outside the specified thirty-day limit and so failed to qualify for the prize.

The first official carriage of mail by air in the U.S.A. was carried by Earl L. Ovington on 23rd September 1911 in a Blériot monoplane from Nassau Boulevard, N.Y., to Mineola, L.I., a distance of 6 miles.

The first air crossing of the Mediterranean was achieved on 23rd September 1913 by a Morane-Saulnier monoplane flown by Roland Garros, who flew 453 miles (700 km) from Saint-Raphaël, France, to Bizerte, Tunisia, in 7 h 53 min.

The first flight from France to Egypt was accomplished by Jules Védrines in a Blériot powered by an 80 hp Gnôme engine, between 29th November and 29th December 1913. Setting out from Nancy, France, his route was via Würzburg, Prague, Vienna, Belgrade, Sofia, Constantinople, Tripoli (Syria), Jaffa and Cairo.

The first scheduled airline using aeroplanes was the Benoist Company airline which started its operations in January 1914, flying between St. Petersburg and Tampa, Florida. The aircraft was a Benoist flying-boat piloted by A. Jannus. The operation lasted four months.

The first passenger to be carried from one city to another in Canada by air was flown in the Curtiss flying-boat *Sunfish* from Toronto to Hamilton and back by Theodore Macaulay on 15th May 1914.

The first flight across the North Sea by an aeroplane was achieved by the Norwegian pilot Tryggve Gran flying a Blériot monoplane on 30th July 1914.

The first British airline company to be registered was Aircraft Transport and Travel Ltd. It was registered in London on 5th October 1916 by George Holt Thomas.

The first scheduled regular international air-mail service in the world was inaugurated between Vienna and Kiev, via Kraków, Lvóv and Proskurov on 11th March 1918. The service was principally for military mails and was operated with Hansa-Brandenburg C I biplanes, continuing until November 1918.

The first air crossing of the Andes was achieved by the Argentine army pilot Teniente Luis C. Candelaria flying a Morane-Saulnier parasol monoplane on 13th April 1918 from Zapala, Argentina, to Cunco, Chile, a distance of approximately 200 km (124 miles). The maximum altitude achieved was about 4,000 m (13,000 ft). Candelaria had attended the fifth military flying course at El Palomar which commenced in September 1916.

Curtiss JN-4D "Jenny"
(Peter M. Bowers)

The first experimental air-mail service in the U.S.A. was flown by War Department Curtiss JN-4 aircraft on 15th May 1918 between Washington, D.C., Philadelphia, Pa., and New York City. Lieutenant Torrey H. Webb was the first pilot.

The first official air-mail flight in Canada was flown on 24th June 1918 in a Curtiss JN-4 from Montreal to Toronto by Captain Brian A. Peck, R.A.F., accompanied by Corporal Mathers.

The first regular air-mail service in the U.S.A. was established on 12th August 1918 by the U.S. Post Office Department between New York City and Washington, D.C. Edward V. Gardner, Max Miller, Maurice Newton and Robert F. Shank were the pilots.

The first West–East crossing of the Andes was reputedly achieved by the Chilean Army pilot Teniente Dn. Dagoberto Godoy of the Chilean Military School of Aviation who flew a Bristol M.1C monoplane fighter from Santiago de Chile to Mendoza in Argentina on 12th December 1918. (For the first-ever crossing of the Andes, see above. There is no record of the Argentinian pilot returning by air, and it is therefore assumed that Teniente Godoy's flight was the first eastward crossing.)

Handley Page o/400 after arrival in India, 1918

The first flight from Egypt to India was made by Captain Ross M. Smith, D.F.C., A.F.C., Major-General W. G. H. Salmond, D.S.O., Brigadier-General A. E. Borton, and two mechanics between 29th November and 12th December 1918, in a Handley Page o/400 from Heliopolis to Karachi via Damascus, Baghdad, Bushire, Bandar Abbas and Chabar. The same aircraft had made **the first flight from England to Egypt** between 28th July and 8th August 1918.

The first sustained commercial daily passenger service was by Deutsche Luft-Reederei, which operated between Berlin and Weimar, Germany, from 5th February 1919.

The first American international air mail was inaugurated between Seattle, Wash., and Victoria, British Columbia, Canada, by the Hubbard Air Service on 3rd March 1919 using a Boeing Type C aircraft. .The service was regularised by contract on 14th October 1920.

Loading mail on the Boeing Type C, 3rd March 1919

The first British aeroplane to carry civil markings (*K-100*) was a de Havilland D.H.6 in 1919. It was sold to the Marconi Wireless Telegraph Co. Ltd., and used for radio trials; it became the second aircraft entered on the British Civil Register (as *G-EAAB*; see below).

The first British civil aeroplane (i.e. the first on the British Civil Register proper) was a de Havilland D.H.9 (*G-EAAA*, previously *C6054*), operated as a mailplane by Aircraft Transport and Travel Ltd., in mid 1919 between London and Paris.

The first British Certificate of Airworthiness was issued on 1st May 1919 to the Handley Page 0/400 (*F5414*) which thereafter became registered as *G-EAAF*, owned by Handley Page Air Transport Ltd.

The Curtiss NC-4

The first Transatlantic crossing by air was achieved by the American Navy/Curtiss NC-4 flying-boat commanded by Lieutenant-Commander A. C. Read between 8th

May and 31st May 1919. Three flying-boats, the *NC-1*, *NC-3* and *NC-4*, under the command of Commander John H. Towers, set out from Rockaway, N.Y., on 8th May, but only *NC-4* completed the crossing, arriving at Plymouth, England, on 31st May, having landed at Chatham, Mass.; Halifax, Nova Scotia; Trepassy Bay, Newfoundland; Horta, Azores; Ponta Delgada, Azores; Lisbon, Portugal; Ferrol del Caudillo, Spain. Total distance flown was 3,925 miles (6,315 km) in 57 flying h, 16 mins, at a speed of 68·4 knots. Both *NC-1* and *NC-3* were forced down on the sea short of the Azores, and *NC-1* sank—its crew being rescued. *NC-3*, with Commander Towers aboard, taxied the remaining 200 miles to the Azores. The crew of the three *NC* boats were:

NC-1: Lieutenant-Commander P. N. L. Bellinger, Commander
Lieutenant-Commander M. A. Mitscher, pilot
Lieutenant L. T. Barin, pilot
Lieutenant Harry Sadenwater, radio operator
Chief Machinist's Mate C. I. Kesler, engineer

NC-3: Commander John H. Towers, Flight Commander
Commander H. C. Richardson, pilot
Lieutenant David H. McCullough, pilot
Lieutenant-Commander R. A. Lavender, radio operator
Machinist L. R. Moore, engineer

NC-4: Lieutenant-Commander A. C. Read, Commander
Lieutenant E. F. Stone, pilot
Lieutenant Walter Hinton, pilot
Ensign H. C. Rodd, radio operator
Lieutenant James W. Breese
Chief Machinist's Mate E. S. Rhoades, engineer

Vimy taking off from Newfoundland, 14th June 1919

The first non-stop air crossing of the Atlantic was achieved on 14th–15th June 1919 by Captain John Alcock and Lieutenant Arthur Whitten Brown who flew in a Vickers Vimy bomber from St. John's, Newfoundland, to Clifden, County Galway, Ireland. Powered by two Rolls-Royce engines, the Vimy was fitted with long-range fuel tanks and achieved a coast-to-coast time of 15 h. 57 min. Total flying time was 16 h 27 min. Both Alcock and Brown were knighted in recognition of this achievement; Sir John Alcock, as Chief Test Pilot of Vickers, was killed on 18th December 1919 in a flying accident in bad weather near Rouen, France.

The first airport at which Customs clearance could be obtained for outward-bound flights from London was Hounslow, Middlesex. It was also the only such aerodrome in operation from July 1919 until March 1920.

The first flight across the Canadian Rocky Mountains was made on 7th August 1919 by a Curtiss "Jenny" flown by Captain Ernest C. Hoy who flew from Vancouver to Calgary via Lethbridge in 16 h 42 min. This was also **the first air-mail flight across the Rockies.**

The first scheduled daily international commercial airline flight anywhere in the world was flown from London to Paris on 25th August 1919 when a de Havilland D.H.16, flown by Cyril Patteson of Aircraft Transport and Travel Ltd., took off from Hounslow with four passengers, and landed at Le Bourget, Paris, 2·5 h later. The fare was £21 for the one-way crossing.

D.H.9 of Aircraft Transport and Travel, under charter to K.L.M.

The first Dutch national airline, K.L.M. (Royal Dutch Airlines), was founded on 7th October 1919. It is the oldest airline in the world still operating under its original name.

The first American international scheduled passenger air service was inaugurated on 1st November 1919 by Aeromarine West Indies Airways between Key West, Florida, and Havana, Cuba. On 1st November 1920 the airline was awarded the first American foreign air-mail contract.

The first flight from Britain to Australia was completed between 12th November and 10th December 1919 by two Australian brothers, Captain Ross Smith and Lieutenant Keith Smith, with two other crew members, in a Vickers Vimy bomber powered by two Rolls-Royce Eagle engines. They set out from Hounslow, Middlesex, England, and flew to Darwin, Australia, a distance of 11,294 miles (18,175 km) in under twenty-eight days. Their feat earned them the Australian Government's prize of £10,000 ($24,000) and knighthoods. Sir Ross Smith was killed in a flying accident near Brooklands Aerodrome, England, on 13th April 1922. By tragic coincidence, both Sir Ross and Sir John Alcock (famous for his Atlantic crossing, see above) were killed in Vickers Viking amphibians.

The first flight from Britain to South Africa was made between 4th February and 20th March 1920 by Lieutenant-Colonel Pierre van Ryneveld and Squadron Leader Christopher Quintin Brand. They set out from Brooklands, England, in a Vickers Vimy bomber on the 4th February, but crashed at Wadi Halfa while attempting an emergency landing. The South African Government provided the pilots with another Vimy aircraft and after eleven days they set off again, only to crash at Bulawayo, Southern Rhodesia, on 6th March. Once again the Government provided an aircraft, a war-surplus D.H.9, and on 17th March they set off again. Finally, on 20th March, they reached Wynberg Aerodrome, Cape Town. They received subsequently £5,000 prize-money and were knighted by H.M. King George V.

Croydon Airport

The first regular use of Croydon as London's air terminal was on 29th March 1920. On that day the main airport facilities were moved from Hounslow (see above) to Croydon—or Waddon, as the airport was originally known. It was officially opened on 31st March 1921.

The first automatic pilot to be fitted in a British commercial aircraft was the Aveline Stabiliser fitted in a Handley Page 0/10 during 1920.

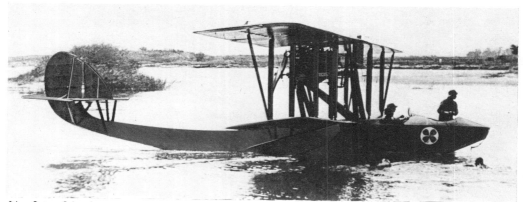

Lévy-Lepen flying-boat

The first regular air services in Equatorial Africa were flown from Kinshasa to N'Gombé, by the Belgian airline SNETA, on 1st July 1920 with a Lévy-Lepen flying-boat; the N'Gombé to Lisala route opened on 3rd March 1921, and the Kinshasa to Stanleyville route opened on 1st July 1921.

The first Australian commercial airline, QANTAS (Queensland and Northern Territory Aerial Service) was registered on 16th November 1920 for air taxi and regular air services in Australia. The Company's first Chairman was Sir Fergus McMaster (1879–1950), and its first scheduled service commenced on 2nd November 1922 with flights between Charleville and Cloncurry, Queensland.

The first fatal accident to a scheduled British commercial flight occurred on 14th December 1920 when a Handley Page 0/400 crashed soon after take-off in fog at Cricklewood, London. The pilot, R. Bager, his engineer and two passengers were killed, but four other passengers escaped.

The first regular scheduled air services in Australia were inaugurated by West Australian Airways on 5th December 1921.

D.H.4 of the U.S. Air Mail Service (Howard Levy)

The first Coast-to-Coast air mail in the United States of America left San Francisco at 04.30 h on 22nd February 1921 and arrived at Mineola, Long Island, New York, at 16.50 h the following day. It was carried from San Francisco to North Platte, Nebraska, by a succession of pilots. At North Platte it was taken over by a pilot named Jack Knight, flying an open-cockpit D.H.4. When he reached Omaha, the pilot scheduled to fly the next stage to Chicago had not put in an appearance. So he carried on through the night over unfamiliar country to Chicago himself, becoming a national hero for "saving the mail service".

The first air collision between airliners on scheduled flights occurred on 7th April 1922 between a Daimler Airways de Havilland D.H.18 (*G-EAWO*) flown by Robin Duke from Croydon, and a Farman Goliath of Grands Express Aériens flown by M. Mier from Le Bourget. The two aircraft, which were following a road on a reciprocal course, collided over Thieuloy-Saint-Antoine 18 miles north of Beauvais. All seven occupants were killed.

A D.H.18

Farman Goliaths at Le Bourget

The first Coast-to-Coast crossing of the United States in a single day was made by Lieutenant James H. Doolittle who flew a modified de Havilland D.H.4B from Pablo Beach, Florida, to Rockwell Field, San Diego, Calif., on 4th September 1922. Actual flying time to cover the 2,163 miles (3,480 km) was 21 h 19 min; elapsed time, with a refuelling stop at Kelly Field, Texas, was 22 h 35 min.

The first Czechoslovak-designed commercial aeroplane was the Aero A-10, whose construction commenced in 1921 at Prague. It was completed in 1922 and entered service with Československé Státni Aerolinie (C.S.A.), flying the Prague–Bratislava–Kosice–Uzhorod route in 1924. Powered by a single 260 hp Maybach Mb IIIa engine, the A-10 carried up to five passengers.

The first scheduled air service between London and Berlin was inaugurated by Daimler Airway on 10th April 1923, with intermediate landings at Bremen and Hamburg.

The first non-stop air crossing of the United States of America by an aeroplane was achieved on 2nd–3rd May 1923 by Lieutenant O. G. Kelly and Lieutenant J. A. Macready of the U.S. Air Service in a Fokker T-2 aeroplane. Taking off from Roosevelt Field, Long Island, at 12.36 h (Eastern Time) on 2nd May, they arrived at Rockwell Field, San Diego, Calif. at 12.26 h (Pacific Time) on 3rd May. They overflew Dayton, Ohio; Indianapolis, Ind.; St. Louis, Mo.; Kansas City, Mo.; Tucumcari, New Mexico; and Wickenburg, Ariz. The distance flown, 2,516 miles (4,050 km), was covered in 26 h 50 min. Kelly and Macready also established a new world's endurance record for aeroplanes on 16th–17th April 1923 in the Fokker T-2, by flying a distance of 2,518 miles (4,052 km) over a measured course in 36 h 5 min.

Macready and Kelly with their Fokker T-2

The first successful in-flight refuelling of an aeroplane was accomplished by Captain L. H. Smith and Lieutenant J. P. Richter in a de Havilland D.H.4B on 27th June 1923 at San Diego, California, U.S.A. Smith and Richter established a world's endurance record by remaining aloft for 37 h 15 min 43·8 s during 27th–28th August 1923, covering a distance of 3,293·26 miles (5,299·9 km) over a measured 50 km course at San Diego, California. Their D.H.4B was flight-refuelled fifteen times.

A duration record was set up at Tirlement, Belgium by Crooy and Groenen who kept the lower of these two D.H.9s airborne for 60 h 7 min 32 s by using the flight refuelling technique pioneered by Smith and Richter (Shell)

The first Czechoslovak national airline was Československé Státni Aerolinie (Č.S.A.) which began operations between Prague and Uzhorod on 28th October 1923.

The first British national airline, Imperial Airways, was formed on 1st April 1924. This was the manifestation of the British Government's determination to develop air transport, and the company was to receive preferential air subsidies, having acquired the businesses of the British Marine Air Navigation Co., Daimler Airway, Handley Page Transport and Instone Air Lines. Its fleet consisted of seven D.H.34s, two Sea Eagles, three H.P. W.8bs, and one Vickers Vimy.

The first recorded flight of a bull was that of the champion animal Nico V carried in a Fokker F.III of K.L.M. from Rotterdam, Holland, to Paris, France, on 9th July 1924. **The first recorded flight by a cow** was that by a Guernsey, Elm Farm Ollie, which was taken aloft over St. Louis, Missouri, on 18th February 1930 during a publicity stunt. She was milked in the air and her milk dispatched to the ground by parachute in sealed paper cartons.

The first successful round-the-world flight was accomplished by Douglas DWC (Douglas World Cruisers) between 6th April and 28th September 1924. Four such aeroplanes set out from Seattle, Washington, and two of these circumnavigated the world. The flagplane (named *Seattle*) only reached Alaska where it crashed on a mountain and the crew returned to the U.S.A.; another (the *Boston*) was forced to give up the flight near The Faeroes. The aircraft and crews were as follows:

Flagplane *Seattle*: Major Frederick Martin, flight commander and pilot
(Aircraft No. 1) Sergeant Alva L. Harvey, mechanic
Chicago: Lieutenant Lowell H. Smith, deputy flight commander
(Aircraft No. 2)   and pilot
Lieutenant Leslie P. Arnold, mechanic and alternate pilot
Boston: Lieutenant Leight Wade, pilot
(Aircraft No. 3) Staff Sergeant Henry H. Ogden, mechanic
New Orleans: Lieutenant Erik Nelson, pilot and engineer officer
(Aircraft No. 4) Lieutenant John Harding, Jr., mechanic and maintenance officer

Douglas World Cruiser

The route flown was as follows:

Seattle, Washington
Prince Rupert, British Columbia
Sitka, Alaska
Seward, Alaska
Chignic, Aleutian Peninsula
Dutch Harbour, Aleutians
Atka, Aleutians
Attu Island
Komandorski, Kamchatka
Paramashiru, Kuriles
Hittokapu, Yetorofu
Kasumiga Ura, Japan
Minato, Japan
Kushimoto, Japan
Kagoshima, Japan
Shanghai, China
Amoy, China
Hong Kong

Haiphong, Indo-China
Tourane, Indo-China
Saigon, Indo-China
Kawrong Island
Bangkok, Siam
Tavoy, Malaya
Rangoon, Burma
Akyab, Burma
Chittagong, India
Allahabad, India
Umballa, India
Multan, W. Pakistan
Karachi, Pakistan
Chabar, Persia
Bandar Abbas, Persia
Bushire, Persia
Baghdad, Mesopotamia
Aleppo, Turkey
Constantinople, Turkey
Bucharest, Romania

Budapest, Hungary
Vienna, Austria
Strasbourg, France
Paris, France
London, England
Brough, England
Kirkwall, Orkneys
Hornafjord, Iceland
Reykjavik, Iceland
Frederiksdal, Greenland
Ivigtut, Greenland
Indian Harbour, Labrador
Hawkes Bay, Newfoundland
Pictou, Nova Scotia
Casco Bay, Maine
Boston, Massachusetts
New York
Washington, D.C.
Eugene, Oregon
Seattle, Washington

The total mileage flown by each of the two aeroplanes (Nos. 2 and 4) which completed the historic flight was 26,345 (42,398 km) and the elapsed time 175 days. The flying time was given as 363 h 7 min.

(*Note on the Douglas DWC amphibians. These aircraft were specially commissioned by the U.S. Army as adaptations of the Douglas DT Navy torpedo bombers. Powered by a single in-line engine, the twin-float biplanes had a span of 50 ft (15·24 m) and a fuel capacity of 600 U.S. gal. Two of the World Cruisers are preserved to this day, one being maintained at the Smithsonian Institution at Washington, the other in the Air Force Museum at Wright-Paterson Air Force Base.*)

The first regular American trans-continental air-mail service, which was flown daily with fourteen intermediate stops, was inaugurated on 1st July 1924. The pilot of the first westward flight was Wesley L. Smith, who took off from New York; the first eastbound pilot was Claire K. Vance who took off from San Francisco, Calif.

The first three-engined all-metal monoplane transport in the world to enter commercial airline service was the Junkers G 23, four of which served with Swedish Air Lines (AB Aerotransport) on the Malmö–Hamburg–Amsterdam route, commencing on 15th May 1925. There is no doubt that this aircraft, built in Germany and Sweden, provided the basis for the Junkers Ju 52/3m, and certainly set the pattern for low-wing multi-engined monoplanes thereafter.

The first aeroplane flight over the North Pole was accomplished by Lieutenant-Commander Richard E. Byrd (U.S.N.), and Floyd Bennett in a Fokker F.VIIA/3m called *Josephine Ford* on 9th May 1926. The total distance flown was 1,600 miles (2,575 km).

The only commercial transport aeroplane designed and built in Belgium was the SABCA S-2 (Société Anonyme Belge de Constructions Aéronautiques) four-passenger high-wing monoplane powered by a single 240 hp Armstrong-Siddeley Puma engine. It was delivered to SABENA in December 1926.

The first light aeroplane flight from London to Karachi, India, was flown by T. Neville Stack in the de Havilland D.H.60 Moth (Cirrus II engine), *G-EBMO*, accompanied by B. S. Leete in a similar aircraft, *G-EBKU*, from Croydon to Karachi between 16th November 1926 and 8th January 1927.

Ryan monoplane Spirit of St. Louis

Charles Lindbergh

The first non-stop solo air crossing of the Atlantic was made by Captain Charles Lindbergh during 20th–21st May 1927 in a single-engine Ryan high-wing monoplane, *Spirit of St. Louis*, from Long Island, New York, to Paris, France. (It is perhaps worth emphasising that this crossing was being made at the same time as Carr was attempting to fly non-stop from England to India, and there is little doubt that had the latter not been forced to alight in the Persian Gulf, Lindbergh's epic flight might well have been eclipsed to some extent.) It took Lindbergh 33 h 39 min to complete the 3,610 mile (5,810 km) journey, at an average speed of 107·5 mile/h (173 km/h).

The first attempt to fly from Great Britain to India non-stop was made on 20th May 1927 by Flight-Lieutenant C. R. Carr, D.F.C. (later Air Marshal Sir Roderick Carr, K.B.E., C.B., D.F.C., A.F.C., R.A.F.(Retd.)) accompanied by Flight-Lieutenant L. E. M. Gillman as navigator. Flying a Hawker Horsley bomber, *J8607*, they took off from Cranwell, Lincolnshire, but were forced down in the Persian Gulf after flying 3,420 miles (5,504 km) in just over 34 h.

Hawker Horsley J8607

The first non-stop aeroplane flight between the United States mainland and Hawaii was achieved by Lieutenant Albert F. Hegenberger and Lieutenant Lester J. Maitland during 28th–29th June 1927, flying an Army Fokker C-2 three-engine monoplane *Bird of Paradise*. They flew the 2,407 miles (3,874 km) from Oakland, California, to Honolulu, Hawaii, in 25 h 50 min.

The first intercontinental charter flight in the world was made by the Fokker F.VIIA *H-NADP*. Chartered by the American W. van Lear Black, the aircraft was flown from Amsterdam to Jakarta and return between 15th June and 23rd July 1927. The crew comprised Captain G. J. Geysendorffer, First Officer J. B. Scholte and Flight-Engineer K. A. O. Weber. The outward journey took 13 days, a flying time of 86 h 27 min, to cover 9,120 miles (14,677 km) and the return journey, 14 days, a flying time of 97 h to cover 9,590 miles (15,433 km).

The first flight by a light aircraft from London to Cape Town, South Africa, was made between 1st and 28th September 1927 by Flight-Lieutenant R. R. Bentley flying a de Havilland D.H.60X Moth, *Dorys*. Bentley made two return flights during the next two years between these points, totalling 51,652 miles (83,126 km).

The first non-stop air crossing of the South Atlantic by an aeroplane was made on 14th–15th October 1927 when Captain Dieudonné Costes and Lieutenant-Commander Joseph Le Brix flew a Breguet XIX aircraft, *Nungesser-Coli*, from Saint-Louis, Senegal, to Port Natal, Brazil, a distance of 2,125 miles (3,420 km) in 19 h 50 min.

The first air service operated by Pan American Airways was inaugurated on 19th October 1927 on the 90 mile (145 km) route between Key West, Florida, and Havana, Cuba.

The first solo flight from Great Britain to Australia was made by Squadron-Leader H. J. L. ("Bert") Hinkler in the Avro 581 Avian prototype light aircraft, *G-EBOV*, flying from Croydon, London, to Darwin, Australia, between 7th and 22nd February 1928. His 11,005 mile (17,711 km) route was via Rome, Malta, Tobruk, Ramleh, Basra, Jask, Karachi, Cawnpore, Calcutta, Rangoon, Victoria Point, Singapore, Bandoeng and Bima. His aircraft was placed on permanent exhibition in the Brisbane Museum.

The first solo flight by a woman from South Africa to London was accomplished by Lady Heath (previously Mrs. Elliott-Lynn) flying an Avro Avian III, *G-EBUG*, from the Cape to Croydon between 12th February and 17th May 1928. She later sold her aircraft to the famous American woman pilot, Miss Amelia Earhart.

The first solo return flight between London and South Africa by a woman was achieved by Lady Bailey who, in a de Havilland Moth (Cirrus II) *G-EBSF*, left London on 9th March 1928. This aircraft was virtually destroyed at Tabora a month later, but the pilot completed the flight to the Cape in a replacement Moth, *G-EBTG*, subsequently flying round Africa and returning to London on 16th January 1929. Her outward flight occupied the period 9th March to 30th April, and her return flight 21st September 1928 to 16th January 1929.

The Australian Flying Doctor Service was inaugurated on 15th May 1928 using the joint services of the Australian Inland Mission and QANTAS at Cloncurry. The first aircraft was a de Havilland D.H.50 *Victory*, modified to accommodate two stretchers; its first pilot was A. Affleck and the first flying doctor was Dr. K. H. Vincent Welsh. The founder of the service was the Reverend J. Flynn, O.B.E.

The Reverend Doctor John Flynn

Charles Kingsford Smith (The Age, *Melbourne*)

The Southern Cross (The Age, *Melbourne*)

The first trans-Pacific flight was made between 31st May and 9th June 1928 by the Fokker F.VIIB-3m *Southern Cross* flown by Captain Charles Kingsford Smith and C.T.P. Ulm (pilots), accompanied by Harry Lyon (navigator) and James Warner (radio operator), from Oakland Field, San Francisco, California, to Eagle Farm, Brisbane, via Honolulu, Hawaii, and Suva, Fiji. The flight covered 7,389 miles (11,890 km), with a flying time of 83 h 38 min. The *Southern Cross* has been preserved and is displayed at Eagle Farm Airport. It was **the first aircraft ever to land in Fiji.**

The first crossing of the Tasman Sea by air was made on 10th–11th September 1928 by the *Southern Cross* (see above), flown from Richmond Aerodrome, Sydney, to Wigram, Christchurch, New Zealand, in 14 h 25 min, by Charles Kingsford Smith and C. T. P. Ulm, accompanied by H. A. Litchfield (navigator) and T. H. McWilliam (radio operator).

The first large-scale airlift evacuation of civilians in the world was undertaken by transport aircraft of the Royal Air Force between 23rd December 1928 and 25th February 1929 from the town of Kabul, Afghanistan, during inter-tribal disturbances. 586 people and 24,193 lb (10,975 kg) of luggage were airlifted over treacherous country using eight Vickers Victoria transports of No. 70 Squadron, R.A.F., and a Handley Page Hinaidi.

The first commercial air route between London and India was opened by Imperial Airways on 30th March 1929. The route was from London to Basle, Switzerland, by air (Armstrong Whitworth Argosy aircraft); Basle to Genoa, Italy, by train; Genoa to Alexandria, Egypt, by air (Short Calcutta flying-boats); Alexandria to Karachi, India, by air (de Havilland D.H.66 Hercules aircraft). The total journey from Croydon to Karachi occupied seven days, for which the single fare was £130. The stage travelled by train was necessary as Italy forbade the air entry of British aircraft, an embargo which lasted several years and substantially frustrated Imperial Airways' efforts to develop the Far East route.

The first non-stop flight from Great Britain to India was accomplished by Squadron Leader A. G. Jones Williams, M.C., and Flight-Lieutenant N. H. Jenkins, O.B.E., D.F.C., D.S.M. (pilot and navigator respectively) between 24th and 26th April 1929. Flying from Cranwell, Lincolnshire, to Karachi, India, in a Fairey Long-range Monoplane, *J9479*, powered by a 530 hp Napier Lion engine, they covered the 4,130 miles (6,647 km) in 50 h 37 min. It had been intended to fly to Bangalore to establish a world distance record but the attempt was abandoned owing to headwinds.

The first airship flight round the world was accomplished by the German *Graf Zeppelin* between 8th and 29th August 1929. Captained by Dr. Hugo Eckener, the craft set out from Lakehurst, New Jersey, and flew via Friedrichshafen, Germany, Tokyo, Japan, and Los Angeles, California, returning to Lakehurst 21 d, 7 h 34 min later.

The two large British commercial airships, *R-100* and *R-101*, were completed at the end of 1929, the *R-101 (G-FAAW)* flying first at Cardington, Bedford, on 14th October, and the *R-100 (G-FAAV)* on 16th December, flying from Howden, Yorkshire, to the Royal Airship Works, Cardington. The *R-100* made a transatlantic flight from Britain to Canada between 29th July and 1st August 1930, returning between 13th and 16th August. The *R-101* was destroyed on 5th October 1930 when it struck a hill near Beauvais, France, during an intended flight from Cardington to India. Commanded by Flight-Lieutenant H. C. Irwin, A.F.C., the *R-101* was carrying fifty-four people, of whom forty-eight were killed or died later, including Lord Thompson, Secretary of State for Air, and Major-General Sir Sefton Brancker, Director of Civil Aviation. This tragedy ended British efforts to develop airships for commercial use.

The first flight over the South Pole was made by Commander R. E. Byrd, U.S. Navy, with Bernt Balchen (pilot), Harold June (radio), and Ashley McKinley (survey), during 28th–29th November 1929, in a Ford 4-AT Trimotor monoplane, named *Floyd Bennett*.

Amy Johnson with Jason

The first solo flight from Great Britain to Australia by a woman was achieved by Miss Amy Johnson between 5th and 14th May 1930, flying a de Havilland D.H.60G Gipsy Moth *Jason* (*G-AAAH*) from Croydon to Darwin.

The first airline stewardess was Ellen Church, a nurse who, with Boeing Air Transport (later absorbed into United Air Lines), made her first flight between San Francisco, Calif., and Cheyenne, Wyom., on 15th May 1930.

Ellen Church (third from left)

The first Coast-to-Coast all-air commercial passenger service in America was opened simultaneously by Transcontinental and Western Air Inc. between New York and Los Angeles, California, on 25th October 1930.

An H.P. 42 (Charles E. Brown)

The first flight of the Handley Page 42E Hannibal four-engine biplane airliner, *G-AAGX*, was made on 14th November 1930, as a prototype, from Radlett, Hertfordshire. The stately H.P. 42 class brought new standards of luxury and reliability to air travel besides providing the backbone of Imperial Airways' fleet during the 1930s. Eight aeroplanes were produced in two versions, the "E" and "W", which could carry twenty-four and thirty-eight passengers respectively.

The first commercial air route between London and Central Africa was opened on 28th February 1931 by Imperial Airways. The route lay from Croydon to Alexandria (using Argosy aircraft from Croydon to Athens, and Calcutta flying-boats from Athens to Alexandria via Crete), and from Cairo to Mwanza, on Lake Victoria (using Argosy aircraft). Passengers were only carried as far as Khartoum, mail being carried over the remainder of the route.

The first non-stop flight from Japan to the United States was made by Clyde Pangborn and Hugh Herndon between 3rd and 5th October 1931, flying from Tokyo to Wenatchee, Washington, in a Bellanca aircraft. The flying time was 41 h 13 min.

"Bert" Hinkler

The first solo flight from New York to London in a light aircraft was made by Squadron Leader H. J. L. Hinkler between 27th October and 7th December 1931 in a de Havilland Puss Moth, *CF-APK*. His flight was via Jamaica (representing the first British crossing of the Caribbean), Jamaica to Venezuela,

Venezuela to Port Natal, and across the South Atlantic to Bathurst, thence to Hanworth, England, via Madrid, Spain. (Hinkler was killed on 7th January 1933 when his Puss Moth crashed in the Alps.)

The first regular commercial passenger air route from London to Cape Town was inaugurated by Imperial Airways on 27th April 1932 by the extension of the England to Central Africa route. The total scheduled time was eleven days and the first service arrived at Cape Town on 8th May. Imperial Airways also inaugurated the first air-mail service from London to Cape Town on 20th January 1932, but the first mail flights encountered a series of misfortunes including accidents to two airliners (*City of Basra* and *City of Delhi*, both de Havilland D.H.66 Hercules aircraft), from which the mail was salvaged on both occasions, to be delivered in London on 16th February. (It is worth recording that between 24th and 28th March 1932, J. A. Mollison flew solo from Lympne, Kent, to Cape Town, South Africa, in 4 d 17 h 50 min—compared with the eleven days for the scheduled Imperial Airways London-to-Cape route.)

The first solo crossing of the North Atlantic by a woman was made by the American pilot Miss Amelia Earhart (Mrs. Putnam) during 20th–21st May 1932, when she flew a Lockheed Vega aircraft from Harbour Grace, Newfoundland, to Londonderry, Northern Ireland.

The first solo east–west crossing of the Atlantic was made by J. A. Mollison during 18th–19th August 1932, flying a special long-range de Havilland Puss Moth, *G-ABXY*, from Portmarnock Strand, near Dublin, to Pennfield Ridge, New Brunswick. Mollison, flying *G-ABXY*, also became **the first man to fly from England to South America, the first man to fly solo across the South Atlantic from east to west, and the first man to cross both the North and South Atlantic,** when he landed at Natal, Brazil, on 9th February 1933 having flown from Lympne, England, in 3 d 10 h 8 min.

Fairey Long-range Monoplane K1991 (Charles E. Brown)

The first non-stop flight from England to South Africa was made by the Fairey Long-range Monoplane, *K1991*, between 6th and 8th February 1933, flown by Squadron Leader O. R. Gayford and Flight-Lieutenant G. E. Nicholetts. The flight of 5,431 miles (8,595 km) from Cranwell, Lincolnshire, to Walvis Bay, South-West Africa, was completed in 57 h 25 min and established a world long distance record.

(above) Santos-Dumont won a prize of 100,000 francs on 19th October 1901, by flying his 110 ft (33·5 m) airship No. 6 from Saint-Cloud to Paris, round the Eiffel Tower and back in thirty seconds under the stipulated limit of half an hour (Science Museum model). Below: This painting by Bernardino de Sousa Pereira, in the museum of the city of São Paulo, Brazil, shows Bartolomeu de Gusmão flying the first model hot-air balloon before King John V of Portugal, the Papal Nuncio and members of the Royal Family and Court, on 8th August 1709

The first ten million miles of flying was completed by Imperial Airways on 18th February 1933. Less than a month later the accident insurance premium rate for air travel was reduced from twelve shillings to one shilling per one thousand pounds for passengers travelling with Imperial Airways, bringing air insurance into line with that for surface travel for the first time.

The first flights over Mount Everest were made on 3rd April 1933 by the Marquess of Clydesdale, flying a Westland PV-3, and by Flight-Lieutenant D. F. McIntyre flying a Westland Wallace, each with one passenger.

The Douglas DC-1 first flew on 1st July 1933 at Clover Field, Santa Monica, Calif. Only one was built, flying mainly in TWA markings. After service during the Spanish Civil War, it was written off in a take-off accident near Malaga, Spain, in December 1940. The DC-1 never killed a passenger.

Wiley Post with his Lockheed Vega Winnie Mae

The first solo flight round the world was achieved by Wiley Post between 15th and 22nd July 1933 when he flew a Lockheed Vega monoplane, called *Winnie Mae*, from the Floyd Bennett Field, New York, for a distance of 15,596 miles (25,099 km) in 7 d 18 h 49 min. His route was via Berlin, Moscow, Irkutsk and Alaska.

Internal air-mail services in the United States were first flown by pilots of the U.S. Army Air Corps on 19th February 1934, following the unsatisfactory use of private contractors. The Corps service was suspended on 10th March after nine fatalities, only to be started again on 19th March, finally ending on 1st June.

The DC-2 was ordered initially by TWA following the success of the DC-1. The first DC-2 (*NC-13711*) was delivered to TWA on 14th May 1934 and entered service on 18th May 1934 between Columbus, Pittsburgh and Newark, New Jersey.

The first regular internal air mail in Great Britain was carried by Highland Airways on 29th May 1934. The de Havilland Dragon *G-ACCE*, flown by E. E. Fresson, carried 6,000 letters from Inverness to Kirkwall, and the service operated thereafter on every week-day.

The first non-stop aeroplane flight from the Canadian mainland to Britain was made during 8th–9th August 1934 by the de Havilland D.H.84 Dragon *Trail of the Caribou* flown by J. R. Ayling and Captain L. Reid. The crew took off from Wasaga Beach, Ontario, for an attempt at a long-distance record flight to Baghdad, but owing to excessive fuel consumption were forced to land at Heston, London, after a flight of 30 h 50 min.

The first flight by an aeroplane from Australia to the United States was made by a Lockheed Altair aircraft flown by Sir Charles Kingsford Smith accompanied by Captain P. G. Taylor from Brisbane to Oakland, Calif., via Fiji and Hawaii, between 22nd October and 4th November 1934.

The first regular weekly air-mail service between Britain and Australia commenced on 8th December 1934 from London to Brisbane via Karachi and Singapore. The airlines participating were Imperial Airways, Indian Trans-Continental Airways and Qantas Empire Airways. Mail which left London on this day reached Brisbane on 21st December.

The first solo flight from Honolulu, Hawaii, to the American mainland by a woman was made by Miss Amelia Earhart on 11th–12th January 1935 in a Lockheed Vega, flying from Honolulu to Oakland, Calif. Her time was 18 h 16 min.

The first through passenger air service between London and Brisbane, Australia, was inaugurated on 13th April 1935 by Imperial Airways and Qantas Empire Airways. The single fare for the 12,754 mile (20,525 km) route was £195. However, owing to heavy stage bookings no through passengers were carried on the inaugural flight. The journey took twelve and a half days.

Sikorsky S-42 flying-boat, used for the first survey flight to Honolulu, April 1935

The first airline flight from the American mainland to Hawaii was made by a flying-boat of Pan American Airways from Alameda, California, to Honolulu on 16th–17th April 1935. The flight, which was part of a company proving flight, occupied 18 h 37 min.

The first non-stop flight from Mexico City to Newark, New Jersey, was made by the American woman pilot, Miss Amelia Earhart, on 19th–20th April 1935; her elapsed time was 14 h 19 min.

The first scheduled air-mail flight across the Pacific was flown by Captain Edwin C. Musick in a Pan American Airways Martin M-130 flying-boat on 22nd November 1935 from San Francisco, Calif., to Honolulu, and afterwards to Midway, Wake Island, Guam and Manila.

The DC-3 was a further development of the DC-1 and DC-2. The first example built made its first flight at 15.00 h on 17th December 1935, flown by Carl A. Cover, at Clover Field, Calif. The first customer for the DC-3 was American Airlines, inaugurating flights between Chicago and Glendale, Calif., on 4th July 1936.

The first direct, solo east-to-west crossing of the North Atlantic by a woman was made by Mrs. Beryl Markham during 4th–5th September 1936, flying from Abingdon, England, to Baleine, Nova Scotia, where she crashed after a flight of 24 h 40 min. She was not hurt.

The first Short C-Type Empire flying-boat *Canopus* (*G-ADHL*) made her first flight on 4th July 1936 with John Lankester Parker, Short's Chief Test Pilot, at the controls. Her first flight with Imperial Airways was made on 30th October 1936. The Empire boats represented the last word in luxury travel before the Second World War and, as their name implied, were flown on the Empire routes to Africa and the Far East.

The first commercial survey flights over the North Atlantic were carried out simultaneously by Imperial Airways and Pan American Airways during 5th–6th July 1937. The former flew the long-range C-Class flying-boat *Caledonia G-ADHM* westwards from Foynes, Ireland, to Botwood, Newfoundland, while the latter flew the Sikorsky S-42 *Clipper III* eastwards.

A Vickers Viscount of B.E.A.

The first turbine-powered airliner in the world to receive an Airworthiness Certificate was the Vickers Viscount V.630 four-turboprop aircraft which was awarded Certificate No. A907 on 28th July 1950. The following day British European Airways operated **the world's first scheduled passenger service to be flown by a gas-turbine-powered airliner.** Piloted by Captain Richard Rymer, the Viscount (*G-AHRF*) took off from London (Northolt) and flew to Paris (Le Bourget) carrying fourteen fare-paying passengers and twelve guests of the airline.

Departure of Comet G-ALYP for Johannesburg, 2nd May 1952

The world's first turbojet airliner to enter airline service was the de Havilland D.H.106 Comet 1 powered by four de Havilland Ghost 50 turbojet engines. **The world's first regular passenger service to be flown by turbojet aircraft** was inaugurated by British Overseas Airways Corporation on 2nd May 1952 using the de Havilland Comet 1 *G-ALYP* between London and Johannesburg, South Africa. Its route was via Rome, Beirut, Khartoum, Entebbe and Livingstone, and the aircraft was captained in turn by Captains A. M. Majendie, J. T. A. Marsden and R. C. Alabaster. It carried thirty-six passengers and the total elapsed time for the 6,724 miles (10,821 km) was 23 h 34 min.

The world's first fatal accident involving a turbojet airliner occurred on 3rd March 1953 when *Empress of Hawaii*, a de Havilland Comet 1, *CF-CUN*, of Canadian Pacific Air Lines crashed on take-off at Karachi, Pakistan, killing all eleven occupants. The accident was stated to have been caused by the pilot lifting the nose too high during take-off, thereby preventing the aircraft from accelerating sufficiently quickly to achieve flying speed.

The first Transatlantic passenger service to be flown by turbine-powered airliners was inaugurated by B.O.A.C. on 19th December 1957 using Bristol Britannia 312 turboprop aircraft. The first flight from London to New York was by *G-AOVC* captained by Captain A. Meagher. The **first Transatlantic service by turbojet airliners** was operated by B.O.A.C. with de Havilland Comet 4s on 4th October 1958. Simultaneous flights were made in each direction, Captain R. E. Millichap being responsible for the London–New York service in *G-APDC*, and Captain T. B. Stoney for the New York–London flight which *G-APDB* completed in a record time of 6 h 11 min.

The first round-the-world passenger service by jet airliners was established by Pan American World Airways during October 1959. The first aircraft flown on this service was a Boeing 707-321, *Clipper Windward*.

CRIME IN THE SKY

Disasters in the Air
The two worst known disasters resulting from criminal violence in aircraft while in flight both involved the *loss of forty-four lives.*

On 1st November 1955 a Douglas DC-6B, operated by United Air Lines, exploded in the air and crashed near Longmont, Colorado, U.S.A., killing all forty-four occupants. It was later established that John G. Graham had introduced a bomb aboard in an insurance plot to murder his mother who was a passenger.

On 7th May 1964 a Fairchild F-27, operated by Pacific Airlines, crashed near Doublin, California, U.S.A., and all forty-four occupants were killed. A tape recording indicated that the pilot was shot by an intruder in the airliner's cockpit.

The first known use of aircraft for violence in civil crime was the dropping of three small bombs on 12th November 1926 by an aeroplane on a farmhouse in Williamson County, Illinois; the raid was carried out by a member of the Shelton gang against members of the rival Birger gang in a Prohibition feud involving illicit supply of beer and rum. The bombs however failed to detonate.

The longest distance flown by a skyjacked airliner was the 6,900 miles (11,095 km) travelled by the Trans-World Airlines Boeing 707 skyjacked by U.S. Marine Lance-Corporal Raphael Minichiello of Seattle, Washington at gunpoint on 31st October 1969. The nineteen-year-old Marine ordered the airliner's pilot, Donald Cook, at 04·42 h to fly to Denver, Colorado, and thence to Kennedy Airport, New York. Here FBI agents attempted to board the aircraft but were persuaded from doing so when Minichiello threatened spectators with his carbine. After permitting two overseas pilots to board, the aircraft was flown to Leonardo da Vinci Airport, Rome, but the Marine was captured shortly afterwards. He was indicted by a New York court for piracy and kidnapping, but continued to be held in Rome's Queen of Heaven Gaol.

Mass hijacking. A B.O.A.C. VC10, a TWA Boeing 707, and a Swissair DC-8 were blown up by Palestinian guerrillas at Dawson's Field, a desert airstrip in Jordan, on 12th September 1970 after being hijacked. Total value of the three aircraft was about £8,500,000 (United Press International)

WORLD POINT-TO-POINT SPEED RECORDS

From	To	Date	Pilot	Nationality	Aircraft	Time	Speed (mile/h km/h)
Amsterdam	Brussels	25th June 1961	Robert W. Fero, Jr.	U.S.A.	North American Sabreliner	9 min 45·1 s	528·48/ 850·50
Anchorage	Chicago	16th October 1963	Lt.-Col. G. A. Andrews	U.S.A.	B-58A Hustler	5 h 36 min 34·8 s	524·12/ 843·49
Anchorage	London	16th October 1963	Major S. J. Kubesch	U.S.A.	B-58A Hustler	5 h 24 min 54 s	826·92/1,330·80
Atlanta	Paris	31st May 1963	Vern F. Peterson	U.S.A.	Lockheed Hercules	12 h 43 min 48·5 s	343·71/ 553·15
Baltimore	Moscow	19th May 1963	Colonel J. B. Swindal	U.S.A.	Boeing 707 (707)	8 h 33 min 45·4 s	563·36/ 906·64
Baltimore	Oslo	19th May 1963	Colonel J. B. Swindal	U.S.A.	Boeing VC-137 (707)	6 h 29 min 47·2 s	591·12/ 951·31
Baltimore	Stockholm	19th May 1963	Colonel J. B. Swindal	U.S.A.	Boeing VC-137 (707)	6 h 58 min 27·1 s	586·76/ 944·30
Beirut	Karachi	2nd January 1962	A. Baig	Pakistan	Boeing 720B	3 h 8 min 27·6 s	633·99/1,020·311
Belfast	Gander	31st August 1951	Roland Beamont	G.B.	English Electric Canberra	4 h 18 min 24·4 s	481·10/ 774·255
Berlin	Hanoi	28th-30th Nov. 1938	A. Henke	Germany	Fw 200 Kondor	34 h 17 min 27 s	151·00/ 243·011
Berlin	New York	10th-11th Aug. 1938	A. Henke	Germany	Fw 200 Kondor	24 h 56 min 12 s	158·76/ 255·499
Berlin	Tokyo	28th-30th Nov. 1938	A. Henke	Germany	Fw 200 Kondor	46 h 18 min 19 s	119·49/ 192·308
Bermuda	London	6th May 1962	M. Gudmundsson	G.B.	Boeing 707-465	6 h 2 min 16 s	572·14/ 920·763
Boston	Bonn	22nd April 1962	Miss Jacqueline Cochrane	U.S.A.	Lockheed Jetstar	10 h 15 min 56 s	349·56/ 562·56
Boston	London	22nd April 1962	Miss Jacqueline Cochrane	U.S.A.	Lockheed Jetstar	9 h 25 min 54·3 s	347·04/ 558·50
Boston	Moscow	19th May 1963	Colonel J. B. Swindal	U.S.A.	Boeing VC-137 (707)	7 h 58 min 15·7 s	562·60/ 905·42
Boston	Oslo	19th May 1963	Colonel J. B. Swindal	U.S.A.	Boeing VC-137 (707)	5 h 54 min 14·7 s	591·94/ 952·63
Boston	Paris	22nd April 1962	Miss Jacqueline Cochrane	U.S.A.	Lockheed Jetstar	9 h 47 min 31 s	351·00/ 564·88
Boston	Shannon	22nd April 1962	Miss Jacqueline Cochrane	U.S.A.	Lockheed Jetstar	8 h 13 min 38 s	351·35/ 565·45
Boston	Stockholm	19th May 1963	Colonel J. B. Swindal	U.S.A.	Boeing VC-137 (707)	6 h 22 min 54·1 s	587·11/ 944·87
Brussels	Amsterdam	25th June 1961	Robert W. Fero, Jr.	U.S.A.	North American Sabreliner	9 min 33 s	537·12/ 864·41
Brussels	Paris	6th June 1963	B. A. Neefs	Belgium	Lockheed F-104G Starfighter	10 min 3·9 s	979·55/1,576·435
Buenos Aires	Washington	13th November 1957	General Curtis E. Le May	U.S.A.	Boeing KC-135	11 h 5 min 0·8 s	471·45/ 758·728
Buenos Aires	Christchurch	16th-17th Nov. 1965	J. L. Martin et al.	U.S.A.	Boeing 707-320	14 h 18 min 37·7 s	430·52/ 692·85
Christchurch	Honolulu	17th November 1965	J. L. Martin et al.	U.S.A.	Boeing 707-320	9 h 1 min 32·9 s	551·08/ 886·88
Copenhagen	London	4th April 1950	Janusz Zurakowski	G.B.	Gloster Meteor	1 h 11 min 17 s	500·67/ 805·752
Fort Worth	Madrid	11th January 1962	Major Clyde P. Evely	U.S.A.	Boeing B-52H	8 h 35 min 24·43 s	577·44/ 929·30
Fort Worth	Saint Louis	21st June 1963	M. E. Payne	U.S.A.	Republic F-47 Thunderbolt	2 h 17 min 37·9 s	248·58/ 400·05
Fort Worth	Washington	11th January 1962	Major Clyde P. Evely	U.S.A.	Boeing B-52H	2 h 0 min 26·66 s	604·44/ 972·75
Gander	Belfast	26th August 1952	Roland Beamont	G.B.	English Electric Canberra	3 h 25 min 18·13 s	605·53/ 974·503
Gander	Bonn	22nd April 1962	Miss Jacqueline Cochrane	U.S.A.	Lockheed Jetstar	5 h 54 min 17·6 s	452·52/ 728·26
Gander	London	22nd April 1962	Miss Jacqueline Cochrane	U.S.A.	Lockheed Jetstar	5 h 3 min 50·5 s	465·48/ 749·11
Gander	Paris	22nd April 1962	Miss Jacqueline Cochrane	U.S.A.	Lockheed Jetstar	5 h 26 min 6·9 s	463·68/ 746·22
Gander	Shannon	22nd April 1962	Miss Jacqueline Cochrane	U.S.A.	Lockheed Jetstar	3 h 52 min 4 s	511·20/ 822·69
Gibraltar	London	19th September 1949	A. G. P. Carver	G.B.	de Havilland Hornet	2 h 30 min 31 s	435·89/ 701·492
Honolulu	Washington	15th November 1965	J. L. Martin et al.	U.S.A.	Boeing 707-320	13 h 54 min 3·3 s	520·45/ 837·58
Havana	Washington	27th November 1947	Woodrow W. Edmondson	U.S.A.	North American P-51	3 h 15 min 13 s	350·33/ 563·800
Cairo	London	11th May 1950	John Cunningham	G.B.	de Havilland Comet I	5 h 39 min 21·7 s	385·89/ 621·026
Cape of Good Hope	London	19th December 1953	A. H. Humphrey	G.B.	English Electric Canberra	13 h 16 min 25·2 s	452·76/ 728·648
Lisbon	Buenos Aires	16th November 1965	J. L. Martin et al.	U.S.A.	Boeing 707-320	11 h 54 min 8·4 s	501·69/ 807·39
Lisbon	Frankfurt	27th October 1963	G. P. Eremea	U.S.A.	North American Sabreliner	2 h 24 min 46·1 s	487·84/ 785·11
London	Aden	30th March 1962	John R. Ward	G.B.	Avro Vulcan	6 h 13 min 59·9 s	589·37/ 948·495
London	Amsterdam	29th July 1954	R. S. Overbury	G.B.	Hawker Sea Hawk		571·51/ 919·76
London	Athens	27th December 1969	Major D. B. O'Conner	Canada	Dassault Fan Jet Falcon	3 h 59 min 17 s	373·25/ 600·69
London	Baghdad	31st July 1955	John Finch	G.B.	Vickers Valiant	4 h 51 min 28·8 s	523·48/ 842·463

From	To	Date	Pilot	Nationality	Aircraft	Time	Speed (mile/h km/h)
London	Basra	8th October 1953	L. E. Burton	G.B.	English Electric Canberra	5 h 11 min 5·6 s	544·33/876·011
London	Bermuda	5th May 1962	G. N. Henderson	G.B.	Boeing 707-465	6 h 53 min 1 s	498·95/802·974
London	Beirut	2nd January 1962	A. Baig	Pakistan	Boeing 720B	3 h 35 min 20·3 s	599·32/964·517
London	Bonn	22nd April 1962	Miss Jacqueline Cochrane	U.S.A.	Lockheed Jetstar	49 min 44·4 s	385·55/620·49
London	Brussels	10th July 1952	David Morgan	G.B.	Supermarine Swift	18 min 3·3 s	665·89/1,071·648
London	Buenos Aires	15th-16th Nov. 1965	J. L. Martin et al.	U.S.A.	Boeing 707-320	16 h 40 min 2·2 s	415·32/668·40
London	Calcutta	27th December 1969	Major D. B. O'Conner	Canada	Dassault Fan Jet Falcon	13 h 29 min 51 s	366·99/590·61
London	Christchurch	8th-9th Oct. 1953	L. E. Burton	G.B.	English Electric Canberra	23 h 50 min 42 s	494·54/795·887
London	Colombo	8th-9th Oct. 1953	L. M. Hodges	G.B.	English Electric Canberra	10 h 23 min 21·5 s	519·47/836·004
London	Copenhagen	4th April 1950	Janusz Zurakowski	G.B.	Gloster Meteor	1 h 5 min 5 s	541·43/871·344
London	Darwin	27th-28th Jan. 1953	L. M. Whittington	G.B.	English Electric Canberra	22 h 0 min 21·8 s	391·19/629·553
London	Johannesburg	23rd-24th Oct. 1957	John Cunningham	G.B.	English Electric Canberra	12 h 59 min 7·3 s	433·91/698·309
London	Karachi	2nd January 1962	A. Baig	Pakistan	Boeing 720B	6 h 43 min 51 s	583·33/938·786
London	Khartoum	16th October 1957	John Cunningham	G.B.	de Havilland Comet 4	5 h 51 min 14·8 s	523·41/842·354
London	Kuwait	2nd February 1964	A. W. Hebborn	G.B.	de Havilland Comet	6 h 0 min 25 s	480·86/773·87
London	Valetta	25th April 1961	Harry Bennett	G.B.	Hawker Hunter	2 h 3 min 8 s	633·33/1,019·24
London	Cairo	13th April 1965	John Cunningham	G.B.	de Havilland Trident	3 h 37 min 44 s	602·10/968·993
London	Cape Town	17th December 1953	G. G. Petty	G.B.	English Electric Canberra	12 h 21 min 12·4 s	486·58/783·078
London	Lisbon	15th-16th Nov. 1965	J. L. Martin et al.	U.S.A.	Boeing 707-320	2 h 21 min 12·4 s	420·75/677·14
London	Los Angeles	13th September 1974	Captain Harold B. Adams	U.S.A.	Lockheed SR-71A	3 h 47 min 35·8 s	1,435·563/2,310·353
London	Melbourne	8th-10th Oct. 1953	W. Baillie	G.B.	English Electric Canberra	35 h 46 min 47·6 s	293·61/472·517
London	Nairobi	28th September 1952	H. P. Conolly	G.B.	English Electric Canberra	9 h 55 min 16·7 s	427·26/687·611
London	New York	27th June 1958	Burl B. Davenport	U.S.A.	Boeing KC-135	5 h 53 min 12·77 s	587·46/945·423
London	Paris	5th July 1953	M. J. Lithgow	G.B.	Supermarine Swift	19 min 5·6 s	669·48/1,077·417
London	Reykjavik	31st July-1st Aug. 1964	Lord Trefgarne et al.	G.B.	de Havilland Dragonfly	32 h 36 min 36 s	36·02/57·966
London	Rome	20th October 1956	A. W. Bedford	G.B.	Hawker Hunter	1 h 34 min 46 s	566·08/911·01
London	Singapore	11th-12th April 1971	Captain L. Bruce et al.	G.B.	Boeing 707-349C	13 h 16 min 46 s	508·22/817·907
London	Sydney	19th-21st Dec. 1969	Captain T. E. Lampitt	G.B.	Beech 99A	49 h 44 min 26 s	212·55/342·068
London	Tripoli	18th February 1952	L. C. E. de Vigne	G.B.	English Electric Canberra	2 h 41 min 49·5 s	538·12/866·021
London	Wellington	21st-24th Aug. 1946	N. H. d'Aeth	G.B.	Avro Lancaster Aries	59 h 50 min	194·66/313·270
Los Angeles	Miami	21st-22nd Dec. 1971	Captain M. C. Wedge	U.S.A.	McDonnell Douglas DC-10	3 h 38 min 32 s	636·77/1,024·78
Los Angeles	New York	5th March 1962	Robert G. Sowers	U.S.A.	B-58A Hustler	2 h 0 min 58·71 s	1,214·64/1,954·79
Los Angeles	Paris	28th-29th May 1953	Ch. Billet	France	Douglas DC-6	20 h 26 min	276·31/444·681
Los Angeles	Stockholm	15th-16th Nov. 1956	Jackson J. Armstrong	U.S.A.	Douglas DC-7C	21 h 39 min 11·88 s	254·85/410·143
Los Angeles	Tokyo	15th-16th Aug. 1966	A. G. Heimerdinger	U.S.A.	Douglas DC-8-61	11 h 30 min 2·4 s	476·62/767·04
Los Angeles	Washington	27th May 1972	Howard M. Keefe	U.S.A.	North American P-51	6 h 25 min 31·5 s	362·35/583·14
Madrid	New York	17th July 1961	Robert W. Fero, Jr.	U.S.A.	North American Sabreliner		371·88/598·48
Moscow	Baltimore	20th-21st May 1963	Colonel J. B. Swindal	U.S.A.	Boeing VC-137 (707)	9 h 47 min 53·2 s	492·30/792·28
Moscow	Boston	20th-21st May 1963	Colonel J. B. Swindal	U.S.A.	Boeing VC-137 (707)	9 h 1 min 7·8 s	497·23/800·21
Moscow	New York	20th-21st May 1963	Colonel J. B. Swindal	U.S.A.	Boeing VC-137 (707)	9 h 24 min 48 s	495·32/797·14
Moscow	Philadelphia	20th-21st May 1963	Colonel J. B. Swindal	U.S.A.	Boeing VC-137 (707)	9 h 35 min 54·9 s	494·13/795·22
Moscow	Washington	20th-21st May 1963	Colonel J. B. Swindal	U.S.A.	Boeing VC-137 (707)	9 h 54 min 48·5 s	490·06/788·67
New Orleans	Bonn	22nd April 1962	Miss Jacqueline Cochrane	U.S.A.	Lockheed Jetstar	13 h 10 min 31 s	375·12/603·69
New Orleans	Boston	22nd April 1962	Miss Jacqueline Cochrane	U.S.A.	Lockheed Jetstar	2 h 54 min 33·6 s	467·28/752·01
New Orleans	Gander	22nd April 1962	Miss Jacqueline Cochrane	U.S.A.	Lockheed Jetstar	4 h 42 min 32·9 s	482·40/776·34
New Orleans	London	22nd April 1962	Miss Jacqueline Cochrane	U.S.A.	Lockheed Jetstar	12 h 20 min 14·9 s	375·12/603·69

From	To	Date	Pilot	Nationality	Aircraft	Time	Speed (mile/h km/h)
New Orleans	New York	22nd April 1962	Miss Jacqueline Cochrane	U.S.A.	Lockheed Jetstar	2 h 31 min 8·5 s	465·12/ 748·53
New Orleans	Paris	22nd April 1962	Miss Jacqueline Cochrane	U.S.A.	Lockheed Jetstar	12 h 42 min 3·9 s	377·64/ 607·75
New Orleans	Shannon	22nd April 1962	Miss Jacqueline Cochrane	U.S.A.	Lockheed Jetstar	11 h 8 min 8·7 s	381·60/ 614·12
New Orleans	Washington	22nd April 1962	Miss Jacqueline Cochrane	U.S.A.	Lockheed Jetstar	2 h 5 min 2·4 s	465·68/ 746·22
New York	Berlin	13th–14th Aug. 1938	A. Henke	Germany	Fw 200 Kondor	19 h 55 min 1 s	199·41/ 320·919
New York	Bonn	22nd April 1962	Miss Jacqueline Cochrane	U.S.A.	Lockheed Jetstar	10 h 39 min 12·5 s	354·24/ 570·09
New York	Karachi	20th–21st October 1974	Captain Mian Abdul Aziz	Pakistan	Douglas DC-10-30	13 h 3 min 53·2 s	556·366/ 895·385
New York	London	1st September 1974	Major James V. Sullivan	U.S.A.	Lockheed SR-71A	1 h 54 min 56·4 s	1,806·987/2,908·026
New York	Los Angeles	5th March 1962	Robert G. Sowers	U.S.A.	Convair B-58A Hustler	2 h 15 min 50·08 s	1,081·81/1,741·00
New York	Moscow	19th May 1963	Colonel J. B. Swindal	U.S.A.	Boeing VC-137 (707)	8 h 15 min 54·1 s	564·12/ 907·86
New York	Oslo	19th May 1963	Colonel J. B. Swindal	U.S.A.	Boeing VC-137 (707)	6 h 11 min 58·8 s	593·14/ 954·56
New York	Paris	26th May 1961	William R. Payne	U.S.A.	Convair B-58A Hustler	3 h 19 min 44·53 s	1,089·30/1,753·068
New York	Shannon	22nd April 1962	Miss Jacqueline Cochrane	U.S.A.	Lockheed Jetstar	8 h 36 min 57·5 s	357·47/ 575·30
New York	Stockholm	19th May 1963	Colonel J. B. Swindal	U.S.A.	Boeing VC-137 (707)	6 h 40 min 36 s	588·31/ 946·79
Oslo	Baltimore	20th–21st May 1963	Colonel J. B. Swindal	U.S.A.	Boeing VC-137 (707)	7 h 39 min 20·9 s	501·89/ 807·71
Oslo	Boston	20th–21st May 1963	Colonel J. B. Swindal	U.S.A.	Boeing VC-137 (707)	6 h 52 min 34·9 s	508·29/ 818·01
Oslo	New York	20th–21st May 1963	Colonel J. B. Swindal	U.S.A.	Boeing VC-137 (707)	7 h 16 min 21 s	505·62/ 813·71
Oslo	Philadelphia	20th–21st May 1963	Colonel J. B. Swindal	U.S.A.	Boeing VC-137 (707)	7 h 27 min 19 s	504·18/ 811·40
Oslo	Washington	20th–21st May 1963	Colonel J. B. Swindal	U.S.A.	Boeing VC-137 (707)	7 h 46 min 18·7 s	498·81/ 802·75
Ottawa	London	27th–28th June 1955	I. G. Broom	G.B.	English Electric Canberra	6 h 42 min 12 s	496·83/ 799·563
Paris	Bonn	22nd April 1962	Miss Jacqueline Cochrane	U.S.A.	Lockheed Jetstar	26 min 5·5 s	576·00/ 926·98
Paris	Frankfurt	27th October 1963	G. P. Eremea	U.S.A.	North American-Sabreliner	35 min 51·4 s	499·96/ 804·61
Paris	Hanoi	15th–18th Nov. 1936	André Japy	France	Caudron Simoun	50 h 59 min 49 s	111·98/ 180·208
Paris	London	5th July 1953	M. J. Lithgow	G.B.	Supermarine Swift	19 min 14·3 s	664·43/1,069·291
Paris	Nice	18th June 1955	Gérard Muselli	France	Dassault Mystère IV-N	41 min 55·8 s	610·46/ 982·433
Paris	Saigon	19th–23rd Dec. 1937	Mlle Maryse Hilsz	France	Caudron Simoun	92 h 36 min	67·93/ 109·316
Paris	Tananarive	21st December 1935	Génin and Robert	France	Caudron Simoun	57 h 35 min 21 s	94·39/ 151·908
Philadelphia	Moscow	19th May 1963	Colonel J. B. Swindal	U.S.A.	Boeing VC-137 (707)	8 h 24 min 36·2 s	563·97/ 907·62
Philadelphia	Oslo	19th May 1963	Colonel J. B. Swindal	U.S.A.	Boeing VC-137 (707)	6 h 20 min 31 s	592·66/ 953·80
Philadelphia	Stockholm	19th May 1963	Colonel J. B. Swindal	U.S.A.	Boeing VC-137 (707)	6 h 49 min 11·6 s	587·88/ 946·10
North Pole	South Pole	15th–17th Nov. 1965	J. L. Martin et al.	U.S.A.	Boeing 707-320	35 h 46 min 20 s	348·04/ 560·11
Portland, Or.	Portland, Mn.	30th July 1967	James F. Nields	U.S.A.	Beech Baron	11 h 40 min 10 s	216·93/ 349·11
Reykjavik	New York	2nd–5th August 1964	Lord Trefgarne et al.	G.B.	de Havilland Dragonfly	77 h 13 min 30 s	33·82/ 54·426
Rome	Addis Ababa	6th–7th March 1939	M. Lualdi	Italy	Fiat BR.20L	11 h 25 min	242·94/ 390·971
Rome	London	25th October 1956	A. W. Bedford	G.B.	Hawker Hunter	1 h 40 min 7 s	533·94/ 859·29
Rome	Rio de Janeiro	24th–25th Jan. 1938	Attileo Biseo	Italy	Savoia-Marchetti SM-79	41 h 32 min	137·92/ 221·966
Saint Louis	Paris	2nd June 1971	Donald L. Mullin	U.S.A.	McDonnell Douglas DC-10	8 h 45 min 27 s	501·15/ 806·52
Seattle	Fort Worth	11th January 1962	Major Clyde P. Evely	U.S.A.	Boeing B-52H	3 h 0 min 24·62 s	552·50/ 889·16
Seattle	Madrid	11th January 1962	Major Clyde P. Evely	U.S.A.	Boeing B-52H	11 h 34 min 9·22 s	456·69/ 734·97
Shannon	Bonn	22nd April 1962	Miss Jacqueline Cochrane	U.S.A.	Lockheed Jetstar	1 h 38 min 15·8 s	426·24/ 685·96
Shannon	London	22nd April 1962	Miss Jacqueline Cochrane	U.S.A.	Lockheed Jetstar	47 min 36·5 s	476·64/ 767·07
Singapore	Darwin	7th–8th August 1955	John Finch	G.B.	Vickers Valiant	1 h 10 min 10·8 s	475·91/ 765·91
Stockholm	Baltimore	20th–21st May 1963	Colonel J. B. Swindal	U.S.A.	Boeing VC-137 (707)	8 h 11 min 33·3 s	518·36/ 834·218
Stockholm	Boston	20th–21st May 1963	Colonel J. B. Swindal	U.S.A.	Boeing VC-137 (707)	7 h 24 min 45·6 s	499·50/ 803·86
Stockholm	New York	20th–21st May 1963	Colonel J. B. Swindal	U.S.A.	Boeing VC-137 (707)	7 h 48 min 31·1 s	505·44/ 813·42

From	To	Date	Pilot	Nationality	Aircraft	Time	Speed (mile/h km/h)
Stockholm	Philadelphia	20th–21st May 1963	Colonel J. B. Swindal	U.S.A.	Boeing VC-137 (707)	7 h 59 min 31·8 s	501·66/ 807·34
Stockholm	Washington	20th–21st May 1963	Colonel J. B. Swindal	U.S.A.	Boeing VC-137 (707)	8 h 18 min 30·8 s	496·66/ 799·29
Sydney	London	21st–26th March 1938	A. E. Clouston	G.B.	de Havilland 88 Comet	130 h 3 min	81·26/ 130·777
Tokyo	Anchorage	16th October 1963	Major S. J. Kubesch	U.S.A.	Convair B-58A Hustler	3 h 9 min 41·8 s	1,093·44/1,759·73
Tokyo	Chicago	16th October 1963	G. A. Andrews	U.S.A.	Convair B-58A Hustler	8 h 38 min 42 s	729·25/1,173·61
Tokyo	Fort Worth	10th–11th Jan. 1962	Major Clyde P. Evely	U.S.A.	Boeing B-52H	11 h 41 min 24·69 s	550·08/ 885·26
Tokyo	London	16th October 1963	Major S. J. Kubesch	U.S.A.	Convair B-58A Hustler	8 h 35 min 20·4 s	692·71/1,114·81
Tokyo	Madrid	10th–11th Jan. 1962	Major Clyde P. Evely	U.S.A.	Boeing B-52H	20 h 22 min 12 s	328·78/ 529·12
Tokyo	Seattle	10th–11th Jan. 1962	Major Clyde P. Evely	U.S.A.	Boeing B-52H	8 h 43 min 40·83 s	549·36/ 884·11
Tokyo	Washington	7th–8th April 1958	William E. Eubank	U.S.A.	Boeing C-135	13 h 45 min 45·5 s	492·26/ 792·219
Tokyo	Winnipeg	18th August 1966	A. G. Heimerdinger	U.S.A.	Douglas DC-8-61	10 h 57 min 23·9 s	510·11/ 820·95
Washington	Bonn	22nd April 1962	Miss Jacqueline Cochrane	U.S.A.	Lockheed Jetstar	11 h 5 min 12·1 s	358·92/ 577·62
Washington	Boston	22nd April 1962	Miss Jacqueline Cochrane	U.S.A.	Lockheed Jetstar	49 min 29·7 s	476·64/ 767·07
Washington	Caracas	22nd February 1958	John W. Hackett	G.B.	English Electric Canberra	4 h 10 min 59·75 s	491·94/ 791·697
Washington	Gander	22nd April 1962	Miss Jacqueline Cochrane	U.S.A.	Lockheed Jetstar	2 h 37 min 48·4 s	497·52/ 800·68
Washington	Havana	25th November 1947	Woodrow W. Edmondson	U.S.A.	North American P-51	3 h 37 min 28·6 s	314·47/ 506·092
Washington	London	22nd April 1962	Miss Jacqueline Cochrane	U.S.A.	Lockheed Jetstar	10 h 15 min 5 s	357·47/ 575·30
Washington	New York	22nd April 1962	Miss Jacqueline Cochrane	U.S.A.	Lockheed Jetstar	26 min 9·6 s	470·88/ 757·80
Washington	Moscow	19th May 1963	Colonel J. B. Swindal	U.S.A.	Boeing VC-137 (707)	8 h 39 min 2·2 s	561·60/ 903·80
Washington	Oslo	19th May 1963	Colonel J. B. Swindal	U.S.A.	Boeing VC-137 (707)	6 h 34 min 49·9 s	589·14/ 948·13
Washington	Stockholm	19th May 1963	Colonel J. B. Swindal	U.S.A.	Boeing VC-137 (707)	7 h 3 min 33·4 s	584·57/ 940·77
Washington	Paris	26th May 1961	William R. Payne	U.S.A.	Convair B-58A Hustler	3 h 39 min 19·08 s	1,048·67/1,687·69
Washington	Shannon	22nd April 1962	Miss Jacqueline Cochrane	U.S.A.	Lockheed Jetstar	9 h 2 min 53·6 s	362·87/ 583·99
Wellington	London	20th–26th March 1938	A. E. Clouston	G.B.	de Havilland 88 Comet	140 h 12 min	83·45/ 134·306

French observation balloon at the Battle of Fleurus, 26th June 1794 (Royal Aeronautical Society)

SECTION V
Lighter-than-Air

In all mankind's modern preoccupation with wing-borne and rocket flight, one perhaps tends to forget that "exploration" of the air had commenced more than one hundred years before the Wright brothers successfully achieved manned, powered flight in their aeroplane; that the advance of science towards the end of the eighteenth century had enabled men (and women) to be carried aloft and float fairly peacefully across country—albeit at the mercy of the elements. For some years after the advent of the Montgolfier hot-air balloons in Paris, opinions were divided on the relative merits of heated air and of hydrogen as the best lifting agent, but inevitably the inherent dangers of carrying a bonfire suspended under the envelope decided early pioneers to resort to the more expensive process of chemical reaction for the generation of hydrogen. It was not until well into the twentieth century that the inert helium gas gained preference over hydrogen (whose use had caused countless aerial tragedies down the years), but was then too late to preserve lighter-than-air travel in the age of the passenger aeroplane.

Nevertheless ballooning during the nineteenth century was undertaken on a far greater scale than is perhaps realised today. Not only were the aeronauts the daring sportsmen of their age, but they were frequently called upon to demonstrate the practical uses to which their craft could be put. Balloons were used in wartime—even on the battlefield—and for the carriage of mail and military despatches; even the English Channel was crossed by air 124 years before Louis Blériot made his perilous flight.

In describing the achievements of those early pioneers it is necessary to remember that the almost total lack of scientific education among the great majority of "civilised" populations allowed an almost medieval fear of the sky to persist; and a man who allowed himself to be carried aloft (as if by magic) would certainly face unknown terrors. Moreover the unheralded arrival of a balloon from the sky might engender widespread hysteria among the local populace. One can learn of similar attitudes of mind towards the aeroplane among primitive tribes in the modern age.

It was the helplessness of those early balloonists, drifting at the whim of the wind, that determined the more constructive and adventurous to seek propulsion and directional control; their success led to the airship or "dirigible", which was at one time regarded as the most destructive harbinger of war as well as the ultimate in safety and comfort in air travel.

Today the balloon and the airship are the playthings of a diminutive band of diehards, swept aside as the chaff of jet and rocket blast.

First successful demonstration of a model balloon took place on 8th August 1709 in the Ambassadors' drawing-room at the Casa da India, Lisbon, in the presence of King John V of Portugal, Queen Maria Anna, the Papal Nuncio, Cardinal Conti (later Pope Innocent III), princes of the Court, members of the Diplomatic Corps, noblemen and courtiers. The balloon, made and demonstrated by Father Bartolomeu de Gusmão, consisted of a small envelope of thick paper inflated with hot air produced by "fire material contained in an earthen bowl encrusted in a waxed-wood tray" which was suspended underneath. The balloon is said to have risen quickly to a height of 12 ft before being destroyed by two valets who feared that it might set the curtains alight. Suggestions that Gusmão became airborne later in a full-scale version of his balloon, although documented, cannot be substantiated. The **Passarola** (Great bird), sometimes illustrated as a peculiar form of flying machine devised by Gusmão, is no more than a fanciful representation of the carriage designed for the full-size balloon.

Hydrogen was first isolated in 1766 by the English scientist Henry Cavendish who referred to it as "inflammable air" or Phlogiston. It was first named hydrogen by the French chemist Lavoisier in 1790.

The Montgolfier balloon at Versailles

The first balloon to leave the ground capable of sustaining a weight equivalent to that of a man was a hot-air balloon made by the brothers Joseph and Étienne Montgolfier (1740–1810 and 1745–1799 respectively). This balloon, calculated as being able to lift 450 lb (205 kg), was released on 25th April

1783, probably at Annonay, France, rose to about 1,000 ft (305 m) and landed about 1,000 yd from the point of lift-off. The balloon had a diameter of about 39 ft (12 m) and achieved its lift using hot air provided by combustion of solid waste (probably paper, straw and wood) below the neck of the envelope.

The first public demonstration by the Montgolfier brothers took place at Annonay on 4th June 1783, when a small balloon of about 36 ft (11 m) diameter, made from linen and paper, rose to a height of 6,000 ft (1,830 m).

The first free ascent of a hydrogen-filled balloon (unmanned) was made on 27th August 1783 from the Champ-de-Mars, Paris when Jacques Alexandre César Charles (1746–1823) launched a 12 ft (3·5 m) balloon. It was filled with hydrogen that Charles had manufactured and was capable of lifting 20 lb (9 kg). The balloon drifted for 45 minutes and came to earth at Gonesse, 15 miles (25 km) from Paris, where it was promptly attacked by a frenzied mob of panic-stricken peasants.

The first living occupants of a balloon to ascend were a sheep, a duck and a cock which rode aloft under a 41 ft (13 m) diameter hot-air Montgolfier balloon at the Court of Versailles on 19th September 1783 before King Louis XVI, Marie-Antoinette and their Court. The balloon achieved an altitude of 1,700 ft (550 m) before descending in the Forest of Vaucresson 8 min later, having travelled about 2 miles. The occupants were scarcely affected by their flight nor by their landing.

The first man carried aloft in a balloon was François Pilâtre de Rozier (born 30th March 1757, died 15th June 1785) who on 15th October 1783 ascended in a tethered 49 ft (15 m) diameter Montgolfier hot-air balloon to 84 ft (26 m) — the limit of the restraining rope. The hot air was provided by a straw-fed fire below the fabric envelope and the balloon stayed up for nearly 4·5 min.

The first men carried aloft in free flight by a balloon were de Rozier (see above) and the Marquis d'Arlandes who rose in the 49 ft (15 m) diameter Montgolfier balloon at 13·54 h on 21st November 1783 from the gardens of the Château La Muette in the Bois de Boulogne. These first aeronauts were airborne for 25 min and landed on the Butte-aux-Cailles, about 5·5 miles (8·5 km) from their point of departure, having drifted to and fro across Paris. Their maximum altitude is unlikely to have been above 1,500 ft (450 m).

François Pilâtre de Rozier

The first men to be carried aloft in free flight by a hydrogen-filled balloon were Jacques Charles and one of the Robert brothers who had helped to make it. They ascended from the gardens of the Tuileries, Paris, at 13·45 h on 1st December 1783, in a balloon 27 ft 6 in (8·6 m) in diameter before a crowd estimated at 400,000. The craft landed 27 miles distant, near the town of Nesles.

The first women to ascend in a balloon (tethered) were the Marchioness de Montalembert, the Countess de Montalembert, the Countess de Podenas and Mademoiselle de Lagarde who rose aloft in a Montgolfier hot-air balloon on 20th May 1784 from the Faubourg-Saint-Antoine, Paris.

The first woman to be carried in free flight in a balloon was Madame Thible who ascended in a Montgolfière with a Monsieur Fleurant on 4th June 1784 from Lyon, France. The balloon, named *Le Gustav*, reached an altitude of 8,500 ft (2,600 m) and was watched by the King of Sweden.

The first balloon ascent in Italy was made on 25th February 1784 by a Montgolfière carrying Chevalier Paul Andreani and the brothers Augustin and Charles Gerli at Moncuco, near Milan, Italy.

The first British aeronaut is claimed to have been James Tytler, a Scotsman, who on 25th August 1784 made a short ascent in a Montgolfier-type balloon, probably from Heriot's Garden, Edinburgh. His maximum altitude is believed not to have exceeded 500 ft (150 m).

The first aerial voyage by a hydrogen balloon made in Great Britain was that of Vincenzo Lunardi, an employee of the Italian Embassy in London, who on 15th September 1784 ascended in a Charlière from the Honourable Artillery Company's training-ground at Moorfields, London. His flight was northwards to the parish of North Mimms (today the site of the village of Welhamgreen), Hertfordshire. Here Lunardi landed his cat and jettisoned his ballast and in so doing ascended again and finally landed at Standon Green End near Ware, Hertfordshire. On the spot where he landed stands a rough stone monument on which a tablet proclaims:

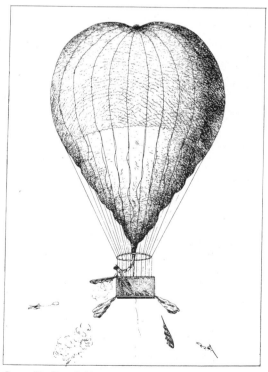

Lunardi's Grand Air Balloon

Let Posterity know
And knowing be astonished!
That
On the 15th day of September, 1784
Vincent Lunardi
of
Lucca in Tuscany
The First Aerial Traveller in Britain
Mounting from the Artillery Ground
in London
And traversing the Regions of the Air
For two Hours and fifteen Minutes
in this Spot
Revisited the Earth.
On this rude Monument
For ages be recorded
That wonderous enterprize, successfully
achieved
By the powers of Chymistry
And the fortitude of man
That improvement in Science
Which
The Great Author of all Knowledge
Patronising by his Providence
The Inventions of Mankind
Hath generously permitted
To their benefit
And
His own Eternal Glory

The first English aeronaut was James Sadler who, on 4th October 1784, flew in a Montgolfier-type balloon of 170 ft (52 m) circumference at Oxford.

Blanchard and Jeffries crossing the Channel

The first aerial crossing of the English Channel was achieved by the Frenchman, Jean-Pierre Blanchard, accompanied by the American, Dr. John Jeffries, who on 7th January 1785 rose from Dover at 13.00 h and landed in the Forêt de Felmores, France, at approximately 15.30 h, having discarded almost all their clothes to lighten the craft *en route*. Their balloon was hydrogen-filled.

The first woman to be carried aloft in a balloon in Britain was Mrs. Letitia Ann Sage who rose aloft in Lunardi's hydrogen balloon from St. George's Fields, London, on 29th June 1785. Lunardi, who had proclaimed that he would be accompanied by three passengers (Mrs. Sage, a Colonel Hastings and George Biggin), discovered that his balloon's lifting power was not equal to the task and, rather than draw attention to the lady's weight (by her own admission, she weighed more than 200 lb), stepped down from the basket with Colonel Hastings. The balloon eventually came to earth near Harrow, Middlesex, where the two occupants were rescued from an irate farmer by the boys from that famous school.

The first aeronaut in the world to be killed while ballooning was François Pilâtre de Rozier who was killed when attempting to fly the English Channel from Boulogne on 15th June 1785 in a composite hot-air/hydrogen balloon. It is believed that when venting hydrogen from the envelope, escaping gas was ignited and the balloon fell at Huitmile Warren, near Boulogne. Also killed was Jules Romain, Pilâtre's companion.

The first free flight by a balloon in the United States of America was made on 9th January 1793 by the Frenchman, Jean-Pierre Blanchard, who ascended in a hydrogen balloon from Philadelphia and landed in Gloucester County, New Jersey, after a flight of 46 min.

The first military use of a man-carrying balloon for aerial reconnaissance was by the French Republican Army at Maubeuge in June 1794. Capitaine Coutelle was the aeronaut and observer.

The first long-distance voyage by air from England was made during 7th–8th November 1836 by a hydrogen balloon—*The Royal Vauxhall Balloon*—manned by Charles Green (English aeronaut) accompanied by Robert Holland, M.P., and Monck Mason, who ascended from Vauxhall Gardens, London, and travelled 480 miles (770 km) to land near Weilberg in the Duchy of Nassau. The balloon was subsequently named the *Great Balloon of Nassau.*

The first balloon bombing raid was carried out on 22nd August 1849 when Austrian hot-air balloons (pilotless), each carrying a 30 lb (14 kg) bomb and time-fuse, were launched against Venice. They caused little damage.

The first long-distance flight by an American balloonist was made in 1859 by John Wise, covering 1,120 miles (1,800 km) from St. Louis to Henderson, N.Y.

Inflating the balloon Intrepid *during the American Civil War Battle of Fair Oaks, 31st May–1st June 1862 (U.S.A.F.)*

The first American Army Balloon Corps was formed on 1st October 1861 with five balloons and fifty men under the command of Thaddeus Sobieski Coulincourt Lowe, Chief Aeronaut of the Army of the Potomac. They were used for reconnaissance and artillery direction.

The first balloon ascent in Australia was made on 29th March 1858 by two men named Brown and Dean in a hydrogen balloon, the *Australasian*, from Cremorne Gardens, Melbourne. (In 1851 a Dr. William Bland, twenty-seven years after he had been transported from India to Australia for killing a ship's purser in a duel, attempted to produce a powered balloon, but there is no evidence that this ever flew.)

The first military use of balloons in an international war outside Europe was by the Brazilian Marquis de Caxias during the Paraguayan War of 1864–1870. This atrocious conflict, which committed the combined forces of Brazil, Argentina and Uruguay against landlocked Paraguay, brought total disaster to the latter nation whose dictator, Francisco Solano López, ordered mass killings among his own people in a savage attempt to compel them towards victory. In the event Brazil occupied Paraguay until 1876; of about 250,000 Paraguayan male nationals before the war, only 28,000 survived in 1871.

The first major balloon operation was carried out during the Franco-Prussian War of 1870–71. The Prussian Army had surrounded Paris and had cut off the city from the rest of France. Inside the city were a few skilled balloonists and material for balloon-making. In an attempt to get despatches out of Paris, Jules Duruog ascended in a balloon on 23rd September 1870. He flew over the Prussian camp and landed at Evreux three hours later. He was followed by Gaston Tissandier, Eugène Godard and Mangin, who were all fired on. Meanwhile inside Paris other balloons were being made from available material and sailors from the French Navy were being trained as pilots. Balloon ascents carried on until 28th January 1871, by which time sixty-six flights had been made carrying 155 persons, nine tons of mail and other cargoes.

A balloon being packed by the Balloon Section of the Royal Engineers on Laffan's Plain, Farnborough, about 1894 (Imperial War Museum)

The first practical development of balloons in the British Army dates from 1878 when the **first "air estimates"** by the War Office allocated the sum of £150 for the construction of a balloon. Captain J. L. B. Templer of the Middlesex Militia (later K.R.R.C.(M)) and Captain H. P. Lee, R.E., were appointed to carry out the necessary development work. Although Captain Templer was thus the **first British Air Commander** and an aeronaut in his own right (and the owner of the balloon *Crusader*, which became the **first balloon used by the British Army** in 1879), the

A Sikorsky S-64 Skycrane helicopter carrying a "people pod" capable of accommodating forty-five combat-equipped troops. Similar pods can be fitted out as mobile hospitals, command posts, communications centres, or any one of a variety of military or civilian interchangeable vans, complete with ventilation, heating, and lighting

Minus pod, an S-64 demonstrates its "flying crane" role by hauling a slung payload. Even prefabricated houses can be delivered in this manner

The go-anywhere versatility of small helicopters, like this Bell 47, suits them well for jobs like power-line patrol and pipe-line inspection

first two aeronauts in the British Army were Lieutenant (later Captain) G. E. Grover, R.E., and Captain F. Beaumont, R.E., who were attached as aeronauts to the Federal Army during the American Civil War from 1862. The **first British Army balloon**, a coal-gas balloon named *Pioneer*, was made during 1879, costing £71 from the £150 appropriation, and had a capacity of 10,000 ft³ (283·2 m³).

The first balloon ascent in Canada was made on 31st July 1879 by a hydrogen balloon manned by Richard Cowan, Charles Grimley and Charles Page at Montreal.

The first military use of a man-carrying balloon in Britain was that by a balloon detachment during military manœuvres at Aldershot, Hants, on 24th June 1880. A balloon detachment accompanied the British military expedition to Bechuanaland, arriving at Cape Town on 19th December 1884, and another accompanied the expeditionary force to the Sudan, departing from Britain on 15th February 1885.

The first air crossing of the North Sea was made during 12th–13th October 1907 by the hydrogen balloon *Mammoth* manned by Monsieur A. F. Gaudron (French aeronaut) accompanied by two others. They ascended from Crystal Palace, London, and landed at Brackan on the shore of Lake Vänern in Sweden. The straight-line distance flown was about 720 miles (1,160 km).

The period 1895–1914 has been termed "the Golden Age" of ballooning. The science and craft of ballooning, for such it had become with the formation of military balloon units in many parts of the world, was now to be joined by ballooning as a respectable sport and recreation. The showmen-aeronauts began to disappear; stunt flights gave way to organised competition. This was becoming the age of the motor car and the aeroplane. International sport blossomed under the watchful eye of respected clubs and societies. Undoubtedly the greatest and longest-lived international ballooning contest was the James Gordon Bennett Trophy, a competition which continued to be held almost every year from 1906 until the Second World War. (See pages 209–212.)

While ballooning as a sport continued to attract the diehards between the world wars, it was not unnatural that science would soon take a hand and, while altitude record-breaking provided something of a spur for human achievement, scientific research of the atmosphere provided the necessary finance.

The first ratified altitude record for balloons in the world was that achieved on 31st June 1901 by Professors Berson and Suring of the Berliner Verein für Luftschiffahrt who attained a height of 35,435 ft (10,800 m). At the time of this record's ratification there was much controversy with those who still firmly believed that James Glaisher had achieved a height of 37,000 ft (11,275 m) on 5th September 1862; as instrumentation to confirm this altitude with any chance of accuracy did not exist at the time, ratification of the Berson and Suring record remained; this record remained unbroken for thirty years (although exceeded on a number of occasions by aeroplanes), and on 11th November 1935 Captain Orvil Anderson and Captain Albert Stevens of the U.S.A. attained an altitude of 72,395 ft (22,066 m) in a balloon in which they ascended from a point 11 miles south-west of Rapid City, South Dakota, and landed 12 miles south of White Lake, South Dakota.

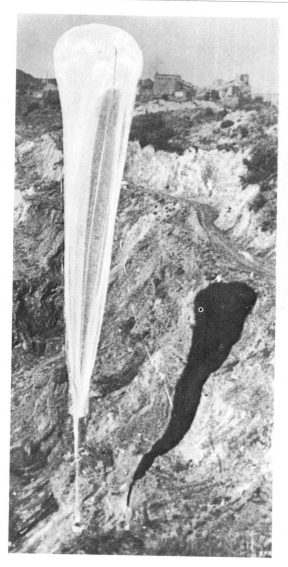

Major David Simons and his balloon. The envelope swelled out to about 200 ft diameter at maximum altitude

The first ratified altitude record for a manned balloon of over 100,000 ft (30,480 m) was achieved by Major David G. Simons, a medical officer of the U.S. Air Force, who reached an altitude of 101,516 ft (30,942 m) on 19th–20th August 1957 in a 3,000,000 ft³ (84,950 m³) balloon *AF-WRI-1*. He took off from Crosby, Minnesota, on 19th August to gather scientific data in the Stratosphere and landed at Frederick, South Dakota, the following day.

The current world altitude record for manned free balloons is held by Commander Malcolm D. Ross of the United States Navy Reserve who, on 4th May 1961, ascended over the Gulf of Mexico to an altitude of 113,739·9 ft (34,668 m) in the Lee Lewis Memorial Winzen Research balloon.

DIRIGIBLES (NAVIGABLE AIRSHIPS)

To many of the adventurous the arrival of the free balloon in 1783 represented the final culmination of man's attempts to fly, albeit without a reliable means of navigation. Of course to others the scarcely predictable nature of this means of travel was something of a frustration and not many years passed before efforts were made to steer and ultimately to propel balloons at speeds greater and in directions other than that of the wind. Although the first elongated and theoretically steerable balloon was attributed to the Frenchman, Lieutenant Jean-Baptiste Marie Meusnier (1754–93), who published a design of such a craft in 1784, it was not until 1852 that a powered dirigible first carried a man into the air.

The world's first powered, manned dirigible made its first flight on 24th September 1852 when the Frenchman, Henri Giffard, rose in a steam-powered balloon from the Paris Hippodrome and travelled approximately 17 miles (27 km) to Trappes, at an average speed of 5 mile/h (8 km/h). The envelope was 144 ft (43·89 m) in length and had a capacity of 88,000 ft³ (2,492 m³); his steam engine developed about 3 hp and drove an 11 ft (3·35 m) diameter three-blade propeller.

The world's first fully controllable powered dirigible was La France, an electric-powered craft which, flown by Captain Charles Renard and Lieutenant Arthur Krebs of the French Corps of Engineers, took off on 9th August 1884 from Chalais-Meudon, France, flew a circular course of about 5 miles (8 km), returned to their point of departure and landed safely. The 9 hp Gramme electric motor drove a 23 ft (7·01 m) four-blade wooden tractor propeller. A maximum speed of 14·5 mile/h (23·5 km/h) was achieved during the 23 min flight.

A later model of the Wölfert airship, also powered by a Daimler engine

The first successful use of a petrol engine in a dirigible was by the German Dr. Karl Wölfert who designed and built a small balloon to which he fitted a 2 hp single-cylinder Daimler engine in 1888. Its **first flight** was carried out at Seelberg, Germany, on Sunday, 12th August that year, probably flown by a young mechanic named Michaël.

The first flight of a Zeppelin dirigible was made by Count Ferdinand von Zeppelin's LZ1 on 2nd July 1900 carrying five people from its floating hangar on Lake Constance near Friedrichshafen. The flight lasted about 20 min.

The first dirigible to fly round the Eiffel Tower and so win a 100,000 franc prize was the No. 6, built and piloted by Santos-Dumont, on 19th October 1901. It had a 12 hp engine and a speed of 15 mile/h (24 km/h).

The first practical dirigible was designed by the Lebaudy brothers and first flew on 12th November 1903. The flight of 38 miles (61 km) was from Moisson to the Champ-de-Mars, Paris. This was the **first controlled air journey in history**.

The first British Army airship, Dirigible No. 1 (popularly known as *Nulli Secundus*), was first flown on 10th September 1907 with three occupants: Colonel John Capper, R.E., pilot; Captain W. A. de C. King, Adjutant of the British Army Balloon School; Mr. Samuel Cody, "in charge of the engine". The engine was a 50 hp Antoinette. The airship was 122 ft (37 m) long, 26 ft (8 m) in diameter and had a capacity of 55,000 ft³ (1,555 m³). The second and third Army airships were *Beta* (35 hp Green engine) and *Gamma* (80 hp Green engine) respectively.

First air service using rigid airships. *See "Route-proving and Commercial Aviation".*

The first dirigible of the U.S. Navy to fly was the DN-1 (A1) which was acquired under contract on 1st June 1915. As originally built with two engines it was too heavy to leave the ground; however, after redesign with only one engine it made its first of three flights in April 1917 at Pensacola, Florida. It was subsequently damaged and not repaired.

The first successful dirigible of the U.S. Navy was the Goodyear FB-1 acquired under contract on 14th March 1917 and first flown from Chicago, Illinois, to Wingfoot Lake, near Akron, Ohio, on 30th May 1917.

The first airship crossing, and double-crossing of the Atlantic were achieved by the British airship R-34 between 2nd and 6th July (westward) and 9th and 13th July (eastward), 1919. Commanded by Squadron Leader G. H. Scott, with a crew of thirty, the R-34 set out from East Fortune, Scotland, and flew to New York, returning afterwards to Pulham, Norfolk, England. At the time the R-34 was the largest airship in the world, and the total distance covered, 6,330 miles (10,187 km) in 183 h 8 min, constituted a world record for airships. (The R-34 was destroyed when it broke up over Hull, England, on 24th August 1921. It was to have been sold to the United States and at the time of the disaster there were seventeen Americans aboard in addition to the crew of thirty-two. All the Americans and twenty-seven of the British lost their lives.)

The first helium-filled American rigid airship was the Zeppelin-type ZR-1 *Shenandoah*, which first flew on 4th September 1923 at Lakehurst, New Jersey, U.S.A. On 3rd September 1925 it was destroyed in a storm over Caldwell, Ohio, with heavy loss of life.

The last commercial airship to be developed by Great Britain was the *R-101* which crashed on 5th October 1930 at Beauvais, France, on a flight from Cardington, Bedfordshire, England, to Egypt and India. The accident, which destroyed the airship and killed forty-eight of the fifty-four occupants (including

Lord Thompson, Secretary of State for Air, and Major-General Sir Sefton Brancker, Director of Civil Aviation), brought to an end the development of passenger-carrying airships in Great Britain.

The R-101

The last major airship disaster involved the destruction of the German *Hindenburg*, then the world's largest airship, on 6th May 1937. It was destroyed by fire when approaching its moorings at Lakehurst, New Jersey, U.S.A., after a flight from Frankfurt, Germany. Thirty-five of the ninety-seven occupants were killed in the fire which engulfed the huge craft and which was attributed to the use of hydrogen—the only gas available to Germany owing to the United States' refusal to supply commercial quantities of helium.

Largest current airship fleet is operated by the Goodyear Tire & Rubber Company of Akron, Ohio, U.S.A. It comprises four non-rigid airships, the *Columbia II* (gross volume 147,300 ft³), *Mayflower III* (147,300 ft³), *America* (202,700 ft³) and *Europa* (202,700 ft³). This last airship, first flown on 8th March 1972 at Cardington, England, and now based in Rome, Italy, is made of two-ply Neoprene-coated Dacron and, like other Goodyear airships, is helium-filled. It carries a pilot and six passengers in an underslung gondola and is powered by two 210 hp Continental piston-engines which give it a cruising speed of 35–40 mile/h. Endurance is from 10 to 23 h. The *Europa* is 192 ft 6 in (58·67 m) long, and 50 ft (15·24 m) wide. On each side of the envelope is a four-colour sign, 105 ft (32·00 m) long and 24 ft 6 in (7·47 m) high, made up of 3,780 lamps to flash static or animated messages.

The world's first hot-air airship, built by Cameron Balloons Ltd. of Bristol, made its maiden flight near Wantage, Berkshire, on 4th February 1973. It is 100 ft (30·5 m) long, with a maximum diameter of 60 ft (18·3 m), and is propelled by a converted Volkswagen engine which was expected to give a maximum speed of 20–25 mile/h (32–40 km/h). Hot air to inflate the light-weight nylon fabric envelope is supplied by an underslung propane gas burner, giving a total operating cost of about £2 per flight.

THE JAMES GORDON BENNETT INTERNATIONAL BALLOON RACE TROPHY

Without doubt the most famous international balloon contest was the Gordon Bennett contest for a trophy and an annual prize of 12,500 francs presented by the expatriate American newspaper magnate, James Gordon Bennett, in 1905 and first contested in 1906. Principal results were as follows:

Date	Starting-point and number of Starters	Winners (Nationality, balloon, qualifying destination and distance)	Remarks
30.9.06	Tuileries, Paris, France (16)	1. Lieutenant Frank P. Lahm, U.S. Army; *United States*; Fylingdales, Yorkshire, England — 402 miles (647 km) 2. Alfredo Vanwiller, Italy; *L'Elfe*; New Holland, Hull, England — 362 miles (583 km) 3. The Hon. C. S. Rolls, England; *Britannia*; Sandringham, Norfolk, England — 289 miles (465 km)	Only these three finishers managed to cross the English Channel, although the Count de la Vaulx was provisionally announced as sharing third place.
1907	St. Louis, Missouri, U.S.A.	1. Oscar Erbslön, Germany; *Pommern* — 849 miles (1,367 km) 2. Leblanc, France; *Île de France* — 848·8 miles (1,366 km) 3. Von Abercron, Germany	Leblanc's time to cover 1,366 km was 44 h and established a new world endurance record.
12.10.08	Berlin, Germany (23)	1. Colonel Schaeck, Switzerland; *Helvetia*; 40 km N. of Molde, Norway — 753 miles (1,212 km) 2. John Dunville, Britain; *Banshee*; Huidding, Schleswig-Holstein — 270 miles (435 km) 3. Geerts, Belgium; *Belgica*; near Huidding, Schleswig-Holstein — 263 miles (423 km)	Many balloons came down in the North Sea. Schaeck's time of 73 h 41 min established a new world endurance record, although he admitted that during the flight his trail rope was caught by fishermen who towed him ashore.
3.10.09	Zürich, Switzerland (17)	1. E. W. Mix, U.S.A., *America II*; Ostrolenka, Poland — 590 miles (950 km) 2. Alfred Leblanc, France; *Île de France*; Zargriva, Hungary — 517 miles (832 km) 3. Captain Messner, Switzerland; *Azurea*; Thule, Silesia — 515 miles (828 km)	Captain Messner was Colonel Schaeck's crew member during his record-breaking flight of 1908.
17.10.10	St. Louis, Missouri, U.S.A.	1. Allan R. Hawley, U.S.A.; *America II*; Lake Tschotogama, Quebec, Canada — 1,171·13 miles (1,884·75 km) 2. Gericke, Germany; *Dusseldorf*; near Quebec, Canada — 1,099 miles (1,769 km) 3. Von Abercron; Germany; *Germania*; near Quebec, Canada — 1,095 miles (1,763 km)	Established a new American distance record.
1911	Kansas City, Kansas, U.S.A.	1. O. Gericke, Germany; Holcombe, Wisconsin, U.S.A. — 468·2 miles (753·5 km) 2. Captain Frank P. Lahm, U.S.A.; La Cross, Wisconsin, U.S.A. — 406 miles (653 km) 3. Vogt, Germany; Austin, Minnesota, U.S.A. — 348 miles (560 km)	
1912	Stuttgart, Germany	1. A. Bienaimé, France; *Picardi*; Ryasan, near Moscow, U.S.S.R. — 1,361 miles (2,191 km) 2. Alfred Leblanc, France; *Île de France*; Kaluga, U.S.S.R. — 1,243 miles (2,001 km) 3. H. E. Honeywell, U.S.A.; *Uncle Sam*; Sapadnaja, U.S.S.R. — 1,118 miles (1,800 km)	One of the longest balloon races in history.

Date	Starting-point and number of Starters	Winners (Nationality, balloon, qualifying destination and distance)		Remarks
1913	Tuileries, Paris, France	1. Ralph Upson, U.S.A.; *Goodyear*; Bempton, Yorkshire, England	384 miles (618 km)	The extraordinary difference in routes followed is explained by the prevailing upper winds used by Upson.
		2. H. E. Honeywell, U.S.A.; *Uncle Sam*; Finisterre, Galicia, Spain;	300 miles (483 km)	
		3. Pastine, Italy; *Roma*; Finisterre, Galicia, Spain	299 miles (481 km)	
24.10.20	Birmingham, Alabama, U.S.A. (8)	1. Lieutenant Ernest E. Demuyter, Belgium; *Belgica*; Lake Champlain, Vermont, N.Y., U.S.A.	1,094 miles (1,760 km)	Honeywell's time of 48 h 26 min established a new American duration record.
		2. H. E. Honeywell, U.S.A.; *Kansas City II*; Lake George, N.Y., U.S.A.	994 miles (1,600 km)	
		3. Major G. del Valle, Italy; *L'Audiens*; Homer, N.Y., U.S.A.	890 miles (1,432 km)	
18.9.21	Brussels, Belgium (14)	1. Captain Paul Armbruster, Switzerland; Lambay Island, Ireland	476 miles (766 km)	Some accounts give Spencer and Upson as tying for second place.
		2. Harry Spencer; Britain; Fishguard, Pembroke, Wales	419 miles (675 km)	
		3. Ralph Upson, U.S.A.; Near Barmouth; Merioneth, Wales	413 miles (664 km)	
6.8.22	Geneva, Switzerland (18)	1. Lieutenant Ernest Demuyter, Belgium; *Belgica*; Oknitsa, Romania	853 miles (1,372 km)	Honeywell, with a time of 26 h 30 min, qualified for the duration prize.
		2. H. E. Honeywell, U.S.A.; Tapio-Szecso, Hungary	659 miles (1,061 km)	
		3. A. Bienaimé, France, *Picardi*; Mór, Hungary	574 miles (923 km)	
23.9.23	Brussels, Belgium (17)	1. Lieutenant Ernest Demuyter, Belgium; *Belgica*; Skillingaryd, Sweden	994 miles (1,600 km)	Race started in thunderstorm, met with disaster, five aeronauts killed, five injured. Collision on start-line, two balloons struck by lightning, and one collided with high-tension cable.
		2. Lieutenant Veenstra, Belgium; *Prince Leopold*; Mellerud, Lake Vänern, Sweden	624 miles (1,005 km)	
		3. Captain Paul Armbruster, Switzerland; *Helvetia*; Northern Schleswig	339 miles (546 km)	
15.6.24	Brussels, Belgium	1. Lieutenant Ernest Demuyter, Belgium; *Belgica*; St. Abbs Head, Berwick, Scotland	466 miles (750 km)	This, the third consecutive win by Belgium, would have qualified that country to retain the trophy outright. The Belgians, however, sportingly announced its renewal for further competition.
		2. Laporte, France; *Ville de Bordeaux*; Brighton, Sussex, England	245 miles (395 km)	
		3. H. E. Honeywell, U.S.A.; *Uncle Sam*; Rouen, France	199 miles (320 km)	

SECOND TROPHY SERIES

Date	Starting-point and number of Starters	Winners		Remarks
1925	Brussels, Belgium	1. Lieutenant Veenstra, Belgium; *Prince Leopold*	841 miles (1,354 km)	In this race Van Orman (U.S. Balloon *Goodyear III*) performed the singular feat of landing on the bridge of a ship at sea; the American balloon, *Elsie*, was hit by a train at Étaples.
		2. Lieutenant Ernest Demuyter, Belgium; *Belgica*	411 miles (661·5 km)	
		3. Colonel G. del Valle, Italy; *Ciampino V*	370 miles (596 km)	

Date	Starting-point and number of Starters	Winners (Nationality, balloon, qualifying destination and distance)		Remarks
30.5.26	Antwerp, Belgium	1. W. T. Van Orman, U.S.A.; *Goodyear III*; Sölvesborg, Sweden	535 miles (861 km)	
		2. Captain H. C. Gray, U.S. Army; *S.16*; Kraków, Poland	370 miles (595 km)	
		3. Lieutenant Ernest Demuyter, Belgium; *Belgica*; near Hamburg, Germany	209 miles (336 km)	
10.9.27	Dearborn, Michigan, U.S.A. (15)	1. E. J. Hill, U.S.A.; *Detroit*; Baxley, Georgia	745 miles (1,199 km)	Some accounts suggest that Herr Kaulen was disqualified; the results quoted are those ratified by the sponsoring body, and later confirmed.
		2. Hugo Kaulen, Germany; *Barmen*; Fort Valley, Georgia	688 miles (1,107 km)	
		3. W. T. Van Orman, U.S.A.; *Goodyear III*; Adrian, Georgia	685 miles (1,102 km)	
30.6.28	Detroit, Michigan, U.S.A. (12)	1. Captain W. E. Kepner, U.S.A.; *U.S. Army*; Kenbridge, Virginia	460 miles (740·3 km)	Herr Kaulen was accompanied by his son, Hugo Kaulen, Jr. Once again the trophy was re-presented for competition, this time by the U.S.A.
		2. Hugo Kaulen, Germany; *Barmen*; Chase City, Virginia	459·4 miles (739·3 km)	
		3. Charles Dollfus, France; *Blanchard*; Walnut Cove, North Carolina	447·9 miles (720·8 km)	

THIRD TROPHY SERIES

Date	Starting-point and number of Starters	Winners (Nationality, balloon, qualifying destination and distance)		Remarks
1929	St. Louis, Missouri, U.S.A.	1. W. T. Van Orman, U.S.A.; Troy, Ohio	339 miles (545 km)	
		2. Captain W. E. Kepner, U.S.A.; *U.S. Army*; Neptune, Ohio	336 miles (541 km)	
		3. Lieutenant T. G. Settle, U.S.A.; *U.S. Navy*; Eaton, Ohio	302 miles (486 km)	
1930	Cleveland, Ohio, U.S.A.	1. W. T. Van Orman, U.S.A.; North Canton, Massachusetts	539 miles (867 km)	No Gordon Bennett Trophy Race was held in 1931 and a fourth series of races was started in 1932.
		2. Captain Ernest Demuyter, Belgium; *Belgica*; North Canton, Massachusetts	445·5 miles (717 km)	
		3. E. J. Hill, U.S.A.		

FOURTH TROPHY SERIES

Date	Starting-point and number of Starters	Winners (Nationality, balloon, qualifying destination and distance)		Remarks
1932	Basle, Switzerland	1. Lieutenant-Commander T. G. Settle, U.S.A.; *U.S. Navy*; Vilna, Lithuania	954 miles (1,536 km)	New series established under Swiss administration.
		2. W. T. Van Orman, U.S.A.; *Goodyear VIII*; Kovno, Lithuania	859 miles (1,383 km)	
		3. Ravaine-Speiss, France; *Petit Mousse*; Tokary, Poland	766 miles (1,233 km)	
1933	Chicago, Illinois, U.S.A.	1. Z. J. Burzynski, Poland; Quebec, Canada	846 miles (1,361 km)	
		2. Lieutenant-Commander T. G. Settle, U.S.A.; *U.S. Navy*; Grove, Long Island, N.Y.	775 miles (1,248 km)	
		3. W. T. Van Orman, U.S.A.; *Goodyear VIII*; Sudbury, Ontario, Canada	492 miles (792 km)	

Date	Starting-point and number of Starters	Winners (Nationality, balloon, qualifying destination and distance)	Remarks
1934	Warsaw, Poland	1. Hynek, Poland; *Kosciuszko*; Finland (location not recorded)	827 miles (1,331 km)	Landing area of first two balloons probably near Savonlinna, Finland.
		2. Z. J. Burzynski, Poland; *Warszawa*; Finland (location not recorded)	810 miles (1,304 km)	
		3. Ernest Demuyter, Belgium; *Belgica*	722 miles (1,162 km)	
15-9-35	Warsaw, Poland	1. Z. J. Burzynski, Poland; *Polonia II*; near Leningrad, U.S.S.R.	1,025 miles (1,650 km)	The leading balloons all landed in a desperately remote area and were not rescued for a fortnight after landing. Burzynski's flight established a world record for balloons of 1,601–2,200 m³.
		2. Janusz, Poland; *Warszawa II*; near Leningrad, U.S.S.R.	971 miles (1,563 km)	
		3. Ernest Demuyter, Belgium; *Belgica*	904 miles (1,455 km)	
1-9-36	Warsaw, Poland	1. Ernest Demuyter, Belgium; *Belgica*; Miedlesza, U.S.S.R.	1,066·15 miles (1,715·8 km)	The veteran Demuyter's flight constituted a world distance record in four balloon categories.
		2. Goetze, Germany	994 miles (1,600 km)	
		3. Z. J. Burzynski, Poland; *Polonia II*	982 miles (1,580 km)	
1937	Brussels, Belgium	1. Ernest Demuyter, Belgium; *Belgica*; Tukumo, Lithuania	889 miles (1,430 km)	
		2. Janusz, Poland; *Warszawa II*; Anec, Lithuania	870 miles (1,400 km)	
1938	Liège, Belgium	1. Janusz, Poland; *L.O.P.P.*; Trojan, Bulgaria	1,013 miles (1,630 km)	
		2. Krzyszkowski, Poland; *Warszawa II*; Catuselle, Romania	913 miles (1,470 km)	
		3. Thonar, Belgium; *S. II*; Vidin, Bulgaria	902 miles (1,451 km)	

Mil Mi-12, the world's largest helicopter in 1973 (Tass)

SECTION VI
Rotorcraft

The first documented reference to the possibility of sustaining or propelling upwards a vehicle by means of rotating surfaces is attributed to Leonardo da Vinci (1452–1519), whose design sketches for such are believed to have originated in about the year 1500. Leonardo was otherwise devoted to the concept of flapping wings (i.e. the ornithopter) to achieve forward flight and he was not aware of the lifting characteristics of aerofoils, nor was he acquainted with the properties of the propeller. As a result his design for a helicopter was based strictly on an "air screw"—literally a rotating helical wing which would "screw" its path upwards through the air.

Numerous attempts to evolve models of helicopters followed during the next four centuries, culminating in the unmanned models of W. H. Phillips who, in 1842, succeeded in launching a steam-driven craft whose rotating *blades* were propelled by tip jets.

It is perhaps useful here to interpose simple definitions of the helicopter and Autogiro. Basically a helicopter achieves vertical flight by means of aerodynamic lift from rotor blades which are rotated under power; to eliminate torque (i.e. to prevent the fuselage of the aircraft from spinning uncontrollably on the axis of the rotor), either coaxial rotors, balanced sets of rotors or small tail-mounted rotors are geared to the power plant. Forward flight is achieved by tilting the rotor "disc" so that its resulting thrust provides a degree of propulsion as well as lift.

An Autogiro, on the other hand, is rather nearer to a conventional aeroplane in that forward motion is achieved by a conventional engine (either jet or piston engine-driven propeller); as forward motion is achieved the freely rotating rotor blades provide lift as aerofoils, enabling the Autogiro to perform short, steep take-offs and landings.

The first helicopter to lift a man from the ground was built by the Breguet brothers of France in 1907. Although the craft lifted off the ground at Douai, France, on 29th September that year, it did not constitute a free flight as four men on the ground steadied the machine with long poles which, while not contributing to the aircraft's lift, constituted a form of control restriction. Power was provided by a 50 hp Antoinette engine.

The Cornu helicopter, 1907

The first true free flight by a man-carrying helicopter was performed by Paul Cornu in his 24 hp Antoinette-powered twin-rotor aircraft near Lisieux, France, on 13th November 1907.

Neither of the above helicopters incorporated cyclic pitch control (hence the problem overcome by Breguet in using external control stabilisation) although G. A. Crocco had in 1906 suggested its necessity. It was J. C. H. Ellehammer, the Danish pioneer aviator, who first produced a helicopter (of only limited application) in 1912 which incorporated cyclic pitch control.

The first helicopters to successfully demonstrate cyclic pitch control were those designed and constructed by the Marquis de Pescara, an Argentinian, in France and Spain between 1919 and 1925. Although demonstrating this feature successfully, these aircraft were directionally unstable as the result of inadequate torque counter-action.

An early Cierva Autogiro in flight

The first successful flight by a gyroplane, the C.4 (commercially named an *Autogiro*) was accomplished by the Spaniard Juan de la Cierva at Getafe, Spain, on 9th January 1923.

The first helicopter flight over a closed 1 kilometre circuit was made on 4th May 1924 by the French Oehmichen No. 2.

The first two-seat Autogiro in the world was the Cierva C.6D which was first flown by F. T. Courtney at Hamble, England, on 29th July 1927. Don Juan de la Cierva, the Spanish inventor, became **the first passenger in the world to ride in a rotating-wing aircraft** when he was taken aloft the following day in this Autogiro.

The first rotating-wing aircraft to fly the English Channel was the Cierva C.8L Mark II (*G-EBYY*) Autogiro flown by Don Juan de la Cierva with a passenger from Croydon to Le Bourget on 18th September 1928.

The first Autogiro flown in America was an aircraft brought to the United States by Harold F. Pitcairn and flown at Willow Grove, Philadelphia, on 19th December 1928.

The first Autogiro to be publicly demonstrated in the U.S.A. was the Cierva C.19 Mark II (*G-AAKY*) which was flown at the Cleveland Air Races, Ohio, during August 1929.

Focke-Wulf Fw.61

The first entirely successful helicopter in the world was the Focke-Wulf Fw 61 twin-rotor helicopter designed by Professor Heinrich Karl Johann Focke during 1932–34. The first prototype Fw 61 V1 (*D-EBVU*) made its first free flight on 26th June 1936 and was powered by a 160 hp Siemens-Halske Sh 14A engine. This aircraft, flown by Ewald Rohlfs in June 1937, established a world's closed-circuit distance record for helicopters of 76·105 miles (122·35 km) and a helicopter endurance record of 1 h 20 min 49 s. On other occasions it set up an altitude record of 11,243 ft (3,427 m) and a speed record of 76 mile/h (122 km/h). It gave a flying demonstration in the Berlin Deutschland-Halle during 1938 in the hands of the famous German woman test pilot Hanna Reitsch.

The first helicopter to go into limited production was the Focke-Achgelis Fa 223. The experimental Focke-Wulf Fw 61 (see page 215) was not commercially exploited, being too heavy structurally to carry a payload. Instead, a commercially developed derivative, the Fa 223 appeared and was put into limited production during 1940, but never achieved service status.

Igor Sikorsky in 1972

Sikorsky VS-300 in an early form with multiple tail rotors

The first successful helicopters to be designed outside Germany were those of the Russian-born American Igor Sikorsky. His first successful helicopter was the VS-300. Powered by a 75 hp engine, it featured full cyclic pitch control and achieved tethered flight on 14th September 1939 in America. Its first recognised free flight was made on 13th May 1940. In May 1941 a 90 hp engine was fitted and the VS-300 set up a new endurance record of 1 h 32 min 26 s. By 1942, after further improvement, the VS-300 became established as the first successful and practical single-rotor helicopter.

The first helicopter designed and built for military service was the Sikorsky XR-4 which was delivered to Wright Field, Dayton, Ohio, in 1942 for military evaluation. As a result of these trials, machines of a small development batch were used for limited service and training in 1944 and 1945, R-4s being the first helicopters to fly in Burma and Alaska, and the first to be flown by the British Fleet Air Arm.

The first helicopter to go into full production and service was the Sikorsky R-4B, at Bridgeport, Connecticut, in 1944.

The first-ever Type-Approval Certificate awarded for a commercial helicopter was for the Bell Model 47 on 8th March 1946; this helicopter made its first flight on 8th December 1945 and provided the design basis for a family of Bell helicopters which has continued in production for more than twenty-seven years.

Bell Model 47 prototype

The first helicopter built in Great Britain to enter service with the R.A.F. was the Sikorsky-designed Westland-Sikorsky Dragonfly (the S-51 built under licence by Westland Aircraft Ltd., Yeovil, England). The first Westland-built S-51 was for commercial use and flew in 1948. The R.A.F.'s first helicopter, a Dragonfly H.C. Mark 2 (*WF308*) powered by an Alvis Leonides engine, was delivered in 1950, and subsequent aircraft equipped No. 194 (Casualty Evacuation) Squadron, **the R.A.F.'s first helicopter squadron**, on 1st February 1953.

The first British-designed and -built production helicopter was the Bristol Sycamore which entered service with both the Army and Air Force. The Army versions were the H.C. 10 ambulance and H.C. 11 communication helicopters, the latter initially flying on 13th August 1950 and being delivered from 29th September 1951. The first R.A.F. version, H.R. 12, was sent to St. Mawgan for trials on 19th February 1952.

By setting up a world speed record of 220·885 mile/h, the Sikorsky S-67 Blackhawk became officially the fastest helicopter of the early 1970s

The largest helicopter in the world in 1973 was the Russian Mil Mi-12 twin-rotor aircraft whose over-all span (over the rotor tips) is 219 ft 10 in (67·00 m), and fuselage length is 121 ft 5 in (37·00 m). It is powered by four 6,500 shp turboshaft engines. First indication of the existence of this enormous helicopter to reach the West was in 1969 when Russia submitted for ratification the lifting of a record payload of 68,410 lb (31,030 kg) to an altitude of 9,678 ft (2,950 m)—approximately the loaded weight of an Avro Lancaster bomber of the Second World War. On 6th August 1969 the Mi-12 beat its own record by lifting a payload of 88,636 lb (40,204·5 kg) to a height of 7,298 ft (2,255 m).

Smallest aeroplane yet built and flown in the U.K., the Ward Gnome spans 15 ft 9 in and is powered by a 14 hp Douglas motor-cycle engine

SECTION VII
Flying for Sport and Competition

In realms of commerce and in times of war it is perhaps often overlooked that flying originally approached maturity before the First World War largely through the enthusiasm and courage of a small band of philanthropic sportsmen who sought satisfaction through a precarious recreation, and the measure of whose success lay in their ability to fly further, faster or higher than their colleagues at home and abroad. The very nature of their sport, eliminating as it did the frontiers that had divided nation from nation, brought airmen of different countries closer together, so that almost at once international competition was keen—yet characterised by something of a universal cameraderie. So powerful was this sense of *entente* between all aerial sportsmen that when, inevitably, the Kaiser's War split nations asunder and they were placed under orders to do battle among one another, there was a reluctance at first to so prostitute their new-found sport by turning their frail craft into machines of destruction. One has only to attend an international flying meeting sixty years later to realise that the old *entente* has not altogether disappeared . . .

This Chapter spans the scope of flying by pilots who, perhaps supported only by limited money, indulged their whims in the private ownership of an aeroplane, and also by pilots who, by their prowess (or perhaps in spite of their lack of it) are encouraged to compete against each other either in organised or in informal sporting events. While of course there have been the classic annual spectacles—the Schneider Trophy, the King's Cup Air Race and the American National Air Races—there have also been great once only competitions, sponsored by big finance, like the Australia Race of 1934 and the Transatlantic Race of 1969. All have contributed greatly both to the progress of aviation and to the better understanding of what, after all, aviation has to offer: the drawing together of nation to nation by time, distance and competition.

The first major prize to be offered in Great Britain for a feat performed in an aeroplane was the £1,000 offered by the *Daily Mail* for the first aeroplane flight across the English Channel. This was won by the Frenchman, Louis Blériot, who crossed from France to England on Sunday, 25th July 1909 (see page 28).

The World's first international air meeting was held at Reims, France, and opened on 22nd August 1909. Promoted and financed by the French Champagne industry, which also offered a number of generous prizes, no fewer than thirty-eight entries were received. Among the aeroplanes which assembled were seven Voisins, six Wright biplanes, five Blériot monoplanes, four Henry Farman biplanes, four R.E.P.s, three Antoinettes, two Curtisses, one Santos-Dumont, one Breguet and one Sanchis. Competition during the meeting consisted of a number of speed, duration and distance events and Henry Farman established world records for duration and distance by flying 112·5 miles (181 km) in a closed circuit in 3 h 4 min 56·4 s. His prize money totalled 63,000 francs. Fastest speed was recorded by Louis Blériot who, flying his Blériot *XII* monoplane, won the 10 km speed contest at 47·8 mile/h (76·95 km/h). *See also "Pioneers".*

The first major prize to be offered in Great Britain for all-British aviation activity was the £1,000 offered by the *Daily Mail* to the first British pilot to complete a circular flight of one mile (1·6 km) in an all-British aeroplane. This prize was won by J. T. C. Moore-Brabazon who, at Shellbeach, flew a Short-built Wright-type biplane powered by a 50–60 hp Green engine over a mile on Saturday, 30th October 1909. This flight is generally regarded as the inauguration of all-British aviation.

While Paulhan waited for the dawn at Lichfield, Grahame-White made his epic night flight (see next page).

The first prize of £10,000 to be offered in Great Britain for an aeroplane flight was again offered by the *Daily Mail* for the first pilot to fly an aeroplane from a point within 5 miles of the newspaper's London offices to a point within 5 miles of its Manchester offices. This prize encouraged Louis Paulhan and Claude Grahame-White to compete in their Henry Farman biplanes, success finally attending the efforts of the former on Thursday, 28th April 1910. The event, which ultimately developed into a race (with Grahame-White resorting to an epic night flight, the first in Europe), fired the imagination of the whole country as supporters and officials hired special trains to follow the progress of the aviators, and reports were flashed to H.M. King Edward VII who was abroad at the time.

The first prize won by an Englishman flying in America went to Claude Grahame-White who, between 6th and 12th September 1910, won a £2,000 prize offered by the *Boston Globe* by flying 33 miles (53 km) cross-country in 40 min 1·6 s. At the same Boston meeting Grahame-White also gained four other first prizes and three seconds, so that his total prize-money amounted to £6,420 for the week.

The first Gordon Bennett international aeroplane race was flown at the end of October 1910 at Belmont Park, New York, and attracted teams from the U.S.A. (Messrs. Brookins, Drexel and Moisant), France (MM Latham and Leblanc) and Great Britain (Messrs. Grahame-White, Ogilvie and Radley). On 29th October the race was won by Claude Grahame-White, flying a Blériot monoplane powered by a 100 hp Gnome rotary engine, who completed the 100 km (62·2 mile) course in 1 h 1 min 4·74 s. Second place was taken by Moisant, also flying a Blériot.

The emphasis placed upon financial reward for competition in the air during the early years of aviation may, by modern definition, tend to detract from the amateur status of the pilots of that time, yet it was the nature of their sport and the absence of national support which threatened to retard their progress by its very cost. It was the far-sighted sponsorship by the Press and by such persons as Archdeacon and the Baron de Forest which not only ensured the survival of competitive aviation, but also spurred European aviation to the efforts which very quickly overhauled those of the pioneering Americans. For example, Claude Grahame-White won in prize-money during 1910 a total of £10,280—much of which was applied to the support of the important Grahame-White Flying Schools.

The first truly international air race (point-to-point) held in Europe was the Circuit of Europe which started on 18th June 1911, whose route was Paris – Reims – Liège – Spa – Liège – Verloo – Utrecht – Breda – Brussels – Roubaix – Calais – Dover – Shoreham – London – Shoreham – Dover – Calais – Amiens – Paris. The field included eight Moranes, seven Deperdussins, six Blériots, three Sommers, three Caudrons, three Henry Farmans, two Maurice Farmans, two Bristols, two Voisins, two Astras, and one each of Antoinette, Barillon, Bonnet-Lab, Danton, Nieuport, Pischoff, R.E.P., Tellier, Train, van Meel and Vinet. The race was won after nineteen days on 7th July by Lieutenant de Vaisseau Conneau flying a Blériot, followed by Roland Garros also in a Blériot. Prize-money totalled £18,300, and only nine aeroplanes completed the course.

The first "Round-Britain" air race was sponsored by the *Daily Mail*, which newspaper presented a £10,000 prize for a race which started from Brooklands on 22nd July 1911. The course, which was flown in five days, followed the route Brooklands – Hendon – Harrogate – Newcastle – Edinburgh – Stirling – Glasgow – Carlisle – Manchester – Bristol – Exeter – Salisbury Plain – Brighton – Brooklands, a distance of 1,010 miles (1,625 km). Only two, French aircraft completed the course in the specified time and the race was won by the French naval officer Lieutenant de Vaisseau Conneau in a Blériot XI, in a time of 22 h 28 min. Jules Vedrines came second, and Samuel Cody completed the course three days late.

The first Schneider Trophy (or to give its formal title, the *"Jacques Schneider Air Racing Trophy for Hydro-Aeroplanes"*) was contested at Monaco on 16th April 1913 over twenty-eight laps of a 10 km course and was organised initially by the Aero Club de France. The first race attracted four starters in the final heat, which was won by Maurice Prevost flying a 160 hp Gnôme-powered Deperdussin. This pilot was the only one to complete the course and was not judged to have flown across the finishing-line correctly. He was accordingly sent off again to complete a further lap which added about another hour to his time, so that his average speed is recorded in the official results as being 45·75 mile/h (73·63 km/h).

The first major British competition for seaplanes was the *Daily Mail* Hydro-Aeroplane Trial of 16th August 1913, and the regulations stated a specified course round Britain, involving a distance to be flown of 1,540 miles (2,478 km) by an all-British aircraft before 30th August. Four aircraft were entered but Samuel Cody had been killed in a crash at Laffan's Plain on 7th August. F. K. McClean withdrew his Short S.68 due to engine trouble, and the Radley-England Waterplane was scratched for the same reason. This left Harry Hawker, accompanied by his mechanic H. A. Kauper, as the only contender, and they left the water at Southampton at 11·47 h in a Sopwith three-seater tractor biplane. The route was from Southampton via Ramsgate, Yarmouth, Scarborough, Aberdeen, Cromarty, Oban, Dublin, Falmouth and back to Southampton. After an abortive attempt, which ended at Yarmouth owing to a cracked engine cylinder, Hawker took off again from Southampton on 25th August. He managed to fly round the course as far as Dublin when, just before alighting on the water, his foot slipped off the rudder-bar and the aircraft struck the water and broke up. The *Daily Mail* prize of £5,000 was not awarded, but Hawker received £1,000 as consolation.

The first British aeroplane to beat all comers in a major international competitive event was the Sopwith Tabloid. Equipped as a landplane towards the end of 1913, this revolutionary aircraft could climb to 1,200 ft in 1 min while carrying pilot, passenger and sufficient fuel for 2·5 h. It was capable of a maximum speed of 92 mile/h (148 km/h). Its outstanding competitive success was its victory in the second contest for the Schneider Trophy held between Monaco and Cap Martin on 20th April 1914 when, equipped as a floatplane, the aircraft was flown by Howard Pixton over the 280 km at an average speed of 86·78 mile/h (139·66 km/h). After completing the racecourse, Pixton continued for two extra laps to establish a new world speed record for seaplanes at 86·6 mile/h (139·37 km/h) over a measured 300 km course.

The first major British aviation competition to be won by an American pilot was the third Aerial Derby, flown in bad weather on 6th June 1914 and won by W. L.

(above) It would be difficult to imagine a more simple aircraft than the Aerosport Rail. Powered by two 33 hp snowmobile engines, it provides exciting flying for one man at up to 95 mile/h (153 km/h) (Howard Levy). (below left) Dornier's eight-seat Do 28 (nearest camera) and fourteen-seat Skyservant are modern air taxis and local-service transports able to operate from short, unprepared airstrips around busy airports. (below right) For those businessmen who can afford it, a Hawker Siddeley 125 baby jet will carry a dozen passengers at airline speeds. Most customers for this British product are based in North America.

Brock in a Morane-Saulnier monoplane powered by an 80 hp Le Rhone engine. Completing the 94·5 mile (152 km) course at an average speed of 71·9 mile/h (115·7 km/h), Brock won the *Daily Mail* Gold Cup and Shell Trophy, as well as £300 in prize-money.

The era of unrestricted flying over Great Britain came to an end with the outbreak of the First World War. On 4th August 1914 the Home Office issued the following order severely curtailing the flying of aeroplanes over the country:

"In pursuance of the powers conferred on me by the Aerial Navigation Acts, 1911 and 1913, I hereby make, for the purposes of the safety and defence of the Realm, the following Order:

"I prohibit the navigation of aircraft of every class and description over the whole area of the United Kingdom, and over the whole of the coastline thereof and territorial waters adjacent thereto.

"This order shall not apply to Naval or Military aircraft or to aircraft flying under Naval or Military orders, nor shall it apply to any aircraft flying within three miles of a recognised aerodrome.

R. McKenna.
One of His Majesty's Principal Secretaries of State."

The return of peace was accompanied by the emergence of commercial air travel and on 30th April 1919 were published the British Air Navigation Regulations (1919) which formulated the regulations by which "civil" aviation would in future be governed. Already a Department of Civil Aviation had, on 12th February 1919, been established within the British Air Ministry, and this in effect brought commercial control under the Civil Service, while the Royal Aero Club continued to administer the sport of aviation.

The first King's Cup Air Race was held on 8th–9th September 1922 from Croydon to Glasgow and back. Originating from a suggestion to hold an annual air race open to British aircraft, and with the object of encouraging sporting flying, H.M. King George V presented what was originally intended as a Challenge Cup. Subsequently, a new King's Cup was awarded each year. The winner of this first race was Captain F. L. Barnard, Commodore of the Instone Airline, flying Sir Samuel Instone's D.H.4A *City of York* (*G-EAMU*). With a total flying time of 6 h 32 min 50 s, Captain Barnard recorded an average speed of 123·6 mile/h (198·9 km/h). Second was Fred Raynham in a Martinsyde F.6 (*G-EBDK*) and third Alan Cobham in a de Havilland D.H.9 (*G-EAAC*).

The only Oxford versus Cambridge University Air Race ever staged was flown on 16th July 1921 and resulted in a flyaway victory for Cambridge. Each team consisted of three S.E. 5As and the course of three laps lay along the route from Hendon via Epping and Hertford, returning to Hendon. Cambridge gained maximum points by achieving the first three places, with the fastest lap being flown at an average speed of 118·55 mile/h (190·79 km/h). One of the Oxford aircraft failed to complete the course.

Spreading the wings of the prototype Moth, G-EBKT. They could be folded for towing behind a car

The first flight of the first de Havilland Moth prototype *G-EBKT* was made by Captain Geoffrey de Havilland on Sunday, 22nd February 1925, from Stag Lane Aerodrome, Edgware, Middlesex. Sir Sefton Brancker, Director of Civil Aviation, was so impressed with the new aircraft that he recommended the formation of five Government-subsidised flying clubs to be equipped with Moths, and the first such aircraft, *G-EBLR*, was delivered to the Lancashire Aero Club by Alan Cobham on 21st July 1925. Moths were subsequently manufactured in Australia, Finland, France, America, Canada and Norway, and the type is regarded as being responsible for the initiation of the flying-club movement round the world.

Scott and Campbell Black arrive at Melbourne

The first "trans-World" air race was the MacRobertson Race from England to Australia which started on 20th October 1934. In March 1933 the Governing Director of MacRobertson Confectionery Manufacturers of Melbourne, Sir Mac-Pherson Robertson offered £15,000 in prize-money for an air race to commemorate the centenary of the foundation of the State of Victoria. (This formed part of a donation of £100,000 placed at the disposal of the Victorian Government in 1933.) The race was won by one of three specially built de Havilland D.H.88 Comets. A two-seat low-wing monoplane, it was powered by two 230 hp Gipsy Six R engines, each driving variable-pitch propellers of unusual design. Set in fine-pitch for take-off, they were moved to the coarse-pitch cruise setting by compressed air after the machine was airborne and at suitable height; they could not be recycled back to the fine-pitch setting. Charles W. A. Scott and Tom Campbell Black were first to cross the finishing line at Flemington Racecourse, Melbourne, in the D.H.88 *Grosvenor House (G-ACSS)*, having completed the 11,333 miles (18,239 km) from Mildenhall, Suffolk, in 70 h 54 min 18 s at an average speed of 158·9 mile/h (255·7 km/h). Second home in the Handicap Race was, surprisingly, the Douglas DC-2 *Uiver (PH-AJU)* passenger transport aircraft of the Dutch airline K.L.M., flown by K. D. Parmentier and J. J. Moll.

The first Transatlantic air race was sponsored by the *Daily Mail* during 1969, for the fastest journey between the top of the Post Office Tower in London and the top of the Empire State Building in New York. The £5,000 first prize was won by the Royal Navy entry flown by Lieutenant-Commander Brian Davies, aged thirty-five, and Lieutenant-Commander Peter Goddard, aged thirty-two, in a McDonnell Douglas F-4K Phantom II. Flying time was 4 h 36 min 30·4 s, and the over-all time between terminal points was 5 h 11 min 22 s.

The Bede BD-5A Micro, able to fly at well over 200 mile/h, is designed to be built at home by amateur constructor-pilots. More than 2,000 orders for plans and kits of parts were received within four months of the first flight of the prototype

AEROBATICS

Aerobatics are almost as old as flying itself, and their development was a measure of the growing confidence in the aeroplane, not only as a flying machine but as a vehicle of sport. The word "aerobatic" is obviously a contraction of the original "aerial acrobatics", and as such found its appeal in the dramatic and spectacular, for no sooner had a pilot extricated himself from an unusual attitude in the air than he set about perfecting the manœuvre in such a manner as to impress his grounded spectators. Of course it was not long before fairly complicated manœuvres came to be developed for necessity—such as, in air combat, the "Immelmann turn"—now thought to have been a climbing half-loop with a roll off the top. Yet for many years aerobatics as such remained no more than a spectacle provided by a skilled, individual pilot, performed to display the manœuvrability of his aeroplane—or simply his own skill and daring. There were certainly few parameters in aerobatics.

Much more recently aerobatics have been pursued more seriously and even "scientifically", and since the Second World War national prestige has been upheld through fairly lavish displays of aerobatics performed by formations of interceptor fighters or jet trainers so that almost every major air force in the world has trained squadrons or flights to provide the spectacle of such displays.

Since 1960 nations have competed in world aerobatic championships, and so complicated and precise have modern aerobatics become in these championship meetings that only a very small handful of specialist aeroplanes, designed and prepared with extreme precision, have been capable—even in the most expert hands—of competing with any chance of success. It is almost certainly true to state that the successful pilots in these championships are the finest exponents of the pure art of flying.

The first aerobatic manœuvre was undoubtedly the spin. Though nowadays not regarded as an aerobatic but simply as a manœuvre in which the aeroplane falls in a stalled condition while rolling, pitching and yawing simultaneously, it was originally performed as a spectacular manœuvre—once the means of recovery had been discovered.

The first British pilot to survive a spin (probably first in the world) was Fred Raynham who, flying an Avro biplane during 1911, stalled while climbing through fog. The stall occurred after he had stooped to adjust his compass as he thought that it was malfunctioning; the next he knew was that he was standing upright on the rudder pedals with his aeroplane whirling round. Quite how he recovered from the spin will never be known, for his recollection was that he *pulled the stick back*; notwithstanding this he caught sight of the ground and was able to perform a controlled landing.

The first pilot to perform, recover from and demonstrate recovery from a spin was Lieutenant Wilfred Parke, R.N., on 25th August 1912 on the Avro cabin tractor biplane during the Military Trials of that year. On this occasion Parke and his observer, Lieutenant Le Breton, R.F.C., were flying at about 600 ft (200 m) and commenced a spiral glide prior to landing; finding that the glide was too steep, Parke pulled the stick back, promptly stalled and entered a spin. With no established procedure in mind for recovery he attempted to extricate himself from the danger by pulling the stick further back and applying rudder *into* the direction of spin, and found that the spin merely tightened. After carefully noting this phenomenon he decided, *when only 50 ft from the ground*—and from disaster—to reverse the rudder, and the machine recovered instantly. Parke was able to give a carefully reasoned résumé of his corrective actions, thereby contributing immeasurably to the progress of aviation.

The first pilot in the world to perform a loop was Lieutenant Nesterov of the Imperial Russian Army who, flying a Nieuport Type IV monoplane, performed the manœuvre at Kiev on 27th August 1913.

The first pilot to fly inverted in sustained flight (as distinct from becoming inverted during the course of the looping manœuvre) was Adolphe Pégoud who, on 21st September 1913, flew a Blériot monoplane inverted at Buc, France. Notwithstanding the above definition, Pégoud's manœuvre involved two "halves" of a loop, in that he assumed the inverted position by means of a half-loop, and after sustained inverted flight recovered by means of a "pull-through". He thus did not resort to a roll or half-roll, which manœuvre had not apparently been achieved at this time. As a means of acclimatising himself for the ordeal of inverted flight, Pégoud had had his Blériot mounted inverted upon trestles and had remained strapped in the cockpit for periods of up to 20 min at a time!

The first British pilot to perform a loop was Benjamin C. Hucks who looped a Blériot monoplane, probably at Hendon in September 1913. Like Adolphe Pégoud (see above), Hucks also sought training for his feat by remaining strapped in an inverted cockpit on the ground.

The first woman in the world to experience a loop in an aeroplane was Miss Trehawke Davis, who was taken aloft for the manœuvre by her protégé, Gustav Hamel (son of an English-naturalised German doctor), at Hendon, probably in September 1913.

The first hesitation roll was probably performed towards the end of or shortly after the First World War. This manœuvre was unlikely to have been performed by a wing-warping aeroplane, but in view of the power available may have been first performed by a Sopwith Camel or Snipe, and would have been a "four-point" hesitation roll.

On the twenty-fifth anniversary of Blériot's cross-Channel flight, Geoffrey Tyson made the crossing inverted in a Tiger Moth

The cartwheel manœuvre (essentially performed in a twin-engined aeroplane) was first demonstrated by Jan Zurakowski in a de Havilland Hornet fighter (two Rolls-Royce Merlin engines) at Boscombe Down, England, in 1945. The same pilot also later gave demonstrations of the manœuvre in a Gloster Meteor IV jet fighter at the annual S.B.A.C. Displays at Farnborough, Hants. It was performed during a vertical full-power climb to the point of near-stall by quickly throttling-back one engine and performing a controlled, vertical wing-over.

The "Derry Turn" was evolved by John Derry, a test pilot of de Havilland Aircraft Co., Ltd., in 1949–50. It was a positive-G turn initiated by rolling in the opposite direction through 270°. It was a fairly spectacular manœuvre, only ultimately made possible by the availability of sufficient excess engine-power allied with rudder control to keep the nose of the aircraft up at the necessary late stage in the rolling manœuvre.

The only known occasions on which inverted spins by high-performance jet aircraft have been demonstrated publicly, were the S.B.A.C. Displays at Farnborough, Hants, in September 1959 and September 1960. At these displays the Hawker Aircraft Ltd. Chief Test Pilot, A. W. ("Bill") Bedford, flying the demonstration Hunter two-seater *G-APUX*, performed inverted spins of twelve or thirteen turns and used coloured smoke to trace the pattern of his recovery in the sky.

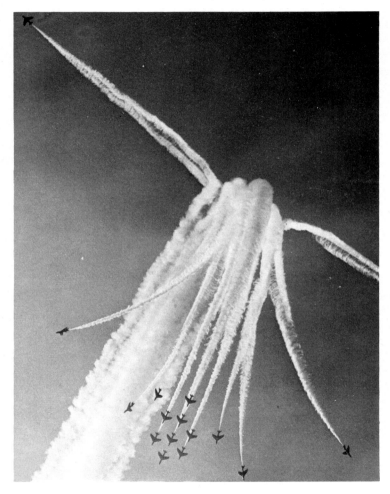

The Black Arrows perform their famous "Bomb-burst". The team consisted of the normal pilots of No. 111 Squadron, R.A.F., in their Hunter fighters (Air Ministry)

PARACHUTING FOR SPECTACLE, SPORT AND NECESSITY

The first demonstration in the world of a quasi-parachute was given by the Frenchman, Sebastien Lenormand, who in 1783 descended from an observation tower at Montpellier, France, under a braced conical canopy.

The first parachute descent ever performed successfully by man from a vehicle was accomplished by the Frenchman, André Jacques Garnerin, who jumped from a balloon at about 3,000 ft (915 m) having ascended from the Parc Monçeau near Paris on 22nd October 1797.

The first parachute descent from a balloon in America was that made by Charles Guille who, on 2nd August 1819, jumped from a hydrogen balloon at a height of about 8,000 ft (2,440 m) and landed at New Bushwick, Long Island, N.Y.

The first parachute descent from an aeroplane in America was performed by Captain Albert Berry who, on 1st March 1912, jumped from a Benoist aircraft flown by Anthony Jannus at 1,500 ft (460 m) over Jefferson Barracks, St. Louis, Mo.

The first parachute descent by a woman from an aeroplane was made by the eighteen-year-old American girl, Georgia ("Tiny") Broadwick who, using an 11 lb (5 kg) silk parachute, jumped from an aircraft flown by Glenn Martin at about 1,000 ft (305 m) over Griffith Field, Los Angeles, Calif., on 21st June 1913.

W. Newell in his take-off position

The Guardian Angel parachute, demonstrated with this jump from Tower Bridge, London, was issued to the crews of British observation balloons, which were a favourite target for enemy fighter pilots

The first parachute drop from an aeroplane over Great Britain was made by W. Newell at Hendon on 9th May 1914 from a Grahame-White Charabanc flown by R. H. Carr. Newell sat on a small rope attached to the port undercarriage, clutching his 40 lb (18 kg) parachute in his lap; when the aeroplane had climbed to 2,000 ft (610 m) F. W. Gooden, seated on the lower wing, prised Newell off his perch with his foot! The parachute was 26 ft (7·9 m) in diameter and the drop occupied 2 min 22 s.

The first successful use of a free parachute (i.e. a "free fall") **from an aeroplane** was made by Leslie Leroy Irvin (1895–1965) on 19th April 1919 using a parachute of the pattern he had developed for the U.S. Army. His descent was made from an aircraft flying at 3,000 ft (915 m). Irvin's parachute consisted of a body-harness, which had a bag attached to the back containing the canopy and rigging-lines. Pulling a ripcord opened the bag, releasing a spring-ejected pilot parachute which pulled the canopy and rigging-lines from the pack.

The first American to escape from a disabled aeroplane by parachute was Lieutenant Harold R. Harris, U.S. Army, who on 20th October 1922 jumped from a Loening monoplane at 2,000 ft (610 m) over North Dayton, Ohio.

The greatest altitude from which anyone has ever jumped without a parachute and survived is 22,000 ft (6,705 m). In January 1942 Lieutenant (now Lieutenant-Colonel) I. M. Chisov of the U.S.S.R. fell from an Ilyushin Il-4 which had been badly damaged. He struck the ground a glancing blow on the edge of a snow-covered ravine and slid to the bottom, sustaining a fractured pelvis and severe spinal damage. (It is estimated that the human body reaches 99 per cent of its low-level terminal velocity after falling 1,880 ft (573 m); this is 117–125 mile/h (188–201 km/h) at normal atmospheric pressure in a random posture, but up to 185 mile/h (298 km/h) in a head-down position.) **The British record** stands at 18,000 ft (5,490 m) set by Flight-Sergeant Nicholas Stephen Alkemade, R.A.F., who jumped from a blazing Lancaster bomber over Germany on 23rd March 1944. His headlong fall was broken by a fir tree, and he landed *without a broken bone* in an 18 in (46 cm) snow-bank.

The first use of an ejection seat, to enable a man to escape from an aircraft in flight, occurred on 24th July 1946. This was the date when the first experimental live ejection was made, using a Martin-Baker ejection seat fitted in a Gloster Meteor. With the aircraft travelling at 320 mile/h (515 km/h), "guinea pig" Bernard Lynch was shot into the air at a height of 8,000 ft (2,440 m). In subsequent tests, Lynch made successful ejections at 420 mile/h (675 km/h) at heights up to 30,000 ft (9,145 m).

The first man to bale out from an aeroplane flying at supersonic speed and live was George Franklin Smith, aged thirty-one, test pilot for North American Aviation Corporation, who ejected from a North American F-100 Super Sabre on 26th February 1955 off Laguna Beach, Calif. After failure of the controls in a dive, Smith fired his ejector seat at an indicated speed of Mach 1·05 or more than 700 mile/h (1,125 km/h). After being unconscious for five days Smith made an almost complete recovery from his injuries which included haemorrhaged eyeballs, damage to lower intestine and liver, knee joints and eye retina. Within nine months he was passed fit to resume flying.

The first member of the Royal Air Force to survive a supersonic ejection (and the second man in the world) was Flying Officer Hedley Molland who escaped from a Hawker Hunter fighter on 3rd August 1955. Flying at 40,000 ft (12,190 m), the aircraft went into an uncontrollable dive. All of Flying Officer Molland's attempts to regain control failed, and by the time he ejected his stricken machine was travelling at an estimated Mach 1·10, its height about 10,000 ft (3,050 m). Descending in the sea he was picked up by a tug, and recovered in hospital from his injuries which included a broken arm (caused by flailing in the slipstream) and a fractured pelvis.

The world's first parachute escape from an aeroplane travelling at speed on the ground was achieved by Squadron Leader J. S. Fifield, D.F.C., A.F.C., on 3rd September 1955 at Chalgrove Airfield, Oxfordshire, when he was ejected from the rear cockpit of a modified Gloster Meteor 7 piloted by Captain J. E. D. Scott, Chief Test Pilot of Martin-Baker Ltd., manufacturers of the ejector seat. Speed of the aircraft at the moment of ejection was 120 mile/h (194 km/h) and the maximum height reached by the seat was 70 ft (21 m) above the runway.

The greatest altitude from which a successful emergency escape from an aeroplane has been made is 56,000 ft (17,070 m). At this altitude on 9th April 1958 an English Electric Canberra bomber exploded over Monyash, Derbyshire, and the crew, Flight-Lieutenant John de Salis, twenty-nine, and Flying Officer Patrick Lowe, twenty-three, fell free in a temperature of −70 °F (−56·7 °C) down to an altitude of 10,000 ft (3,050 m) at which height their parachutes were deployed automatically by barometric control.

Lieutenant-Colonel William H. Rankin (U.S. Marine Corps)

The longest recorded parachute descent was that by Lieutenant-Colonel William H. Rankin of the U.S. Marine Corps who, on 26th July 1959, ejected from his LTV

F8U Crusader naval jet fighter at 47,000 ft (14,326 m). Falling through a violent thunderstorm over North Carolina, his descent took 40 min instead of an expected time of 11 min as he was repeatedly forced *upwards* by the storm's vertical air currents.

The greatest altitude from which a man has fallen and the longest delayed drop ever achieved by man was that of Captain Joseph W. Kittinger, D.F.C., aged thirty-two, of the U.S. Air Force, over Tularosa, New Mexico, U.S.A., on 16th August 1960. He stepped out of a balloon gondola at 102,200 ft (31,150 m) for a free fall of 84,700 ft (25,816 m) lasting 4 min 38 s, during which he reached a speed of 614 mile/h (988 km/h) despite a stabilising drogue and experienced a minimum temperature of −94 °F (−70 °C). His 28 ft (8·5 m) parachute deployed at 17,500 ft (5,334 m) and he landed after a total time of 13 min 45 s. The step by the gondola door was inscribed "This is the highest step in the world."

The speed of 614 mile/h (988 km/h) reached by Kittinger during his fall represents a Mach No. of 0·93 in the Stratosphere and would have been reached at an altitude of about 60,000 ft (18,300 m); thereafter his fall would have been retarded fairly rapidly to less than 200 mile/h (322 km/h) as he passed through the Tropopause at about 36,000 ft (11,000 m). The speed of 614 mile/h (988 km/h) almost certainly represents the greatest speed ever survived by a human body not contained within a powered vehicle beneath the interface (i.e. within the earth's atmosphere).

The longest delayed drop by a woman was 46,250 ft (14,100 m) made by the Russian woman parachutist, O. Komissarova, on 21st September 1965.

The world's "speed record" for parachute jumping is held by Michael Davis, aged twenty-four, and Richard Bingham, aged twenty-five, who made eighty-one jumps in 8 h 22 min at Columbus, Ohio, U.S.A., on 26th June 1966.

The British record for a delayed drop by a group of parachutists stands at 39,183 ft (11,942 m), achieved by five Royal Air Force parachute jumping instructors over Boscombe Down, Wiltshire, on 16th June 1967. They were Squadron Leader J. Thirtle, Flight-Sergeant A. K. Kidd, and Sergeants L. Hicks, P. P. Keane and K. J. Teesdale. Their jumping altitude was 41,383 ft (12,613 m).

The greatest number of parachute jumps made by one man is over 5,000 by Lieutenant-Colonel Ivan Savkin of the U.S.S.R., born in 1913, who reached 5,000 on 12th August 1967. It has been calculated that since 1935 Savkin has spent 27 h in free fall, 587 h floating and has dropped 7,800 miles (12,550 km). **The largest number of jumps made by a Briton** is believed to be the 1,601 descents made by Flight-Lieutenant Charles Agate, A.F.C. (born March 1905), all with packed parachutes, between 1940 and 1946.

The most northerly parachute jump was that by the Canadian, Ray Munro, aged forty-seven, of Lancaster, Ontario, who on 31st March 1969 descended on to the polar ice cap at 87° 30′ N. His eyes were frozen shut instantly in the temperature of −39 °F (−39·5 °C).

The greatest landing altitude for a parachute jump was 23,405 ft (7,134 m), the height of the summit of Lenina Peak on the borders of Tadzhikistan and Kirgiziya in Kazakhstan, U.S.S.R. It was reported in May 1969 that ten Russians had parachuted on to this mountain peak but that four had been killed.

Apollo 17 astronaut Eugene Cernan driving a Lunar Roving Vehicle on the Moon (NASA)

SECTION VIII
Rocketry and Spaceflight

One of the oldest known forms of artificial propulsion, the rocket for hundreds of years possessed one serious drawback, the uncontrollable nature of its combustion; it was essentially a matter of lighting the fuse and standing back. In the seventeenth and eighteenth centuries chemists were able to demonstrate the action of acids as potential propulsive agents, yet still the advance in metallurgy was inadequate to enable these agents to be contained within a suitable combustion chamber. Even today, in the extraordinary development of acceleration associated with space travel, one sees an almost clinical approach to the handling of rocket fuels, so powerful is their interaction.

Opel's glider

The first rocket-powered aeroplane in the world was the sailplane *Ente* ("Duck"), powered by two Sander slow-burning rockets and built by the Rhön-Rossitten

Gesellschaft of Germany. Piloted by Friedrich Stamer, it made a flight of just over 0·75 mile near the Wasserkuppe Mountain in about 1 min on 11th June 1928. The rocket-powered glider flown by Fritz von Opel at Rebstock, near Frankfurt, is often stated as being the world's first rocket aeroplane but did not fly until 30th September 1929. (See Appendix I.)

The first successful liquid-fuel rocket aircraft in the world was the German DFS 194 which, having been conceived by the Sailplane Research Institute in 1938 under Professor Alexander Lippisch, was taken over by Messerschmitt A.G. at Augsburg and flown in 1940 by Heini Dittmar. It was powered by a 600 lb (272 kg) thrust Walter rocket.

The world's first operational rocket-powered fighter was the Messerschmitt Me 163 Komet, first flown by Heini Dittmar at Peenemünde, Germany, in 1941. On one early flight Dittmar far exceeded what was then the official world speed record, attaining a speed of 571 mile/h (919 km/h); on 2nd October 1941, after having been towed to 13,000 ft (4,000 m), he started the rocket motor and 2 min later recorded a speed of 623 mile/h (1,001 km/h) in level flight. It was the success of these early trials that led to the Me 163 being developed as an operational rocket-powered interceptor. (See "Military Aviation", page 97.)

The first combat sortie flown by a rocket-powered interceptor is believed to have been flown against Allied bombers over Germany on 16th August 1944. The only Luftwaffe unit equipped with Messerschmitt Me 163B Komet aircraft was Jagdgeschwader 400, whose first two operational Staffeln moved to Brandis, near Leipzig, in July 1944. (See "Military Aviation".)

The first American rocket-powered military aircraft was the Northrop MX-324, which was first flown under rocket power by Harry Crosby on 5th July 1944. It was powered by an Aerojet XCAL-200 motor fuelled by monoethylaniline. It had originally flown as a glider, being first flown by John Myers on 2nd October 1943.

Bell XS-1. In this aircraft, Captain Charles Yeager became the first person to fly faster than the speed of sound on 14th October 1947

The first manned supersonic aeroplane in the world was the rocket-powered American Bell XS-1. The second prototype made its first powered flight on 9th December 1946, piloted by Chalmers Goodlin, after being air-launched from a Boeing B-29 Superfortress. Flown by Captain Charles "Chuck" Yeager, U.S.A.F., the XS-1 was taken progressively nearer to "the speed of sound" and finally, on 14th October 1947, escaped from the buffeting of near-sonic compressibility into the smooth airflow of supersonic flight. The speed recorded for that historic occasion was 670 mile/h (1,078 km/h) at a height of 42,000 ft (12,800 m), the equivalent Mach number being 1·015.

Larry Bell congratulates "Chuck" Yeager after reaching 1,650 mile/h in the Bell X-1A

The fastest aeroplane ever flown is the rocket-powered North American X-15A-2 research aircraft. Three X-15s were built during the late 1950s and the first free flight was made on 8th June 1959. Just over three months later, on 17th September, the second craft made the first powered flight. Because the 60,000 lb (27,215 kg) thrust Thiokol XLR99-RM-2 rocket engine was not ready, two XLR11-RM-5 engines powered X-15 No. 2. Despite the fact that these gave a combined thrust of only 33,000 lb (15,000 kg), a speed of Mach 2·3 was recorded. By December 1963, then powered by the XLR99, speed had climbed to Mach 6·06, and a surface skin temperature of 1,320 °F (715·6 °C) had confirmed yet another problem associated with very high-speed flight. Following a landing accident to No. 2, it was re-built and various modifications introduced. Redesignated X-15A-2, this machine made its first flight on 28th June 1964. The highest altitude it attained was 354,200 ft (67·08 miles) on a flight by J. A. Walker on 22nd August 1963, and the highest speed was 4,534 mile/h (Mach 6·72) by W. J. Knight on 3rd October 1967. A full list of the progressive speeds achieved by these aircraft are given in an Appendix.

North American X-15 being launched from its B-52 "mother-plane"

ROCKETS AND ROCKET MISSILES

The world's first liquid-propellant rocket was launched by the American Professor R. H. Goddard, on 16th March 1926, at Auburn, Massachusetts.

Rockets for research and commerce. During the period 1931–34 a number of Europeans conducted experiments with rockets fired from the ground with the principal object of developing solid- and liquid-fuel motors as reliable power plants for air and surface vehicles. Some went further to suggest a commercial application. **The first successful firing of a ground-launched rocket in Europe for research measurements** was achieved on 13th March 1931 by the German, Karl Poggensee, who fired a solid-fuelled rocket to a height of 1,500 ft (460 m) near Berlin. It carried cameras and an altimeter and was recovered by parachute. Also using solid fuel, Reinhold Tiling achieved a height of 6,600 ft (2,010 m) and a speed of about 700 mile/h (1,100 km/h) with a rocket launched at Osnabrück in April 1931 and which burned for about 11 s. Shortly afterwards he may have achieved an altitude of about 32,000 ft (9,750 m) with another solid-fuelled rocket launched from the Frisian Island of Wangerooge. **The first attempt at a ground-to-ground rocket flight in the British Isles** was undertaken by the German, Gerhard Zucker, on 31st July 1934. An attempt to fire a powder rocket from Harris to Scarp, in the Western Isles of Scotland, failed when the rocket exploded before take-off. Zucker had put forward the idea of sending mail by rocket across the English Channel, but his scheme never materialised.

The initial development work which led to the German V-2 rocket commenced at Kummersdorf, near Berlin, during 1933–34, after Wernher von Braun had been invited to complete a thesis on rocket combustion in 1932. **The first German Army rocket**, the A-1, was developed at Kummersdorf in 1933 but this was destroyed in an explosion. Two A-2 rockets were fired from Borkum in December 1934 and achieved an altitude of about 6,500 ft (2,000 m). In April 1937 the Kummersdorf site was abandoned and von Braun took his team to Peenemünde on the Baltic coast. Here the A-3 and A-5 rockets were developed in preparation for the A-4. It was better known as the "V-2", the initial V standing for *Vergeltungswaffe* ("reprisal weapon"). The first so-called "reprisal weapon" was the V-1 flying-bomb, better known to the British as the "Doodlebug".

V-2 rockets ready for launch

The world's first strategic rocket surface-to-surface missile was the German V-2, developed under the supervision of Wernher von Braun. The first firing of a V-2 took place on 13th June 1942, but the rocket failed, went out of control and crashed. **The first successful launching of a V-2** occurred on 3rd October 1942 when the rocket burned for just under 1 min, lifting it to over 50 miles (80 km) before it returned to earth nearly 120 miles (190 km) away down-range from Peenemünde. The operational V-2 was 46 ft 2 in (14·1 m) long and weighed 28,400 lb (12,880 kg), which included 19,300 lb (8,754 kg) of alcohol and liquid oxygen propellants, and a warhead containing 2,150 lb (975 kg) of explosive. Its range was between 190 and 200 miles (306 and 322 km).

The first country in the world to be subjected to an assault by ballistic rocket missiles was France. On the morning of 8th September 1944 the first V-2 rocket was fired against Paris. At about 18.40 h on the same day the **first V-2 to land in Britain** fell in Chiswick, London, killing two people and injuring ten. The last rocket to fall in Britain fell at Orpington, Kent, at 16.54 h on 27th March 1945, killing one person and injuring twenty-three. Between the two dates 1,115 rockets fell on Britain (of which about 500 hit London), killing 2,855 and seriously injuring 6,268. **The worst incident** is believed to have occurred when a V-2 fell upon a Woolworth store at Deptford, killing 160 and injuring 135. **The worst-hit country** was, however, Belgium, more than 1,500 rockets being launched against Antwerp alone.

The first ballistic missile to enter service in the United States was the Firestone SSM-A-17 Corporal, a liquid-fuelled rocket-propelled (unboosted) missile which entered service with the U.S. Army during the early 1950s and subsequently with the British Army. It had a range of about 75–100 miles (120–160 km).

The first Swedish surface-to-surface guided missile was the Robot 315 which was conceived in 1946 but on which work did not start until 1949. It was a subsonic weapon, boosted by four solid-fuel rockets and sustained by a pulse-jet. The first test firing of the complete weapon was accomplished from the Swedish destroyer *Halland* in January 1954, and three years later it became operational on board the *Halland* and *Smaland*.

Matador launch

The first surface-to-surface weapon to enter service with the U.S. Air Force was the Martin TM-61A Matador "flying-bomb" which joined Tactical Missile Wings in the U.S.A., Germany and Taiwan during the early 1950s. By 1957 Martin's Baltimore factory had delivered 1,000 Matadors.

The first British ballistic missile was the Hawker Siddeley Dynamics Blue Streak which, though started in 1955, was cancelled as a military project in 1960. It was, however, adopted as the launch vehicle for the E.L.D.O. (European Launcher Development Organisation, or Conseil Européen pour la Construction de Lanceurs d'Engins Spatiaux C.E.C.L.E.S.). Its first test launch was conducted on 5th June 1964, but in 1970 British participation in E.L.D.O. was withdrawn.

The first operational sub-surface-to-surface ballistic missile in the world was the American Lockheed Polaris F.B.M.S. ("Fleet Ballistic Missile System"), of which the first test firing was carried out in 1959. Sixteen such missiles were carried aboard each of the special class of nuclear-powered submarines built for the U.S. Navy and Royal Navy.

Loading a Soviet "Styx" missile on to a fast patrol-boat of the Russian Navy. Missiles of this kind were used by the Egyptians to sink the Israeli destroyer Eilat *on 21st October 1967*

GROUND-TO-AIR MISSILES

The first British commercial organisation to engage in the development of surface-to-air guided missiles was the Fairey Aviation Company which, in 1944, started work on a missile to counter Japanese suicide aircraft. The outcome of this was a general-purpose test vehicle named "Stooge".

Only ten years after man first journeyed into space, with a single orbit round the Earth, America's Apollo 15 landed a vehicle on the Moon. Each of the last three Apollos transported a Lunar Roving Vehicle, built by Boeing, to increase the mobility of their astronaut-explorers. Unladen weight of the L.R.V. was 462 lb (209 kg). It could carry a total of 1,080 lb (490 kg), comprising two astronauts, their life-support systems, and 280 lb (127 kg) of experiments and lunar rock and soil samples (NASA)

Most spectacular of all America's space launches was the departure of Apollo 17 for the Moon on 7th December 1972. For the first time the launch took place at night, amid high drama when a signalled fault caused a lengthy hold only thirty seconds before the original count-down was scheduled to end (NASA)

Nike-Ajax battery

The first American surface-to-air anti-aircraft guided missile was the Western Electric SAM-A-7 Nike-Ajax, development of which was started by Bell Telephone Laboratories in 1945. Before the weapon entered service more than 1,500 test rounds were fired, and by 1959 10,000 had been delivered. Its place was taken in 1959–60 by the Nike-Hercules.

The first operational pilotless long-range ground-to-air interceptor was the Boeing IM-99 Bomarc. The first prototypes, designated XF-99s, were tested in 1952. Launched vertically, the Bomarc was powered by two Marquardt RJ43-MA ramjets and incorporated a Westinghouse guidance system. Its cruising speed was Mach 2·8 and maximum range varied from 200 miles (320 km) for the IM-99A to 400 miles (640 km) for the IM-99B.

The first operational French ground-to-air guided missile was the D.E.F.A. (Direction des Etudes et Fabrications d'Armement) P.A.R.C.A. (Projectile Autopropulsé Radioguidé Contre Avions) liquid-fuel rocket weapon which entered service with the French Army in about 1957. It had an effective ceiling of 82,000 ft (25,000 m).

The first British surface-to-air guided missile to enter service was the Bristol/Ferranti Bloodhound (code-named "Red Duster"), powered by two Bristol Thor ramjets (and four solid-fuel booster rockets), which equipped the experimental R.A.F. missile station at North Coates, Lincolnshire, in June 1958. **The first British surface-to-air guided missile ordered for the British Army** was the English Electric Thunderbird (code-named "Red Shoes") which entered evaluation service in 1959.

AIR-TO-AIR GUIDED MISSILES

For many years the traditional armament of fighters was the machine-gun and, later on, the so-called cannon (20 mm calibre and over).

Generally speaking this type of weapon was effective but demanded that the interceptor close right up to its target, assuming that it possessed the speed, rate of climb and high altitude performance to reach its target before the bomber dropped its bombs. In time bombers, by reason of their greater size, came to carry such equipment as tail warning radar, pressure cabins, and gun-laying radar, and were powered by such powerful engines that on detecting the approach of an interceptor they could fight back or take effective evasive action. As, by the end of the 1950s, bomber speeds had risen so high that the conventionally armed interceptor could do little more than perhaps "pick off" an occasional bomber, dependence was placed upon a type of missile that could take over the interception and destruction of the intruder at greater range.

Ever since the early introduction of the first "air-to-air" rockets (of which the first were Le Prieur anti-balloon and anti-airship weapons, used during the First World War), efforts have been made to improve the range and accuracy of the missile, as well as its target-seeking capabilities and destructive power. Today we have the missile which, carried into the approximate area of the incoming bomber, can be released to continue climbing, homing through infra-red detection of the enemy bomber's jet-engine exhaust and exploding sufficiently close to ensure the total destruction of its target.

The first successful use of air-to-air rockets against aeroplanes is believed to have taken place on the afternoon of 20th August 1939 when five Polikarpov I–16 Type-10 fighters, each fitted with underwing rails for eight 82 mm RS 82 rockets, went into action against Japanese fighters over the Khalkin Gol area of Mongolia. The unit, commanded by Captain Zvonariev, claimed the destruction of two Mitsubishi A5M fighters on this occasion.

The first widespread operational use of air-to-air rockets against aeroplanes was by the Luftwaffe, probably by III/JG7 either in late 1944 or early 1945. The R4M unguided rockets, of which twenty-four were carried on racks under the wings of Messerschmitt Me 262A-1b jet fighters, were 55 mm folding-fin missiles aimed through a standard Revi gunsight. Fired in salvoes their effect was devastating, especially against the American formations of B-17 Fortress and B-24 Liberator bombers.

Falcon missiles exposed for firing from the wingtip pods of a Scorpion

The first air-to-air guided missile to be adopted by the U.S. Air Force was the Hughes GAR-1 Falcon, six of which were carried in wing-tip pods on the Northrop F-89H Scorpion all-weather fighter. They entered operational service in 1956.

The first British air-to-air guided missile to destroy a target aircraft was the Fairey Fireflash (code-named "Blue Sky"). Work on this started in 1949 but it never achieved operational status; it was however ordered into production and, fitted to Swift Mark 7 fighters, used by an R.A.F. squadron to develop interception tactics using missiles. Fireflash was a "beam-riding" missile which in fact carried no sustainer motor but was boosted by two cordite rockets and then coasted along a coded radar beam.

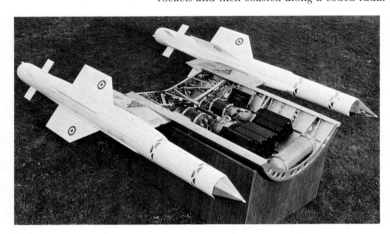

Firestreak missile pack for a Lightning interceptor

The first British air-to-air guided missile to achieve operational status was the de Havilland Firestreak (code-named "Blue Jay"). Incorporating an infra-red heat-seeking guidance system the Firestreak equipped squadrons of Gloster Javelin 7s and 8s of the R.A.F. in 1958 and 1959, and also de Havilland Sea Vixens of the Fleet Air Arm. It continues to arm R.A.F. Lightnings.

The first-ever firing of a nuclear-tipped air-to-air missile was carried out on 19th July 1956 when a Northrop F-89J Scorpion discharged a Douglas MB-1 Genie at 15,000 ft (4,500 m) above Yucca Flat, Nevada, in the U.S.A. This missile incorporated a warhead of about 1·5 kilotons yield and the fighter turned away sharply to avoid the missile's blast. The warhead was detonated after having travelled about 3 miles horizontally, but U.S.A.F. observers standing directly below the explosion reported no ill-effects from fall-out.

AIR-TO-SURFACE GUIDED MISSILES

Just as recourse to guided weapons was sought to overcome the inherent inaccuracy of the gun in air-fighting tactics, so the guided "bomb" was developed to improve on the accuracy available from the conventional bombsight and free-falling bomb. Inevitably the bomb acquired wings and engines, thereby enabling the bomber to "stand off" from its target and avoid the defences.

The first American air-to-surface radar-guided missile was the Bat, an impowered glide-bomb developed by Hugh L. Dryden. Carrying a 1,000 lb warload, the missile was about 12 ft (3·65 m) long and, on being launched from its carrier air-craft, used radar to home on its target. It possessed a range of about 20 miles (30 km), and in April 1945 one such missile succeeded in sinking a Japanese destroyer at this range.

The Bat

The world's first true stand-off bomb to achieve operational status was the Bell GAM-63 Rascal on which, under the original designation XB-63, work started in 1946. Powered by three liquid-fuel rockets, this bomb was first delivered to the U.S. Strategic Air Command at Pinecastle Air Force Base, Florida, on 30th October 1957, and was carried operationally under Boeing DB-47E Stratojet bombers of S.A.C. Its warhead was either atomic or thermonuclear, as required, and its range was about 100 miles (160 km).

The Blue Steel missile in position under the belly of a Vulcan bomber

The first operational British stand-off bomb was the Hawker Siddeley Dynamics Blue Steel, of which test firings were made from Avro Vulcan and Handley Page Victor bombers in mid 1960. It entered service with Vulcan Mark 2s of No. 617 (Bomber) Squadron in 1962, becoming operational in February the following year. Initially powered by a 16,000 lb (7,260 kg) thrust Bristol Siddeley Stentor BSSt.1 liquid-fuel rocket, it had a stand-off range of about 200 miles (320 km).

SPACEFLIGHT

From the moment that Dr. Wernher von Braun's first A-4 (V-2) ballistic rocket succeeded in lifting a payload into the upper atmosphere above the Baltic during the Second World War, space flight by mankind became a realistic possibility. Nevertheless that war left all but two nations, the U.S.A. and the U.S.S.R., so economically exhausted that only they could apply their resources to pursue this hitherto-fictional adventure. Von Braun himself went to America to continue his work, while other Germans found themselves working in Russia; yet more than a dozen years were to pass before the first man-made object could be placed in orbit round the Earth. *Only twelve years later, man first placed his foot upon the Moon!*

Dr. Wernher von Braun
(NASA)

The first man-made satellite, "Sputnik I", to enter an orbit round the Earth was rocket-launched from the Soviet Union on 4th October 1957. Weighing 184·3 lb (83·6 kg), the satellite was a metal sphere 23 in (58·42 cm) in diameter which orbited the earth in 96 min at 142–588 miles (228·5–945·6 km) perigee and apogee. Its purpose was to measure and transmit information on the density and temperature of the upper atmosphere, as well as to measure the concentration of electrons in the ionosphere. It completed about 1,400 circuits of the earth before re-entering the lower atmosphere and burning up on 4th January 1958.

The first living creature carried into space from Earth to experience orbital flight was a Russian bitch, Laika, which was carried aloft in the second Russian satellite, launched on 3rd November 1957. The purpose of this satellite was to measure and transmit readings of cosmic radiation and on the behaviour of the creature during space flight. The satellite weighed 1,120·6 lb (508·3 kg) and orbited the earth in 103·7 min at 140–1,038 miles (225–1,670 km) perigee and apogee. By regulated feeding, supply of oxygen and by other devices, the dog was kept alive for seven days in space, during which time telemetered information on respiration and heart behaviour was transmitted back to earth. This satellite completed 2,370 orbits of the earth before it re-entered the denser atmosphere and burned up on 14th April 1958.

The first living creatures carried into earth orbit and safely recovered were the bitches Belka and Strelka. Launched on 19th August 1960, the *Sputnik 5* (Spaceship 2) which carried them for seventeen orbits of the earth, re-entered the atmosphere on the following day. The capsule containing the two dogs separated from the re-entry vehicle and when it was opened Belka and Strelka were found to have survived their ordeal in space without coming to any harm.

The first human to enter space was the Russian cosmonaut, Flight-Major Yuriy Alexeyevich Gagarin (aged twenty-seven, born Friday, 9th March 1934 near Gzatsk, died in a jet crash on Wednesday, 27th March 1968). Launched at 09.07 h, Moscow time on 12th April 1961, from Baikonur, East Kazakhstan, in the 10,417 lb (4,725 kg) *Vostok 1* spacecraft, Gagarin completed a single orbit of the earth, making a safe landing in the U.S.S.R. 1 h 48 min later.

Flight-Major Yuriy Alexeyevich Gagarin

The first American to enter space was Alan B. Shepard who, on 5th May 1961, was fired in a sub-orbital trajectory of 302 miles (486 km). In his 15 min journey in the Mercury capsule *Freedom 7*, Shepard had attained a height of 115 miles (185·1 km) and travelled at a speed of 5,188 mile/h (8,350 km/h).

The first woman to enter space was the Russian cosmonaut Junior Lieutenant Valentina Vladimirovna Tereshkova, aged twenty-six, who, in *Vostok 6*, was placed in earth orbit on 16th June 1963 and completed forty-eight orbits in 70 h 50 min.

The first human to set foot on the Moon was the American astronaut, Mr. Neil Armstrong, aged thirty-eight, late of the U.S. Navy (born on Tuesday, 5th August 1930 at Wapakoneta, Ohio). At 02.56 h 20 s G.M.T. on Monday, 21st July 1969 Armstrong stepped on to the moon's surface from the lunar module *Eagle*, an event watched through television by 600 million viewers 232,000 miles away on earth. Shortly afterwards his colleague Edwin Aldrin joined him on the moon, while Michael Collins remained in moon orbit in the command module *Columbia*. The entire flight to the moon had been a complete success, and the safe return to earth was terminated with splash-down at 16.49 h G.M.T. on 24th July, 940 miles (1,510 km) south-west of Honolulu in the Pacific Ocean.

In his Special State of the Union Message of 25th May 1961, the late President John F. Kennedy addressed to Congress a request for additional funds to accelerate space research:

"I believe this nation should commit itself to achieving the goal before this decade is out, of landing a man on the moon and returning him to earth. No single space project in this period will be more exciting, or more impressive, or more important for the long-range exploration of space; and none will be so difficult or expensive to accomplish. Including necessary supporting research, this objective will require an additional $531,000,000 this year and still higher sums in the future. We propose to accelerate development of the appropriate lunar space craft. We propose to develop liquid and solid boosters much larger than any now being developed . . . We propose additional funds for other engine development and for unmanned explorations, which are particularly important for one purpose which this nation will never overlook—the survival of the man who first makes this daring flight. But in a very real sense, it will not be one man going to the moon—it will be an entire nation. For all of us must work to put him there."

After the expenditure of $24,000,000,000 Neil Armstrong brought success to the President's proposal.

First unmanned spacecraft to land on the moon's surface and take off again successfully, after taking lunar soil samples for analysis, was the Soviet *Luna 16*. Launched on 12th September 1970, the spacecraft was controlled from earth during its lunar activities. A successful recovery of the craft was made on 24th September 1970.

First mobile vehicle on the moon's surface to be remotely controlled from earth was the eight-wheeled *Lunokhod 1* moon vehicle, landed on the lunar surface by the Soviet spacecraft *Luna 17*. Following initial deployment on 17th November 1970, it made a 300 ft (96 m) trip on the following day.

First vehicle to be driven by man on the moon's surface was the Boeing Lunar Roving Vehicle, carried to its surface by the lunar module *Falcon* as part of the *Apollo 15* mission. First used on 31st July 1971.

The Russian Lunokhod 1 automatic lunar roving vehicle, which was carried to the Moon by the Luna 17 spacecraft and travelled six and a half miles between 17th November 1970 and mid-August 1971. The results of its exploration were sent back to Earth by TV and radio (Tass)

The longest journey ever started by a man-made object is that on which the American space probe Pioneer 10 was launched on 2nd March 1972, by a three-stage Atlas-Centaur rocket, from Cape Kennedy, Florida. On 25th May Pioneer 10 crossed the orbit of Mars and entered a region of space never previously explored. In July it entered the Asteroid Belt, passing safely through it in about seven months. Scheduled to reach Jupiter, largest planet in our solar system, on 3rd December 1973, the probe will be swung around the planet by gravitational pull, past the orbit of the planet Uranus in 1979, to escape from the solar system. It might then travel on for *two million years* before approaching the star Aldebaran. On board Pioneer 10 is a plaque designed in such a way that it would indicate the nature of the probe's builders, and the part of the galaxy from which it was launched, to any beings who might retrieve the spacecraft in the remote future.

The longest period spent in space, at the time of writing, was 84 days 1 h 15 min 30·8 sec by the crew of *Skylab 4*, Gerald P. Carr (Commander), Dr Edward G. Gibson (science pilot) and William R. Pogue (pilot), after their launch on 16th November 1973. The mission to Skylab station, which had been launched on 14th May 1973, was to reactivate and man the station, to obtain medical data for use in extending the duration of manned space flights, and to perform in-orbit experiments. The mission ended on 8th February 1974, the crew having travelled 55,474,039 km.

Date	Country	Spacecraft	Crew Members	Flight Duration H Min	No. of Orbits	Remarks
12th April 1961	U.S.S.R.	*Vostok 1*	Flt.-Maj. Yuriy Alexeyevich Gagarin (27)	1 48	1	First man in space. Flight represented progressive world altitude record of 203·2 st. miles (327·0 km).
5th May 1961	U.S.A.	MR-3, *Freedom 7*	Cdr. Alan B. Shepard (37) U.S. Navy	15	Sub-orbital	First American in space; launched by Redstone rocket and reached height of 115 miles (185·1 km).
21st July 1961	U.S.A.	MR-4, *Liberty Bell 7*	Capt. Virgil Ivan Grissom (34) U.S. Air Force	16	Sub-orbital	Spacecraft sank on splashdown; launched by Redstone rocket and reached height of 118 miles (190·0 km).
6th–7th Aug. 1961	U.S.S.R.	*Vostok 2*	Maj. Gherman Stepanovich Titov (26)	25 18	17	To study effects of prolonged weightlessness; believed to have made final descent by parachute.
20th Feb. 1962	U.S.A.	MA-6, *Friendship 7*	Lt.-Col. John Herschel Glenn (40), U.S. Marine Corps	4 55	3	First American manned spacecraft to enter earth orbit. Launched by Atlas rocket.
24th May 1962	U.S.A.	MA-7, *Aurora 7*	Lt.-Cdr. Malcolm Scott Carpenter (37) U.S. Navy	4 56	3	Duplicated Glenn's first flight; reached speed of 17,532 mile/h (28,215 km/h).
11th–15th Aug. 1962	U.S.S.R.	*Vostok 3*	Maj. Andrian Grigoryevich Nikolayev (32)	94 22	64	First man-operated television from space; travelled 1,640,000 miles (2,639,320 km).
12th–15th Aug. 1962	U.S.S:R.	*Vostok 4*	Col. Pavel Romanovich Popovich (31)	70 57	48	Among other purposes, flight was to "obtain data on establishing contact" with *Vostok 3*.
3rd Oct. 1962	U.S.A.	MA-8, *Sigma 7*	Cdr. Walter Marty Schirra (39), U.S. Navy	9 13	6	Launched by Atlas rocket; splashed down in Pacific north-west of Midway. Near-tragedy with spacesuit.
15th–16th May 1963	U.S.A.	MA-9, *Faith 7*	Maj. Leroy Gordon Cooper (36), U.S. Air Force	34 20	22	Launched by Atlas; manual re-entry after failure of automatic control system. Splashdown in Pacific.
14th–19th June 1963	U.S.S.R.	*Vostok 5*	Lt.-Col. Valeriy Fyodorovich Bykovsky (28)	119 66	81	Call-sign "Hawk" in two-way communication with *Vostok 6* (q.v.).
16th–19th June 1963	U.S.S.R.	*Vostok 6*	Junior Lt. Valentina Vladimirovna Tereshkova (26)	70 50	48	First woman in space. Call-sign "Seagull". Came within 3 miles of *Vostok 5*.
12th–13th Oct. 1964	U.S.S.R.	*Voskhod 1*	Col. Vladimir Mihailovich Komarov (37); Commander; Lt. Boris Borisovich Yegorov (37), Space Physician; Konstantin Petrovich Feoktistov (38), Engineer-scientist.	24 17	16	First three-man crew in space. The purpose of the flight was, *inter alia* "to examine the capacity for work and interaction during spaceflight of a group of cosmonauts consisting of specialists in different fields of science and technology".
18th–19th Mar. 1965	U.S.S.R.	*Voskhod 2*	Lt.-Col. Aleksey Arkhipovich Leonov (30); Col. Pavel Ivanovich Belyayev (39)	26 2	17	Leonov became world's first man to leave his spacecraft and float in outer space (for a total of 20 min).
23rd March 1965	U.S.A.	GT-3, *Gemini 3*	Maj. Virgil Ivan Grissom (38), U.S. Air Force; Lt.-Cdr. John Watts Young, U.S. Navy	4 53	3	First American two-man spaceflight, launched by Titan rocket; splashed down east of the Bahamas in the Atlantic.

Date	Country	Spacecraft	Crew Members	Flight Duration H Min	No. of Orbits	Remarks
3rd–7th June 1965	U.S.A.	GT-4, *Gemini 4*	Maj. James Alton McDivitt (35), U.S. Air Force; Maj. Edward Higgins White (34), U.S. Air Force	97 56	62	First American "space walk" by White (which occupied 21 min); also longest space-flight by multi-man crew.
21st–29th Aug. 1965	U.S.A.	GT-5, *Gemini 5*	Lt.-Col. Leroy Gordon Cooper (38), U.S. Air Force; Lt.-Cdr. Charles Conrad (35), U.S. Navy	190 56	120	Longest spaceflight to date. This was Cooper's second earth-orbital flight, thus having spent more time in space than any other man.
4th–18th Dec. 1965	U.S.A.	GT-7, *Gemini 7*	Lt.-Col. Frank Borman (37), U.S. Air Force; Cdr. James Arthur Lovell (37), U.S. Navy	330 35	206	Longest spaceflight to date; rendezvoused with *Gemini 6* which, after one failure to launch on 12th December, was successfully put into orbit on 15th December.
15th–16th Dec. 1965	U.S.A.	GT-6, *Gemini 6*	Cdr. Walter Marty Schirra (43), U.S. Navy; Maj. Thomas P. Stafford (35), U.S. Air Force	25 51	15	Approached to within 10 ft (3 m) of *Gemini 7* and flown for two earth orbits side-by-side. Splashed down in Atlantic south-west of Bermuda.
16th March 1966	U.S.A.	GT-8, *Gemini 8*	Mr. Neil Alden Armstrong (35); Major David Randolph Scott (34), U.S. Air Force	10 42	6½	Intended three-day flight; first docking between manned and unmanned spacecraft (Agena-7); flight terminated prematurely due to failure of manoeuvring rockets.
3rd–6th June 1966	U.S.A.	GT-9, *Gemini 9*	Lt.-Col. Thomas P. Stafford (36), U.S. Air Force; Lt.-Cdr. Eugene Andrew Cernan (32), U.S. Navy	72 21	21	Longest space walk to date (129 min by Cernan); it had also been intended to attempt a docking with the A.T.D.A. (Augmented Target Docking Adapter) but this failed owing to failure of docking mechanism on the A.T.D.A.
18th–21st July 1966	U.S.A.	GT-10, *Gemini 10*	Cdr. John Watts Young, U.S. Navy; Maj. Michael Collins, U.S. Air Force	70 47	43	Space walk by Collins (30 min); rendezvous with two Agena craft in different orbits. Flight represented altitude record of 474·6 miles (763·8 km).
12th–15th Sept. 1966	U.S.A.	GT-11, *Gemini 11*	Cdr. Charles Conrad (36), U.S. Navy; Lt.-Cdr. Richard F. Gordon, U.S. Navy	71 17	44	Space walk by Gordon (44 min); docking tests with Agena. Photographs taken through open hatch of earth and stars.
11th–15th Nov. 1966	U.S.A.	GT-12, *Gemini 12*	Cdr. James Arthur Lovell (38), U.S. Navy; Maj. Edwin Eugene Aldrin (36), U.S. Air Force	94 35	59	Record E.V.A. (extra-vehicular activity). 5·5 h by Aldrin; more open-hatch photography; docking with Agena.
22nd–23rd Apr. 1967	U.S.S.R.	*Soyuz 1*	Air Engineer Colonel Vladimir Mihailovich Komarov (40)	26 45	18	First Russian to make two space flights; was killed, landing parachute tangled. First man killed during space flight.
11th–22nd Oct. 1968	U.S.A.	*Apollo VII*	Capt. Walter Marty Schirra (45), U.S. Navy; Maj. Donn F. Eisele (38), U.S. Air Force; R. Walter Cunningham (36), civilian scientist	260 9	163	First American three-man space flight; launched by Saturn 1-B rocket. This was first flight of capsule designed for ultimate seven-day voyage to the moon. Included numerous safety features not previously used.

Date	Country	Spacecraft	Crew Members	Flight Duration H Min	No. of Orbits	Remarks
26th–30th Oct. 1968	U.S.S.R.	*Soyuz 3*	Col. Georgiy T. Beregovoiy (47)	94 51	61	Rendezvous with unmanned *Soyuz 2*. Col. Beregovoiy was the oldest man yet to travel in space.
21st–27th Dec. 1968	U.S.A.	*Apollo VIII*	Col. Frank Borman (40), U.S. Air Force; Cdr. James Arthur Lovell (40), U.S. Navy; Maj. William A. Anders (35), U.S. Air Force	147 0	1½ (earth) 10 (moon)	The first men in history to break free from the earth's gravitational field and the first to orbit the moon; launched by Saturn-5 rocket. Splashdown in mid-Pacific. Christmas radio messages from astronauts while in moon orbit. This flight set up an altitude record of 234,772 miles (377,828 km).
14th–17th Jan. 1969	U.S.S.R.	*Soyuz 4*	Lt.-Col. Vladimir Shatalov (41); Alexei Yeliseyev (34), civilian engineer; Lt.-Col. Yevgeny Khrunov (35);	71 14	48	Successful docking manoeuvre in earth-orbit with *Soyuz 5*. Orbits of both spacecraft altered under manual control. This flight provided the first joining of two manned spacecraft in orbit and the first transfer of crew (Yeliseyev and Khrunov transferring to and landing in *Soyuz 5*).
15th–18th Jan. 1969	U.S.S.R.	*Soyuz 5*	Lt.-Col. Boris Volynov (34)	72 46	49	
3rd–13th March 1969	U.S.A.	*Apollo IX*	Col. James Alton McDivitt (39), U.S. Air Force; Col. David Randolph Scott (36), U.S. Air Force; Mr. Russell Louis Schweikart (33), U.S. Air Force Reserve	241 1	151	First trial of lunar module (manned) in space; transfer of crew through interior connection. Also the first flight of all three components (Command, Service and Lunar Modules). Splashdown in Atlantic.
18th–26th May 1969	U.S.A.	*Apollo X*	Col. Thomas P. Stafford (38), U.S. Air Force; Cdr. John Watts Young (38), U.S. Navy; Cdr. Eugene Andrew Cernan (35), U.S. Navy	192 3	1½ (earth) 31 (moon)	Lunar module (*Snoopy*) flown by Stafford and Cernan to within 9·4 miles (15·13 km) of moon, while Young remained with Command and Service Module (*Charlie Brown*). Flight set up new altitude record of 246,960 miles (397,443 km).
16th–24th July 1969	U.S.A.	*Apollo XI*	Mr. Neil Alden Armstrong (38), Flight Commander; Col. Edwin Eugene Aldrin, Jr., (39), U.S. Air Force, Lunar Module Pilot; Lt.-Col. Michael Collins, U.S. Air Force, Command Module Pilot	195 18	1½ (earth) 30 (moon)	First moon landing by man (Armstrong, first E.V.A., 2 h 14 m; Aldrin, second, E.V.A., 1 h 33 min). Lunar Module (*Eagle*) landed in south-west corner of Sea of Tranquillity at 02·56 h, G.M.T., on 21st July 1969. Col. Collins remained in Command Module (*Columbia*). 48 lb moon rock returned.
11th–16th Oct. 1969	U.S.S.R.	*Soyuz 6*	Lt.-Col. Giorgiy Shonin (34); Valery N. Kubasov (34), engineer	118 42	75	Rendezvous and formation trials and experiments carrying out simulated assembly techniques for manufacture of space-stations (including arc welding, electron beam welding and electrode welding in depressurised compartment). Total of thirty-one manoeuvring operations carried out during the flight.
12th–17th Oct. 1969	U.S.S.R.	*Soyuz 7*	Lt.-Col. Anatoly V. Filipchenko (41); Lt.-Col. Viktor V. Gorbatko (35); Vladislav N. Volkov (34)	118 41	75	
13th–18th Oct. 1969	U.S.S.R.	*Soyuz 8*	Col. Vladimir A. Shatalov (41); Alexei N. Yeliseyev (35), engineer	118 41	75	

Date	Country	Spacecraft	Crew Members	Flight Duration H Min	No. of Orbits	Remarks
14th–24th Nov. 1969	U.S.A.	Apollo XII	Cdr. Charles Conrad (39), U.S. Navy; Cdr. Richard F. Gordon (40), U.S. Navy; Cdr. Alan L. Bean (37), U.S. Navy	244 36	· 1½ (earth) 45 (moon)	Second moon landing by man (Conrad, total E.V.A., 7 h 53 min; Bean, total E.V.A., 6 h 50 min) Lunar Module (Intrepid) landed on Ocean of Storms while Command Module (Yankee Clipper) stayed in moon orbit. 73 lb moon soil returned.
11th–17th Apr. 1970	U.S.A.	Apollo XIII	Captain James Arthur Lovell (41), U.S. Navy; Mr. Fred W. Haise; Mr. John L. Swigert	142 54	1½	Projected moon landing abandoned after near-catastrophic failure of Service Module en route, 205,000 miles (329,915 km) from earth. Crew occupied Lunar Module for remainder of flight, but returned to Command Module for splashdown.
31st Jan–9th Feb. 1971	U.S.A.	Apollo XIV	Capt. Alan B. Shepard, U.S. Navy; Cdr. Stuart A. Roosa, U.S. Navy; and Maj. Edgar J. Mitchell, U.S. Air Force	214 2	—	Third moon landing by man. Lunar Module (Antares) landed north of the Fra Mauro crater in the Sea of Rains. Use of a golf-cart-like Modular Equipment Transporter aids the collection of 96 lb (43·5 kg) of rock samples in two E.V.As totalling 9 h 29 min.
23rd–25th April 1971	U.S.S.R.	Soyuz 10	Vladimir Shatalov, Alexei Yeliseyev and Nikolai Rukavishnikov			Rendezvous and docking exercise with the Salyut 1 space-station.
6th–30th June 1971	U.S.S.R.	Soyuz 11	G. Dobrovolsky, V. Volkov and V. Patseyev	569 40		Rendezvous and docking with Salyut 1. Cosmonauts on board Salyut carried out a programme involving earth-resources survey, meteorological, space physics and biological studies. During the re-entry phase of the return to earth, on 30th June, the spacecraft suffered decompression and the crew died.
26th July–7th Aug. 1971	U.S.A.	Apollo XV	Alfred Worden, David Scott and James Irwin	271 12	1½ (earth) 75 (moon)	Fourth moon landing by man. Lunar Module (Falcon) landed in the Apennine Mountains/Hadley Rille area. First use of Boeing Lunar Roving Vehicle. Three E.V.A.s, totalling 18 h 36 min, made possible by its use.
16th–27th April 1972	U.S.A.	Apollo XVI	Capt. John W. Young, U.S. Navy; Lt.-Cdr. Thomas K. Mattingly, U.S. Navy; and Lt.-Col. Charles F. Duke, U.S. Air Force	265 50	—	Fifth moon landing by man. Lunar Module (Orion) landed north of the crater Descartes. Three E.V.A.s, totalling almost 20 h, were made with the aid of an L.R.V., and some 245 lb (110 kg) of rock samples collected.
7th–19th Dec. 1972	U.S.A.	Apollo XVII	Eugene A. Cernan; Ronald E. Evans; and Harrison H. Schmitt	301 52	—	Final Apollo mission. Sixth moon landing by 2 men. Lunar Module (Challenger) landed at pre-selected Taurus-Littrow site in the Sea of Serenity. Three E.V.A.s, totalling 22 h 6 min, were made by L.R.V., during which 22 miles (35 km) were travelled and 249 lb (113 kg) of lunar material was collected.

Date	Country	Spacecraft	Crew Members	Flight Duration H Min	No. of Orbits	Remarks
25th May–22nd June 1973	U.S.A.	*Skylab 2*	Charles Conrad, Dr. Joseph Kerwin, Paul Weitz	654 48		Mission was to repair damage to Skylab station caused during launch, and to man the station.
28th July–25th September 1973	U.S.A.	*Skylab 3*	Alan L. Bean, Dr Owen K. Garriott, Jack R. Lousma	1,427 9	858	Mission objectives were to obtain medical data on crew for use in extending the duration of space flights, and to perform in-orbit experiments.
16th Nov. 1973–8th Feb. 1974	U.S.A.	*Skylab 4*	Gerald P. Carr, Dr Edward G. Gibson, William R. Pogue	2,016 15	1,214	See page 246.
3rd–19th July 1974	U.S.S.R.	*Soyuz 14*	Col. Pavel Popovich, Lt.-Col. Yuri Artyukhin	15¾ days		First manned flight to *Salyut 3* space station.
26th–28th Aug. 1974	U.S.S.R.	*Soyuz 15*	Lt.-Col. Gennady Sarafanov, Col. Lev Demin	under 2 days		Second manned flight to *Salyut 3* failed when booster burned too long and cosmonauts overshot station.
2nd–8th Dec. 1974	U.S.S.R.	*Soyuz 16*	Col. Anatoli Filipchenko, Nikolai Rukavishnikov	6 days		Rehearsal for joint U.S.–Soviet ASTP mission.

Appendix 1

ADDENDA

The first woman to lose her life in an aerial disaster was Madame Blanchard, widow of the pioneer French aeronaut Jean-Pierre Blanchard (who had died after a heart attack, suffered while ballooning, on 7th March 1809). Madame Blanchard was killed when her hydrogen balloon was ignited during a firework display which she was giving at the Tivoli Gardens, Paris, on 7th July 1819.

The first flight by a powered and navigable lighter-than-air craft (i.e. a dirigible) was made on 24th September 1852 by Henri Giffard from Paris to Trappes—about 17 miles (27 km). The craft, coal-gas filled, was powered by a steam engine.

The man whose aircraft have probably contributed most to British sporting flying was the late Sir Geoffrey de Havilland, O.M., C.B.E., A.F.C. His first aircraft was a failure, but the second was a success and was bought by the British Government. He then started to design aircraft at the Royal Aircraft Factory which were to serve with the R.F.C. The B.E. 2 series of aircraft were designed during this period, but when the First World War started he moved to the Aircraft Manufacturing Company Ltd., and designed the first aircraft bearing a D.H. designation. After the end of the war Airco changed its name to de Havilland Aircraft Company and started designing and remodelling aircraft for civilian use. Several aircraft were built before the D.H. 60 Moth established de Havilland as the designer of the first practical aircraft for private use. Several versions of the Moth were built and were used in clubs, for racing and for record-breaking attempts. Geoffrey de Havilland was born in 1882 and died on 21st May 1965.

The inventor of the first aircraft jet engine to run was Sir Frank Whittle, who was born on 1st June 1907 at Coventry. In 1928, while a Cadet at Cranwell, he published a thesis entitled *Speculation* which put forward the basic equations of thermodynamics for this system. Although the Air Ministry showed an interest, the idea was not taken up, and it was not until 1935 that Whittle had some success when R. D. Williams started a company called Power Jets Ltd. to exploit the invention. On 12th April 1937 Whittle ran **the first aircraft turbojet in the world** (although a gas-turbine engine had been made previously, he was the first person to make one for aircraft propulsion). The Ministry, in March 1938, gave Whittle a contract for an engine, and on 15th May 1941 a Gloster E 28/39, powered by this engine, took off at Cranwell flown by Flight-Lieutenant P. E. G. Sayer. This was **the first British jet aeroplane**. By 1944 Gloster Meteor squadrons were being formed, and flew **the first jet combat sorties**, destroying German V-1 flying -bombs.

The first occasion on which four people lost their lives in an air accident was on 25th September 1909 when the French dirigible *Republique* lost a propeller which pierced the gasbag; the craft fell from 400 ft (122 m) at Avrilly, near Moulins, the crew of four being killed.

The first occasion on which five people lost their lives in an air accident was on 13th July 1910 when a German non-rigid dirigible, of the Erbsloch type, suffered an explosion of the gasbag and fell from 920 ft (280 m) near Opladen, Germany. The crew of five, including Oscar Erbsloch, were killed.

The first gyroscopic automatic stabiliser was successfully demonstrated by the Americans, Lawrence B. Sperry and Lieutenant Patrick Nelson Lynch Bellinger, in a Curtiss F flying-boat in 1913. The aircraft was longitudinally and laterally stabilised.

The first composite (i.e. "pickaback") aeroplane experiments were conducted on 17th May 1916 in Britain, using a Bristol Scout "C" mounted atop a Felixstowe Baby three-engined flying-boat, with a view to developing a means of intercepting Zeppelin airship raiders. On that day the pair of aircraft took off from Felixstowe, Suffolk, the lower component captained by John Cyril Porte and the

Lawrence Sperry began experimenting with a gyro-stabiliser for aeroplanes in 1912, fitting his devices in a Curtiss flying-boat. By 1914 he had progressed to an automatic pilot which held the aircraft so steady in flight that he could stand up in the cockpit while his companion calmly walked along the wings

Bristol occupied by Flight-Lieutenant M. J. Day, R.N.A.S. When flying at 1,000 ft (300 m) over Harwich, Day released the Bristol and climbed away, landing at Martlesham Heath. Although successful, the experiment was not repeated.

The first Bolivian military pilots were Capitáns José Alarcón and Renato Parejas, and Sub-Lieutenant Horacio Vasquez who were sent to the Argentine to learn their flying at El Palomar in 1916, attending the Fifth Flying Course. Capitán Alarcón was however killed on 23rd January 1917 while flying a Farman.

The first Mexican pilot to be awarded a Mexican Pilot's Certificate was Samuel C. Rojas who gained Mexican Military Certificate No. 1 in 1918.

The first variable-incidence variable-geometry aeroplane in the world was the Swedish Pålson Type 1 single-seat sporting aircraft of 1918–19. It is said that the aircraft featured a system of cranks to alter the position of the biplane's top wing as well as its angle of incidence as a means of achieving optimum lift/drag in cruising flight. It is not known what success attended flight trials (if any).

The first flight across Australia was made during the period 16th November–12th December 1919 by a B.E.2e flown by Captain H. N. Wrigley, D.F.C., accompanied by Lieutenant A. W. Murphy, D.F.C., from Melbourne to Darwin to meet Ross and Keith Smith. They covered the 2,500 miles (4,000 km) in 46 h flying time.

The Australian Air Force was established by Proclamation on 31st March 1921, pending passage of the Air Defence Act. H.M. King George V approved the designation as Royal Australian Air Force on 13th August 1921.

The New Zealand Air Force was formed on 14th June 1923. It was reorganised in 1934 and restyled the Royal New Zealand Air Force on 1st April 1937.

The first lightplane competition to be organised in Great Britain was that held at Lympne, Kent, between 27th September and 4th October 1924, organised by the Royal Aero Club and for which prizes worth £3,000 were offered by the Air Ministry. The competition was won by Mr Piercey on the Beardmore Wee Bee monoplane which was powered by a Bristol Cherub engine. The lightest aircraft entered was the Hawker Cygnet biplane, also a two-seater, whose tare weight was 373 lb (169·2 kg).

The first occasion on which an heir to the British throne crossed the English Channel by air was on 4th May 1926 when H.R.H. The Prince of Wales flew in an Imperial Airways Handley Page W.10 piloted by Captain O. P. Jones from London to Le Bourget, Paris.

The first rocket-propelled aeroplane to fly with a degree of success was an aircraft designed and flown by the German, Fritz von Opel. He flew his aeroplane on 30th September 1929 for a distance of about 2,000 yd (1,830 m), attaining a speed of 100 mile/h (161 km/h) for a short period.

The first film (movie picture) shown in an aeroplane in flight was demonstrated in a Ford aircraft of Transcontinental Air Transport Inc., flying at 5,000 ft (1,500 m) over land in America on 8th October 1929. The entire film projector and equipment weighed less than 34 lb (16 kg).

The first electrical-mechanical flight simulator was the Link Trainer, which represented a replica of an aeroplane with full controls and instruments, but which did not leave the ground; instead it was "attached" to a mechanical crab which traced a path over a large-scale map in such a way as to represent heading, speed and time of the replica aircraft "flown" by its occupant. It was invented by Edward Albert Link who sold his first model in 1929; it was adopted by the U.S. Navy in 1931, and by the U.S. Army in 1934. By 1939 there was scarcely an air force in the world that was not using Link Trainers, and there can be no doubt that they were the forerunners of today's complex flight simulators.

The first fighter to enter service with the Royal Air Force capable of a maximum level speed of more than 200 mile/h (322 km/h) was the Hawker Fury I biplane. Powered by a 525 hp Rolls-Royce Kestrel IIS liquid-cooled engine and armed with two synchronised Vickers machine-guns, the Fury had a top speed of 207 mile/h (333 km/h) at 14,000 ft (4,270 m). Designed by the late Sir Sydney Camm, it entered service in May 1931.

The first commercial British aeroplane to be fitted with a retractable undercarriage was the Airspeed A.S.5 Courier which first flew on 11th April 1933 at Portsmouth Airport. The test pilot was Flight-Lieutenant G. H. Stainforth. The second was the General Aircraft Monospar ST-6 which first flew several weeks later.

The first commercial use of composite aeroplanes in the world occurred during 21st–22nd July 1938 when the Short S.21 *Maia* flying-boat and the Short S.20 *Mercury* seaplane took off from Foynes, Ireland, the upper component then separating and flying the Atlantic non-stop to Montreal, Canada, with a load of mail and newspapers. It covered 2,930 miles (4,715 km) in 20 h 20 min, at an average speed of 140 mile/h (225 km/h). The pilot of *Mercury* was Captain D. C. T. Bennett (later Air Vice-Marshal, C.B., C.B.E., D.S.O.). Numerous composite flights and separations were carried out and the pair of aircraft continued to operate on the Southampton to Alexandria air route until the outbreak of the Second World War. After brief service with a Dutch seaplane squadron (No. 320) serving with the R.A.F., *Mercury* was broken up late 1941; *Maia* was destroyed by a German bomb on the night of 11th May 1941 while moored in Poole Harbour, Dorset.

The first operational use of stand-off bombs was by twelve Dornier Do 217s of II Gruppe, Kampfgeschwader 100, commanded by Hauptmann Molinus, on 25th August 1943 in an attack

The Short-Mayo Composite was built as a means of getting a heavily loaded seaplane into the air. When launched from its "mother-plane" Maia, the seaplane Mercury carried sufficient petrol to fly 5,997·5 miles (9,652 km) from Dundee, Scotland, to the Orange River, South Africa. In doing so, on 6th–8th October 1938, it set up a record that has never been beaten

against seven anti-U-boat ships of the Royal Navy in the vicinity of Cape Finisterre, Spain. The German weapons were Henschel Hs 293 rocket-boosted glider-bombs. On this occasion the bombs were released about six miles from the ships but no hits were scored, only H.M.S. *Bideford* being damaged by a near miss. **The first ship to be sunk in action by the Henschel Hs 293 stand-off bomb** was H.M.S. *Egret*, a corvette of the Royal Navy, which was hit in the same area as the above action two days later, on 27th August 1943. A Canadian destroyer, the *Athabaskan*, and the corvette *Rother* were damaged.

The first documented sighting of an Unidentified Flying Object (U.F.O. or "flying saucer") by a qualified flying person was reported by an American private pilot, Kenneth Arnold, who in June 1947 reported seeing from his cockpit nine "saucer-shaped things" flying among the peaks in the Mount Rainier area.

The smallest piloted aeroplane ever flown is the Stits Skybaby biplane, designed, built and flown by Ray Stits at Riverside, Calif., in 1952. It had a wing span of 7 ft 2 in (2·18 m) and a length of 9 ft 10 in (3·00 m). Powered by an 85 hp Continental C85 engine, it weighed 452 lb (205 kg) empty and had a top speed of 185 mile/h (298 km/h).

The first woman in the world to fly faster than the speed of sound was Miss Jacqueline Cochrane, an American cosmetics tycoon, who, flying a North American F-86 Sabre, exceeded the speed of sound on 18th May 1953, and on the same day established a world's speed record for women of 652 mile/h (1,049 km/h).

The world's first aircraft to be fitted with a hinged tail for rear loading, the Canadair CL-44D-4, was flown for the first time on 16th November 1960. Powered by four Rolls-Royce Tyne 515/10 two-shaft two-spool turboprops, each rated at 5,730 ehp, it had a range of 5,660 miles (9,110 km) with a 37,300 lb (16,920 kg) payload. Its maximum payload was 66,048 lb (29,960 kg).

Aviation's richest man. The progress of aviation has been constantly sponsored and nurtured by some of the wealthiest men (and women) of the age. Not surprisingly, aviation has also made many men very wealthy. Without question, the richest man associated with aviation is Howard Hughes, who shares with Paul Getty the distinction of being the richest man in the world. Hughes's assets have been estimated, conservatively, at $985,500,000 (£369,000,000). When he sold his shares in Trans World Airlines, he realised the sum of $546,549,771 (£227,729,070), which, incidentally stands as a world record for the largest cash sum to be paid to an individual by cheque. His own two major companies, Hughes Aircraft and Hughes Tool contribute share holdings conservatively estimated in 1968 at $387,500,000 (£161,458,000). Thirteen years older than Hughes, Jean Paul Getty is also an American citizen but is resident in Surrey, England. With visible assets once estimated at $957,404,289 (£398,918,500), Getty's fortune lies principally in oil, although the Sarah C. Getty Trust owns stock valued at $2,832,812 (£1,180,330) in the Spartan Aircraft Company.

The lightest aeroplane built and flown in Great Britain is the Ward P46 Gnome, built by Michael Ward of North Scarle, Lincolnshire, and flown on 4th August 1967. Empty it weighs 210 lb (95·3 kg), with a maximum take-off weight of 380 lb (172 kg). Its ceiling, officially imposed at 10 ft (3·05 m) because of the use of materials not covered by air regulations, is probably the **lowest ceiling of any aeroplane!**

The Hovey Whing Ding II

The lightest aeroplane yet flown is the Hovey Whing Ding II, the prototype first flying in February 1971. It was designed and built by Mr R. W. Hovey of Saugus, Calif. and weighs only 123 lb (55·5 kg) including fuel. Several examples are now flying.

The world's first aircraft apprentice was Mr Howard "Dinger" Bell who joined Short Brothers in 1909 and worked on **the world's first aircraft production line** making six Short-Wright biplanes for the Wright brothers. He died in December 1972 at the age of seventy-seven.

Appendix 2

PROGRESSIVE WORLD ABSOLUTE SPEEDS ACHIEVED BY MAN IN THE ATMOSPHERE

Those entries marked with an asterisk represent accurately measured speeds not ratified as World records by the Fédération Aéronautique Internationale. These speeds were often achieved during one run of several, from which the mean was submitted for ratification as a record; they are included to indicate the progressive highest speed achieved by man.

Speed mile/h	km/h	Pilot	Nationality	Aircraft	Location of achievement	Date
(25·65*)	41·27	Alberto Santos-Dumont†	France	Santos-Dumont "14bis"	Bagatelle, France	12th Nov. 1906
(32·73*)	52·66	Henry Farman	France	Voisin biplane	Issy-les-Moulineaux, France	26th Oct. 1907
34·04	54·77	Paul Tissandier	France	Wright biplane	Pau, France	20th May 1909
43·35	69·75	Glenn Curtiss	U.S.A.	Herring-Curtiss biplane	Reims, France	23rd Aug. 1909
46·18	74·30	Louis Blériot	France	Blériot monoplane	Reims, France	24th Aug. 1909
47·85	76·99	Louis Blériot	France	Blériot monoplane	Reims, France	28th Aug. 1909
48·21	77·57	Hubert Latham	France	Antoinette monoplane	Nice, France	23rd Apr. 1910
66·19	106·50	Léon Morane	France	Blériot monoplane	Reims, France	10th July 1910
68·20	109·73	Alfred Leblanc	France	Blériot monoplane	Reims, France	29th Oct. 1910
69·48	111·79	Alfred Leblanc	France	Blériot monoplane	Belmont Park, Long Island, U.S.A.	29th Oct. 1910
74·42	119·74	Édouard Nieuport	France	Nieuport biplane		12th Apr. 1911
77·68	124·99	Alfred Leblanc	France	Blériot monoplane		11th May 1911
80·82	130·04	Édouard Nieuport	France	Nieuport biplane	Châlons, France	16th June 1911
82·73	133·11	Édouard Nieuport	France	Nieuport biplane	Châlons, France	21st June 1911
90·20	145·13	Jules Védrines	France	Deperdussin monoplane	Pau, France	13th Jan. 1912
100·23	161·27	Jules Védrines	France	Deperdussin monoplane	Pau, France	22nd Feb. 1912
100·95	162·53	Jules Védrines	France	Deperdussin monoplane	Pau, France	29th Feb. 1912
103·66	166·79	Jules Védrines	France	Deperdussin monoplane	Pau, France	1st Mar. 1912
104·34	167·88	Jules Védrines	France	Deperdussin monoplane	Pau, France	2nd Mar. 1912
106·12	170·75	Jules Védrines	France	Deperdussin monoplane		13th July 1912
108·18	174·06	Jules Védrines	France	Deperdussin monoplane	Chicago, Illinois, U.S.A.	9th Sept. 1912
111·74	179·79	Maurice Prévost	France	Deperdussin monoplane		17th June 1913
119·25	191·87	Maurice Prévost	France	Deperdussin monoplane	Reims, France	27th Sept. 1913
126·67	203·81	Maurice Prévost	France	Deperdussin monoplane	Reims, France	29th Sept. 1913
First World War: No reliable international records						
171·05	275·22	Sadi Lecointe	France	Nieuport-Delage monoplane		7th Feb. 1920
176·15	283·43	Jean Casale	France	Blériot monoplane		28th Feb. 1920
181·87	292·63	Baron de Romanet	France	Spad biplane		9th Oct. 1920
184·36	296·94	Sadi Lecointe	France	Nieuport-Delage 29		10th Oct. 1920
187·99	302·48	Sadi Lecointe	France	Nieuport-Delage 29		20th Oct. 1920
192·02	308·96	Baron de Romanet	France	Spad biplane		4th Nov. 1920
194·53	313·00	Sadi Lecointe	France	Nieuport-Delage 29		12th Dec. 1920

†Brazilian, but resident in France

Speed mile/h	km/h	Pilot	Nationality	Aircraft	Location of achievement	Date
(210·64*	339·00	Sadi Lecointe	France	Nieuport-Delage 29	Villesauvage, France	25th Dec. 1921
205·24	330·23	Sadi Lecointe	France	Nieuport-Delage 29	Villesauvage, France	20th Sept. 1922
211·91	341·00	Sadi Lecointe	France	Nieuport-Delage 29	Villesauvage, France	21st Sept. 1922
222·98	358·77	Brig.-Gen. William A. Mitchell	U.S.A.	Curtiss HS D-12	Detroit, Michigan, U.S.A.	13th Oct. 1922
(243·94*	392·64	Brig.-Gen. William A. Mitchell	U.S.A.	Curtiss HS D-12	Detroit, Michigan, U.S.A.	18th Oct. 1922
233·03	374·95	Sadi Lecointe	France	Nieuport-Delage 29		15th Feb. 1923
236·59	380·67	Lieutenant R. L. Maughan	U.S.A.	Curtiss R-6		29th Mar. 1923
259·16	411·04	Lieutenant A. Brown	U.S.A.	Curtiss HS D-12	Mitchell Field, N.Y., U.S.A.	2nd Nov. 1923
266·60	429·96	Lieutenant Alford J. Williams	U.S.A.	Curtiss R-2 C-1	Mitchell Field, N.Y., U.S.A.	4th Nov. 1923
(270·50*	435·30	Lieutenant Alford J. Williams	U.S.A.	Curtiss R-2 C-1	Mitchell Field, N.Y., U.S.A.	4th Nov. 1923
(274·20*	441·30	Lieutenant A. Brown	U.S.A.	Curtiss HS D-12	Mitchell Field, N.Y., U.S.A.	4th Nov. 1923
278·47	448·15	Adjutant Chef A. Bonnet	France	Ferbois V-2	Istres, France	11th Dec. 1924
(284·21*	457·39	Flying Officer Sidney Webster, A.F.C.	G.B.	Supermarine S.5	Venice, Italy	26th Sept. 1927
297·83	479·21	Major Mario de Bernardi	Italy	Macchi M-52	Venice, Italy	4th Nov. 1927
(313·59*	504·67	Major Mario de Bernardi	Italy	Macchi M-52	Venice, Italy	6th Nov. 1927
318·64	512·69	Major Mario de Bernardi	Italy	Macchi M-52bis	Venice, Italy	30th Mar. 1928
(348·60*	561·00	Major Mario de Bernardi	Italy	Macchi M-52bis	Venice, Italy	30th Mar. 1928
(>370·00*	>595·40	Flying Officer R. D. Waghorn, A.F.C.	G.B.	Supermarine S.6	Solent, England	7th Sept. 1929
*		Flying Officer R. L. R. Atcherley	G.B.	Supermarine S.6	Solent, England	12th Sept. 1929
357·75	575·62	Squadron Leader A. H. Orlebar	G.B.	Supermarine S.6	Ryde, Isle of Wight, England	12th Sept. 1929
(388·00*	624·00	Flight-Lieutenant G. H. Stainforth, A.F.C.	G.B.	Supermarine S.6B	Ryde, Isle of Wight, England	13th Sept. 1931
407·02	654·90	Flight-Lieutenant G. H. Stainforth, A.F.C.	G.B.	Supermarine S.6B	Ryde, Isle of Wight, England	29th Sept. 1931
(415·20*	668·20	Flight-Lieutenant G. H. Stainforth, A.F.C.	G.B.	Supermarine S.6B	Ryde, Isle of Wight, England	29th Sept. 1931
423·85	681·97	Warrant-Officer Francesco Agello	Italy	Macchi-Castoldi 72	Lago di Garda, Italy	10th Apr. 1934
(430·32*	692·53	Warrant-Officer Francesco Agello	Italy	Macchi-Castoldi 72	Lago di Garda, Italy	10th Apr. 1934
(>434·96*	>699·85	Colonel Bernascori	Italy	Macchi-Castoldi 72	Desenzano, Italy	18th Apr. 1934
440·69	709·07	Lieutenant Francesco Agello	Italy	Macchi-Castoldi 72	Lago di Garda, Italy	23rd Oct. 1934
(441·22*	710·07	Lieutenant Francesco Agello	Italy	Macchi-Castoldi 72	Lago di Garda, Italy	23rd Oct. 1934
463·92	746·45	Flugkapitän Hans Dieterle	Germany	Heinkel He 100V-8	Oranienburg, Germany	30th Mar. 1939
469·22	754·97	Flugkapitän Fritz Wendel	Germany	Messerschmitt Bf 109R	Augsburg, Germany	26th Apr. 1939
(486·00*	781·97	Flugkapitän Fritz Wendel	Germany	Messerschmitt Bf 109R	Augsburg, Germany	29th Apr. 1939
			Second World War: No reliable international records			
(603·00*	970·23	Squadron Leader P. Stanbury, D.F.C.	G.B.	Gloster Meteor F.4	Moreton Valence, England	19th Oct. 1945
606·38	975·67	Group Captain H. J. Wilson, A.F.C.	G.B.	Gloster Meteor F.4	Herne Bay, Kent, England	7th Nov. 1945
(611·20*	983·42	Group Captain H. J. Wilson, A.F.C.	G.B.	Gloster Meteor F.4	Herne Bay, Kent, England	7th Nov. 1945
615·78	990·79	Group Captain E. M. Donaldson, D.S.O., A.F.C.	G.B.	Gloster Meteor F.4	Rustington, Sussex, England	7th Sept. 1946
(623·45*	1003·31	Group Captain E. M. Donaldson, D.S.O., A.F.C.	G.B.	Gloster Meteor F.4	Rustington, Sussex, England	7th Sept. 1946

Speed mile/h	km/h	Pilot	Nationality	Aircraft	Location of achievement	Date
623·74	1003·60	Colonel Albert Boyd	U.S.A.	Lockheed P-80R Shooting Star	Muroc, California, U.S.A.	19th June 1947
640·74	1030·95	Commander Turner F. Caldwell, U.S.N.	U.S.A.	Douglas D-558 Skystreak	Muroc, California, U.S.A.	20th Aug. 1947
650·92	1047·33	Major Marion E. Carl, U.S.M.C.	U.S.A.	Douglas D-558 Skystreak	Muroc, California, U.S.A.	25th Aug. 1947
670·98	1079·61	Major Richard L. Johnson U.S.A.F.	U.S.A.	North American F-86A Sabre	Muroc, California, U.S.A.	15th Sept. 1948
698·50	1123·89	Captain J. Slade Nash, U.S.A.F.	U.S.A.	North American F-86D Sabre	Salton Sea, California, U.S.A.	19th Nov. 1952
(699·94*	1126·20	Captain J. Slade Nash, U.S.A.F.	U.S.A.	North American F-86D Sabre	Salton Sea, California, U.S.A.	19th Nov. 1952)
715·75	1151·64	Lieutenant-Colonel William F. Barnes, U.S.A.F.	U.S.A.	North American F-86D Sabre	Salton Sea, California, U.S.A.	16th July 1953
727·63	1170·76	Squadron Leader Neville Duke, D.S.O., O.B.E., D.F.C., A.F.C.	G.B.	Hawker Hunter 3	Littlehampton, Sussex, England	7th Sept. 1953
(741·66*	1193·33	Squadron Leader Neville Duke, D.S.O., O.B.E., D.F.C., A.F.C.	G.B.	Hawker Hunter 3	Littlehampton, Sussex, England	31st Aug. 1953)
735·70	1183·74	Lieutenant-Commander Michael Lithgow, O.B.E.	G.B.	Supermarine Swift 4	Libya, Africa	25th Sept. 1953
752·94	1211·48	Lieutenant-Commander James B. Verdin, U.S.N.	U.S.A.	Douglas F4D-1 Skyray	Salton Sea, California, U.S.A.	3rd Oct. 1953
755·15	1215·04	Lieutenant-Colonel Frank K. Everest, U.S.A.F.	U.S.A.	North American YF-100A Super Sabre	Salton Sea, California, U.S.A.	29th Oct. 1953
822·27	1323·03	Colonel H. A. Hanes, U.S.A.F.	U.S.A.	North American F-100C Super Sabre	Edwards Air Force Base, California, U.S.A.	20th Aug. 1955
1132·00	1821·39	Lieutenant Peter Twiss, O.B.E., D.S.C.	G.B.	Fairey Delta 2	Chichester, Sussex, England	10th Mar. 1956
1207·60	1943·03	Major Adrian Drew, U.S.A.F.	U.S.A.	McDonnell F-101A Voodoo		12th Dec. 1957
1404·09	2259·18	Captain Walter W. Irvin, U.S.A.F.	U.S.A.	Lockheed F-104A Starfighter	Southern California, U.S.A.	16th May 1958
1483·83	2387·48	Colonel Georgiy Mosolov	U.S.S.R.	Mikoyan Type E-66	Sidorovo, Tyumenskaya, U.S.S.R.	31st Oct. 1959
1525·95	2455·74	Major Joseph W. Rogers, U.S.A.F.	U.S.A.	Convair F-106A Delta Dart	Edwards Air Force Base, California, U.S.A.	15th Dec. 1959
1606·51	2585·43	Lieutenant-Colonel Robert B. Robinson	U.S.A.	McDonnell F4H-1F Phantom II	Edwards Air Force Base, California, U.S.A.	22nd Nov. 1961
1665·89	2681·00	Colonel Georgiy Mosolov	U.S.S.R.	Mikoyan Type E-166	Sidorovo, Tyumenskaya, U.S.S.R.	7th July 1962
2070·10	3331·51	Colonel Robert L. Stephens	U.S.A.	Lockheed YF-12A	Edwards Air Force Base, California, U.S.A.	1st May 1965

The record speed achieved by Colonel Stephens on 1st May 1965 has survived to date as the highest ratified speed record attained by an aeroplane which took off under its own power from the earth's surface. Between 1960 and 1967 however the U.S. Air Force conducted a substantial programme of manned flight trials with the North American X-15 and X-15A-2. Powered by a liquid oxygen and ammonia rocket engine, the X-15 was carried to altitude by a Boeing B-52 before embarking upon ultra-high-speed and altitude flights, as summarised overleaf:

Progressive maximum speeds achieved by the X-15:

mile/h	km/h	Mach No.	Pilot	Date
2111	3397	3·19	J. A. Walker	12th May 1960
2196	3534	3·31	J. A. Walker	4th Aug. 1960
2275	3613	3·50	R. M. White	7th Feb. 1961
2905	4675	4·43	R. M. White	7th Mar. 1961
3074	4947	4·62	R. M. White	21st Apr. 1961
3300	5311	4·90	J. A. Walker	25th May 1961
3603	5798	5·27	R. M. White	23rd June 1961
3614	5816	5·25	J. A. Walker	12th Sept. 1961
3620	5826	5·25	F. S. Petersen	28th Sept. 1961
3647	5869	5·21	R. M. White	11th Oct. 1961
3900	6276	5·74	J. A. Walker	17th Oct. 1961
4093	6587	6·04	R. M. White	9th Nov. 1961
4104	6605	5·92	J. A. Walker	27th June 1962 (X-15A-2)
4250	6840	6·33	W. J. Knight	18th Nov. 1966 (X-15A-2)
4534	7297	6·72	W. J. Knight	3rd Oct. 1967

Appendix 3

FOUR REMARKABLE AIRCRAFT

The Boeing 747

The Boeing 747, currently referred to as the first of a new generation of "jumbo-jets", is the largest aircraft in commercial airline service in the world. It was conceived in 1965 to cope with the world-wide explosion in the demand for intercontinental passenger travel, as airlines came to realise that saturation of airways and air traffic patterns was rapidly approaching. Apart from its sheer size, its development was something of a technical masterpiece; from the date of first airline orders being placed to that of the first airline deliveries was only three years and eight months, and regular airline service followed only five months later.

The size of the Boeing 747 is emphasised by this photograph of a Pan Am example parked by a Boeing 707, which was itself regarded once as a "big jet"

The first airline to order the Boeing 747 was Pan American World Airways which ordered twenty-five aircraft on 13th April 1966, at a cost of $525 million (£218,750,000), or $21 million (£8,750,000) each.

The first Boeing 747 made its first flight on 9th February 1969 from Paine Field, near Seattle, Washington. There was no prototype and this first aircraft was representative of the type scheduled for airline delivery. **The first Boeing 747-136 ordered by B.O.A.C. flew for the first time** on 15th March 1970 and was handed over to the airline on 20th April.

At the time of writing, orders for the huge aeroplane totalled 223, for delivery to the following airlines:

K.L.M.	7	Sabena	2	Iberia		3
Pan American	33	Lufthansa	6	El Al		3
American Airlines	16	Air Canada	3	S.A.S.		2
United Airlines	18	National Airlines	2	Condor		2
Continental	4	Air India	4	T.A.P. (Portugal)		2
Trans-World Air Lines	15	Qantas	6	Korean Air Lines		1
Eastern Air Lines	4	Alitalia	5	C.P. Air (Canada)		2
Braniff	1	Swissair	2	World Airlines		3
Delta Air Lines	5	South African		Wardair		1
Northwest Orient	15	Airways	5	Singapore Airlines		2
Air France	14	Japan Air Lines	20			
B.O.A.C.	13	Irish International	2			

In terms of size, weight and load-carrying capacity the Boeing 747 is indeed impressive. The standard current passenger version provides accommodation for 382 passengers—74 First Class and 308 Economy Class; other versions include one for 447 Economy Class passengers seated nine abreast, and one for 500 seated ten abreast. Compare this accommodation with that of the Short Sandringham flying-boat of twenty-five years ago (at 25 passengers) and with that of the de Havilland Comet which, with accommodation for 60–81 passengers, entered service on the transatlantic run fifteen years ago.

The weight of the Boeing 747 at maximum take-off load is 775,000 lb (351,540 kg). This weight is equivalent to the *total take-off weight of nine Lancaster bombers each loaded with a 22,000 lb "Grand Slam" bomb!* Its fuel capacity of 42,466 Imperial gal (193,050 ls), is sufficient to run sixty family saloon cars each for 20,000 miles (33,000 km), or forty cars round the world.

The engines, of which four power the Boeing 747, each develop between 43,500 and 47,000 lb thrust (19,730 to 21,320 kg) depending on the aircraft variant. This is more than ten times the power of the jet engines fitted to the first jet fighters which entered service with the R.A.F. and U.S.A.F. twenty-nine years ago.

By way of summing up the Boeing 747, it is an aeroplane capable of carrying more than 400 passengers (equivalent to a fairly good attendance at a cinema show) from New York to London in about six hours, together with their baggage, feeding them, and entertaining them with a film show as they cruise at nearly 600 mile/h (975 km/h) seven miles above the earth!

Harrier V/STOL fighter taking off for a simulated strike mission, carrying a large bomb under its fuselage

The Hawker Siddeley Harrier

In a totally different sphere of aviation lies the Hawker Siddeley Harrier, a British military fighter aircraft capable of vertical and short take-off and landing. Developed directly from the Hawker P.1127 Kestrel, **the Harrier was the world's first operational, high-performance V/STOL fighter**, entering service with No. 1 (Fighter) Squadron, Royal Air Force, early in 1969. Powered by a single Rolls-Royce Bristol Pegasus vectored-thrust turbofan (initially developing 19,000 lb; 8,620 kg, thrust), the Harrier is capable of taking off vertically and flying at more than 735 mile/h (1,185 km/h). At the time of writing over two hundred Harriers were on order, half of them destined for the U.S. Marine Corps.

The P.1127 (prototype for the Harrier) was the world's first high-performance, fixed-wing aeroplane to achieve vertical take-off and landing. Its first untethered vertical take-off was performed on 19th November 1960, and its first conventional take-off on 13th March 1961. Its first transition from hovering to conventional flight and vice versa occurred in September 1961. Supersonic speed was achieved in dives during 1962, the aircraft thus becoming **the world's first VTOL aeroplane to fly faster than the speed of sound.**

The Kestrel was the world's first VTOL high-performance fixed-wing aircraft to be evaluated under service conditions, was the first to be flown by Service pilots of the R.A.F., the Luftwaffe, the U.S.A.F., the U.S. Navy, the U.S. Army and the U.S. Marine Corps, under field conditions. It was the first such aircraft to be exported anywhere in the world when, in 1966, ex-evaluation aircraft were passed to the American Services for further trials in the U.S.A. It was the first such aircraft to perform night take-offs and landings, and the first to operate to and from an aircraft carrier. The Harrier is the world's first fully operational fixed-wing high-performance V/STOL military aircraft to achieve world-wide combat capability, and the two-seater trainer version (the T. Mark 2) is the first fully-developed fixed-wing high-performance V/STOL trainer in the world.

Concorde 002

The BAC/Aérospatiale Concorde

Development of this supersonic transport aircraft was undertaken by two companies, British Aircraft Corporation based at Filton and Aérospatiale (S.N.I.A.S.) at Toulouse. Construction of the two prototypes began in February 1965, the 001 from Aérospatiale first flying on 2nd March 1969 and the 002 from B.A.C. flying on 9th April 1969.

The test programme includes the two prototypes, two pre-production aircraft and three production Concordes, on which about 3,320 flying hours will be completed.

Concorde is powered by four Rolls-Royce/SNECMA Olympus 593 turbojet engines, developing 38,050 lb (17,260 kg) thrust each. It has a maximum cruising speed of Mach 2·2 at 54,500 ft (16,600 m) and will carry between 128 and 144 passengers. It is due to enter service in 1975.

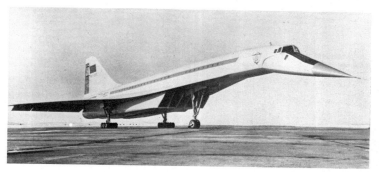

Tu-144 prototype (Tass)

The Tupolev Tu-144

The Tu-144 is a Russian supersonic transport aircraft similar in configuration to the Concorde, although it has a greater wing span. The prototype was assembled at the Zhukovsky Plant, near Moscow, and became the first such aircraft to fly on 31st December 1968.

The first public showing of the aircraft was on 21st May 1970, at Sheremetyevo Airport, Moscow. One of the first, largely redesigned production Tu-144s crashed during a demonstration flight at the Paris Air Show on 3rd June 1973. The airliner is now expected to enter service in 1975. It is powered by four Kuznetsov NK-144 turbofan engines, developing 44,090 lb (20,000 kg) thrust each, with reheat. The cruising speed is similar to that of Concorde and it will carry up to 140 passengers.

Appendix 4

AVIATION'S WORST DISASTERS

The following table presents details of all known air disasters involving the loss of more than fifty persons' lives.

Date	Loss of life	Location of Accident	Aircraft involved
24.8.21	62	Hull, Yorkshire, England; airship broke in two and fell in flames.	British airship *R-38*
21.12.23	52	Mediterranean Sea; airship crashed in sea.	French airship *Dixmude*
4.4.33	73	Off New Jersey coast; airship crashed in sea during storm.	U.S. airship *Akron*
23.8.44	76	Freckleton, Preston, England; bomber hit school in storm.	U.S.A.F. Liberator bomber
30.5.47	53	Near Fort Deposit, Maryland.	Eastern Air Lines DC-4
24.10.47	52	Boyce Canyon, Utah; aircraft caught fire and crashed.	United Air Lines DC-6
1.11.49	55	Washington, D.C.; collided with P-38 fighter.	Eastern Air Lines DC-4
12.3.50	81	Sigginston, South Wales; crashed while preparing to land at Llandow.	Chartered Avro Tudor V
24.6.50	58	Lake Michigan; crashed in storm.	Northwest Airlines DC-4
31.8.50	55	Near Cairo, Egypt; crashed and burned.	TWA Constellation
23.3.51	53	Atlantic Ocean; only wreckage found.	U.S.A.F. C-124
16.12.51	56	Elizabeth River, New Jersey.	Miami Airlines C-46
11.4.52	52	Off San Juan, Puerto Rico.	Pan American DC-4
20.12.52	87	Moses Lake, Washington; crashed and burned.	U.S.A.F. C-124
18.6.53	129	Tachikawa A.F.B., Tokyo, Japan; crashed after engine failure on take-off.	U.S.A.F. C-124
12.7.53	58	Off Wake Island, Pacific.	Transocean Air Lines DC-6B
22.3.55	66	Honolulu; aircraft hit cliff.	U.S. Navy DC-6
11.8.55	66	Near Stuttgart, Germany; two aircraft collided.	Two U.S.A.F. C-119
6.10.55	66	West of Laramie, Wyoming; hit mountain.	United Air Lines DC-4
20.2.56	52	In desert near Cairo, Egypt.	T.A.I. (French) DC-6B
20.6.56	74	In sea off Ashbury Park, New Jersey.	Venezuelan Super Constellation
30.6.56	128	Grand Canyon, Arizona; two airliners collided.	TWA Super Constellation and United Air Lines DC-7
10.10.56	59	Lost at sea about 150 miles north of the Azores.	U.S.A.F. (MATS) C-118
9.12.56	62	British Columbia; crashed in mountains.	Trans-Canada DC-4
21.3.57	67	Lost at sea over Pacific Ocean.	U.S.A.F. (MATS) C-97
16.7.57	56	Off New Guinea.	K.L.M. Super Constellation
11.8.57	79	Quebec, Canada; aircraft crashed in swamp.	Maritime Central Airways DC-4
8.12.57	62	Near Bolivar, Argentina.	Aerolineas Argentinas DC-4
18.5.58	65	Casablanca, Morocco.	SABENA DC-6B
14.8.58	99	Lost at sea 130 miles west of Ireland.	K.L.M. Super Constellation
17.10.58	75	Kanash, Chuvashskaya A.S.S.R., U.S.S.R.	Aeroflot Tu-104
16.1.59	51	Mar del Plata, Argentina.	Austral Curtiss Commando
3.2.59	65	East River, New York City	American Airlines Electra
26.6.59	68	Near Milan, Italy; aircraft crashed in storm.	TWA Super Constellation
24.9.59	53	Near Bordeaux, France.	Transports Aeriens DC-4
5.2.60	59	Near Cochabamba, Bolivia.	Bolivian DC-4
25.2.60	61	Air collision near Rio de Janeiro.	U.S. Navy R6D transport and Brazilian Real aircraft
17.3.60	63	Air explosion over Tell City, Indiana.	Northwest Airlines Electra
24.6.60	51	Guanabara Bay, Brazil.	Brazilian Real Convair
29.8.60	55	Lost at sea off Dakar, Senegal.	Air France Super Constellation
19.9.60	78	Burst into flames after take-off at Guam.	World Airways DC-6B
4.10.60	61	Boston, Massachusetts; crashed on take-off.	Eastern Air Lines Electra

Date	Loss of life	Location of Accident	Aircraft involved
22.7.73	78	Papeete, Tahiti; crashed into sea.	Pan American Boeing 707
31.7.73	88	Boston, U.S.A.; struck sea wall in fog.	Delta Air Lines DC-9
13.8.73	85	Corunna, Spain; crashed during fourth approach in bad weather.	Aviaco Caravelle
22.12.73	105	Tangier; crashed into high ground.	Sobelair Caravelle
26.1.74	65	Izmir, Turkey; take-off crash and fire.	THY F.28 Fellowship
31.1.74	97	Pago Pago, Samoa; touch-down and crash short of runway.	Pan American Boeing 707
3.3.74	346	Paris, France; explosive decompression caused by cargo door failure.	THY DC-10
4.4.74	77	Botswana; take-off accident.	Wenela DC-4
22.4.74	106	Bali, Indonesia; impacted at 4,000 ft volcano.	Pan American Boeing 707
27.4.74	118	Leningrad, U.S.S.R.; take-off accident.	Aeroflot Il-18
8.9.74	88	Ionian Sea; explosion resulting from sabotage.	TWA Boeing 707
11.9.74	70	Douglas, N.C., U.S.A.; crashed and caught fire during approach.	Eastern Air Lines DC-9
15.9.74	71	Between Da Nang and Singapore; blown up after hijacking.	Air Vietnam Boeing 727
20.11.74	59	Nairobi, Kenya; lost height during take-off, crashed and caught fire.	Lufthansa Boeing 747
1.12.74	92	West Virginia, U.S.A.; struck high ground during approach.	TWA Boeing 707
4.12.74	191	Sri Lanka; impacted high ground during approach.	Martinair DC-8
22.12.74	77	Maturin, Venezuela; engine failure at take-off.	Avensa DC-9

Bibliography

Abbas, A.: *Till We Reach the Stars: The Story of Yuriy Gagarin*; Asia Publishing House, Bombay, 1961.

Air Ministry: *The Rise and Fall of the German Air Force, 1933–1945*; Air Ministry, London, 1948.

Authors, Various: *Aircraft Profiles* (Seven Volumes, 204 aircraft described); Profile Publications, Leatherhead, England, 1965–67.

Babington-Smith, Constance: *Testing Time: The Story of British Test Pilots and their Aircraft*; Harper, New York, 1961.

Barnes, C. H.: *Bristol Aircraft Since 1910*; Putnam, London, 1970.

Barnes, C. H.: *Shorts Aircraft Since 1900*; Putnam, London, 1967.

Benecke, Th., and Quick A. W.: *History of German Guided Missile Development*; Verlag E. Appelhaus, Brunswick, Germany, 1957.

Bergman, Jules: *Ninety Seconds to Space: The X-15 Story*; Doubleday, New York, 1960.

Bowers, Peter M.: *Boeing Aircraft since 1916*; Putnam, London, 1965.

Brabazon of Tara, Lord: *The Brabazon Story*; Heinemann, London, 1956.

Braun, Wernher von, and Ordway III, Frederick I.: *History of Rocketry and Space Travel*; Thomas Nelson & Sons, Camden, New Jersey, U.S.A., 1966.

Brett, R. D.: *The History of British Aviation, 1908–1914*; Hamilton, London, 1934.

Brewer, Griffith: *Ballooning and its Application to Kite Balloons*; The Air League of the British Empire, London (11th Edition), 1940.

Broke-Smith, Brigadier P. W. L.: *The History of Early British Military Aeronautics*; L. A. Academic Reprint, Chivers, Bath, England, 1968.

Bruce, J. M.: *British Aeroplanes, 1914–1918*; Putnam, London, 1957.

Canby, C.: *History of Rockets and Space*; Manhasset, New York, 1963.

Carpenter, M. S. *(et al.):* *We Seven*; Simon and Schuster, New York, 1962.

Chapman, J. L.: *Atlas: The Story of a Missile*; Harper, New York, 1960.

Cornish III, Joseph Jenkins: *The Air Arm of the Confederacy*; Richmond Civil War Centennial Committee, Richmond, Virginia, U.S.A. 1963.

Davies, R. E. G.: *The History of the World's Airlines*; Oxford University Press, London, 1964.

Dixon, C.: *Parachuting*; Sampson Low, London, 1930.

Dollfus, Charles: *Balloons*; Prentice-Hall International (Transl. Mason), London, 1961.

Dollfus, Charles; Beaubois, Henry; Rougeron, Camille: *L'homme, l'air et l'espace*; Les Editions de l'Illustration, Paris, 1965.

Dorian, A. F., and Osenton, James (eds.): *Dictionary of Aeronautics* (six languages); Elsevier, London, 1964.

Feeney, William D.: *In Their Honour*; Duell, Sloan and Pearce, New York, 1963.

Francillon, René J.: *Japanese Aircraft of the Pacific War*; Putnam, London, 1970.

Fricker, John, and Green, William: *The Air Forces of the World*; Macdonald, London, 1958.

Gagarin, Yuriy: *Road to the Stars*; Foreign Languages Publishing House, Moscow, 1962.

Garber, Paul E.: *The National Aeronautical Collections*; The Smithsonian Institution, Washington, 1956.

Gatland, Kenneth W.: *Development of the Guided Missile*; Philosophical Library, New York, 1952.

Gatland, Kenneth W.: *Spacecraft and Boosters*; Iliffe, London, 1964.

Gibbs-Smith, Charles: *Aviation*: Her Majesty's Stationery Office, London, 1970.

Goldberg, Alfred: *A History of the United States Air Force, 1907–1957*; D. Van Nostrand Co. Inc., New Jersey, 1957.

Haddow, G. W., and Grosz, Peter M.: *The German Giants*; Putnam, London, 1969.

Hodgson, J. E.: *The History of Aeronautics in Great Britain*; Oxford University Press, London, 1924.

Hoeppner, Von: *Deutschlands Krieg in der Luft*; Berlin, 1920.

Howard, William E., and Barr, James: *Spacecraft and Missiles of the World*; Harcourt, Brace and World, New York, 1966.

Hurren, B. J.: *Fellowship of the Air 1901–1951*; Iliffe and Sons Ltd., London, 1951.

Ingells, Douglas J.: *The Plane that changed the World*; Aero Publishers Inc., California, 1966.

Inoguchi, Rikihei; Nakajima, Tadashi, and Pineau, Roger: *The Divine Wind*; Hutchinson, London, 1959.

Jackson, A. J.: *British Civil Aircraft, 1919–59* (two volumes); Putnam, London, 1960.

Jackson, A. J.: *De Havilland Aircraft Since 1915*; Putnam, London, 1962.

Jackson, A. J.: *Avro Aircraft Since 1908*; Putnam, London, 1965.

Jackson, A. J.: *Blackburn Aircraft Since 1909*; Putnam, London, 1968.

Jones, H. A., and Raleigh, Sir Walter: *The War in the Air* (six volumes); Oxford University Press, London, 1922–37.

Josephy Alvin M. (Jr): *The Adventure of Man's Flight*; Putnam, London.

Kerr, Mark: *Land, Sea and Air*; Longmans, Green, London, 1927.

King, H. F.: *Aeromarine Origins*; Putnam, London.

Klee, Ernst, and Merk, Otto: *The Birth of the Missile*; Dutton, New York, 1960.

Lewis, Peter: *British Aircraft, 1809–1914*; Putnam, London, 1962.

Lewis, Peter: *British Racing and Record-Breaking Aircraft*; Putnam, London.

Ley, Willy: *Rockets, Missiles and Space Travel*; Viking, New York, 1961.

Marsh, W. Lockwood: *Aeronautical Prints and Drawings*; Halton and Truscott Smith, London, 1924.

Mason, Francis K.: *Hawker Aircraft Since 1920*; Putnam, London, 1971.

Mason, Francis K., and Windrow, Martin C.: *Battle Over Britain*; McWhirter Twins, London, 1969.

Mason, H. M.: *The Lafayette Escadrille*; Random House, New York, 1967.

McDonough, Kenneth: *Atlantic Wings 1919–1939*; Model Aeronautical Press Ltd., Herts, 1966.

McWhirter, Norris and Ross: *The Guinness Book of Records* (and U.S. Edition, *The Guinness Book of World Records*) Editions; Guinness Superlatives Ltd., London, 1955–1972.

Moyes, Philip: *Bomber Squadrons of the R.A.F.*; Macdonald, London, 1964.

Neumann: *Die Deutschen Luftstreitkräfte in Weltkriege*; Berlin, 1920.

Nowarra, H. J., and Brown, K. S.: *Von Richthofen and the Flying Circus*; Harleyford Publications Ltd., Herts, 1958.

Obermaier, Ernst: *Die Ritterkreuzträger der Luftwaffe: Jagdflieger, 1939–45*; Verlag Dieter Hoffmann, Mainz, Germany, 1966.

Peaslee, B. J.: *Heritage of Valor: The Eighth Air Force in the Second World War*; Lippincott, New York, 1964.

Penrose, Harald: *British Aviation: The Pioneer Years*; Putnam, London, 1967.

Penrose, Harald: *British Aviation: The Great War and Armistice*; Putnam, London, 1969.

Phelan, Joseph A.: *Heroes and Aeroplanes of the Great War, 1914–1918*; Barker, London, 1968.

Pierce, P. N., and Schuon, Karl: *John H. Glenn: Astronaut*; Franklin Watts, New York, 1962.

Price, Alfred: *Instruments of Darkness*; Kimber, London, 1967.

Price, Alfred: *German Bombers of the Second World War* (two volumes); Lacy, Windsor, 1969.

Priller, Josef: *Geschichte eines Jagdgeschwaders: Das JG 26 "Schlageter" 1937–1945*; Kurt Vowinckel Verlag, Heidelberg, Germany, 1956.

Rawlings, J.: *Fighter Squadrons of the R.A.F.*; Macdonald, London, 1969.

Richards, Denis, and Saunders, H. St. J.: *Royal Air Force 1939–1945* (three volumes); H.M.S.O., London, 1953–56.

Richthofen, General Baron von: *Personal Diary*; Karlsruhe Collection, Hamburg, 1941–44.

Robertson, Bruce, and others: *Air Aces of the 1914–18 War*; Harleyford Publications Ltd., Herts.

Robertson, Bruce: *British Military Aircraft Serials 1911–1971*; Ian Allan, Shepperton, 1971.

Robinson, Douglas H.: *The Zeppelin in Combat*; G. T. Foulis and Co. Ltd., Oxfordshire, 1971.

Rolt, L. T. C.: *The Aeronauts: A History of ballooning, 1783–1903*; Longmans, Green, London, 1966.

Schweibert, Ernest G.: *A History of the United States Air Force Ballistic Missiles*; Praeger, New York, 1965.

Seemen, Gerhard von: *Die Ritterkreuzträger, 1939–45*; Podzun-Verlag, Bad Nauheim, Germany, 1955 et seq.

Sims, Edward H.: *American Aces of the Second World War*; Macdonald, London, 1958.

Stewart, O.: *First Flights*; Routledge and Kegan Paul, London, 1957.

Stewart, O.: *Of Flights and Flyers*; Newnes, London, 1964.

Stroud, John: *Annals of British and Commonwealth Air Transport, 1919–1960*; Putnam, London, 1962.

Stroud, John: *European Transport Aircraft Since 1910*; Putnam, London, 1966.

Stroud, John: *Soviet Transport Aircraft Since 1945*; Putnam, London, 1968.

Swanborough, Gordon, and Taylor, J. W. R.: *British Civil Aircraft Register*; Ian Allan, Shepperton, 1970.

Swanborough, F. G., and Bowers, P. M.: *United States Military Aircraft Since 1908*; Putnam, London, 1972.

Swanborough, F. G., and Bowers, P. M.: *United States Navy Aircraft Since 1911*; Putnam, London, 1968.

Taylor, H. A.: *Airspeed Aircraft Since 1931*; Putnam, London, 1970.

Taylor, J. W. R.: *Aircraft Aircraft*; Hamlyn, London, 1972.

Taylor, J. W. R.: *Air B.P.*; 1956–73.

Taylor, J. W. R.: *A Picture History of Flight*; Hulton Press, London.

Taylor, J. W. R.; Jane, Fred T.; Grey, C. G.; Bridgman, Leonard: (ed.): *Jane's All The World's Aircraft* (various editions, 1909–1973); Sampson Low, et al.

Taylor, J. W. R.: *C.F.S.*; Putnam, London, 1958.

Taylor, J. W. R., and Swanborough, Gordon: *Civil Aircraft of the World*; Ian Allan, Shepperton, 1972.

Taylor, J. W. R., and Munson, Kenneth: *History of Aviation*; New English Library, 1971–72.

Taylor, J. W. R. and Allward, M. F.: *Westland 50*; Ian Allan, London, 1965.

Thetford, Owen J.: *Aircraft of the R.A.F. Since 1918*; Putnam, London, 1971.

Thetford, Owen J.: *British Naval Aircraft Since 1912*; Putnam, London, 1971.

Thetford, Owen J., and Gray, Peter: *German Aircraft of the First World War*; Putnam, London, 1962.

Wallace, Graham: *Flying Witness: Harry Harper and the Golden Age of Aviation*; Putnam, London, 1958.

Windrow, Martin C.: *German Fighters of the Second World War* (Two Volumes); Lacy, Windsor, England, 1968–69.

Vassiliev, M., and Dobronravov, V. V.: *Sputnik into Space*; Souvenir Press, London, 1958.

Ziegler, Mano: *Rocket Fighter*; London, 1963.

Index

Notes:

Ranks quoted for serving
officers are those held
at the time of their first entry
in this volume

Initials, in brackets, after certain entries indicate the following:

A—airline
AC—aircraft carrier
AF—aircraft, fixed wing
AR—aircraft, rotary wing

M—missile
P—power plant
S—satellite, spacecraft or space vehicle
W—weapon

A

A-1 rocket (M), 236
A-1 seaplane, Curtiss (AF), 136, 137
A-2 rocket (M), 236
A-3 rocket (M), 236
A-3 Skywarrior, Douglas (AF), 159, 160, 165
A3D Skywarrior, Douglas (AF), 159, 160, 165
A-4 rocket (M), 236, 244
A-4 Skyhawk, Douglas (AF), 122, 165
A-5 rocket (M), 236
A-5 Vigilante, North American (AF), 160, 166
A5M 'Claude', Mitsubishi (AF), 148, 162, 241
A6M1 Zero-Sen, Mitsubishi (AF), 81, 154, 163
A6M2 Type O, Mitsubishi (AF), 81, 112, 151
A-7A Corsair II, LTV (AF), 166
A-10, Aero (AF), 175
A.74.RC.38, Fiat (P), 81
AB Aerotransport (A), 178
AB flying-boat, Curtiss (AF), 49, 138
AB-2 flying-boat, Curtiss (AF), 140
AB-3 flying-boat, Curtiss (AF), 49
AD Skyraider, Douglas (AF), 156
An-2, Antonov (AF), 123
Ar 234B Blitz, Arado (AF), 96
A.S.5 Courier, Airspeed (AF), 254
Abingdon, Berkshire, 189
Abu Dhabi Air Force, 122
Aces of the First World War, 56, 57, 58, 59, 60, 61, 62, 63, 64, 69, 70, 71, 72, 73, 74, 75, 76, 77
Aces of the Second World War, 99, 100, 101, 102, 103, 104, 105, 106, 107, 109, 114, 115
Achernar, S.S., 154
Ademeit, Maj. Horst, 109
Ader, Clément, 15
Aerial Steam Carriage, 11
Aero A-10 (AF), 175
Aéro-Club de France, 20, 33, 43, 221
Aero Club of America, 45
Aero Club of Great Britain, 25, 27, 31
Aero Club of Sweden, 34
Aerodrome (AF), 12, 17
Aerojet XCAL-200 (P), 234
Aeromarine West Indies Airways (A), 172
Aeronautical Society of Great Britain, 15, 25
Aeronautica Militar Española, 127
Aérospatiale (S.N.I.A.S.), 263
Aérospatiale Alouette (AR), 123

Affleck, A., 181
Africa, H.M.S., 136, 138
Agate, Flt.-Lt. Charles, 232
Agusta-Bell 206A JetRanger (AR), 122
Aichi D3A Val (AF), 151, 163
Airacomet, Bell (AF), 93
Air Canada (A), 261
Air cargo, 37
Airco (Aircraft Manufacturing Co. Ltd.), 251
Aircraft carrier, first, 129
Aircraft carriers, 149
Aircraft Manufacturing Co. Ltd. (Airco), 251
Aircraft Transport and Travel Ltd. (A), 168, 170, 172
Air Force of the German Democratic Republic, 124
Air Force of the Southern Yemen People's Republic, 127
Air Forces, origin of, 122
Air France (A), 261
Air India (A), 261
Air Mail, 36, 37, 167
Airship, first round-the-world flight, 182
Airspeed A.S.5 Courier (AF), 254
Air-to-air missile, 240
Air-to-surface missile, 242
Air Volunteer Group (A.V.G.), 100
Akagi (AC), 149
Akron, airship, 147
Akron, Ohio, 207, 208
Alabama, U.S.S., 145
Alabaster, Capt. R. C., 190
Alameda, California, 188
Alarcon, Capt. José, 253
Albacore, Fairey (AF), 163
Albanian Air Force, 122
Albatros B.II (AF), 62
Albatros C.I (AF), 63, 75
Albatros D.I (AF), 63, 64
Albatros D.II (AF), 62, 63
Albatros D.III (AF), 45, 48, 62
Albatros D.V (AF), 70
Albatross, Grumman (AF), 164
Alcock, Capt. John, 171, 172
Aldershot, Hampshire, 204
Aldrin, Edwin, 246
Alexandria, Egypt, 182, 184, 254
Alitalia (A), 261
Alizé, Breguet (AF), 165
Alkemade, Flt. Sgt. Nicholas S., 230
Allahabad, India, 36
Allen, Brig. Gen. James, 21
Allied pilots, high-scoring, Battle of Britain, 89
Allmenröder, Leutnant Karl, 45, 74
All-metal aeroplane, 38

Almirante Cochrane, 145
Alouette, Aérospatiale (AR), 123
Alpine, U.S.S., 154
Altair, Lockheed (AF), 188
Alvis Leonides (P), 217
Ambrogi, Sgt. Marius, 65
America, airship, 208
American Airlines (A), 189, 261
American Army Balloon Corps, 201
American Civil War, 129, 204
Amiens, France, 50
Amsterdam, Netherlands, 178, 180
Ancillotto, Tenente Giovanni, 58
Anderson, Capt. Orvil, 204
Andreani, Chevalier Paul, 199
Anjou, France, 33
Anne, HMS, 139
Annonay, France, 198
Anson I, Avro (AF), 79
Antoinette aircraft (AF), 28, 29, 30, 31, 207, 214, 219, 220
Antoinette engine (P), 20, 21, 25, 30, 207, 214
Antonov An-2 (AF), 123
Antwerp, Belgium, 51, 237
Anzani engine (P), 31
Apollo 15 mission (S), 245
Appleby, John, 14
Arab, Sunbeam (P), 143
Arado Ar 234B Blitz (AF), 96
Archdeacon, Ernest, 22, 23, 220
Archdeacon Prize, 20
Archilla, Dr Arstóbulo, 123
Argentine Air Force, 122
Argosy, Armstrong Whitworth (AF), 182, 184
Argus, Canadair (AF), 165
Argus engine (P), 40
Argus, H.M.S. (AC), 142, 143, 149
Arigi, Offizierstellvertreter Julius, 58
Ark Royal, H.M.S. (AC), 140, 149, 150
Armainvilliers, France, 15
Armstrong, Neil, 246
Armstrong-Siddeley Puma (P), 179
Armstrong-Siddeley Sapphire (P), 119
Armstrong Whitworth Argosy (AF), 182, 184
Armstrong Whitworth Whitley (AF), 85, 86, 88
Arnhem, Netherlands, 103
Arnold, Kenneth, 255
Arnold, Lt. Leslie P., 177
Arrowsmith, Cpl. V., 85
Astra aircraft (AF), 220
Athabaskan, 254
Athens, Greece, 184
Atlantic, Breguet (AF), 166
Atlantic crossing, first non-stop, 171

Atlantic crossing, first non-stop solo, 179
Atomic bomb, 42, 120, 121
Attacker, Supermarine (AF), 158, 164
Aubrun, Emil, 32
Auburn, Massachusetts, 235
Auckland, New Zealand, 36
Audemars, Edmond, 38
Augsburg, Germany, 234
Australasian, balloon, 202
Australian Air Force, 253
Australian Inland Mission, 181
Austrian Air Force, 123
Autogiro, C.4, Cierva (AR), 215
Auvours, France, 26
Auxi-le-Château, France, 75
Aveline stabiliser, 173
Avenger, TBF, Grumman (AF), 151, 163
Avian, Avro (AF), 180
Avian III, Avro (AF), 181
Aviatik aircraft (AF), 51, 68, 70
Aviatik R-type aircraft (AF), 55
Aviation Nationale Khmere (A), 125
Aviation's worst disasters, 264, 265, 266
Avion III (AF), 15
Avon, Rolls-Royce (P), 119
Avro Anson I (AF), 79
Avro Avian (AF), 180
Avro Avian III (AF), 181
Avro biplane (AF), 226
Avro Lancaster (AF), 92, 93, 98, 217, 230, 262
Avro Lancaster Mk IV (AF), 120
Avro Lincoln (AF), 120
Avro Vulcan (AF), 120, 243
Ayling, J. R., 188

B

B.II, Albatros (AF), 62
B5N2 'Kate', Nakajima (AF), 112, 151, 162
B-17 Flying Fortress, Boeing (AF), 91, 92, 96, 106, 241
B-24 Liberator, Consolidated (AF), 106, 241
B-29 Superfortress, Boeing (AF), 118, 234
B-52 Stratofortress, Boeing (AF), 42, 120, 121
B-57A, Martin (AF), 119
BAC (British Aircraft Corporation), 263
BAC Pembroke (AF), 128
BAC/Aérospatiale Concorde (AF), 7, 263
B.E.1, Royal Aircraft Factory (AF), 44
B.E.2a, Royal Aircraft Factory (AF), 46, 50
B.E.2c, Royal Aircraft Factory (AF), 64
B.E.2e, Royal Aircraft Factory (AF), 54
Bf 109, Messerschmitt (AF), 79, 82, 83, 85, 87, 101, 102, 103, 105, 110
Bf 110, Messerschmitt (AF), 85, 87
BMW 003 engine (P), 98
B.R.20, Fiat (AF), 82, 90
B.S.1, Royal Aircraft Factory (AF), 44

Baby, Felixstowe (AF), 252
Baby, N. 1B, Supermarine (AF), 162
Baddeck Bay, Nova Scotia, 27
Baden-Powell, Maj. B. F. S., 25
Bader, Douglas, 103
Bagatelle, Paris, 26
Bager, R., 174
Baghdad, Iraq, 188
Baikonur, East Kazakhstan, 245
Bailey, Lady, 181
Balchen, Bernt, 183
Baldwin, F. W. "Casey", 29
Baleine, Nova Scotia, 189
Ball, Capt. Albert, 56, 64
Balsley, H. Clyde, 53
Baltimore, Maryland, 119, 238
Bangalore, India, 182
Bangladesh Defence Force (Air Wing), 123
Banshee, McDonnell (AF), 164
Bär, Oberstleutnant Heinz, 97, 106, 107, 109, 118
Baracca, Maggiore Francesco, 58, 68
Baracchini, Tenente Flavio T., 58
Barber, Horatio, 37, 167
Barillon aircraft (AF), 220
Barin, Lt. L. T., 171
Barker, Maj. William G., 45, 56, 68
Barkhorn, Maj. Gerhard, 109
Barling XNBL-1 (AF), 78
Barlow, Airman R. K., 50
Barnard, Capt. F. L., 223
Baron de Forest Prize, 36
Basle, Switzerland, 182
Basse und Selve engines (P), 56
Bat, Dryden (M), 242
Bat glider (AF), 16
Battle of Britain, 41, 42, 88, 89, 90, 102, 103
Battle of Jutland, 140
Battle of Midway, 151
Battle of the Coral Sea, 151
Batz, Maj. Wilhelm, 109
Bauer, Oberst Victor, 115
Bäumer, Leutnant Paul, 57
Baylies, 2nd.-Lt. F. L., 58
Bean, Capt. Alan, 250
Bearcat, XF8F-1, Grumman (AF), 164
Beardmore Inflexible (AF), 83
Beardmore, William, and Co., 83
Beardmore Wee Bee (AF), 253
Béarn (AC), 146, 149
Beauchamp-Proctor, Capt. A. W., 56
Beaumont, Belgium, 36
Beaumont, Capt. F., 204
Beauvais, France, 174, 182, 207
Bedford, A. W. "Bill", 228
Beerenbrock, Lt. Franz J., 115
"Beethoven-Gerät", 101
Beetle glider (AF), 16
Beisswenger, Oberleutnant Hans, 114
Belem, Portugal, 32
Belfast, Ireland, 31
Belka, dog, 245
Bell GAM-63 Rascal (M), 243
Bell XB-63 (M), 243
Bell XS-1 (AF), 234
Bell, Mr Howard "Dinger", 7, 256

Bell airacomet (AF), 93
Bell Model 47 (AR), 216
Bell Telephone Laboratories, 240
Bellanca aircraft (AF), 184
Bellinger, Lt. P. N. L., 49, 171, 252
Belmont Park, New York, 220
Ben-My-Chree, H.M.S., 139, 140
Bennett, Capt. D. C. T., 254
Bennett, Floyd, 179
Benoist aircraft (AF), 229
Benoist Company (A), 168
Benoist flying-boat (AF), 168
Benoit, M., 37
Bentley, Flt.-Lt. R. R., 180
Benz engine (P), 55
Berlin, Germany, 15, 38, 85, 88, 169, 175, 236
Berry, Capt. Albert, 229
Berry, Sqdn. Ldr. Joseph, 99
Berson, Professor, 204
Berthold, Hauptmann Rudolf, 48, 57
Beryl, Metrovick (P), 157
Beta, airship, 207
Bettington, Lt. C. A., 39
Betty, G4M, Mitsubishi (AF), 163
Beverley, Blackburn (AF), 119
Bibliography, 267, 268, 269
Bideford, H.M.S., 254
Biggin, George, 200
Bikini Atoll, Pacific Ocean, 121
Bingham, Richard, 232
Birch, Lt. W. C., 52
Bird of Paradise, Fokker (AF), 180
Birkner, Lt. Hans J., 115
Birksted, Gp. Capt. Kaj, 99
Birmingham, U.S.S., 130, 138
Bishop, Capt. William A., 45, 56, 73
Bitsch, Hauptmann Emil, 115
Bizerte, Tunisia, 168
Black, W. van Lear, 180
Blackburn N.A.39 (AF), 161
Blackburn Beverley (AF), 119
Blackburn Buccaneer (AF), 161
Blackburn Firebrand (AF), 163
Blackburn Iris (AF), 162
Blackburn Roc (AF), 163
Blackburn Skua (AF), 150
Blackpool, Lancashire, 31, 35
Bladud, 9th King of Britain, 9
Blanchard, Jean-Pierre, 200, 201, 251
Blanchard, Madame, 251
Bland, Dr William, 202
Blenheim IV, Bristol (AF), 85
Blériot, Louis, 20, 21, 29, 31, 38, 196, 219
Blériot Flying School, 34, 37
Blériot monoplane (AF), 23, 31, 32, 33, 34, 35, 37, 38, 43, 50, 54, 167, 168, 219, 220, 226, 227
Blériot VII monoplane (AF), 20, 21
Blériot XI monoplane (AF), 29, 30, 221
Blériot XII monoplane (AF), 30, 219
Blériot XIII monoplane (AF), 30
Blitz, Ar 234B, Arado (AF), 96
Blitzkreig, 87
"Block-buster" bomb (W), 90
Bloodhound, Bristol/Ferranti (M), 240
"Blue Jay", de Havilland (M), 242

Blue Max, 62
"Blue Sky", Fairey, (M), 242
"Blue Steel", Hawker Siddeley
  Dynamics (M), 243
"Blue Streak", Hawker Siddeley
  Dynamics (M), 238
Boehme, Leutnant, 63
Boeing B-17 Flying Fortress (AF), 91,
  92, 96, 241
Boeing B-29 Superfortress (AF), 118,
  234
Boeing B-52 Stratofortress (AF), 120,
  121
Boeing DB-47 Stratojet (AF), 243
Boeing F4B-1 (AF), 162
Boeing IM-99 Bomarc (M), 240
Boeing XF-99 (M), 240
Boeing Air Transport (A), 183
Boeing Lunar Rover Vehicle (S), 246
Boeing Model 69 (AF), 162
Boeing Model 707 (AF), 190, 191
Boeing Model 747 (AF), 261, 262
Boeing Type C (AF), 169
Boelcke, Leutnant Oswald, 48, 57, 61,
  62, 63
Bolivian Cuerpo de Aviación, 123
Bolshoi biplane (AF), 40
Bomarc, IM-99, Boeing (M), 240
Bong, Maj. Richard I., 99, 100, 104,
  112
Bonnet-Lab aircraft (AF), 220
Boomerang, CA-12, Commonwealth
  (AF), 92
Borchers, Maj. Adolf, 114
Bordelon, Lt. Guy, 159
Borkum, Germany, 236
Borton, Brig.-Gen. A. E., 169
Boscombe Down, Wiltshire, 227, 232
Boston, Douglas DWC (AF), 177
Boston Globe, 220
Botwood, Newfoundland, 189
Boulogne, France, 201
Bournemouth Aviation Week, 34
Boxer, U.S.S. (AC), 158
Box-kite structure, 16
Boxted, Suffolk, 112
Boyd, Flt.-Lt. R. F., 89
Boyington, Lt.-Col. G., 100
Brabazon of Tara, Lord, 27
Brackan, Sweden, 204
Braham, Wing Cdr. J.R.D., 100
Brancker, Maj.-Gen. Sir Sefton, 182,
  208, 224
Brand, Sqdn. Ldr. Christopher Q., 173
Brändle, Maj. Kurt, 109
Braniff (A), 261
Brazilian Army Air Service, 123
Breda-SAFAT machine-gun (W), 81
Breese, Lt. James W., 171
Breguet XIX (AF), 180
Breguet, Louis, 21, 37
Breguet aircraft (AF), 30, 37, 219
Breguet Alizé (AF), 165
Breguet Atlantic (AF), 166
Breguet biplane (AF), 38
Breguet brothers, 214
Breguet-Richet Gyroplane No. 1 (AR),
  21

Bremen, Germany, 175
Brendel, Hauptmann Joachim, 109
Brest, France, 11, 15
Brewer, Griffith, 25
Brewster XF2A-1 Buffalo (AF), 162
Brewster XSB2A-1 Buccaneer (AF), 163
Bridgeport, Connecticut, 216
Brisbane, Australia, 180, 188
Brisbane Museum, Australia, 180
Bristol aircraft (AF), 220
Bristol F.2B (AF), 48, 122
Bristol M.1C (AF), 169
Bristol Blenheim IV (AF), 85
Bristol Boxkite (AF), 37
Bristol Britannia (AF), 190
Bristol Centaurus (P), 119, 153
Bristol Cherub (P), 253
Bristol monoplane (AF), 39
Bristol Scout "C" (AF), 252
Bristol Sycamore H.C.10/11 (AR), 217
Bristol Sycamore H.R.12 (AR), 217
Bristol Thor ramjet (P), 240
Bristol/Ferranti Bloodhound (M), 240
Bristol/Ferranti "Red Duster" (M), 240
Bristol Siddeley Stentor (P), 243
Britannia, Bristol (AF), 190
British Aerial Derby, 221
British Aircraft Corporation (BAC), 263
British Army Aeroplane No. 1 (AF), 25, 27,
  29
British Army Balloon School, 207
British European Airways (A), 189
British Marine Air Navigation
  Company (A), 177
British Overseas Airways Corporation
  (A), 190, 261
Britten-Norman Islander (AF), 122
Broadlees, Dover, Kent, 33
Broadwick, Georgia "Tiny", 229
Brocke, W. L., 223
Brompton Hall, Yorkshire, 13, 14
Brookins, Mr., 220
Brooklands, Surrey, 37, 39, 172, 173, 221
Broussard, Max Holste (AF), 124, 125,
  127
Brown, Capt. A. Roy, 62
Brown, Lt.-Cdr. E. M., 156
Brown, Lt. Russel J., 118
Brown, Mr., 202
Browning, John, 15
Browning machine-gun (W), 80
Bruges, Belgium, 53
Brumowski, Hauptmann Godwin, 58
Buc, France, 226
Buccaneer, Blackburn (AF), 161
Buccaneer, Hawker-Siddeley (AF), 166
Buccaneer, XSB2A-1, Brewster (AF),
  163
Bucharest, Romania, 31
Buchet engine (P), 12
Büchner, Leutnant Franz, 57
Büchner, Oberfeldwebel Hermann, 97
Buckeye, North American, (AF), 166
Buenos Aires, Argentina, 32
Buerling, Sqdn. Ldr. G. F., 99, 100
Buffalo, XF2A-1, Brewster (AF), 162
Buhligen, Oberstleutnant Kurt, 106,
  107, 115

Bulawayo, Southern Rhodesia, 173
Bulgarian Army Aviation Corps, 123
Bullet, Morane (AF), 71
Bull, flight of, 177
Burbank, California, 104
Butler, Frank H., 25
Byrd, Lt.-Cdr. Richard E., 179, 183

C

C-Type flying-boat, Short (AF), 189
C.I, Albatros (AF), 63, 75
C.I, Hansa-Brandenburg (AF), 168
C-2, Fokker (AF), 180
C.II, Roland (AF), 64, 75
C-2A Greyhound, Grumman (AF), 166
C.4 *Autogiro*, Cierva (AR), 215
C.6D, Cierva (AR), 215
C.8L Mk II, Cierva (AR), 215
C.19 Mk II, Cierva (AR), 215
C-47 Skytrain, Douglas (AF), 123, 125,
  127, 128
C.85, Continental (P), 255
C.200 Saetta, Macchi (AF), 81
CA-12 Boomerang, Commonwealth
  (AF), 92
C.E.C.L.E.S. (Conseil Européen pour
  la Construction de Lanceurs
  d'Engins Spatiaux), 238
CL.III, Hannover (AF), 75
CL-44D-4, Canadair (AF), 255
CR. 32, Fiat (AF), 82, 83
CR. 42, Fiat (AF), 90
Cairo, Egypt, 9, 31, 168, 184
Cairo Museum, Egypt, 9
Calais, France, 28, 34, 53
Calcutta, India, 36
Calcutta, Short (AF), 182, 184
Calder, Sqdn. Ldr. C. C., 98
Caldwell, Gp. Capt. C. R., 99, 100
Caldwell, Ohio, 207
Caledonia, Short (AF), 189
Calgary, Canada, 172
Camel, Sopwith (AF), 62, 68, 75, 139,
  143, 144, 145, 227
Camerman, Lt., 43
Cameron Balloons Ltd., 208
Cameroun Air Force, 123
Camm, Sir Sydney, 78, 254
Campania, H.M.S., 141
Campbell, Lt. Douglas, 55, 65, 76
Campbell Black, Tom, 225
Canadair CL-44D-4 (AF), 255
Canadair Argus (AF), 165
Canadian Pacific Air Lines (A), 190
Canberra, English Electric (AF), 231
Canberra B.Mk.2, English Electric
  (AF), 119
Candelaria, Teniente Luis C., 168
Canopus, Short (AF), 189
Cantacuzino, Capt. Prince Constantine, 99
Cap Blanc Nez, France, 29
Cape Finisterre, Spain, 254
Cape Town, South Africa, 173, 180,
  181, 185, 204
Cap Gris-Nez, France, 38
Capper, Col. John, 207

Carbury, Flg. Off. B. J. G., 89
Cardington, Bedfordshire, 182, 207, 208
Carey, Gp. Capt. F. H. R., 100
Caribou, DHC (de Havilland Canada)
    (AF), 122
Carmichael, Lt. P., 157
Carr, Flt.-Lt. C. R., 179
Carr, Gerald P., 246
Carr, R. H., 229
Cartagena, Spain, 83
Carver, Lt. L. V., 150
Casa da India, Lisbon, 197
Castoldi, Dr Mario, 81
Catalina, PBY, Consolidated (AF), 148,
    162
Catapult, compressed-air, 137
Caudron, M., 37
Caudron, René, 137
Caudron aircraft (AF), 49, 220
Caudron G. IIIA-2 (AF), 123
Caudron G.IV (AF), 70
Cavendish, Henry, 197
Cayley, Sir George, 10, 11, 13, 14
Cederström, Baron Carl, 34
Centaurus, Bristol (P), 119, 153
Centocelle, Italy, 27
Cerutti, Sgt. Marziale, 58
Ceskoslovenské Státni Aerolinie (A),
    175, 177
Cessna 185 Skywagon (AF), 125
Cessna U-17A (AF), 127
Chalais-Meudon, France, 206
Chalgrove, Oxfordshire, 231
Châlons, France, 26, 31
Chambers, Capt. W. I., 137
Chance Vought F4U Corsair (AF), 107,
    150, 159
Chance Vought (LTV) F-8 Crusader
    (AF), 159, 165, 232
Chance Vought (LTV) F8U Crusader
    (AF), 159, 165, 232
Chance Vought XF8U-1 (AF), 159, 187
Chanute, Octave, 12, 15, 16
Chapman, Victor E., 53
Charabanc, Grahame-White (AF), 229
Chard, Somerset, 14
Charles, Jacques A. C., 198
Charleville, Queensland, 174
Chatham, Massachusetts, 171
Chavez, Georges, 35
Cherub, Bristol (P), 253
Chevalier, Lt.-Cdr., 146
Cheyenne, Wyoming, 183
Chicago, Douglas DWC (AF), 177
Chicago, Illinois, 174, 189, 207
Chilean Air Force, 123
Chinese Army Air Arm, 123
Chipmunk, de Havilland (AF), 125
Chisov, Lt.-Col. I. M., 230
Chiswick, London, 237
Cholmondeley, Lt. R., 49
Christchurch, New Zealand, 182
Christmas Island, Pacific Ocean, 121
Chronology of man in space, 247, 248,
    249, 250
Chungking, China, 81
Church, Ellen, 183
Churchill, Winston S., 138

Cierva C.4 Autogiro (AR), 215
Cierva C.6D (AR), 215
Cierva C.8L Mk II (AR), 215
Cierva C.19 Mk II (AR), 215
Cinematographer, first airborne, 27
Circuit of Europe, 220
City of Basra, de Havilland D.H.66
    (AF), 185
City of Delhi, de Havilland D.H.66
    (AF), 185
City of York, de Havilland (AF), 223
Clark, Julie, 38
"Claude", A5M, Mitsubishi (AF), 148,
    162, 241
Clausens, Maj. Erwin, 114
Cleveland, Ohio, 215
Cleveland Air Races, 215
Clifden, Ireland, 171
Clipper III, Sikorsky (AF), 189
Clipper Windward, Boeing (AF), 190
Cloncurry, Queensland, 174, 181
Clostermann, Sqdn. Ldr. Pierre H., 99,
    100
Clover Field, California, 189
Clutterbuck, Lt. L. C. F., 48
Clydesdale, Marquess of, 187
Cobham, Alan, 223, 224
Cochrane, Miss Jacqueline, 255
Cody, Mrs. S. F., 29
Cody, Samuel F., 25, 27, 29, 36, 207,
    221
Coli, Capt., 73
College Park, Maryland, 44
Collett, Flt.-Lt., 51
Collins, Gen. Michael, 125
Collins, Michael, 246
Collishaw, Flt.-Sub.-Lt. Raymond, 45,
    56, 74, 75
Colmore, Lt. G. C., 130
Cologne, Germany, 51, 138
Columbia, command module (S), 246
Columbia II, airship, 208
Columbus, Mexico, 53
Columbus, Ohio, 76, 187, 232
Comet, D.H.88, de Havilland (AF), 225
Comet 1, D.H.106, de Havilland (AF),
    190, 262
Comet 4, de Havilland (AF), 190
Commonwealth CA-12 Boomerang
    (AF), 92
Composite (pickaback) aircraft (AF),
    101, 252, 252
Concorde, BAC/Aérospatiale (AF), 7, 263
Condor (A), 261
Condor II, Rolls-Royce (P), 84
Congolese Air Force, 123
Conneau, Lt. de Vaisseau, 220, 221
Conrad, Charles, 250
Conran, Capt. E. L., 52
Conseil Européen pour la Construction
    de Lanceurs d'Engins Spatiaux
    (C.E.C.L.E.S.), 238
Consolidated B-24 Liberator (AF), 106,
    241
Consolidated PBY Catalina (AF), 148,
    162
Constantinople, Turkey (Istanbul), 71,
    168

Conte Rosso, S.S., 142
Conti, Cardinal, 197
Continental (A), 261
Continental engines (P), 208
Continental C.85 (P), 255
Cook, Donald, 191
Cook, Miss Edith M., 33
Coppens, 2nd.-Lt. Willy, 59
Cornu, Paul, 21, 214
Corporal, SSM-A-17, Firestone (M),
    237
Corsair, F4U, Chance Vought (AF),
    107, 150, 159
Corsair II, A-7A, LTV (AF), 166
Costes, Capt. Dieudonné, 180
Cougar, Grumman (AF), 165
Courbet, 101
Courageous, H.M.S. (AC), 149
Courier, A.S.5, Airspeed (AF), 254
Courtney, F. T., 215
Courtrai, Belgium, 52
Coutelle, Capt., 201
Coventry, Warwickshire, 33
Cover, Carl A., 189
Cowan, Richard, 204
Cranfield, Bedfordshire, 90
Cranwell, Lincolnshire, 179, 182, 185,
    251
Cremorne Gardens, Melbourne, 202
Crete, Greece, 91
Cricklewood, London, 174
Crinius, Lt. Wilhelm, 115
Crissy, Lt. Myron S., 43
Crocco, G. A., 214
Crosby, Harry, 234
Crosby, Minnesota, 205
Croydon, Surrey, 173, 174, 179, 180,
    181, 182, 183, 184, 215, 223
Crusader, F-8, Chance Vought (LTV)
    (AF), 159, 165
Crusader, F8U, Chance Vought (LTV)
    (AF), 159, 165, 232
Crusader, balloon, 202
Crystal Palace, London, 15, 204
Cuban Revolutionary Air Force, 123
Cuckoo, Sopwith (AF), 142, 143
Cuerpo de Aeronautica del Perú, 126
Cuerpo de Aeronautica Militar
    (Guatemala), 124
Cuerpo de Aviadores Militares
    (Ecuador), 124
Cuffley, Hertfordshire, 89
Culdrose, Scotland, 161
Culley, Lt. Stuart, 139, 143
Culmhead, Somerset, 95
Cunco, Chile, 168
Cunningham, Lt. Alfred A., 137
Curtiss, Glenn H., 23, 26, 43, 130, 135
Curtiss A-1 seaplane (AF), 136, 138
Curtiss AB flying-boat (AF), 49, 138
Curtiss AB-2 flying-boat (AF), 140
Curtiss AB-3 flying-boat (AF), 49
Curtiss F flying-boat (AF), 252
Curtiss F9C Sparrowhawk (AF), 147
Curtiss HS-1 flying-boat (AF), 144
Curtiss JN aircraft (AF), 53, 126, 168,
    169, 172
Curtiss SBC Helldiver (AF), 147

Curtiss XF12C-1 (AF), 147
Curtiss XSB2C-1 (AF), 163
Curtiss XSC-1 Seahawk (AF), 164
Curtiss aircraft (AF), 30, 34, 137, 168, 219
Curtiss biplane (AF), 38, 43, 130, 135
Curtiss "hydroaeroplane" (AF), 135, 137
Cutlass, Vought (AF), 165
Cygnet, Hawker (AF), 253
Cyprus National Guard, Air Wing, 123
Czechoslovak Army Air Force, 124

D

D.I, Albatros (AF), 63, 64
D.I, Phönix (AF), 68
D.II, Albatros (AF), 62, 63
D.III, Albatros (AF), 45, 48, 62
D3A Val, Aichi (AF), 151, 163
D4Y, Yokosuka (AF), 163
D.V, Albatros (AF), 70
D.VII, Fokker (AF), 45, 48, 70
D.VIII, Fokker (AF), 55
D.XXI, Fokker (AF), 86, 88, 92
D.371, Dewoitine (AF), 83
D.500, Dewoitine (AF), 83
D.510, Dewoitine (AF), 83
DB-3 (AF), 92
DB-47 Stratojet, Boeing (AF), 243
DC-1, Douglas (AF), 187, 189
DC-2, Douglas (AF), 187, 189, 225
DC-3, Douglas (AF), 189
DC-6B, Douglas (AF), 191
D.E.F.A., P.A.R.C.A. (Projectile Autopropulsé Radioguidé Contre Avions) (M), 240
DFS 194 (rocket-powered) (AF), 234
DFS 230 (glider) (AF), 91
D.H.2, de Havilland (AF), 62, 75
D.H.4, de Havilland (AF), 54, 126, 223
D.H.4 type, American-built (AF), 54, 126, 146, 174, 175, 176
D.H.6, de Havilland (AF), 170
D.H.9, de Havilland (AF), 170, 173, 223
D.H.16, de Havilland (AF), 172
D.H.18, de Havilland (AF), 174
D.H.34, de Havilland (AF), 177
D.H.50, de Havilland (AF), 181
D.H.60 Moth, de Havilland (AF), 179, 180, 181, 183, 251
D.H.66 Hercules, de Havilland (AF), 182, 185
D.H.84 Dragon, de Havilland (AF), 187, 188
D.H.88 Comet, de Havilland (AF), 225
D.H.106 Comet 1, de Havilland (AF), 190, 262
DHC-3 Otter (AF), 123
DHC-4 Caribou (AF), 122
DN-1, dirigible, 207
Do 17, Dornier (AF), 82, 85, 86, 87, 103
Do 18, Dornier (AF), 85, 87, 150
Do 215, Dornier (AF), 87
Do 217, Dornier (AF), 96, 254
Dr I, Fokker (AF), 48, 56, 62
DT, Douglas (AF), 178

DWC, Douglas (AF), 177
Dacre, Flt.-Lt. G. B., 140
Daedalus, 9
Dahl, Oberst Walther, 107, 114
Dahlbeck, Lt. C. O., 37
Daily Mail Gold Cup, 223
Daily Mail prizes, 27, 28, 32, 219, 220, 221, 223, 225
Daimler Airway (A), 174, 175, 177
Daimler engine (P), 206
Dalkeith, Scotland, 86
Dallas, Texas, 150
Dammers, Lt. Hans, 115
Danish Army Air Corps, 124
Danton aircraft (AF), 220
Dardanelles, Turkey, 139, 140
d'Argueeff, Capt. P. V., 59
d'Arlandes, Marquis, 198
Darwin, Australia, 172, 180, 183, 253
Dassault Etendard IV-M (AF), 166
Dassault Mirage (AF), 122
Dauntless, SBD, Douglas (AF), 151
Davies, Lt.-Cdr. Brian, 225
da Vinci, Leonardo, 9, 10, 213
Davis, Flg. Off. C. R., 89
Davis, Michael, 232
Davis, Miss Trehawke, 227
Dawes, Capt. G. W. P., 43
Day, Flt.-Lt. M. J., 253
Dayton, Ohio, 26, 42, 230
Deal, Kent, 38
Dean, Flg.-Off., 95
Dean, Mr., 202
de Caters, Baron, 31
de Caxias, Marquis, 202
de Forest, Baron, 220
de Forest Chandler, Charles, 44
Defries, Colin, 31
de Gusmao, Bartolomeu, 7, 197
de Havilland D.H.2 (AF), 62, 75
de Havilland D.H.4 (AF), 54, 126, 223
de Havilland D.H.6 (AF), 170
de Havilland D.H.9 (AF), 170, 173, 223
de Havilland D.H.16 (AF), 172
de Havilland D.H.18 (AF), 174
de Havilland D.H.34 (AF), 177
de Havilland D.H.50 (AF), 181
de Havilland D.H.60 Moth (AF), 179, 180, 181, 183, 251
de Havilland D.H.66 Hercules (AF), 182, 185
de Havilland D.H.84 Dragon (AF), 187, 188
de Havilland D.H.88 Comet (AF), 225
de Havilland D.H.106 Comet 1 (AF), 190, 262
de Havilland, Geoffrey, 44, 224, 251
de Havilland Jr., Geoffrey, 116
de Havilland Aircraft Company Ltd., 227, 251
de Havilland "Blue Jay" (M), 242
de Havilland Chipmunk (AF), 125
de Havilland Comet 4 (AF), 190
de Havilland Dragon (AF), 187
de Havilland Firestreak (M), 242
de Havilland Ghost (P), 117, 190
de Havilland Gipsy Moth (AF), 124, 125, 183

de Havilland Gipsy Six (P), 225
de Havilland Gyron Junior (P), 161
de Havilland Hornet (AF), 116, 227
de Havilland Puss Moth (AF), 184, 185
de Havilland Rapide (AF), 125
de Havilland Sea Hornet F.20 (AF), 155, 164
de Havilland Sea Mosquito (AF), 153
de Havilland Sea Vampire (AF), 156
de Havilland Sea Venom (AF), 159
de Havilland Sea Vixen (AF), 160, 165, 242
de Havilland Vampire (AF), 123, 156
de la Cierva, Juan, 215
de Lagarde, Mademoiselle, 198
Delagrange, Léon, 22, 23, 24, 26, 31
de la Meurthe, Henry Deutsch, 22
de Laroche, Mme. la Baronne, 32
Delta Air Lines (A), 261
de Meulemeester, Adj. André, 59
Demon, McDonnell (AF), 165
de Montalembert, Countess, 198
de Montalembert, Marchioness, 198
den Schkrouff, Van, 29
Denver, Colorado, 38, 191
Department of Civil Aviation, 223
Deperdussin aircraft (AF), 220, 221
de Pescara, Marquis, 214
de Podenas, Countess, 198
Deptford, London, 237
de Rozier, Francois Pilâtre, 198, 201
Derry, John, 227
der Spuy, Maj. Van, 127
Derwent 5, Rolls-Royce (P), 116
Derwent 8, Rolls-Royce (P), 116
de Salis, Flt.-Lt. John, 231
Dessau, Germany, 53
Deutsche Luft-Reederei (A), 169
Deutschland-Halle, Berlin, 215
Devastator, TBD, Douglas (AF), 151, 162
Devyatayev, Lt. Michael, 93
de Witt Milling, Lt. Thomas, 44
Dewoitine D.371 (AF), 83
Dewoitine D.500 (AF), 83
Dewoitine D.510 (AF), 83
di Calabria, Capt. Fulco R., 58
Dickfield, Oberst Adolf, 114
Dickson, Capt. Bertram, 33
Digger's Rest, Victoria, Australia, 31
Dittmar, Heini, 234
Dixon, Lt.-Cdr. Robert, 151
Dobrovolsky, G, 250
Doe, Plt. Off. R. F. T., 89
Donaldson, Gp. Capt. E. M., 116
Doncaster, Yorkshire, 31
Dons, Lt. Hans E., 38
"Doodlebug", 236
Doolittle, James H., 175
Doran, Flt.-Lt. K. C., 85
Dornier Do 17 (AF), 82, 85, 86, 87, 103
Dornier Do 18 (AF), 85, 87, 150
Dornier Do 215 (AF), 87
Dornier Do 217 (AF), 96, 254
Dörr, Hauptmann Franz, 114
Dortmund-Ems Canal, Germany, 90
Dorys, de Havilland Moth (AF), 180
Douai, France, 21, 37, 38, 54, 63, 64, 214

Green engine (P), 207, 219
Grislawski, Feldwebel Alfred, 101, 114
Gregory, Lt. R, 135
Greyhound, C-2A, Grumman (AF), 166
Griffin, Cdr. Virgil C., 146
Grimley, Charles, 204
Grosvenor House, de Havilland Comet (AF), 225
Ground-to-air missile, 238
Grover, Lt. G. E., 204
Grumman C-2A Greyhound (AF), 166
Grumman F4F Wildcat (AF), 150, 151
Grumman F6F Hellcat (AF), 112
Grumman F7F-1 Tigercat (AF), 153, 164
Grumman F9F-2 Panther (AF), 158, 164
Grumman F9F-9 (AF), 159
Grumman F11F-1 Tiger (AF), 159, 165
Grumman F-14 Tomcat (AF), 166
Grumman FF-1 (AF), 147
Grumman TBF Avenger (AF), 151, 163
Grumman XF2F-1 (AF), 162
Grumman XF4F-2 (AF), 162
Grumman XF6F-1 (AF), 163
Grumman XF7F-1 (AF), 153
Grumman XF8F-1 Bearcat (AF), 164
Grumman XF9F-2 (AF), 158
Grumman XF10F-1 Jaguar (AF), 120
Grumman XFF-1 (AF), 147
Grumman XJF-1 Duck (AF), 162
Grumman XS2F-1 Tracker (AF), 165
Grumman XTBF-1 (AF), 151
Grumman XTB3F-1 Guardian (AF), 164
Grumman Albatross (AF), 164
Grumman Cougar (AF), 165
Grumman Hawkeye (AF), 166
Grumman Intruder (AF), 166
Grumman Martlet (AF), 150
Guantánamo Bay, Cuba, 145
Guardian, XTB3F-1, Grumman (AF), 164
Guidoni, Capt., 136
Guille, Charles, 229
Guinea Air Force, 124
Gull glider (AF), 16
Gusmão, Bartolomeu de, 7
Guynemer, Capt. Georges M. L. J., 58, 65, 71
Gyron Junior, de Havilland (P), 161

H

H.2 Hercules, Hughes (AF), 157
HD-1, Hanriot (AF), 68, 145
He 51b, Heinkel (AF), 81
He 59, Heinkel (AF), 85
He 111, Heinkel (AF), 82, 85, 86, 87, 93
He 162 Salamander, Heinkel (AF), 98
He 280, Heinkel (AF), 91
HeS 8A, Heinkel-Hirth (P), 91
H.M. King George V, 37, 173, 223
H.M.S. *Africa*, 136, 138
H.M.S. *Anne*, 139
H.M.S. *Argus* (AC), 142, 143, 149
H.M.S. *Ark Royal* (AC), 140, 149, 150

H.M.S. *Ben-My-Chree*, 139, 140
H.M.S. *Bideford*, 254
H.M.S. *Campania*, 141
H.M.S. *Courageous* (AC), 149
H.M.S. *Eagle* (AC), 145, 149
H.M.S. *Egret*, 254
H.M.S. *Foyle Bank*, 89
H.M.S. *Furious* (AC), 141, 142, 149, 150
H.M.S. *Glorious* (AC), 149
H.M.S. *Hermes* (AC), 138, 146, 149
H.M.S. *Hibernia*, 137, 138
H.M.S. *Manxman*, 141
H.M.S. *Ocean* (AC), 156
H.M.S. *Philomel*, 138
H.M.S. *Pomone*, 138
H.M.S. *Raven* II, 139
H.M.S. *Redoubt*, 143, 144
H.M.S. *Repulse*, 141
H.M.S. *Somali*, 85
H.M.S. *Spartan*, 96
H.M.S. *Uganda*, 96
H.M.S. *Warrior*, 141
H.M.S. *Warspite*, 96
H.M.S. *Yarmouth*, 141, 142
H.P.42E Hannibal, Handley Page (AF), 184
HS-1 flying-boat, Curtiss (AF), 144
HS 12Y-31, Hispano-Suiza (P), 80
HS 14 Ab 10/11, Hispano-Suiza (P), 88
HS 59 20mm cannon (W), 80
Hs 123, Henschel (AF), 82, 85, 87
Hs 126, Henschel (AF), 85, 87
Hs 129, Henschel (AF), 92
Hs 293, Henschel (M), 254
HT-2, Hindustan (AF), 124
HWK 109-509A-2 rocket motor, Walter (P), 97
Hachtel, Oberleutnant August, 97
Hackl, Maj. Anton, 109
Hafner, Oberleutnant Anton, 109
Hahn, Maj Hans, 115
Haitian Corps d'Aviation, 124
Halberstadt Flying School, 62
Hales bombs (W), 51
Halland, 237
Hamble, Hampshire, 215
Hamburg, Germany, 175, 178
Hamel, Gustav, 37, 227
Hamilton, Canada, 168
Hamilton Field, California, 104
Hammondsport, New York, 27, 130
Hampden, Handley Page (AF), 86, 88, 90
Hampton Roads, Virginia, 130
Handley Page H.P.42E Hannibal (AF), 184
Handley Page O/10 (AF), 173
Handley Page O/400 (AF), 55, 169, 170, 174
Handley Page W.8b (AF), 177
Handley Page W.10 (AF), 253
Handley Page Air Transport Ltd. (A), 170, 177
Handley Page Hampden (AF), 86, 88, 90
Handley Page Heyford (AF), 84
Handley Page Hinaidi (AF), 182
Handley Page Victor (AF), 243
Hanlon, Lt. D. R., 52

Hannibal, H.P.42E, Handley Page (AF), 184
Hannover CL.III (AF), 75
Hanriot HD-1 (AF), 68, 145
Hansa-Bradenburg C.I (AF), 168
Hanson, Lt. R. M., 100
Hanworth, Middlesex, 185
Harbour Grace, Newfoundland, 185
Harding, Lt. John, 177
Hargrave, Lawrence, 16
Harrier, Hawker Siddeley (AF), 262
Harris, Lt. Harold R., 230
Harris, Inverness, 236
Harrow, Middlesex, 200
Hartmann, Maj. Erich, 99, 101, 104, 105, 109, 110
Harvard, North American (AF), 124
Harvey, Sgt. Alva L., 177
Harvey-Kelly, Lt. H. D., 50, 51
Harwich, Essex, 144, 253
Hastings, Col., 200
"Hat-in-the-Ring" Squadron, 76
Havana, Cuba, 172, 180
Hawk glider (AF), 16
Hawker, Harry, 221
Hawker, Maj. Lanoe G., 62
Hawker P.1040 Sea Hawk (AF), 164
Hawker P.1127 Kestrel (AF), 262, 263
Hawker Aircraft Ltd., 228
Hawker Cygnet (AF), 253
Hawker Fury (AF), 78, 164, 254
Hawker Horsley (AF), 179
Hawker Hunter (AF), 227, 230
Hawker Hurricane (AF), 80, 86, 89, 90, 110
Hawker, Maj. Lanoe G., 62
Hawker Sea Fury (AF), 123, 157, 164
Hawker Sea Hurricane (AF), 150
Hawker Siddeley Buccaneer (AF), 166
Hawker Siddeley Harrier (AF), 262
Hawker Siddeley Nimrod (AF), 166
Hawker Siddeley Dynamics Blue Steel (M), 243
Hawker Siddeley Dynamics Blue Streak (M), 238
Hawkeye, Grumman (AF), 166
Hazell, Maj. T. F., 56
Hearst, William R., 167
Heath, Lady, 181
Heavier-than-air flight, 13, 14
Hegenberger, Lt. Albert F., 180
Heglund, Flt. Lt. Svein, 99
Heinkel He 51b (AF), 81
Heinkel He 59 (AF), 85
Heinkel He 111 (AF), 82, 85, 86, 87, 93
Heinkel He 162 Salamander (AF), 98
Heinkel He 280 (AF), 91
Heinkel-Hirth HeS 8A (P), 91
Heliopolis, Egypt, 169
Helium-filled airship, 207
Hellcat, F6F, Grumman (AF), 112
Helldiver, SBC, Curtiss (AF), 147
Henderson, New York, 201
Hendon, Middlesex, 17, 37, 64, 223, 227, 229
Henschel Hs 123 (AF), 82, 85, 87
Henschel Hs 126 (AF), 85, 87
Henschel Hs 129 (AF), 92

Henschel Hs 293 (M), 254
Henson, William Samuel, 11, 14
Hercules, D.H.66, de Havilland (AF), 182, 185
Hercules, H.2, Hughes (AF), 157
Hermes, H.M.S. (AC), 138, 146, 149
Herndon, Hugh, 184
Herne Bay, Kent, 116
Herring, Augustus M., 16
Hervé, Capt., 49
Heston, Middlesex, 188
Hewitt-Sperry biplane (AF), 54
Hewlett, Mrs. Hilda B., 37
Hewlett, Sub.-Lt. F. E. T., 37
Heyford, Handley Page (AF), 84
Hibernia, H.M.S., 137, 138
Hicks, Sgt. L., 232
Hidessen, Leutnant F., 51
Highland Airways (A), 187
Hinaidi, Handley Page (AF), 182
Hindenburg airship, 208
Hindustan HT-2 (AF), 124
Hingham, Norfolk, 54
Hinkler, Sqdn. Ldr. H. J. L. "Bert", 180, 184
Hinton, Lt. Walter, 171
Hiroshima, Japan, 42, 104
Hiryu (AC), 149
Hispano cannon (W), 88
Hispano-Suiza HS 12Y-31 (P), 80
Hispano-Suiza HS 14 Ab 10/11 (P), 88
Hispano-Suiza engine (P), 143
Hoffmann, Lt. Gerhard, 114
Holland, Robert, 201
Hollowday, Aircraftsman V., 99
Holyhead, Anglesey, 35
Honolulu, Hawaii, 180, 181, 188, 189
Hornet, de Havilland (AF), 116, 227
Hornum, Germany, 86
Horsham St. Faith, Norfolk, 116
Horsley, Hawker (AF), 179
Hosho (AC), 146, 149
Hot-air airship, 208
Hot-air balloon, 197, 198
Hotchkiss, 2nd Lt. E., 39
Hotchkiss machine-gun (W), 51
Houdini, Harry, 31
Hounslow, Middlesex, 172
Hove, Sussex, 37, 167
Hovey, Mr. R. W., 256
Hovey Whing Ding II (AF), 256
Howard Wright biplane (AF), 35, 36
Howard Wright monoplane, 35
Howden, Yorkshire, 182
Hoxie, A. 35
Hoy, Capt. Ernest C., 172
Hrabak, Oberst Dietrich, 114
Hubbard, Wg. Cdr. K. G., 121
Hubbard Air Service (A), 169
Hucks, Benjamin C., 227
Hughes, Howard, 157, 256
Hughes, Flt.-Lt. P. C., 89
Hughes GAR-1 Falcon (M), 241
Hughes H.2 Hercules (AF), 157
Hughes Aircraft and Tool Company, 256
Hull, Yorkshire, 207
Humber biplane (AF), 36
Humber monoplane (AF), 43

Hunaudières, France, 26
Hungarian Air Force, 124
Hunstanton, Norfolk, 52
Hunter, Hawker (AF), 228, 230
Hurricane, Hawker (AF), 80, 86, 89, 90, 110
"Hydroaeroplane", Curtiss (AF), 135
Hydro-Aeroplane Trial, 221
Hydrogen balloon, 198
Hydrogen bomb, 121

I

I-15, Polikarpov (AF), 83
I-16, General Electric (P), 155
I-16 Ishak, Polikarpov (AF), 79, 83, 241
Il-2, Ilyushin (AF), 102
Il-4, Ilyushin (AF), 230
Il-14, Ilyushin (AF), 123
Il-28, Ilyushin (AF), 122
IM-99 Bomarc, Boeing (M), 240
Iberia (A), 261
Icarus, 9
Ihlefeld, Oberst Herbert, 114
Ilya Mourometz (AF), 49
Ilyushin Il-2 (AF), 102
Ilyushin Il-4 (AF), 230
Ilyushin Il-14 (AF), 123
Ilyushin Il-28 (AF), 122
Immelmann, Leutnant Max, 48, 62, 63, 64
Imperial Airways (A), 177, 182, 184, 185, 187, 188, 189, 253
Imperial Ethiopian Air Force, 124
Indian Air Force, 124
Indian Trans-Continental Airways (A), 188
Indonesian Republican Air Force, 124
Inflexible, Beardmore (AF), 83
In-flight refuelling, 176
Ingalls, Lt. David S., 144
Inouye, Vice-Adm. Shigeyoshi, 151
Instone Air Line (A), 177, 223
Instone, Sir Samuel, 223
International Aviation Meeting, 30
Intruder, Grumman, 166
Inverness, Scotland, 187
Iran Army Air Department, 125
Iris, Blackburn (AF), 162
Irish Army Air Corps, 125
Irish International (A), 261
Irish Sea, 35
Irvin, Leslie L., 230
Irwin, Flt.-Lt. H. C., 182
Ishak, I-16, Polikarpov (AF), 79, 83, 241
Islander, Britten-Norman (AF), 122
Israeli Air Force, 125
Issy-les-Moulineaux, France, 20, 22, 26, 37
Italia, 96
Italian Air Force, 125
Ivanhov, M. I., 117
Ivory Coast Air Force, 125

J

J.1, Junkers (AF), 53
J2M 'Jack', Mitsubishi (AF), 163
J-29, Saab (AF), 117
J40, Westinghouse (P), 120

J57, Pratt & Whitney (P), 159, 160
J65, Wright (P), 159
J79, General Electric (P), 159, 160
J.A.P. engine (P), 28, 31
JN aircraft, Curtiss (AF), 53, 126, 168, 169, 172
Ju 52/3M, Junkers (AF), 65, 81, 85, 87, 88, 91, 179
Ju 87, Junkers (AF), 82, 85, 87, 110
Ju 88, Junkers (AF), 87, 88, 98, 101, 150
Jabara, Capt. James, 118
'Jack', J2M, Mitsubishi (AF), 163
Jacobs, Leutnant Josef, 57
Jacquet, Capt. Fernand, 59
Jaguar M, S.E.P.E.C.A.T. (AF), 166
Jaguar, XF10F-1, Grumman (AF), 120
Jahnow, Oberleutnant Reinhold, 50
Jamaica Defence Force, Air Wing, 125
Jannus, Anthony, 168, 229
Japan Air Lines (A), 261
Japanese Air Self-Defence Force, 125
Japan to United States, first non-stop flight, 184
Jason, Gipsy Moth (AF), 183
Jatho, Carl, 7, 12, 13
Javelin, Gloster, 119, 242
Jeffries, Dr. John, 200
Jenkins, Flt.-Lt. N. H., 182
Jet fighter, first, 91
JetRanger, Model 206A, Agusta-Bell (AR), 122
Johannesburg, South Africa, 190
Johannisthal, Germany, 52
Johnson, Miss Amy, 183
Johnson A. M. "Tex", 120
Johnson Gp. Capt. James E., 99, 100, 103, 110
Johnson, Lt.-Col. R. S., 100
Jones, Capt. J. I. T., 56
Jones, Capt. O. P., 253
Jones Williams, Sqdn. Ldr. A. G., 182
Jope, Maj. Bernhard, 96
Josephine Ford (AF), 179
Josten, Oberleutnant Günther, 109
Jullerot, Henri, 36
"Jumbo-jets", 261
Jumo 109-004B-1, Junkers (P), 95, 96
Jumo 210D, Junkers (P), 79
June, Harold, 183
June Bug, Curtiss (AF), 23
Junkers, Hugo, 53
Junkers F-13 (AF), 125
Junkers J.1 (AF), 53
Junkers G.23 (AF), 178
Junkers Ju 52/3M (AF), 65, 81, 85, 87, 88, 91, 179
Junkers Ju 87 (AF), 82, 85, 87, 110
Junkers Ju 88 (AF), 87, 88, 98, 101, 150
Junkers Jumo 109-004B-1 (P), 95, 96
Junkers Jumo 210D (P), 79
Jupiter (later *Langley*), U.S.S. (AC), 145, 146
Jutland, Denmark 52
Juutalainen, Flt. Master E. I., 99

K

K.L.M. (Royal Dutch Airlines) (A), 172, 177, 225, 261

Kabul, Afghanistan, 182
Kaga (AC), 149
Kamanin, Gen., 83
Kamikaze, 154, 155
Karachi, Pakistan, 169, 179, 182, 188, 190
Kastner, Hauptmann, 63
"Kate", B5N2, Nakajima (AF), 112, 151, 162
Kauper, H. A., 221
Kawanishi N1K1-J "George" (AF), 163
Kazakov, Staff. Capt. A. A., 59, 68
Kazarinova, Maj. Tamara A., 93
Keane, Sgt. P. P., 232
Kelb, Oberleutnant Fritz, 97
Kelly, Lt. O. G., 175
Kelly Field, Texas, 175
Kennedy, President John F., 246
Kennedy Airport, New York, 191
Kenney, Gen. George C., 104
Kenya Air Force, 125
Kerwin, Dr Joseph, 250
Kesler, Chief Machinist's Mate C. I., 171
Kestrel, P.1127, Hawker (AF), 262, 263
Kestrel II, Rolls-Royce (P), 78, 254
Kestrel III, Rolls Royce (P), 84
Kestrel V, Rolls-Royce (P), 79
Key West, Florida, 172, 180
Khan, Reza, 125
Khartoum, Sudan, 184
Kiaochow Bay, China, 138
Kidd, Flt.-Sgt. A. K., 232
Kiel, Germany, 24
Kiev, Russia, 52, 168, 226
Kill Devil Hills, Carolina, 7, 11, 18, 26
Kimberley, South Africa, 127
Kindley, Capt. F. E., 58
King, Capt. W. A. de C., 207
King Amanullah, Afghanistan, 122
King Edward VII, H.M., 220
Kingfisher, XOS2U-1, Vought (AF), 163
King George V, H.M., 37, 137, 173, 223
King John V of Portugal, 197
King Louis XVI of France, 198
King's Cup Air Race, 218, 223
Kingsford Smith, Capt. Charles, 181, 182, 188
King's Lynn, Norfolk, 52
Kirkwall, Orkney, 187
Kirschner, Hauptmann Joachim, 109
Kiss, Leutnant Josef, 58
Kittel, Oberleutnant Otto, 109
Kittinger, Capt. Joseph W., 232
Kitty Hawk, Carolina, 7, 11, 18
Knight, Jack, 174
Knight, W. J., 235
Knoke, Hauptmann Heinz, 107
Komet, Me 163, Messerschmitt (AF), 97, 234
Komissarova, O., 232
König, Hauptmann Hans H., 107
Korean Air Lines (A), 261
Korean People's Armed Forces Air Corps, 125
Korean War, 103, 116, 118, 157
Korts, Lt. Berthold, 115

Kowalewski, Oberstleutnant Robert, 96
Kozhedub, Guards Col. Ivan, 99, 110
Kraków, Poland, 84
Krebs, Lt. Arthur, 206
Krupinski, Maj. Walter, 109
Kukkonen, Sgt., 86
Kummersdorf, Germany, 236
Kuwait Air Force, 125
Kuznetsov NK-144 (P), 263

L

L-1011 TriStar, Lockheed (AF), 7
La-5FN, Lavochkin (AF), 110
LaGG-3, Lavochkin (AF), 102
LTV A-7A Corsair II (AF), 166
LVG CV (AF), 45, 64
Lacey, Sgt. J. H., 89, 100
Laffan's Plain, Hampshire, 27, 29, 221
La Force Aérienne Belge, 123
La France, dirigible, 206
Laguna Beach, California, 230
Laika, dog, 244
Lake Constance, Germany, 207
Lakehurst, New Jersey, 182, 207, 208
Lake Victoria, Uganda, 184
Lambert, Oberleutnant August, 115
Lancashire Aero Club, 31, 224
Lancaster, Avro (AF), 92, 93, 98, 217, 230, 262
Lancaster Mk IV, Avro (AF), 120
Lancaster, Ontario, 232
Landis, Maj. R. G., 58
Landskrona, Sweden, 34
Lang, Hauptmann Emil, 109
Langley, Dr Samuel Pierpont, 12, 17
Langley, U.S.S. (AC), 145, 146, 149
Larkhill, Wiltshire, 49
l'Armée de l'Air, 124
Latham, Hubert, 28, 29, 30, 31, 33, 220
Lavender, Lt.-Cdr. R. A., 171
Lavochkin La-5FN (AF), 110
Lavochkin LaGG-3 (AF), 102
Lea Marshes, Essex, 28
Learoyd, Flt.-Lt. R. A. B., 90
Lebanese Air Force, 125
Lebaudy brothers, 207
Leblanc, M., 220
Le Blond, Señor, 32
Le Bourget, France, 172, 174, 189, 215, 253
Le Breton, Lt., 226
Le Brix, Lt.-Lt. R. A. Joseph, 180
Lee, Capt. H. P., 202
Leefe Robinson, Lt. W., 89
Leete, B. S., 17
Lefebvre, Eugène, 30
Legagneux, G., 27, 29
Legion Condor, 82
Le Havre, France, 73
Leie, Oberstleutnant Erich, 115
Leipzig, Germany, 234
Lemke, Hauptmann Wilhelm, 114
Lenina Peak, Kazakstan, 232
Lent, Oberst Helmont, 115

Le Oiseau Blanc (AF), 73
Leonardo da Vinci Airport, Rome, 191
Lenormond, Sebastien, 228
Leonides, Alvis (P), 217
Le Prieur rockets (W), 241
Le Rhone engine (P), 223
Les Baraques, France, 29
"Les Cigognes", 60, 65, 69, 70, 71
Leuchars, Scotland, 116
Levasseur P.L.8 (AF), 73
Levasseur Company, 73
Lévy-Lepen flying-boat (AF), 173
Lewis, 2nd.-Lt. D. G., 62
Lewis machine-gun (W), 44, 51, 69
Lexington, USS (AC), 145
Liberator, B-24, Consolidated (AF), 106, 241
Liberty engine (P), 78, 144
Libyan Republican Air Force, 125
Lighter-than-air flight, 196
Lightning, P-38, Lockheed (AF), 104, 112
Lilienthal, Otto, 12, 15, 16
Lincoln, Avro (AF), 120
Lindbergh, Capt. Charles, 179
Link, Edward Albert, 253
Link Trainer, 253
Linke-Crawford, Oberleutnant Frank, 58
Linke-Hofman R.II (AF), 56
Lion, Napier (P), 182
Lipfert, Hauptmann Helmut, 109
Lippisch, Professor Alexander, 234
Lisbon, Portugal, 171
Lisieux, France, 21, 214
Litchfield, H. A., 182
Little, Capt. R. A., 56
Litvak, Jr. Lt. Lydia, 92
Lock, Plt. Off. E. S., 89, 100
Lockheed F-80C Shooting Star (AF), 118
Lockheed L-1011 TriStar (AF), 7
Lockheed P2V-1 Neptune (AF), 156, 164
Lockheed P-3 Orion (AF), 166
Lockheed P-38 Lightning (AF), 104, 112
Lockheed P-80 Shooting Star (AF), 104
Lockheed PV Ventura (AF), 163
Lockheed S-3A Viking (AF), 166
Lockheed Altair (AF), 188
Lockheed Polaris (M), 238
Lockheed Vega (AF), 185, 187, 188
Loening monoplane (AF), 230
Loerzer, Hauptmann Bruno, 57
Loewenhardt, Oberleutnant Erich, 57
Loire-Nieuport 46 (AF), 83
London, England, 53, 170, 172, 175, 179
London Gazette, 107
Londonderry, Northern Ireland, 185
Long Island, New York, 179, 229
Longmont, Colorado, 191
Longmore, Lt. A. M., 135, 136, 138
Long-range Monoplane, Fairey (AF), 182, 185
Lopez, Francisco S., 202
Loraine, Robert, 35

Los Angeles, airship, 147
Los Angeles, California, 157, 182, 183, 229
Lossiemouth, Scotland, 161
Lousma, Maj. Jack, 250
Lowe, Flg. Off. Patrick, 231
Lowe, Thaddeus S. C., 129, 201
Lucas, Hauptmann Werner, 115
Lufbery, Maj. Raoul, 55, 58, 65, 76
Lufthansa (A), 261
Luke, 2nd-Lt. Frank, 58, 77
Luke Field, Arizona, 104
Luna 16 (S), 246
Luna 17 (S), 245
Lunardi, Vicenzo, 199, 200
Lunar Roving Vehicle, Boeing (S), 246
Lunokhod 1 (S), 245
Lushington, Lt. G. V. W., 135
Lützow, Oberst Günther, 115
Luukkanen, Lt. Eino, 86
Lwow, Poland, 84
Lynch, Bernard, 230
Lympne, Kent, 185, 253
Lyon, Harry, 181

M

M.1C, Bristol (AF), 169
M.8, Fokker (AF), 63
M22 (P), 79
M-130, Martin (AF), 189
MAC machine-gun (W), 80, 88
MB-1 Genie, Douglas (M), 242
MB-2, Martin (AF), 145
Mb IIIa, Maybach (P), 175
Me 163B Komet, Messerschmitt (AF), 97, 234
Me 262A, Messerschmitt (AF), 95, 96, 241
Me 262-2a Sturmvogel, Messerschmitt (AF), 95, 96
Mi-12, Mil (AR), 217
MiG-15, Mikoyan (AF), 118, 122, 124, 157, 158
MiG-17, Mikoyan (AF), 122, 123, 124
MiG-19, Mikoyan (AF), 123
MiG-21, Mikoyan (AF), 122
MG 17 machine-gun (W), 79
MK 108 30mm cannon (W), 95, 97
M-S 405, Morane-Saulnier (AF), 80
M-S 406, Morane-Saulnier (AF), 80
MX-324, Northrop (AF), 234
MXY7 Ohka, Yokosuka (AF), 154, 164
McCampbell, Capt. D., 100, 112
Macaulay, Theodore, 168
Macchi C.200 Saetta (AF), 81
McClean, F. K., 38, 221
McClellan, Gen., 129
McConnell, Capt. Joseph, 118
McCubbin, 2nd.-Lt. G. R., 63
McCudden, Capt. James T. B., 45, 48, 56, 75
McCullough, Lt. David H., 171
McCurdy, J. A. D., 27, 29, 34
McDonald, Col. C. H., 100
McDonnell F4H Phantom II (AF), 166
McDonnell FH-1 Phantom (AF), 156, 157

McDonnell XFD-1 (AF), 156, 164
McDonnell Banshee (AF), 164
McDonnell Demon (AF), 165
McDonnell, Lt.-Cdr. Edward O., 145
McDonnell Douglas F-4K Phantom II (AF), 225
McDowall, Sgt. A., 89, 95
McElroy, Capt. G. E. H., 56
Macewicz, Brig.-Gen., 127
McGubbin, Lt. G. R., 63
McGuire, Maj. T. B., 100
McIntyre, Flt.-Lt. D. F., 187
McKellar, Flt.-Lt. A. A., 89
McKenna, R., 223
McKinley, Ashley, 183
MacLaren, Maj. D. R., 56
McMaster, Sir Fergus, 174
McMullen, Flg. Off. D. A. P., 89
McPherson, Flg. Off. A., 85
Macready, Lt. J. A., 175
McRobertson Race, 225
Macon, airship, 147
McWilliam, T. H., 182
Mader, Dr., 53
Madon, Capt. Georges F., 58
Madrid, Spain, 185
Magdeburg, Germany, 24
Magennis, C. S., 31
Maia, Short (AF), 254
Maitland, Lt. Lester J., 180
Majendie, Capt. A. M., 190
Malaga, Spain, 187
Malagasy Air Force, 126
Malan, Gp. Capt. A. G., 100
Malmédy, Belgium, 50
Malmö, Sweden, 178
Mamet, Señor, 32
Mammoth, balloon, 204
Mangin, M., 202
Manly, Charles M., 17
Manly-Balzer engine (P), 17
Mannert L. Abele, U.S.S., 154
Mannock, Maj. Edward, 56, 71
Manston, Kent, 79, 95
Mantle, Act. Seaman J. F., 89
Manxman, H.M.S., 141
Maralinga, South Australia, 119, 121
Marconi Wireless Telegraph Co. Ltd., 170
Marham, Norfolk, 118
Marie-Antoinette, 198
Mariner, XPBM-1, Martin (AF), 163
Marix, Flt.-Lt. R. L. G., 51, 139
Market Harborough, Leicestershire, 16
Markham, Mrs Beryl, 189
Marlin, Martin (AF), 165
Marquardt RJ43-MA ramjet (P), 240
Marquardt, Oberfeldwebel Heinz, 115
Marsden, Capt. J. T. A., 190
Marseille, Hauptmann Hans J., 102, 106, 109, 110
Martigues, France, 32, 130
Martin B-57A (AF), 119
Martin M-130 (AF), 189
Martin MB-2 (AF), 145
Martin TM-61A Matador (M), 238
Martin XBTM-1 Mauler (AF), 164
Martin XPBM-1 Mariner (AF), 163

Martin, Maj. Frederick, 177
Martin, Glenn, 229
Martin Marlin (AF), 165
Martin-Baker ejection seat, 230, 231
Martin-Baker Ltd., 231
Martinsyde F.6 (AF), 223
Martinsyde Type A (AF), 125
Martlesham Heath, Suffolk, 83, 253
Martlet, Grumman (AF), 150
Mason, Monck, 201
Matador, TM-61A, Martin (M), 238
Mathers, Cpl., 169
Mauberge, France, 51, 201
Mauler, XBTM-1, Martin (AF), 164
Maurice Farman S.11 (AF), 61
Max Holste Broussard (AF), 124, 125, 127
Maxim, Sir Hiram, 12, 17
May, 2nd.-Lt. W. R., 62
Maybach Mb IIIa (P), 175
Mayer, Oberstleutnant Egon, 106, 107, 115
Mayflower III airship, 208
Meagher, Capt. A., 190
Melbourne, Australia, 225, 253
Melilla, Spain, 82
Mendoza, Argentina, 169
Menin, Belgium, 52
Mercedes engine (P), 56
Mercury, Short (AF), 254
Mercury VI S.2, P.Z.L. (P), 84
Merlin II, Rolls-Royce (P), 80
Merlin III, Rolls-Royce (P), 80
Merlin 85, Rolls-Royce (P), 120
Merlin 130/131, Rolls-Royce (P), 116, 227
Merlin 133, Rolls-Royce (P), 155
Merlin 134, Rolls-Royce (P), 155
Messerschmitt AG., 234
Messerschmitt Bf 109 (AF), 79, 82, 83, 85, 87, 101, 102, 103, 105, 110
Messerschmitt Bf 110 (AF), 85, 87
Messerschmitt Me 163 Komet (AF), 234
Messerschmitt Me 163B Komet (AF), 97
Messerschmitt Me 262A (AF), 95, 96, 241
Messerschmitt Me 262A-2A Sturmvogel (AF), 95, 96
Messiha, Dr Khalil, 9
Meteor, Gloster (AF), 93, 230, 251
Meteor 7, Gloster (AF), 231
Meteor F.4, Gloster (AF), 116, 227
Meteor F.8, Gloster (AF), 116
Metrovick, Beryl (P), 157
Meurisse, M., 31
Meusnier, Lt. Jean-Baptiste M., 206
Mexican Air Force, 126
Mia Mia, Victoria, Australia, 34
Michael, Herr, 206
Michelin Prize, 26, 36
Mier, M., 174
Miethig, Hauptmann Rudolf, 115
Mikoyan MiG-15 (AF), 118, 122, 124, 157, 158
Mikoyan MiG-17 (AF), 122, 123, 124
Mikoyan MiG-19 (AF), 123

Mikoyan MiG-21 (AF), 122
Mil Mi-12 (AR), 217
Milan, Italy, 26, 199
Mildenhall, Suffolk, 225
Military Biplane (AF), 36
Military Flying School, Nanyuen, Peking, 37
Military Trials, 226
Miller, Max, 169
Millichap, Capt. R. E., 190
Mineola, Long Island, New York, 31, 167, 174
Minichiello, Lance-Cpl. Raphael, 191
Mirage, Dassault (AF), 122
Mississippi, U.S.S., 49, 138
"Mistel-Programm", 101
Mitchell, Brig.-Gen. "Billy", 129, 145
Mitscher, Lt.-Cdr. M. A., 171
Mitsubishi A5M "Claude" (AF), 148, 162, 251
Mitsubishi A6M1 Zero-Sen (AF), 81, 154, 163
Mitsubishi A6M2 Type 0 (AF), 81, 112
Mitsubishi G3M "Nell" (AF), 162
Mitsubishi G4M "Betty" (AF), 163
Mitsubishi J2M "Jack" (AF), 163
Model 47, Bell (AR), 216
Model 69, Boeing (AF), 162
Model 185 Skywagon, Cessna (AF), 125
Model 206A JetRanger, Agusta-Bell (AR), 122
Model 707, Boeing (AF), 190, 191
Model 747, Boeing (AF), 261, 262
Moisant, J. B., 34
Moisant, Mr., 220
Moisson, France, 207
Mölders, Oberst Werner, 102, 115
Molinus, Hauptmann, 254
Moll, J. J., 225
Molland, Flg. Off. Hedley, 230
Mollison, J. A., 185
Monaco, Europe, 37, 221
Monoethylaniline, 234
Montgolfier balloon, 196, 197, 198, 199, 200
Montgolfier brothers, 7, 197, 198
Montoya, Guardia M. I., 54
Montpellier, France, 228
Montreal, Canada, 169, 204, 254
Monyash, Derbyshire, 231
Moore, Machinist L. R., 171
Moore-Brabazon, J. T. C., 27, 219
Moorfields, London, 199
Morane aircraft (AF), 68, 220
Morane Bullet (AF), 71
Morane-Saulnier M-S 405 (AF), 80
Morane-Saulnier M-S 406 (AF), 80
Morane-Saulnier Monoplane (AF), 168, 223
Morane-Saulnier Parasol (AF), 53, 75, 168
Morane Type M monoplane (AF), 51
Morocco, North-west Africa, 49
Morris, 2nd.-Lt. L. B. F., 62
Mosca, (I-16) (AF), 83
Moscow, U.S.S.R., 263
Moth, D.H.60, de Havilland (AF), 179, 180, 181, 251

Mould, Pil. Off. P. W., 86
Moulins, France, 251
Mount Everest, Nepal-Tibet, 187
Mount Everest, first flight over, 187
Mourmelon, France, 31
Mozhaisky, Alexander, 11
Mulberry Harbour, 101
Müller, Oberstleutnant Friedrich K., 114
Müncheburg, Maj. Joachim, 106, 114
Munchen Gladbach, Germany, 88
Munro, Ray, 232
Murphy, Lt. A. W., 253
Muscat and Oman, Sultan of, 126
Musick, Capt. Edwin C., 189
Mustang, P-51, North American (AF), 96, 102
Myers, John, 234

N

N.18 Baby, Supermarine (AF), 162
N1K1-J 'George', Kawanishi (AF), 163
N3N-3, Naval Aircraft Factory (AF), 161
N.A.39 Blackburn (AF), 161
NC-1, Navy/Curtiss (AF), 162, 171
NC-3, Navy/Curtiss (AF), 171
NC-4, Navy/Curtiss (AF), 170, 171
NK1C Sakae 12, Nakajima (P), 81
NK-144, Kuznetsov (P), 263
No. 2, Oehmichen (AR), 215
No. 6 Dirigible, Santos-Dumont, 207
NS-23 machine-gun (W), 117
Nagasaki, Japan, 42
Nakajima B5N2 "Kate" (AF), 112, 151, 162
Nakajima NK1C Sakae 12 (P), 81
Nanaimo, British Columbia, 74
Nancy, France, 168
Napier Lion (P), 182
Natal, Brazil, 185
National Airlines (A), 261
Naval Aircraft Factory N3N-3 (AF), 161
Naval Aircraft Factory PN-9 (AF), 146
Naval Aircraft Factory TS-1 (AF), 145
Naval Aircraft Factory XN3N-3 (AF), 162
Naval Wing, R.F.C., 37
Navy/Curtiss NC-1 (AF), 162, 171
Navy/Curtiss NC-3 (AF), 171
Navy/Curtiss NC-4 (AF), 170, 171
"Nell", G3M, Mitsubishi (AF), 162
Nelson, Lt. Erik, 177
Nene, Rolls-Royce (P), 158
Neptune, P2V-1, Lockheed (AF), 156, 164
Nesterov, Staff Capt. Petr. N., 51, 226
Netheravon, Wiltshire, 50
Neumann, Leutnant Klaus, 97
Newell, W., 229
Newark, New Jersey, 187, 188
New Brunswick, Canada, 185
New Jersey, U.S.S., 145
New Orleans, Douglas DWC (AF), 177
Newton, Maurice, 169
New York, N.Y., 167, 168, 169, 178, 183, 207

New Zealand Air Force, 253
Nicaraguan Air Force, 126
Nice, France, 32
Nicholetts, Flt.-Lt. G. E., 185
Nicolson, Flt.-Lt. J. B., 90
Niehoff, Leutnant Rolf, 86
Nieuport 11 (AF), 61, 68
Nieuport 17 (AF), 46, 65, 73
Nieuport 28 (AF), 65, 145
Nieuport aircraft (AF), 220
Nieuport Flying School, 44
Nieuport Scout (AF), 64
Nieuport Type IV (AF), 226
Night flight, 32, 49
Nijmegen, Netherlands, 88
Nike-Ajax SAM-A-7, Western Electric (M), 240
Nike-Hercules (M), 240
Nimrod, Hawker Siddeley (AF), 166
Nishizawa, Sub. Off. Hiroyoshi, 99
Noakes, Sqdn. Ldr. J., 83
Nordholz, Germany, 52
Norrkoping, Sweden, 117
North American A-5/RA-5C Vigilante (AF), 160, 166
North American F-86 Sabre (AF), 118, 156, 255
North American F-100 Super Sabre (AF), 230
North American FJ-1 Fury (AF), 156, 158, 164
North American FJ-2 Fury (AF), 165
North American FJ-4 Fury (AF), 165
North American P-51 Mustang (AF), 96, 102
North American T-28 Trojan (AF), 165
North American X-15A-2 (AF), 235
North American Aviation Corporation, 230
North American Buckeye (AF), 166
North American Harvard (AF), 124
North Carolina, U.S.S., 140
North Coates, Lincolnshire, 240
Northfall Meadow, Dover, Kent, 29
Northolt, Middlesex, 80, 189
North Platte, Nebraska, 174
North Pole, Arctic Ocean, 179
Northrop F-89 Scorpion (AF), 241, 242
Northrop MX-324 (AF), 234
North Scarle, Lincolnshire, 256
Norwegian Army Air Service, 126
Northwest Orient (A), 261
Norz, Lt. Jakob, 115
Nottingham, Nottinghamshire, 64
Nowotny, Maj. Walter, 95, 96, 99, 109
Nudelman-Suranov NS-23 machine-gun (W), 117
Nulli Secundus airship, 207
Nungesser, Lt. Charles E. J. M., 58, 65, 72
Nungesser-Coli, Breguet (AF), 180

O

0/10, Handley Page (AF), 173
0/400, Handley Page (AF), 55, 169, 170, 174
Oakland, California, 180, 188

Oberkanone, 61
Oberursel engine (P), 55, 56
Obleser, Oberleutnant Friedrich, 115
Ocean, H.M.S. (AC), 156
Odessa, Russia, 29
Odiham, Hampshire, 119
Oehmichen No. 2 (AR), 215
Oerlikon cannon (W), 81
Oesau, Oberst Walter, 114
Ogden, Staff-Sgt. Henry H., 177
Ogilvie, Mr., 220
O'Hare, Lt. Edward H., 151
Ohka, MXY7, Yokosuka (AF), 154, 164
Okinawa, Japan, 154, 155
Olieslagers, Lt. Jan, 32, 59
Olivari, Tenente Luigi, 58
Olympus 593, Rolls-Royce/SNECMA (P), 263
Omaha, Nebraska, 174
Ontario, Canada, 73, 188
Opladen, Germany, 252
Ordre Pour le Mérite, 57, 62, 63
Origone, 2nd.-Lt. Manuel, 45
Orion, P-3, Lockheed (AF), 166
Ornithopter, 213
Orpington, Kent, 237
Ortmans, Flt.-Lt. Vicki, 99
Oslo Fjord, Norway, 38
Osnabrück, Germany, 236
Ostend, Belgium, 53
Osterkamp, Leutnant Theo, 55
Ostermann, Oberleutnant Max H., 115
Ostfriesland, battleship, 145
Otter, DHC-3, de Havilland Canada (AF), 123
Ovington, Earl L., 167
Oxford, Oxfordshire, 39, 200

P

P2V-1 Neptune, Lockheed (AF), 156
P-3 Orion, Lockheed (AF), 166
P.11, P.Z.L. (AF), 84
P.24, P.Z.L. (AF), 90
P-35, Seversky (AF), 79
P-38 Lightning, Lockheed (AF), 104, 112
P.46 Gnome, Ward (AF), 256
P-47 Thunderbolt, Republic (AF), 112
P-51 Mustang, North American (AF), 96, 102
P-80 Shooting Star, Lockheed (AF), 104
P.1040 Sea Hawk, Hawker (AF), 164
P.1127 Kestrel, Hawker (AF), 262, 263
PBY Catalina, Consolidated (AF), 148, 162
P.L.8, Levasseur (AF), 73
PN-9, Naval Aircraft Factory (AF), 146
PO-2 biplane (AF), 93
PS-1, Shin Meiwa (AF), 166
PV Ventura, Lockheed (AF), 163
PV-3, Westland (AF), 187
P.Z.L. P.11 (AF), 84
P.Z.L. P.24 (AF), 90
P.Z.L. Mercury VI S.2 (P), 84
Pablo Beach, Florida, 175
Pacific Airlines (A), 191
Page, Charles, 204

Paine Field, Washington, 261
Palson Type 1 (AF), 253
Panamanian Air Force, 126
Pan American Airways (A), 180, 188, 189, 190, 261
Pangbourn, Clyde, 184
Panhard motor car, 22
Panther, F9F-2, Grumman (AF), 158, 164
Parachute, 228
Paraguayan War, 202
Parasol, Morane-Saulnier (AF), 53, 75
Parejas, Capt. Renato, 253
Paris, France, 20, 51, 70, 170, 172, 177, 179, 189, 196, 198, 202, 206, 207, 228, 237, 251
Parke, Lt. Wilfred, 226
Parke, Sub.-Lt., 150
Parke Custis, G. W. (AC), 129
Parker, John L., 153, 189
Parmalee, Phillip O., 43
Parmentier, K. D., 225
Parschau, Leutnant, 63
Pasadena, California, 167
Pasha, Mustafa Kemâl, 139
Passarola, 197
Patseyev. V, 250
Patteson, Cyril, 172
Pattle, Sqdn. Ldr. M. T. St. J., 99, 100
Pau, France, 33, 34, 71
Paulhan, Louis, 32, 37, 220
Pearce, Senator George, 122
Pearl Harbor, Oahu, 112, 147
Peck, Capt. Brian A., 169
Peenemünde, Germany, 42, 234, 236, 237
Pegasus, Rolls-Royce/Bristol (P), 262
Pégoud, Adolphe, 226, 227
Peltier, Madame Thérèse, 24
Pembroke, Hunting (AF), 128
Penn-Gaskell, Lt. L.da C., 51
Pennsylvania, U.S.S., 135
Pensacola, Florida, 207
Pensacola Bay, Florida, 140
Pequet, Henri, 36
Percival Prentice (AF), 126
Pershing, Gen. John, 53, 76
Peter, Kapitan, 98
Petewawa, Ontario, 29
Petrograd, Russia, 49
Phantom, FH-1, McDonnell (AF), 156, 157
Phantom II, F4H, McDonnell (AF), 166
Phantom II, F-4K, McDonnell (AF), 225
Philadelphia, Pennsylvania, 161, 168
Philipp, Oberstleutnant Hans, 109
Philippine Air Force, 127
Phillips, Horatio, 20
Phillips, W. H., 213
Philomel, H.M.S., 138
Phoenix, Arizona, 77
Phönix D.I (AF), 68
Piazza, Capt., 43
Piccio, Tenente-Col. Pier R., 58
Piercey, Mr., 253
Pig, flight of, 27
Pilcher, Percy S., 12, 15, 16

Pinecastle AFB, Florida, 243
Pioneer 10 (S), 7
Pioneer balloon, 204
Pioneers of the air, 9
Pischoff aircraft (AF), 220
Pitcairn, Harold F., 215
Pittsburgh, Pennsylvania, 187
Pixton, Howard, 221
Plymouth, Devonshire, 171
Poelcapelle, Belgium, 72
Poggensee, Karl, 236
Pogue, William R., 246
Poillot, Señor, 32
Polaris, Lockheed (M), 238
Polikarpov I-15 (AF), 83
Polikarpov I-16 Ishak (AF), 79, 83, 241
Polish Air Force, 127
Pomone, H.M.S., 138
Ponche, M., 38
Pond, Capt. C. F., 135
Poniatowski, Jan, 99
Ponta Delgada, Azores, 171
Poole, Dorsetshire, 254
Port Aviation, Juvisy, 30
Port Moresby, New Guinea, 151
Port Natal, Brazil, 180
Porte, John C., 144, 253
Porte/Felixstowe Fury (AF), 144
Portuguese Air Force, 127
Post Office Tower, London, 225
Post, Wiley, 187
Potez XXV (AF), 127
Potez 63/II (AF), 88
Potez 630 (AF), 88
Potez 631 (AF), 88
Potomac River, Maryland, 12, 17, 129
Power Jets Ltd., 251
Póznań, Poland, 84
Prague, Czechoslovakia, 175, 177
Pratt & Whitney J57 (P), 159, 160
Pratt & Whitney R-1830 (P), 79, 92
Pratt & Whitney R-2800 (P), 150, 153
Pratt & Whitney R-4360 (P), 157
Preddy, Maj. G. E., 100
Prentice, Percival (AF), 126
Prévost, Maurice, 221
Prier, Pierre, 37
Priller, Oberst Josef, 106, 115
Primard, M., 38
Prince of Wales, H.R.H., 27, 253
Progress in Flying Machines, 16
Projectile Autopropulsé Radioguidé Contre Avions (P.A.R.C.A.), D.E.F.A. (M), 240
Protzel, Aspirant Guillermo, 54
Pulham, Norfolk, 207
Pulse-jet (P), 237
Puma, Armstrong Siddeley (P), 179
Pup, Sopwith (AF), 74, 141, 142
Puss Moth, de Havilland (AF), 184, 185
Putnam, Lt. D. E., 58, 65
Pyramids, Egypt, 11

Q

Qantas (Queensland and Northern Territory Aerial Service) (A), 174, 181, 188, 261

Qatar Public Security Forces Air Arm, 127
Queen Maria Anna of Portugal, 197
Queensland and Northern Territory Aerial Service (Qantas) (A), 174, 181, 188, 261
Quénault, Cpl., 51
Quimby, Harriet, 38

R

R-4, Sikorsky (AR), 216
R4M 55mm rocket (W), 95, 241
R-34 airship, 207
R-100 airship, 182
R-101 airship, 182, 207
R-1820, Wright (P), 155
R-1830, Pratt & Whitney (P), 79, 92
R-2800, Pratt & Whitney (P), 150, 153
R-3350, Wright (P), 157
R-4360, Pratt & Whitney (P), 157
RA-5C Vigilante, North American (AF), 160
RD-10 engine (P), 116, 117
RD-500 engine (P), 116
REP aircraft (AF), 30, 219, 220
RJ43-MA ramjets, Marquardt (P), 240
Ro 37, Romaine (AF), 82
RS B2 (M), 241
R-type bomber aircraft (AF), 49, 55
Rademacher, Lt. Rudolf, 97, 114
Radio, 34
Radlett, Hertfordshire, 84, 184
Radley, Mr., 220
Radley-England Waterplane (AF), 221
Rafael Shafrir (M), 121
Rall, Maj. Gunther, 109
Ranger, U.S.S. (AC), 149
Rangoon, Short (AF), 162
Rankin, Lt.-Col. William H., 231
Ranza, Tenente Ferruccio, 58
Rapid City, South Dakota, 204
Rapide, de Havilland (AF), 125
Rascal, GAM-63, Bell (M), 243
Rata (AF), 83
Raven II, HMS, 139
Rawlinson, A., 32
Raynham, Fred, 223, 226
Read, Lt.-Cdr. A. C., 170
Reali, Sgt. Antonio, 58
Red Baron, 61, 62
Redoubt, H.M.S., 143, 144
"Red Duster", Bristol/Ferranti (M), 240
"Red Shoes", English Electric (M), 240
Rees, Lt. T., 62
Reid, Capt. L., 188
Reims (Rheims), France, 26, 51, 219
Reims International Aviation Meeting, 30, 219
Reinert, Oberleutnant Ernst W., 109
Reitsch, Hanna, 215
Renard, Capt. Charles, 206
Renaux, A., 37
Republic of Korea Air Force, 125
Republic P-47 Thunderbolt (AF), 112
Republique, dirigible, 251
Repulse, H.M.S., 141

Reuter, Otto, 53
Revi gunsight, 241
Rhinower Hills, Germany, 15
Rhoades, Chief Machinist's Mate E. S., 171
Rhodesian Air Force, 127
Rhodes-Moorhouse, 2nd.-Lt. W. B., 38, 52
Rhön-Rossiten Gesellschaft, 233
Richardson, Cdr. H. H., 171
Richter, Lt. J. P., 176
Richthofen Circus, 54, 62
Rickenbacker, Capt. E. V., 54, 55, 58, 65, 76
Riihimäki, Finland, 92
Rio de Janeiro, Brazil, 72
Riverside, California, 255
Riviera, S.S., 138
Robert brothers, 198
Roberts, Lt., 77
Robertson, Sir MacPherson, 225
Robinson, Mr., 37
Robot 315 (M), 237
Roc, Blackburn (AF), 163
Rochester, Kent, 153
Rockaway, New York, 171
Rockets and rocket missiles, 235
Rockwell Field, San Diego, California, 175
Rodd, Ensign H. C., 171
Rodgers, Calbraith P., 167
Roe, Alliot V., 28
Roëland, M., 49
Rohlfs, Ewald, 215
Rohrbach, Dr. Adolf, 83
Roland C.II (AF), 64, 75
Rolls, Hon. C. S., 25, 33, 34
Rolls-Royce Ltd., 7, 33
Rolls-Royce W.2B/23 Welland I (P), 93
Rolls-Royce Avon (P), 119
Rolls-Royce Condor (P), 84
Rolls-Royce Derwent 5 (P), 116
Rolls-Royce Derwent 8 (P), 116
Rolls-Royce Eagle (P), 144, 172
Rolls-Royce Kestrel II (P), 78, 254
Rolls-Royce Kestrel III (P), 84
Rolls-Royce Kestrel V (P), 79
Rolls-Royce Merlin II (P), 80
Rolls-Royce Merlin III (P), 80
Rolls-Royce Merlin 85 (P), 120
Rolls-Royce Merlin 130/131 (P), 116, 227
Rolls-Royce Merlin 133 (P), 155
Rolls-Royce Merlin 134 (P), 155
Rolls-Royce Nene (P), 158
Rolls-Royce Spey (P), 161
Rolls-Royce Tyne 515/10 (P), 255
Rolls-Royce/Bristol Pegasus (P), 262
Rolls-Royce/SNECMA Olympus 593 (P), 263
Rollwage, Oberleutnant Herbert, 107, 115
Roma, battleship, 96
Romain, Jules, 201
Romaine Ro 37 (AF), 82
Romanian Flying Corps 127
Rome, Italy, 208
Roosevelt, President Theodore, 35

Roosevelt Field, Long Island, New York, 175
Ross, Cdr. Malcolm D., 205
Rother, 254
Rotterdam, Netherlands, 88, 177
Rouen, France, 92, 172
Round Britain Air Race, 221
Round-the-world flight, first airship, 182
Round-the-world flight, first solo, 187
Round-the-world flight, first successful, 177
Royal Aero Club of Great Britain, 31, 37, 223, 253.
Royal Aircraft Factory B.E.1 (AF), 44
Royal Aircraft Factory B.E.2a (AF), 46, 50
Royal Aircraft Factory B.E.2c (AF), 64
Royal Aircraft Factory B.E.2e (AF), 54
Royal Aircraft Factory B.S.1 (AF), 44
Royal Aircraft Factory F.E.2b (AF), 54, 61, 63
Royal Aircraft Factory F.E.2d (AF), 75
Royal Aircraft Factory S.E.5a (AF), 46, 48, 69, 71, 73, 75, 223
Royal Aircraft Factory, Farnborough, 251
Royal Afghan Air Force, 122
Royal Air Force, 75, 103, 124
Royal Airship Works, 182
Royal Australian Air Force, 92, 116, 123
Royal Brunei Malay Regiment Air Wing, 123
Royal Canadian Air Force, 123
Royal Ceylon Air Force, 123
Royal Dutch Airlines (K.L.M.) (A), 172, 177, 225, 261
Royal Flying Corps, 38, 44, 63, 64, 71, 73, 75
Royal Hellenic Army Air Wing, 124
Royal Hong Kong Auxiliary Air Force, 124
Royal Iraqi Air Force, 125
Royal Jordanian Air Force, 125
Royal Laos Air Force, 125
Royal Malaysian Air Force, 126
Royal Moroccan Air Force, 126
Royal Naval Air Service, 74
Royal Naval Armoured Car Force, 139
Royal Navy, 41
Royal Netherlands Air Force, 126
Royal New Zealand Air Force, 126
Royal Pakistan Air Force, 126
Royal Rhodesian Air Force, 127, 128
Royal Saudi Air Force, 127
Royal Siamese Flying Corps, 128
Rugere, M., 37
Rudat, Hauptmann Horst, 101
Rudel, Maj. Hans V., 110
Rudorffer, Maj. Erich, 97, 109
Ruhrstahl Fritz-X (W), 96
Ruiz, 2nd.-Lt. Enrique, 54
Rumey, Leutnant Fritz, 57
Rumpler aircraft (AF), 70
Russian Air Force, 128
Russian Baltic Railway Car Factory, 49
Russian Revolution, 49

Rutland, Flt.-Lt. F. J., 140, 141
Ryan FR-1 Fireball (AF), 155
Ryan monoplane (AF), 179
Rymer, Capt. Richard, 189
Ryujo (AC), 149

S

S-2, SABCA (AF), 179
S-3A Viking, Lockheed (AF), 166
S.11, Maurice Farman (AF), 61
S.20, Short (AF), 254
S.21, Short (AF), 254
S.27, Short (AF), 136
S-42, Sikorsky (AF), 189
S-51, Sikorsky (AR), 158, 217
S-58, Sikorsky (AR), 161
S.68, Short (AF), 221
SABCA S-2 (AF), 179
SABENA (A), 179, 261
SAM-2 (M), 122
SAM-A-7 Nike-Ajax, Western Electric (M), 240
SAS (A), 261
SB-2, Tupolev (AF), 83, 86
S.B.A.C. Display, 227
SBC Helldiver, Curtiss (AF), 147
SBD Dauntless, Douglas (AF), 151
S.E.5a, Royal Aircraft Factory (AF), 46, 48, 69, 71, 73, 75, 223
Sh 14A, Siemens-Halske (P), 215
ShKAS machine-gun (W), 79
SM.79, SIAI-Marchetti (AF) 82
SM.81, SIAI-Marchetti (AF), 82
SNETA (A), 173
SPAD VII (AF), 65
SPAD XIII (AF), 65, 68
SR.A/1, Saunders-Roe (AF), 157, 164
S.S. *Achernar*, 154
S.S. *Conte Rosso*, 142
S.S. *Empress*, 138
S.S. *Engadine*, 138, 141
S.S. *Riviera*, 138
S.S. *Tyrell*, 154
S.S. *Wakamiya Maru*, 138, 140
SSM-A-17 Corporal, Firestone (M), 237
Su-7, Sukhoi (AF), 122
Saab-91D Safir (AF), 128
Saab J-29 (AF), 117
Sabot-type shells (W), 92
Sabre, F-86, North American (AF), 118, 156, 255
Sachsenberg, Lt. Heinz 115
Sadenwater, Lt. Harry, 171
Sadler, James, 200
Sage, Mrs. Letita A., 200
Saetta, C-200, Macchi (AF), 81
Safir, Saab-91D (AF), 128
Safonov, Lt. M., 59
Sailplane Research Institute, 234
Saint-Cyr, France, 70
St. J. Pattle, Sqdn. Ldr. M. T., 99, 100, 110
St. John's, Newfoundland, 171
St. Lo, U.S.S. (AC), 154
St. Louis, Missouri, 35, 177, 201, 229
Saint-Louis, Senegal, 180

St. Mawgan, Cornwall, 216
St. Moritz, Switzerland, 32
St. Petersburg, Florida, 168
St. Petersburg, Russia, 40
St-Raphaël, France, 137, 168
Sakae 12, NK1C, Nakajima (P), 81
Sakai, Petty Off. 1st Class, Saburo, 112
Salamander, He 162, Heinkel (AF), 98
Salinas, Maj. Alberto, 45
Salisbury Plain, Wiltshire, 37, 39, 44
Salmond, Maj.-Gen. W. G. H., 169
Salvator, Archduke Léopold, 35
Salyut 1 (S), 246
Samson, Cdr. Charles R., 45, 135, 136, 137, 138, 143, 144
Sanchis aircraft (AF), 219
Sander rockets (P), 233
San Diego, California, 135, 176
Sandringham, Short (AF), 262
San Fernando, Uruguay, 128
San Francisco, California, 43, 135, 146, 174, 178, 181, 183, 189
Sangatte, France, 28, 29, 33
Santa Monica, California, 187
Santiago de Chile, Chile, 169
Santos-Dumont, Alberto, 20, 22, 26, 207
Santos-Dumont 14-*bis* aircraft (AF), 20, 22
Santos-Dumont No. 6 dirigible, 207
Santos-Dumont aircraft (AF), 219
Sapphire, Armstrong-Siddeley (P), 119
Sarafand, Short (AF), 162
Saratoga, U.S.S. (AC), 145, 146, 149
Saugus, California, 256
Saunders-Roe SR.A/1 (AF), 157, 164
Savanna, U.S.S., 96
Savkin, Lt.-Col. Ivan, 232
Sayer, Flt.-Lt. P. E. G., 251
Scapa Flow, Orkney, 150
Scaroni, Tenente Silvio, 58
Scarp, Inverness, 236
Schack, Hauptmann Günther, 109
Schall, Hauptmann Franz, 96, 97, 114
Schenk, Maj. Wolfgang, 96
Schmidt, Hauptmann Heinz, 109
Schnaufer, Maj. Heinz W., 114
Schneider Trophy, 218, 221
Schnörrer, Leutnant Karl, 97
Scholte, First Officer J. B., 180
Schroer, Maj. Werner, 106, 107, 115
Schuck, Oberleutnant Walter, 97, 109
Schutte-Lanz airship, 89
Schwann, Cdr. O., 136
Science Museum, London, 11
Scimitar, Supermarine (AF), 161, 165
Scorpion, F-89, Northrop (AF), 241, 242
Scott, Charles W. A., 225
Scott, Sqdn. Ldr. G. H., 207
Scott, Capt. J. E. D., 231
Scout "C", Bristol (AF), 252
Seaford, Short (AF), 164
Sea Fury, Hawker (AF), 123, 157, 164
Seagull, Supermarine (AF), 162
Sea Hawk, P.1040, Hawker (AF), 164
Seahawk, XSC-1, Curtiss (AF), 164
Sea Hornet F.20, de Havilland (AF), 155, 164

Sea Hurricane, Hawker (AF), 150
Sea Mosquito, de Havilland (AF), 153
Sea Otter, Supermarine (AF), 163
Seaplane competition, 37
Seattle, Douglas DWC (AF), 177
Seattle, Washington, 169, 177, 191
Sea Vampire, de Havilland (AF), 156
Sea Venom, de Havilland (AF), 159
Sea Vixen, de Havilland (AF), 160, 165, 242
Seelberg, Germany, 206
Seely, Col., 39
Seiler, Maj. Reinhard, 115
Seki, Lt. Yukio, 154
Selassie, Emperor Haile, 124
Selfridge, Lt. Thomas E., 25, 42
Senegal Air Force, 127
SEPECAT Jaguar M (AF), 166
Serbian Military Air Service, 128
Sergeivsky, Capt. B., 59
Setz, Maj. Heinrich, 114
Seversky, Lt.-Cdr. A. P., 59
Seversky P-35 (AF), 79
Shafrir (M), 121
Shakhovskaya, Princess Eugenie M., 52
Shank, Robert F., 169
Sheepshead Bay, New York, 34, 43
Shellness, Isle of Sheppey ("Shellbeach"), 27, 219
Shell Trophy, 223
Shenandoah, ZR-1, airship, 207
Shepard, Alan B., 245
Sheremetyevo Airport, Moscow, 263
Sheringham, Norfolk, 52
Shetland, Short (AF), 153, 164
Shimpu, Special Attack Corps, 154
Shin Meiwa PS-1 (AF), 166
Shoho (AC), 151
Shokaku (AC), 151
Shooting Star, F-80C, Lockheed (AF), 118
Shooting Star, P-80, Lockheed (AF), 104
Shoreham, Sussex, 37, 167
Short 184 seaplane (AF), 140
Short C-Type Empire flying-boat (AF), 189
Short S.20 (AF), 254
Short S.21 (AF), 254
Short S.27 (AF), 136
Short S.68 (AF), 221
Short biplane (AF), 38, 130, 136, 137, 138
Short Bros. Ltd., 27, 256
Short Calcutta (AF), 182, 184
Short-Mayo Composite (AF), 254
Short Rangoon (AF), 162
Short Sandringham (AF), 262
Short Sarafand (AF), 162
Short Seaford (AF), 164
Short Shetland (AF), 153, 164
Short Singapore (AF), 162
Short Sunderland (AF), 162
Short-Wright biplane (AF), 27, 33, 219, 256
Sidewinder (M), 159
Siemens-Halske Sh 14A (P), 215
Siemens-Shuckert D.III (AF), 48
Siemens-Shuckert R.VIII (AF), 56

Signals Corps, U.S. Army aviation section, 25, 42, 44, 49
Sikorsky, Igor, 40, 49, 216
Sikorsky R-4 (AR), 216
Sikorsky S-42 (AF), 189
Sikorsky S-51 (AR), 158, 217
Sikorsky S-58 (AR), 161
Sikorsky VS-300 (AR), 216
Sikorsky XR-4 (AR), 216
Silver Dart biplane (AF), 27
Simons, Maj. David G., 205
Singapore Air Defence Command, 127
Singapore, Short (AF), 162
Six Day War, 119
Skene, 2nd.-Lt. R. B., 50
Skua, Blackburn (AF), 150
Skybaby, Stits (AF), 255
Skyhawk, A-4, Douglas (AF), 122, 165
Skylab (S), 246, 250
Skynight, F3D-2, Douglas (AF), 158, 165
Skyraider, AD, Douglas (AF), 156
Skyray, Douglas (AF), 165
Skytrain, C-47, Douglas (AF), 123, 125, 127, 128
Skywagon 185, Cessna (AF), 125
Skywarrior, A-3, Douglas (AF), 160, 165
Skywarrior, A3D, Douglas (AF), 159, 165
Skywarrior, XA3D-1, Douglas (AF), 159, 165
Smaland, 237
Smart, Flt.-Sub.-Lt. B. A., 142
Smirnoff, Lt. I. W., 59
Smith, George Franklin, 230
Smith, Lt. Keith, 172, 253
Smith, Lt. Lowell H., 176, 177
Smith, Capt. Ross M., 169, 172, 253
Smith, Wesley L., 178
Snipe, Sopwith (AF), 227
Society of British Aerospace Companies (S.B.A.C.), 227
Soesterburg, Netherlands, 126
Somali, H.M.S., 85
Sommer, Roger, 37
Sommer aircraft (AF), 37, 220
Sondergeräte 113A Forstersonde (W), 92
Sopwith, T. O. M., 35, 36
Sopwith 1½-Strutter (AF), 74
Sopwith 7F.1 Snipe (AF), 46
Sopwith biplane (AF), 221
Sopwith Camel (AF), 62, 68, 75, 139, 143, 144, 145, 227
Sopwith Cuckoo (AF), 142, 143
Sopwith Pup (AF), 74, 141, 142
Sopwith Snipe (AF), 227
Sopwith Tabloid (AF), 51, 139, 221
Sopwith Triplane (AF), 46, 74
Soryu (AC), 149
South African Air Force, 127
South African Airways (A), 261
South African Aviation Corps, 127
Southampton, Hampshire, 90, 221, 254
South Atlantic, first non-stop crossing, 180
Southern Cross, Fokker, 181, 182

South Pole, Antarctica, 183
Southport, Lancashire, 35
Soyuz (S), 249, 250
Space, chronology of man in, 247, 248, 249, 250
Space flight, 244
Spandau machine-gun (W), 55
Spanish Civil War, 81, 82, 187
Sparks, 2nd.-Lt. H. J., 48
Sparrowhawk, F9C, Curtiss (AF), 147
Spartan, H.M.S., 96
Spartan Aircraft Company, 256
Späte, Maj. Wolfgang, 97
"Spencer, Viola", Miss, 33
"Spencer-Kavanagh", Miss, 33
Spenser-Grey, Cdr. D. A., 51
Sperrle, Maj.-Gen., 82
Sperry, Lawrence B., 252
Spey, Rolls-Royce (P), 161
Spirit of St Louis, Ryan (AF), 179
Spitfire, Supermarine (AF), 86, 89, 103, 110, 124
Springs, Capt. E. W., 58
Sputnik 1 (S), 244
Sputnik 5 (S), 245
Squadrons, first British, 44
Squires Gate, Blackpool, 31, 34
Stack, T. Neville, 179
Stag Lane aerodrome, Edgware, Middlesex, 224
Stamer, Friedrich, 234
Stapf, General, 42
Stapleford Tawney, Essex, 103
Start aircraft (AF), 38
State of Victoria, Australia, 225
Steinbatz, Oberfeldwebel Leopold, 101
Steinhoff, Oberst Johannes, 97, 109
Stentor, Bristol Siddeley, (P), 243
Sterr, Oberleutnant Heinrich, 114
Stevens, Capt. Albert, 204
Stits, Ray, 255
Stits Skybaby (AF), 255
Stockholm, Sweden, 29, 34
Stöllen, Germany, 15
Stone, Lt. E. F., 171
Stoney, Capt. T. B., 190
"Stooge", Fairey (M), 238
Stotz, Hauptmann Max, 109, 114
Strange, 2nd.-Lt. L. A., 51
Stratofortress, B-52, Boeing (AF), 120, 121
Stratojet, DB-47, Boeing (AF), 243
Stratosphere, 232
Strelka, dog, 245
Stringfellow, John, 14
Sturm, Hauptmann Heinrich, 114
Sturmvogel, Me 262A-2A, Messerschmitt (AF), 95
Sudanese Air Force, 128
Sukhoi Su-7 (AF), 122
Sultan of Oman's Air Force, 126
Sunbeam Arab (P), 143
Sunderland, Short (AF), 162
Sunfish, Curtiss (AF), 168
Superfortress, B-29, Boeing (AF), 118, 234
Supermarine Attacker (AF), 158, 164
Supermarine Baby, N.1B (AF), 162

Supermarine Scimitar (AF), 161, 165
Supermarine Seagull (AF), 162
Supermarine Sea Otter (AF), 163
Supermarine Spitfire (AF), 86, 89, 103, 110, 124
Supermarine Swift Mk 7 (AF), 242
Supermarine Walrus (AF), 162
Super Sabre, F-100, North American (AF), 230
Suring, Professor, 204
Süss, Oberfeldwebel, 101
Suva, Fiji, 181
Swaab, Capt. J. M., 58
Swedish Air Force, 128
Swedish Air Lines (A), 178
Swift Mk 7, Supermarine (AF), 242
Swissair (A), 261
Swiss Air Force, 128
Swordfish, Fairey (AF), 150
Sycamore H.C.10/11, Bristol (AR), 217
Sycamore H.R.12, Bristol (AR), 217
Sydney, Australia, 31, 182
Szentgyörgyi, 2nd.-Lt. Dezjö, 99

T

T-2, Fokker (AF), 175
T-28 Trojan, North American (AF), 165
T.55 Vampire, de Havilland (AF), 123
T.A.P. (Portugal) (A), 261
TBD Devastator, Douglas (AF), 151
TBF Avenger, Grumman (AF), 151
TM-61A Matador, Martin (M), 238
TS-1, Naval Aircraft Factory (AF), 145
Tu-2, Tupolev (AF), 116
Tu-12, Tupolev (AF), 116
Tu-144, Tupolev (AF), 263
Tabloid, Sopwith (AF), 51, 139, 221
Tabor, Tarrant (AF), 144
Tafari, Ras, 124
Taj Mahal, India, 11
Takagi, Vice.-Adm. Takeo, 151
Tampa, Florida, 168
Tangmere, Sussex, 78, 90, 103, 116
Tanzer, Leutnant Kurt, 114
Tarrant Tabor (AF), 144
Tasman Sea, 182
Taube aircraft (AF), 27, 51, 126
Taylor, Capt. P. G., 188
Teesdale, Sgt. K. J., 232
Tegtmeier, Leutnant Fritz, 114
Tellier aircraft (AF), 220
Templer, Capt. J. L. B., 202
Tereshkova, Jr. Lt. Valentina V., 245
Texas, U.S.S. (AC), 145
Thible, Madame, 199
Thieffry, 2nd.-Lt. Edmond, 59
Thiokol XLR11-RM-5 (P), 235
Thiokol XLR99-RM-2 (P), 235
Thirimont, Belgium, 36
Thirtle, Sqdn. Ldr. J., 232
Thomas, George Holt, 168
Thompson, Cdr., 85
Thompson, Lord, 182, 208
Thor ramjets, Bristol (P), 240
Thulin, Dr. Enoch, 34
Thulin Aircraft Works, 24

Thunderbird, English Electric (M), 240
Thunderbolt, P-47, Republic (AF), 112
Thyben, Oberleutnant Gerhard, 114
Tiger, F11F-1, Grumman (AF), 159, 165
Tigercat, F7F-1, Grumman (AF), 153, 164
Tiling, Reinhold, 236
Tissandier, Gaston, 202
Tivoli Gardens, Paris, 251
Tokyo, Japan, 182, 184
Tomcat, F-14, Grumman (AF), 166
Tomson, Ensign E. M., 59
Toronto, Canada, 168, 169
Toul, France, 65, 86
Toulouse, France, 263
Tower Bridge, London, 38
Tower of London, 53
Towers, Cdr. John H., 171
Tracker, XS2F-1, Grumman (AF), 65
Trail of the Caribou, de Havilland (AF), 188
Train aircraft (AF), 220
Transatlantic Air Race, 218, 225
Transcontinental Air Transport Inc. (A), 253
Transcontinental and Western Air Inc (T.W.A.) (A), 183, 187
Trans-Pacific, first flight, 181
Trans-World Airlines (T.W.A.) (A), 191, 256, 261
Trappes, France, 206, 251
Trenkel, Hauptmann Rudolf, 114
Trewin, Asst. Paymaster G. S., 140
Trimotor, 4-AT, Ford (AF), 183
Triplane, Roe, 28
Triplane, Sopwith (AF), 46, 74
TriStar, L-1011, Lockheed (AF), 7
Trojan, T-28, North American, (AF), 165
Tropopause, 117, 232
Truculent Turtle (AF), 156
Tubavion monoplane (AF), 38
Tuck, Flt.-Lt. R. S. S., 89, 100
Tularosa, New Mexico, 232
Tunisian Air Force, 128
Tupolev SB-2 (AF), 83, 86
Tupolev Tu-2 (AF), 116
Tupolev Tu-12 (AF), 116
Tupolev Tu-144 (AF), 263
Turin, Italy, 24, 88
Turkish Flying Corps, 128
Tyne 515/10, Rolls-Royce (P), 255
Type 0, A6M2, Mitsubishi (AF), 81, 112, 151
Type 003, BMW (P), 98
Type 1, Palson (AF), 253
Type IIIC, Fairey (AF), 175
Type IV, Nieuport (AF), 226
Type 4-AT Trimotor, Ford (AF), 183
Type IV-M Etendard, Dassault (AF), 166
Type 11, Nieuport (AF), 61, 68
Type 14 Ab 10/11, Hispano-Suiza (P), 88
Type 17, Nieuport (AF), 46, 65, 73

Type XIX, Breguet (AF), 180
Type XXV, Potez (AF), 127
Type 28, Nieuport (AF), 65, 145
Type 46, Loire-Nieuport (AF), 83
Type 63/II, Potez (AF), 88
Type 97 machine-gun (W), 81
Type 99 20 mm cannon (W), 81
Type 184, Short (AF), 140
Type 230, DFS (AF), 91
Type 630, Potez (AF), 88
Type 631, Potez (AF), 88
Type A, Martinsyde (AF), 125
Type C, Boeing (AF), 169
Type F, Curtiss (AF), 252
Type M, Morane (AF), 51
Tyrell, S.S., 154
Tyson, Geoffrey, 153
Tytler, James, 199

U

U-17A, Cessna (AF), 127
UFO (Unidentified Flying Object), 255
U.S.S. Alabama, 145
U.S.S. Alpine, 154
U.S.S. Birmingham, 130, 138
U.S.S. Boxer (AC), 158
U.S.S. Enterprise (AC), 149, 160
U.S.S. Essex, 112
U.S.S. Franklin D. Roosevelt (AC), 156
U.S.S. Jupiter (later Langley) (AC), 145, 146
U.S.S. Langley (AC), 145, 146, 149
U.S.S. Lexington (AC), 145, 146, 149, 151
U.S.S. Mannert L. Abele, 154
U.S.S. Mississippi, 49, 138
U.S.S. New Jersey, 145
U.S.S. North Carolina, 140
U.S.S. Pennsylvania, 135
U.S.S. Ranger (AC), 149
U.S.S. St. Lo (AC), 154
U.S.S. Saratoga (AC), 145, 146, 149
U.S.S. Savanna, 96
U.S.S. Texas, 145
U.S.S. Valley Forge (AC), 158
U.S.S. Virginia, 145
U.S.S. Wake Island (AC), 156
U.S.S. Washington, 145
U.S.S. West Virginia, 154
U.S.S. Yorktown (AC), 149, 151
Ubben, Maj. Kurt, 115
Udet, Oberleutnant Ernst, 48, 57
Ugaki, Adm. Matome, 155
Uganda, H.M.S., 96
Uganda Army Air Force, 128
Uiver, Douglas, 225
Ulm, C. T. P., 181, 182
Unidentified Flying Object (UFO), 255
Union of Burma Air Force, 123
United Air Lines (A), 183, 191, 261
United States Air Force, 128
United States, first non-stop crossing, 175
Universal (A), 261
Universal Postal Exhibition, 36

University Air Race, 223
Unwin, Flt.-Sgt. G. C., 89
Upavon, Wiltshire, 49
Upper Heyford, Oxfordshire, 84
Upton, Plt.-Off. H. C., 89
Uruguay Department of Military Aviation, 128
Urbanowicz, Fg. Off. W., 89
Utrecht, Netherlands, 88

V

V-bomber, 119
V-1 flying-bomb, 95, 99, 236, 251
V-2 rocket (M), 236, 237, 244
V.10, Fokker (AF), 56
VE-7, Vought (AF), 145
VS-300, Sikorsky (AR), 216
Vahrenwalder Heide, Germany, 7
"Val", D3A, Aichi (AF), 151, 163
Valiant, Vickers (AF), 119, 121
Valkyrie monoplane (AF), 37, 167
Valley Forge, U.S.S. (AC), 158
Vampire, de Havilland (AF), 123, 156
van Arkel, Lt.-Col., 99
Vance, Claire K., 178
Vancouver, Canada, 172
van de Haegen, Oberleutnant Otto, 53
Van Meel aircraft (AF), 220
van Ryneveld, Lt.-Col. Pierre, 173
Vasquez, Sub.-Lt. Horacio, 253
Vaughan, Lt. G. A., 58
Vauxhall Gardens, London, 201
Vechtel, Oberleutnant Bernhard, 115
Védrines, Jules, 168, 221
Vega, Lockheed (AF), 185, 187, 188
Velazco, Guardia M. R., 54
Venezuelan Military Air Service, 128
Venice, Italy, 201
Ventura, PV, Lockheed (AF), 163
Vera Cruz, Mexico, 49
Verdun, France, 53
Vergeltungswaffen, reprisal weapons, 42, 236
Versailles, Court of, 198
Vickers machine-gun (W), 78, 254
Vickers Valiant (AF), 119, 121
Vickers, Victoria (AF), 182
Vickers Viking amphibian (AF), 172
Vickers Vimy (AF), 171, 172, 173, 177
Vickers Viscount (AF), 189
Vickers Wellington (AF), 88, 90
Victor, Handley Page (AF), 243
Victoria, British Columbia, 169
Victoria, Vickers (AF), 182
Victoria and Albert, Royal yacht, 137
Victoria Cross, 38, 45, 52, 53, 69, 71, 73, 75, 89, 90, 107
Victory, DH.50 (AF), 181
Vienna, Austria, 27, 168
Vienna-Schwechat, Austria, 98
Vietnamese Air Force, 128
Vigilante, A-5/RA-5C, North American (AF), 160, 166
Viipuri, Finland, 86
Viking amphibian, Vickers (AF), 172
Viking, S-3A, Lockheed (AF), 166

Villa, Flg. Off. J. W., 89
Villa Nova da Rainha, Portugal, 127
Vimy, Vickers (AF), 171, 172, 173, 177
Vindicator, XSB2U-1, Vought (AF), 162
Vinet aircraft (AF), 220
Viper, Wolseley (P), 143
Virginia, U.S.S., 145
Visconti, Maj. Adriano, 99
Viscount, Vickers (AF), 189
Voisin aircraft (AF), 16, 22, 24, 27, 29, 30, 31, 32, 34, 51, 72, 219, 220
Voisin brothers, 16, 22
Volkov V., 250
Volksjäger, 98
Volkswagen engine (P), 208
von Braun, Wernher, 236, 244
von Fassong, Hauptmann Horst G., 114
von Fernbrugg, Oberleutnant Benno F. Ritter, 58
von Opel, Fritz, 234, 253
von Porat, Capt. G., 44
von Richthofen, Overleutnant Lothar, 57, 69
von Richthofen, Rittmeister Manfred, 48, 57, 61
von Rosenthal, Leutnant Baron, 51
von Tiedemann, Lt. Richard, 43
von Zeppelin, Count Ferdinand, 207
Voss, Leutnant Werner, 48, 57
Vostok 1 (S) 245
Vostok 6 (S), 245
Vought VE-7 (AF), 145
Vought XOS2U-1 Kingfisher (AF), 163
Vought XSB2U-1 Vindicator (AF), 162
Vought Cutlass (AF), 165
Vulcan, Avro (AF), 120, 243

W

W.2B/23 Welland I, Rolls-Royce (P), 93
W.8b, Handley Page (AF), 177
W.10, Handley Page (AF), 253
Waalhaven, Netherlands, 88
Waddington, Lincolnshire, 92, 120
Wade, Lt. Leight, 177
Wade, Wg. Cdr. L. C., 100
Wadi Halfa, Sudan, 173
Wakamiya Maru, S.S., 138, 140
Wake Island, U.S.S. (AC), 156
Walden, Dr. Henry W., 31
Walden III monoplane (AF), 31
Waldmann, Oberleutnant Hans, 114
Walker, J. A., 235
Wallace, Westland (AF), 187
Waller, Cpl. J. H., 63
Walrus, Supermarine (AF), 162
Walsh, Vivian C., 36
Walter HWK 109-509A-2 (P), 97
Walter rocket, 234
Walvis Bay, South-west Africa, 185
Wantage, Berkshire, 208
Wapakoneta, Ohio, 246
Wapiti, Westland, (AF), 124
Warchalovski brothers, 35
Ward, Michael, 256

Ward P.46 Gnome (AF), 256
Ware, Hertfordshire, 199
Warneford, Flt.-Sub.-Lt. R. A. J., 53
Warner, James, 181
Warrior, H.M.S., 141
Warsaw, Poland, 84
Warsprite, H.M.S., 96
Wasaga Beach, Ontario, 188
Washington, D.C., 168, 169
Washington B.Mk 1, Boeing (AF), 118
Washington Naval Treaty, 145
Washington, U.S.S., 145
Waterplane, Radley-England (AF), 221
Waterton, Sqdn. Ldr. W. A., 119
Webb, Lt. Torrey H., 168
Weber, Lt. Eng. K. A. O., 180
Weber, Hauptmann Karl H., 114
Wee Bee, Beardmore (AF), 253
Wehner, Lt., 77
Weilberg, Nassau, 201
Weimar, Germany, 169
Weiss, Ehrich, 31
Weiss, Hauptmann Robert, 114
Weissenberger, Maj. Theodor, 97, 109
Weitz, Paul, 250
Welland I, W.2B/23, Rolls-Royce (P), 93
Wellington, Vickers (AF), 88, 90
Welsh, Dr. K. H. Vincent, 181
Wenatchee, Washington, 184
Wenham, F. H., 15
Wernicke, Lt. Heinz, 115
Wernitz, Leutnant Ulrich, 115
Wessex, Westland (AR), 161
West, Ensign Jake C., 155
West Australian Airways (A), 174
Western Electric SAM-A-7 Nike-Ajax (M), 240
Western Isles, Scotland, 236
Westinghouse, J40 (P), 120
Westland PV-3 (AF), 187
Westland Aircraft Ltd., 217
Westland Wallace (AF), 187
Westland Wapiti (AF), 124
Westland Wessex (AR), 161
Westland Whirlwind 3 (AR), 127
Westland Whirlwind 10 (AR), 123
Westland/Sikorsky Dragonfly (AR), 158, 217
West Virginia, USS, 154
Whing Ding II, Hovey (AF), 256
Whirlwind 3, Westland (AR), 127
Whirlwind 10, Westland (AR), 123
White Lake, South Dakota, 204
Whitley, Armstrong Whitworth (AF), 85, 86, 88
Whitten Brown, Lt. Arthur, 171
Whittle, Sir Frank, 251
Wiener-Neustadt, Austria, 27, 35
Wiese, Maj. Johannes, 114
Wilcke, Oberst Wolf D., 109
Wildcat, F4F, Grumman (AF), 150, 151, 162
Wilhelmshaven, Germany, 85, 91
Williams, R. D., 251
Williamson County, Illinois, 83, 191
Willow Grove, Philadelphia, 215
Wilson, Gp. Capt. H. J., 116
Windsor, Berkshire, 37

Windham, Capt. W. G., 36
Wind tunnel, 15
Winnie Mae, Lockheed Vega (AF); 187
Wise, John, 201
Wisseman, Leutnant, 72
Woidich, Oberleutnant Franz, 115
Wolf, German raider, 139
Wolf, Oberleutnant Albin, 114
Wölfert, Dr. Karl, 206
Wolfrum, Oberleutnant Walter, 114
Wolseley Viper (P), 143
Wolverhampton, Staffordshire, 43
Woolworth store, 237
World absolute speed records, 257, 258, 259, 260
World point-to-point speed records, 192, 193, 194, 195
World's Air Forces, 122, 123, 124, 125, 126, 127, 128
World's fastest aeroplane, 235
Wright J65 (P), 159
Wright R-1820 (P), 155
Wright R-3350 (P), 157
Wright biplane (AF), 7, 25, 27, 30, 31, 34, 35, 41, 42, 43, 44, 167, 219
Wright brothers, 7, 11, 12, 13, 16, 17, 18, 23, 24, 42, 196, 256
Wright Field, Dayton, Ohio, 79, 216
Wright Flyer (AF), 18, 20, 22, 34
Wright, Orville, 25, 42
Wright Type A (AF), 30
Wright, Wilbur, 25, 26, 27
Wrigley, Capt. H. N., 253
Wurmheller, Maj. Josef, 115
Württemberg, Germany, 101

X

X-15A-2, North American (AF), 235
XA3D-1 Skywarrior, Douglas (AF), 159, 165
XB-63, Bell (M), 243
XBT2D-1, Douglas (AF), 157, 164
XBTM-1 Mauler, Martin (AF), 164
XCAL-200 Aerojet (P), 234
XF2A-1 Buffalo, Brewster (AF), 162
XF2F-1, Grumman (AF), 162
XF4F-2, Grumman (AF), 162
XF6F-1, Grumman (AF), 163
XF7F-1, Grumman (AF), 153
XF8F-1 Bearcat, Grumman (AF), 164
XF8U-1, Chance Vought (AF), 159
XF9F-2, Grumman (AF), 158
XF10F-1 Jaguar, Grumman (AF), 120
XF12C-1, Curtiss (AF), 147
XF-99, Boeing (M), 240
XFD-1, McDonnell (AF), 156, 164
XFF-1, Grumman (AF), 147
XIX, Breguet (AF), 180
XJF-1 Duck, Grumman (AF), 162
XLR11-RM-5, Thiokol (P), 235
XLR99-RM-2, Thiokol (P), 235
XN3N-3, Naval Aircraft Factory (AF), 162
XNBL-1, Barling (AF), 78
XOS2U-1 Kingfisher, Vought (AF), 163

XPBM-1 Mariner, Martin (AF), 163
XR-4, Sikorsky (AR), 216
XS-1, Bell (AF), 234
XS2F-1 Tracker, Grumman (AF), 165
XSB2A-1 Buccaneer, Brewster (AF),
    163
XSB2C-1, Curtiss (AF), 163
XSB2U-1 Vindicator, Vought (AF),
    162
XSC-1 Seahawk, Curtiss (AF), 164
XTB3F-1 Guardian, Grumman (AF),164
XTBD-1, Douglas (AF), 162
XTBF-1, Grumman (AF), 151

                    Y

Yak fighter, Yakovlev (AF), 92
Yak-1, Yakovlev (AF), 93
Yak-3, Yakovlev (AF), 117, 122
Yak-7B, Yakovlev (AF), 93
Yak-9, Yakovlev (AF), 93

Yak-11, Yakovlev (AF), 123
Yak-15, Yakovlev (AF), 117
Yak-18, Yakovlev (AF), 123
Yakovlev, Alexander S., 117
Yakovlev Yak fighter (AF), 92
Yakovlev Yak-1 (AF), 93
Yakovlev Yak-3 (AF), 117, 122
Yakovlev Yak-7B (AF), 93
Yakovlev Yak-9 (AF), 93
Yakovlev Yak-11 (AF), 123
Yakovlev Yak-15 (AF), 117
Yakovlev Yak-18 (AF), 123
Yalu River, Korea, 118
Yarmouth, H.M.S., 141, 142
Yeager, Capt. Charles "Chuck", 234
Yeovil, Somerset, 217
Yeovilton, Somerset, 159, 160
Yokosuka D4Y (AF), 163
Yokosuka MXY7 Ohka (AF), 154, 164
Yokoyama, Lt. T., 81
Yom Kippur War, 121

Yorktown, U.S.S. (AC), 149, 151
Yucca Flat, Nevada, 242

                    Z

ZR-1 *Shenandoah*, airship, 207
Zambian Air Force, 128
Zapala, Argentina, 168
Zeebrugge, Belgium, 140
Zee Yee Lee, 37
Zeppelin airship, 41, 51, 52, 53, 124,
    139, 141, 142, 144, 167, 252
Zeppelin Staaken R aircraft (AF), 55
Zero-Sen, A6M2, Mitsubishi (AF), 81,
    151, 154, 163
Zink, Fräulein Lola, 48
Zucker, Gerhard, 236
Zuikaku (AC), 151
Zurakowski, Jan, 227
Zvonariev, Capt., 241
Zwernemann, Oberleutnant Josef, 114